A YEAR TO REMEMBER
Sources We Forget

A YEAR TO REMEMBER
Sources We Forget

*52 contemplative messages
on 12-step recovery and Christianity and
19 sermons specifically relating
AA principles with Biblical precepts*

Bruce Van Blair

Xlibris

OTHER BOOKS BY BRUCE VAN BLAIR

In a Nut's Shell
The Believer's Road
Eli and the Tiger

To inquire, contact:
Melchizedek Publications
1104 Madison Street
Port Townsend, WA 98368
360.385.6853
nimba@olympus.net

Published by Xlibris

Second Edition
Library of Congress Catalog Card Number: 87-73383
ISBN :   Softcover   1-4134-0821-4

Edited by Joey Moschetti
Cover photograph by Robert Hansen
Photograph of the author by Cindy Dupuie
Cover design by Barbara Goss Anderson

*Dedicated to the members of the
Mercer Island United Church of Christ,
who kept putting up with me.*

CONTENTS

SECTION ONE—WINTER

SECTION TWO—SPRING

SECTION THREE—SUMMER

SECTION FOUR—AUTUMN

THE STEPS THROUGH LENT, AND BEYOND

AUTHOR'S NOTE

I was surprised when Pat Moriarty wanted to publish these sermons in the first place. I thought they had too much alcohol in them for the Christian community, and too much "church" in them for the AA community. And essentially that is still the case. But Steve and Jim and a few others keep recommending this book to folk—so we ran out. Now Glen Abbey Books has merged and moved on, but there are other ways to get a book out. So we will try to keep a supply on hand for those who still want it. Meanwhile, we have added a series of sermons relating the Twelve Steps to Christian teachings. These were written several years later, after time for reflection and experience had a chance to "season" (but not lessen) some of the early delight in the two programs. My thanks to Barbara Anderson, Cindy Dupuie, Joey Moschetti and Jeanette Ripp for making this happen a second time. And if you are a reader recovering from alcohol, or sin, or whatever, God bless.

Bruce Van Blair

PREFACE

A person might ask, "Why publish a book on recovery for Christian people?" Or, "Why publish a book on Christianity for recovering people?" There seems to be an underlying assumption that either group might be offended by a relationship with the other. *A Year To Remember* is a milestone achievement for bringing these two groups together. The import of this coming together lies in the fact that there is so much to be gained by the relationship between the recovering person and the Church. *A Year To Remember* captures on a week-to-week basis the thrill of life discovery that comes to anyone who has ever struggled through an addiction experience, one day at a time. At the same time, the message of Christianity speaks loud and clear to ears that are open to hear the unmistakable message of life, love and fulfillment.

Reverend Bruce Van Blair is a recovering alcoholic. As such, he was spared no pain or misery in his own coming to grips with his faith and his life. His own struggle to make sense out of a battered and shattered life was no less than that of anyone coming off the street to seek help with his or her alcoholism. Van Blair began his journey with Step One. The gift to the recovery field of his book is the manner in which he uses both twelve-step recovery and the Christian message to invigorate his journey, his recovery. He swings the door of the Church open to the addict. At the same time, he invites church people to consider their need for recovery.

A Year To Remember has fifty-two messages that are totally devoid of moralistic judgments and high-handed platitudes of what people ought to be like. The book quite simply grounds twelve-step recovery in the faith from which such programs were spawned, and illuminates the Christian way as a fantastic resource for recovering people. I experienced in *A Year To Remember* a kind of enthusiasm and

inspiration that set me off at a very deep level. We who are recovering
need an infusion of spirituality on a regular basis. We go to meetings,
we call other recovering people, we work our program. We do it all
so that we might continue to stay sober and live happy, joyous and
free. Even more importantly, we are called to carry the message to
others who still suffer, for it is our experience that we cannot keep
what we have gained if we do not give it away. It is precisely our own
cure that we not only want to share, but indeed must share, if we are
to stay cured.

This sense of hope and salvation was precisely the spirit-
filled enthusiasm that the early Church embodied as it carried
the Christian message to all corners of the world. Before the Church
became embroiled in a struggle over dogma, doctrine and
institutions, there was a sense of purpose and destiny that bears
remarkable similarity to the recovering community. It is precisely
at this point of convergence that *A YEAR TO REMEMBER* was written.

Reverend Bruce Van Blair has written a wonderful book that,
if nursed over the course of a year, will provide you with weekly
doses of deep spiritual insights. You can feel him wrestling with
his own faith and recovery, discovering exciting new connections
between them, and sharing it all very openly with his
congregation. You may find yourself feeling more deeply in touch
with your own spirituality as a result. (You need not worry about
being converted to anything.) You *will* experience being put more
deeply in touch with your life. We believe that as a direct result,
the artificial barriers which have separated these two great
communities will come down, and that they can appreciate each
other in a rich and rewarding way.

Therefore, afford yourself the gift of this treasure. Open your
heart, your mind, your soul each week, as slowly as you like. You
will soon discover, we believe, that you, too, have *A Year To
Remember.*

Pat Moriarty
Glen Abbey Books

INTRODUCTION

J. Golden Kimball was one of the most colorful characters of the early frontier days in Utah. One day he commented, "All you have to do to live a long and fruitful life is just get yourself an incurable disease—and then take care of it."

After chuckling over that comment for a while, I began to wonder why it seemed so true. Was it that age inevitably brings us all to one ailment or another? That must be it.

It also seems true that humans do better when something forces them to a conscious surrender—when some "unfortunate circumstance" moves them out of willful, self-centered choices and brings them to a steady, disciplined, more humble way of life.

It is my assumption that everybody who picks up this book has run into a giant somewhere along the way. If you are like me, you've slung lots of rocks at it, and maybe even returned to work or home thinking somebody would crown you king for such heroic deeds against "Goliath." Only, this giant never really fell, never went away. And though, in time, we may have learned that life is still possible, or even better than before, we also have discovered that this giant will never really go away, never sleep, never promise to leave us alone. A few careless moves, and we will be in big trouble again, probably bigger than before—very possibly too big.

So we have our incurable disease, our nemesis. Life can't be our way, or on our terms anymore. Many of us have discovered, to our amazement, that these "unfortunate circumstances" (or whatever we call our dis-ease) have also been the necessary ingredients for getting us onto a spiritual path. We know, at last, that we need help. It is the First Step. It is the First Beatitude.

Knowing this, we also discover that there is more help available than we had ever imagined, and from more than human sources.

Another surprise for many of us is that spiritual paths have been all around us all of our lives, only they were camouflaged. People call them funny names, like "church" or "temple." Even the people in and around such places do not always realize that they are "fronts" for a spiritual path. We finally get on a spiritual path because we are desperate for help, and then we begin to discover incredible connections with those familiar places we have known since our youth.

Several years ago, my congregation was informed, one Sunday morning, that I would not be there to preach for a few weeks because I was in an alcoholic treatment center. The last thing I wanted to do, when I came out of that hospital, was to stand in a pulpit and say anything to anybody!

But there was no other plan running, and I certainly hadn't had a chance to devise one. So Sunday came, and there I was. There seemed to be nothing for it but to continue doing what I had been doing, at least until we all had a chance to regroup. I assumed that meant the church would find a new minister, and I would find a new vocation.

Sunday morning came, and it was as strange and painful as I had imagined it would be. But the days after came swiftly, and other things began to happen. I was going to twelve-step meetings and church meetings and Bible Study groups. Rather quickly, people came to counsel with me again, only now some of them talked even more freely than before. Soon all of these things kept getting mixed up together until it was hard to tell where church left off and the twelve-step program began; where helping others left off and getting help myself began; where sharing in a meeting left off and preaching began.

As the weeks passed and nobody asked for my resignation, I found less and less opportunity to plan or look for my next career. It also seemed to me that the precepts of the Christian Faith were getting clearer and more personal and more practical than ever.

I had to be careful not to mention the twelve-step program too much in the church—or the church too much in twelve-step meetings. While the two seemed ever more closely related to me, there were those in the church who resented or feared the twelve-step program. And there were numerous people in the twelve-step program who feared, resented or were angry toward the church. (Very interesting, and for many interesting reasons, but we won't get into that.)

Eventually some church members discovered that twelve-step programs were a lifesaver. Eventually some twelve-step friends discovered that the church was the source, and an endless resource, of the wisdom and power that flow in the twelve-step program.

It has been particularly fascinating for me to find myself on both sides of the fence—trying to recover and trying to preach—and finding a similar "Path" being spoken of in both places and in both "Big Books."

I write the thoughts in these pages as straightforward musings about the Christian Way, yet with the "giant" dogging my steps . . . and "The Program" ringing in one ear, even as the Scriptures of another "Program" ring in the other. Whatever your giant, whatever your program of recovery, I hope you will find connections in these pages that will seem as encouraging and exciting to you as they do to me.

I would also like to thank Pat Moriarty and Steve White for envisioning and encouraging this book. Pat has worked on it almost as hard as I have.

SECTION ONE

WINTER

Acts 2:25-28

Week One

IT IS HARD TO SEE THE DRAGON
THAT HAS SWALLOWED YOU

I've been thinking all month about what I would say to you when this moment finally came. The thing is, it kept changing every few days, all month long. Part of the time, I thought maybe I should just wait for the moment and then say whatever came to mind off the top of my head. Glad I didn't decide to do that. What comes to mind right now, off the top of my head, is "I need a drink."

I've seen movies and read books from time to time that portrayed a minister standing before the congregation in shame and disgrace after some personal sin or weakness had come to light. (Do you remember Richard Burton in *Night of the Iguana?*) I never figured it would happen to me, but sometimes after seeing or reading such a story, I would get nightmares about it. It seemed like about the worst thing that could happen. But the way you folks have pulled together and handled things, and the way you have treated me . . . well, it doesn't seem like such a nightmare after all.

I have always secretly longed for some dramatic moment of success in my ministry—something, I suppose, to reassure me that the energy and effort were really worthwhile. Now that I have had the dramatic failure instead, I'm not sure but what I was after the wrong thing. I'm already wondering, should things get cold and distant again in the future—what will I do for encores?

Sorry I wasn't here to welcome Carol as our new Choir Director last Sunday. Hi Carol. I've been hearing good things about you. Church musicians, you know, spend more time than most folk realize trying not only to provide the best music they can, but also trying to choose appropriate music to match the theme of the service. Carol was already trying to find out what today would be like so she could choose some appropriate music. What could I tell her? I can hardly wait to see what the anthem will be.

A favorite old anecdote popped into my head. Back in the days just before prohibition, one Sunday a powerful hellfire preacher was pouring it on about the evils of drink. He got more and more eloquent as he got more and more excited. Finally he wound things up by saying that the authorities should pass a law requiring all liquor-store owners and manufacturers of every kind of booze to take every drop of booze and pour it in the river. The congregation then rose to sing the final hymn, "Shall We Gather At The River."

It's an old hymn, and I couldn't find a copy to send you, Carol. You're on your own for next Sunday too. But after that, I promise to keep coordinated.

On the secular calendar, it says that today is Halloween. I identify with that. A crazy, ghoulish, happy day for me, since I get to come back and be among you. On the other hand, coming back before you as a marked alcoholic feels very Halloweenish indeed. Only, I don't get to take the costume off after the party is over. It is a title I am having quite a struggle getting used to.

On the church calendar, it says that today is Reformation Sunday. I identify with that too! And somehow the bizarre mixture of the two strikes my funny bone, as well as some very tender spots that nonetheless have considerable meaning to me. So I don't know what kind of a day you are having, but I am having a good day. A little strange, bizarre, difficult, wonderful—but a good day.

You have been super-great to Mariana and to me during this past month. I wish I could let you each know how much your letters and prayers have meant to me. I hope somebody told you why I couldn't respond to them before. I guess part of my sickness was the notion that forgiveness was okay for everybody but the minister. Apparently you don't agree with that, and I am very grateful. Personally, I still have trouble equating alcoholism with a sickness or disease—even if it is the number-two killer in the nation. Most of you already seem to have known that, even if I didn't. I guess if you're sick and don't know it, or can't admit it, you're probably an alcoholic. Either that or a sinner. The two seem to have a lot of patterns in common.

Anyway, if there are visitors or returning vacationers here who don't know what I'm talking about: The first Sunday of October, this congregation was surprised to see a stranger in the pulpit. Later in the service, Mariana stood up to explain that I was in the alcoholic treatment center at Cabrini Hospital, and would not be around for several weeks. Most of you were somewhere between surprise and shock. You hadn't seen me drink very much. Matter of fact, I hadn't been drinking very much since I came to Mercer Island—at least not in comparison to former days. In some of your letters, you wondered why I didn't say something—share some of the load like I always tell you to do. Hey, you think *you* were surprised! You should have been inside my head those first days I was in Cabrini! I checked into the hospital a perfectly normal, rational human being. Three days later, I was an alcoholic. My head is still spinning. Apparently Denial & Defensiveness is my middle name. "It is hard to see the dragon that has swallowed you."

My first few days at Cabrini, I wrote my letter of resignation. It's still available whenever you want it. I kissed my old life goodbye, and started making plans to follow the Way of the Tao. Then one day I didn't get all my armor quite in place, and I started feeling your prayers. I used to be able to do that, but I had closed it out—at least the ones that had to do with me. Some of you mix your prayers with a lot of fear and sorrow, but behind that was some stuff I really needed, so I dropped a few more plates of armor to let more of it in. Things have been changing, happening almost too fast, ever since.

By the way, some of you also feel guilty when you don't pray as often as you mean to. I could pick up some of that too. But you don't understand that once you set up some of that energy, it is there for me to draw on. It's like you open the channel. You don't have to kick at it all the time to keep it open. Anyway, then your letters started coming. A lot of them felt like the visible evidence and continuation of your prayers. Wish I had some way to tell you what a difference it made.

My head now knows that I am an alcoholic. But my emotions, at least the deep ones, cannot accept it. They wake up in the night, and even sometimes during the day, and scream NO! That is what I am watching and working on most right now, with the help of a twelve-step program. If anything in me gets through this period unbelieving, the chances are apparently about one hundred to one that I will be right back where I started. So I'm not trying to tell you anything this morning. Just trying to tell me.

I took my first drink twenty-two years ago—one quart of 100-proof bourbon. I must have been an alcoholic in some past life, and it's been progressing ever since. That first drink was an incredible experience. I had never been unable to control my faculties before. It was eleven o'clock the next morning, swimming in the ocean off Cape Breton Island in Nova Scotia, before I started feeling like myself again. It had been a planned drunk—penance for having refused the wine of Christ's communion. It started a new life for me of being more accepting and loving of other people. I lost the "virginity" of my self-righteousness. I would rather die a drunk than go back to the way I was before that day.

Anyway, I drank against all the "don'ts" of my upbringing, and refused to pay attention to the guilt, knowing it was only my old moral pride. I drank claiming grace and the right to be human, and it was good . . . for a long time. I also started a game with alcohol. I was fascinated by its effect. It couldn't do that to me! Often thereafter, when I could, I drank in a contest to see how long I could stay in control against the effects. I lost a lot of rounds. But inside, I also knew that I had put up a pretty good fight. It was fun.

In the early days, I also had many experiences of close times and good conversations with people who didn't have much use for the church until after we started drinking together. Many of them became excellent members and leaders in the church.

Also, I didn't turn into a beast, as I had been taught I would if I ever touched alcohol. I loved people more, God more, Mariana more. I had the same feelings I had had before, only they came welling up with beauty and power from somewhere within. I had the courage to share the things I usually kept to myself. People quipped that they could learn a lot from me in six months of counseling—or in one night, if they could get me drinking. The old Oracle Syndrome.

Looking back, it was about ten years ago that the pattern started changing. Sometimes I wasn't sharp and insightful anymore when I drank—just repetitive, dull and argumentative. I began to be wary. I started pulling back, drinking only with a few I knew wouldn't care (or remember) how I acted. I didn't know it consciously, but I was on the run. How to keep drinking—but avoid the painful experiences and repercussions? Inevitably, that came down to drinking alone. And it took a lot of pain and shame to do that—and fear.

I did not move from California to Mercer Island to escape, at least not consciously. That is in answer to some of the questions in your letters. I was not asked to leave Redlands, I was begged to stay. Frankly, I kept wondering why I had been so close to so many there, and so distant from most folk here. Often, I figured it was because I drank with the people there, and had decided not to do that here. Anyway, my pattern changed when I got here. I didn't drink for six months. After the flurry of a new position wore off, I took to rewarding myself once or twice a week—one bottle of sherry or a half bottle of brandy in the late evening (looking forward to vacation breaks, when I could "do it right"). At the "intervention" that got me into Cabrini, most of the evidence of my problem was two years old or older. (Naturally, I was saying to myself, "Why now?") All, that is, except for one kind of evidence: I had changed. I was more and more closed off and alone. Dealing with people, trying to care and be helpful seventy to eighty hours a week . . . but still alone. I didn't want intimacy, friendship, closeness with anybody. Inwardly angry, bitter, discouraged—I went on working. My alcohol input was drastically reduced (both amount and frequency), but my head and heart were still getting more and more "alcoholic." Do you know how it feels? I AM A LEPER—DON'T TOUCH ME!

I took inventory, all right. All the time. And the reality was that I gave more than I got—with everybody. And everything would be fine if people would just listen and act on the wisdom I provided. That's the real ugliness. PRIDE. Too proud to receive anything—from anybody—even God.

Some of you wondered, "Why didn't you pray, like you told us to do?" What do you think kept me going?! Only, I wasn't praying about what was under my cloud or behind my armor. I didn't know how. It was closed off to me—off limits. I prayed for other things . . . for some of you . . . for purpose and guidance and wisdom . . . and for the church—but not about my own need, because I couldn't face, see or admit it. You know why, of course. I am not an alcoholic; I am a Christian minister, and a very dedicated one too—even gifted in some ways. And since you cannot be an alcoholic and a minister at the same time, therefore I am not an alcoholic. Simple logic . . . that has cost me ten years of anguish. "It is hard to see the dragon that has swallowed you." But for Mariana, it would doubtless have been another ten years.

Some of you obviously know it already, but others asked, "Why didn't you just use more discipline, or willpower?" If I didn't have so much willpower—another name for it is "willfulness"—the disease probably would have been arrested long ago. But once inside the alcoholic pattern, willpower or self-discipline is turned to the needs of the drinking pattern. You don't use it outside. Drinking still seems like a harmless and, in fact, beneficial friend. In time, it seems like about the only friend you have left. Anyway, don't tell me about discipline. Every day or night that any of you saw me without a drink in my hand, you were watching pure willpower in action. Then at 10:30 p.m., or whenever you didn't need me for a while, that same willpower would say, "Good, that was for them. Now for me."

Anyhow, I seek surrender—again—like I had back when I took that first drink. Back to where I was, twenty-two years ago . . . only for the opposite reason. And opposites have a way of being almost similar. I haven't found it yet, but I seek it: the brokenness—or death—that leads to Life.

I have always walked with God—even through the last ten years. It is how I have survived. I just have a hard time remembering, sometimes, which one of us should go first. I have also learned, once again, with your help, that there is no justice. Thank God!

I don't know if any of you have comments or curiosity about any of this. If so, I wish you would feel free to speak it. I'd kind of like to get everything cleared that needs clearing, so we can move on . . . if that is God's will.

II Timothy 2:23-25

Week Two

DRY DRUNKS & DRY CHRISTIANS

Not many of you are recovering alcoholics. Statistically, nine out of ten of you will not abuse alcohol, and drinking can be for you a pleasant and celebrative part of normal life. Sometimes I get so enthralled, however, by what I am seeing and learning through recovery from alcoholism that I can't help wanting to share it with you. Today is one of those days.

There are endless corollaries, I'm finding, between alcoholism and sin, between twelve-step recovery programs and the church, between sobriety and reconciliation. I don't really care if you learn more about alcoholism, but I do care that we learn more and more about the Christian Faith. Sometimes comparisons lift up things we have half-forgotten through sheer familiarity, or neglect.

For instance, denial is the most difficult problem for the alcoholic. We prefer to do things our own way, claiming that we are in control and managing just fine, thank you. The notion that we need help, treatment, the fellowship of twelve-step recovery . . . is irritating and repulsive in the extreme, usually for years. Nevertheless, without such help, an alcoholic will eventually lose everything and die.

Well, denial is also the most difficult problem for sinners. Sinners also prefer to do things their own way, claiming they are in control and managing life just fine. The notion that we need a Savior, a new way of life, the fellowship of the church . . . is irritating and repulsive in the extreme. It's okay if we want it, freely choose it, participate because it is good for society or our children or people in general. But the notion that we ourselves need it—that we will lose everything, die to everything that matters, without it—that is offensive and brings out strong denial.

An alcoholic must come to the point of recognition: "My way is not working. My need is absolute and without equivocation. I must have help or all is lost." Many people come to the program but cannot make this admission, and so they drift back out again. Many people come to the church but cannot make the admission of their sin, and so they drift back out again. Neither twelve-step recovery programs nor the church are designed for people who can "take it or leave it alone."

Some twelve-step groups become in-grown and stale. The members stop working the steps, stop growing in the program, stop trying to help other alcoholics to recover, or forget their reason for being. Such groups lose their power and begin to dwindle away. Their members must either find another group or go back to drinking. As I said, the parallels are endless.

There is no such thing as a recovered alcoholic. There are only alcoholics and recovering alcoholics. There is no such thing as a recovered sinner. There are only sinners and recovering sinners, at least in this world. A Christian is a recovering sinner. If this awareness is lost, all is lost. There is no recovering from sin without the grace and help of God. All the creeds and rituals in the world will not help the alcoholic or the sinner if either one tries to go back to living their own way. Getting and staying on the program, whether you like it or understand it or not, is the only hope there is.

Perhaps we should take a moment to clarify terms. Some twelve-step recovery programs have people who come, stop drinking, but don't work the program. They are called dry drunks. They aren't drunks anymore, but there's no joy in their lives either. None of their inner attitudes or goals or purposes have changed. A recovering alcoholic is one who seeks sobriety. Sobriety is a different quality of life, one in which everything that contributes to drinking is slowly changed. No alcoholic who has experienced real sobriety wants to return to the drinking days. If there are relapses, they will not last for long, if sobriety has truly been tasted.

A sinner is one who is not completely in tune with God. A sinner is one alienated or separated from God. A sinner who merely tries to control unhelpful behavior patterns is like a dry drunk. A recovering sinner seeks reconciliation with God. Everything that contributes to distance or alienation from God is slowly eliminated. A different quality of life is sought, to the core of all inner attitudes, values and purposes. (The Christian word for sobriety is "salvation." The Christian word for serenity is "peace.")

It was a wonderful day for me when this distinction finally broke through my thick resistances. I had stopped drinking lots of times. Nothing changed, that I could see. It hadn't improved anything. Why stop drinking if nothing is improved? Some could add, "Why go to church, or study Scripture, if nothing is improved?" I stopped drinking, but nothing inside changed to match. I was just a dry drunk. So, thinking I had tried the other way and found nothing, I kept going back to my own way. Perhaps if drinking had been landing me in jail or in traffic court, I would have been able to see the improvement.

Sinners who don't get into serious trouble because of their alienation from God have the same difficulty. Why worry about self-will, or a life that avoids God's purpose and authority, if it isn't causing obvious and serious problems that we can see at the moment?

It finally came clear, with a lot of help, that "not drinking" was only "the way in"—essential, but not the real issue. Sobriety was the real issue. (Serenity and surrender may seem closer to the right words for you.) Morality isn't the real issue either. Christian precepts of behavior are also a way in. But reconciliation—life in communication with God—is the real issue. So I could "not drink" forever and no good would come of it, like some people "don't lie, steal, commit adultery" forever, and no good comes from it. No harm either, but you can say the same for any fencepost. Big deal! Abstinence from drink is not sobriety. Abstinence from bad deeds is not the Christian life, or reconciliation, or joy, or love. Dry drunks and dry Christians. A real sinner may repent. A real alcoholic may hit bottom. But what do you do with a dry drunk, or a dry Christian?

The most appalling story I have run across so far is about a man who stopped drinking for twenty years. He didn't get help or treatment, or participate in twelve-step recovery; he just stopped drinking. He was about to lose his job and family, and he had young children to raise, so he decided he had to stop drinking, and he did. He worked hard, became successful, provided for his children. He was also a grim, joyless man who made no friends, had few pleasures, and never learned to relate much, even with his own family. At the end of twenty years, with his children raised and his retirement secure, he said, "That's over, now I can go back to drinking." Six months later, he was dead. The disease had gone right on progressing through the twenty years.

Mere abstinence has no effect on spiritual issues. Only a changed inner life does. There is a distinction between a dry drunk and a recovering alcoholic. There is a difference between a dry Christian and a person finding reconciliation with God.

Life's real principles have a way of repeating themselves again and again throughout every area of life. The Designer was cagey that way. If you find an authentic truth, no matter where or how or in what area, you can find it repeated endlessly in all other aspects of life. When we skip or miss an essential lesson, it keeps plaguing us wherever we go, no matter what the circumstances or whom we are with. Hence the saying that expresses the positive side of it: "If you can learn to make a perfect cup of coffee, you can reach Nirvana."

Some people know the joy of work, and others put in time for a paycheck. Some students find the true fascination of seeking knowledge, and others spend time making grades. Even if they become teachers, they are still dry learners. There are dry marriages, dry parents, dry friendships and, of course, dry Christians. The form without the passion and purpose is dry.

Between two ways of life, between every dimensional breakthrough, between wherever we are and where we need to go in life, there seems always to be an arid place, a neutral zone, a limbo, a kind of "no-man's land." I have only used the dry drunk as one illustration. We are forever getting stuck in this place between—too aware to stay where we are, and too frightened or stubborn to move on. This strange buffer zone is everywhere. Some of you have seen it with your children. They do okay in school, but somehow you know it isn't clicking. They do the work, but somehow you know the power is cut. They put in the time, they say they study as hard as they can, but it's grim effort. Then one day, as if by magic, they find a whole new level. Performance triples, effort seems almost to diminish, and they say it's easy, fun. They don't know why it seemed so hard before. Of course, they still work at it, probably more, but it isn't grim anymore.

Inventors, artists, athletes, everybody experiences this phenomenon in some fashion. Why don't we learn to expect it, and refuse to get stuck in the desert places in between? Perhaps more than in any other area of life, we humans get stuck in the dry places between the secular life and the spiritual life—weary and discontent with secular reality, but unwilling to let it go and move on through to the spiritual life. Why do we call it faith when we choose to walk a spiritual path? Because it seems so uncertain and scary.

Being a dry drunk is very hard work. It takes constant effort. It is never pleasant, or flowing, or natural. The desire to go back to the old way is persistent and powerful. To be a recovering alcoholic is not hard at all. It is easy and simple. It flows and feels natural and gets better and better. That is always the way when we finally get past one of the dry places. It is called grace. Yet, standing in the dry place, looking forward, we would swear that the journey is impossible, that one more step would be unbearable. What we cannot see or know from the buffer zone, the dry place, is that one more step is breakthrough! That is also why they call it faith. Some places the mind cannot go, only the feet can. It is not a closer *thinking* about God. Just a closer walk with God.

In twelve-step recovery programs, they say you can't just talk the talk, you have to walk the walk: get on the program and stay on it, work the twelve steps, keep coming to meetings, turn life over to the Higher Power, and don't drink between times.

They got it straight from the church, of course, and it works for everybody who does it. My question is: Why has the church forgotten?

A similar image of comparison came to mind the other day. I found myself trying to picture what it would be like if a twelve-step group went on a "membership drive" the way a lot of churches do. All the members would be out saying to people, "Hey, it doesn't matter if you drink or not; it doesn't make any difference if you want to go on drinking; it doesn't matter if you work the program; you don't have to care about sobriety—just come and join our group. You'll find a lot of nice people there, and we serve refreshments after the meeting." Can you imagine what would happen to a group if it started caring about attendance records instead of about sobriety? How very bizarre!

Actually, a twelve-step group puts tremendous emphasis on attending meetings. Even an old-time traditional church looks flabby by comparison. Twelve-step people tell each other, "If you stop coming around, you'll be drinking again." That's twelve-step language for, "If you don't come to church regularly, you're going to go to hell." It makes me nervous how so many of us ministers take poor church attendance as an inevitable reality we can do nothing about. In twelve-step recovery, however, the point is never that "we wanted a big turnout" or "we hoped fifty people would show up and only thirty-five came out." People don't think or talk like that until they have absolutely lost sight of their purpose and no longer know what they are doing, or why they are doing it.

Do you tithe, do you pray and study Scripture, do you keep coming to meetings, do you try to help other sinners who want to be recovering? We don't want it that simple. We want something more grand and glorious, not humble and true. Or maybe it is back to that First Step: We cannot admit that our own need is great enough to keep us on the program. As long as that is true, the church will be full of dry Christians. That means all the work and discipline—without the joy or the love or the grace.

Dry drunks and dry Christians are in limbo, caught halfway between two worlds. Go back, or go on, but do not stay in limbo. Nothing good comes from limbo.

Luke 17:11-19; Colossians 3:12-17

Week Three

AN ATTITUDE OF GRATITUDE

I get greeted often these days with the question, "How are you doing?" Maybe it's just my new ears, or maybe it's partly you, but the query seems to come with a new dimension of earnest caring. As a matter of fact, it goes both ways. I really want to know how you are doing too.

Anyway, I am having an astounding and wonderful time. I'm almost afraid to say how good I feel because I know how irritating that can be to someone who may be in a hard place at the moment. But for myself, the best word I can think of is "renewal." Everything I have known in the past seems to be circling back with new clarity. On the inside, it feels like old logjams are starting to break up, and the stream of life is starting to flow again. And it doesn't seem like I am doing any of it. In fact, I know more surely than ever that I don't know how to do such a thing. I'm just watching with fascination, and trying to keep out of the way.

I don't seem to have lost any of the normal problems. The bills keep coming, the leaves keep falling, the day is too short, I can't handle all the requests and complaints. I preach about tithing, and you can't hear me. Nothing has changed. And yet everything is different. Some people think I'm just temporarily high on too little to drink. Or as they say at Cabrini: "Reality is just an illusion caused by lack of alcohol." But that is just the tip of it. Somewhere along the way, I don't know how or why, in the midst of anger, resentment, aloneness and determined self-will, I tripped . . . and fell into gratitude.

Gratitude is an old friend I hadn't seen in a long time. I had missed him terribly, but it had been so long I had forgotten what he looked like, and didn't know where he lived anymore. Suddenly there he was again—out of nowhere I could imagine—

calm and smiling and confident as ever. I was terribly embarrassed. I had neglected him badly. I should have looked him up long ago. I didn't want him to see me in my condition. Shy and apologetic, I suggested that maybe he should go on his way, and look me up again in a few months when I had had a chance to get myself fixed up. He laughed and said he didn't care what I looked like. We should walk together again, and see the wonders of life together again. "After all," he said, "what are friends for if they can't share the hard times?" "Don't be ridiculous," I replied. "With you around, there can't be any hard times. And I'm heading into a really hard time." Then he really laughed. "Well," he said finally, still chuckling, "I'm glad to see you still know the truth, even if you don't act like it."

He just plain flat refused to leave. I don't know how he found me, and the attitude I was in at the time should have driven him off, if anything could. But he wouldn't leave. And that's why I'm still here. Of course, I have my suspicions about who really sent him. That just makes me even more grateful.

I don't know why I'm telling you this. Talking about gratitude doesn't make anybody grateful. At least it never worked that way with me. But I just have to tell somebody. I stumbled onto that passage in Colossians the other day, for instance, and it just leapt out at me that one of the things the early Christians were doing a lot of—was feeling grateful. Then I began to realize that, in a way, that was the *only* thing they were doing. At least, everything that mattered seemed to be coming from thankfulness and gratitude.

You know how sometimes the inner fog seems to blow away for a minute and things seem to get into their true perspective—kind of like the flash of a vision or something? Well, that's the way it seemed to me for a while. I saw that everything I had ever done which did not spring from a genuine thankfulness was tainted and corrupted. The only deeds that matter anywhere on earth are those which come out of some sincere gratitude. That's a bit more than my little mind can comprehend. Nevertheless, I saw it for a moment. And it was beautiful and true.

That sort of sweeps through and throws a lot of my life into the trash bin. It also leaves some rather surprising things still standing. But that doesn't matter. Better to have seen it than never to have seen it. I even saw that Jesus went to the Cross in gratitude—gratitude to God for being stronger in Him than the fear of what men could do to Him. I knew He was courageous and obedient. But this was even bigger. He was grateful for a Kingdom most of us but dimly see. And gratitude is the highest and purest motive power in the universe—except for the love of God itself. That overwhelms me. I'd like to talk more about it, but don't know enough to say any more about it right now. But consider some lesser things.

I.) GRATITUDE IS AN ATTITUDE—NOT AN EVENT

Somewhere along the line, most of us pick up the notion that gratitude is the result of some outer event. Something good happens to us, and then we feel grateful. Something bad happens, and we are ungrateful and sad. Therefore, our thankfulness— and behind that, our happiness—depends on what is happening to us. It is caused by events from outside. Therefore, we have a tendency, along with the rest of our culture, to look for and to hope for good things coming our way. And in fact, it is commonly believed that if we work for it correctly, we can cause the good events to come our way. Then, of course, we have no reason to be grateful, because we worked for it, and deserve it.

Somehow, despite the logic of these assumptions, life doesn't bear out such expectations. Looking around us, it is glaringly obvious that gratitude bears no correlation to outward circumstances. Some people who "have everything," as we say, are indeed grateful people. But if anything, they are rare among their kind. We do not have to observe life for very long to discover that things on the outside do not make people happy. Most of us know and say that for years before we believe it, but it is obvious. People can have a great overabundance of every kind of outward blessing, and still be ungrateful, miserable and unhappy.

The reverse is even stranger to behold. Many people who

live in circumstances we consider to be harsh or difficult or meager
are also ungrateful and unhappy. But the correlation does not
hold. We also meet many among them who seem, inexplicably, to
be immensely grateful people.

One of the most grateful people I have ever known was a boy
named Richy Bravacos. He spread love and joy and appreciation
like perfume spreads its scent. Yet, he struggled for every breath
he took, and died at age nineteen of cystic fibrosis.

Thanksgiving Day itself was born out of a poverty and need
that would make many people today feel anything but grateful.
Some of the folk involved weren't feeling very grateful either.
None of the plans were working out. Some wondered if God had
deserted them, or if they were being punished for their unorthodox
faith. It certainly looked like it! Landing at Plymouth was a
mistake. Landing in December was a disaster. By springtime,
forty-four of the one hundred were dead. It didn't appear that
God had gone out of his way to bless them. But facing another
winter, counting up the harvest in November, it appeared that if
food were carefully rationed, those who survived would have seed
enough for the spring planting. So they got together to celebrate
and give thanks to God. It makes some of our present
Thanksgiving Day celebrations seem almost a mockery.

Martin Rinkart was pastor of the Lutheran Church in
Eilenberg, Saxony, during the Thirty Years' War. Into his city
came the refugees from the surrounding territory, with famine
and plague close behind. In 1637 alone, eight thousand people
died of the fever in Eilenberg. Rinkart was finally the only pastor
left in the city, and he buried four thousand people in one terrible
year. As the ordeal was ending, he wrote a hymn that is still sung
today, though with little comprehension of its profound faith. In
fact, you just sang it: "Now Thank We All Our God."

Paul thanks God from prisons and beatings and trials that
look to us like utter defeat and devastation. Stephen thanks God
as they hurl the stones that will kill him. Thankfulness is not
linked to outward circumstances, good or bad. Gratitude is an
attitude—not an event. It comes from within, not from without.

The bad news is, we cannot just go get some. The good news is, if once we find it, this world cannot take it away.

II.) GRATITUDE IS AN OVERALL RESPONSE, NOT A SPECIFIC JUDGMENT

Again, I'm not of the notion that you do not know such things. Rather, I am enthralled with the rediscovery of them myself. Saying "thank you" for isolated items or favors does not make me a thankful person. On many occasions, "counting our blessings" can leave us less grateful than when we started. It gets us to focusing on our personal opinions of what we like or dislike, want or don't want. Perhaps you don't fall into this trap, but pretty soon I get to thinking that I was born into this world to give my personal opinion about everything. I like this kind of food, I don't like that kind of food. I like this kind of tree, I don't like that kind of tree. I like this kind of person, I don't like that kind of person. Without realizing it, I'm soon starting to use a very low-grade form of gratitude as a way to judge everything around me according to my whims of what pleases or displeases me. Every minute I remain in that mode, my gratitude is actually diminishing. I'm playing God, and only God can get away with that.

I like this kind of day . . . I don't like that kind of day . . . and if I don't get the kind of day I want, then I have a right to withhold my thanks, and to let everybody know how displeased I am. That is perhaps a slight caricature or exaggeration. But very slight!

Thankfulness, by its very inner meaning, is a response to God and, therefore, to all of life. Gratitude, by its very nature, implies that we are aware of something or someONE beyond and greater than ourselves. Thankfulness is always the mark of those who in some fashion recognize purpose and caring and blessings that are more than can be attributed to human effort alone. As such, thankfulness is the core and key to all true worship, personal or corporate. It is therefore also the source of faith. Faith means trusting God. There is a difference between trust and gratitude, but the two are inseparable. We trust God to precisely the degree that we are grateful. And we are grateful to the precise degree that we trust God. Gratitude comes from surrender—acknowledged dependence. Therefore, grateful people stop trying to put their personal stamp of approval on all the various items and events of life. Gratitude is a response to the whole show—to everything that comes, for everything that happens.

My personal likes and dislikes begin to fade to insignificance. Nobody really asked me my opinion anyway. I am here to learn and experience Life, not to judge or grade it. And thankfulness wells up when I begin to trust its Author for the design, the meaning, the outcome—the whole thing. Then I become a grateful person.

Counting our blessings is still a good thing to do, if we start out from an attitude of gratitude. Thanking people for the efforts they make on our behalf is a good thing to do also. Only, I have to be careful not to turn that into a little courtroom scene inside my head—where I am merely judging everything from my own notions of what I want or like. It wouldn't be so dangerous, I'm sure, if I had the wisdom to know what my blessings were. Looking back, I'm always amazed at how often I was thankful for things that had no real importance—sometimes even for things that turned out to be a curse. And how also I severely complained so many times at things that turned out to be great blessings. Some of you may have had the same experience.

The day the Redlands church split was one of the darkest days in my life. I made it dark, that is. It turned out to be an unspeakable blessing. Recently, I had an equally startling experience along the same line. But you know about that one.

III.) THE OPPOSITE OF PRIDE IS GRATITUDE

I don't know if it's true, but it seems to me that there are two kinds of power in the world. I don't mean physical energy, but motive power. Everything that humans do is being motivated from either the principle of pride, or the principle of gratitude. It is coming from the urge to power, the need to gain control, the desire for domination—or it is coming from the response of thankfulness. People do things to get into a god-like position—

or people do things in gratitude to God. Gratitude is the fuel of faith. It is the purest energy source for human endeavor.

And gratitude is the only motivation uncorrupted by human pride. If we do a person a service or a favor out of gratitude to God and to Life, they will end up blessed. If our action comes for any other reason, they will end up the worse for our attention— manipulated, controlled or dehumanized in some way, obvious or subtle. The deeds may even be identical on the surface. But the source from which they spring is either pride or gratitude. That will make all the difference in the end. I won't try to carry that thought any further, though it goes into endless places. Just wanted to leave it with some of you for a Thanksgiving Day meditation. Gratitude, or thankfulness, is the only motivation the saints of God will touch. Everything else leads to corruption.

One of the ten lepers felt thankful and turned back, praising God aloud. He was cured twice over. The other nine were merely cured of a physical disease. The tenth man realized that he had been loved. That cured him of the most deadly of all diseases. His thankfulness was not only the mark and proof of his cure, it was part of the cure itself.

Nine men got clean bodies. They lost the white marks of physical disaster. The tenth man lost that too—but in his thankfulness, he lost more. What stopped him in his tracks as he headed for the priests so they could declare him cured?

"Where is it coming from? And why me? Is it an accident? Whence cometh this sudden miraculous blessing?" In the simplicity of childlike logic, he knew, and stopped in his tracks. "It couldn't be an accident! Something cared! Somebody up there likes me, and I finally ran into some of his agents. I am loved!" And so he didn't just lose the white marks of the present leprosy, but all the marks of fear and aloneness and despair that crush our souls, warp our deeds, and deform our futures.

"Stand up—go your way—your faith has cured you." Indeed it had, for faith is knowing that you are loved. And thankfulness is the response and the motive power that come from that knowing.

They say some people are in love with love. Maybe it's foolish, but I find myself being very grateful for stumbling back into gratitude. I still can't figure out how it happened. Which is, I guess, even more reason for being grateful. Anyway, I know one grateful leper. How are you?

Acts 4:32-5:12

Week Four

TAKING CARE OF IT

When I was in treatment, one of the sayings of the colorful Mormon leader, J. Golden Kimball, kept coming to mind. It took on a new level of meaning, as things have a way of doing sometimes. "All you have to do to live a long and fruitful life is just get yourself an incurable disease, and then take care of it." I want to tell you what that statement now means to me.

The crucial first step in dealing with any disease is diagnosis. Do I have a disease? What is it? What is its nature? What will it do to me? The world is full of sad tales about disease that was never diagnosed or that was misdiagnosed. Things go from bad to worse and nothing is done, or the wrong things are done. People suffer needlessly, and often die, from diseases that could have been taken care of.

My own incurable disease, alcoholism, is a natural illustration. One in twenty-eight alcoholics today makes the correct diagnosis and learns to take care of their disease. Ten years ago, it was one in thirty-five. The number-one killer—stress, usually diagnosed as heart trouble—is another obvious illustration. People who do not admit the stress and learn to take care of it also die early, of heart attacks.

I am particularly fascinated, at the moment, with the phenomenon of denial. Nobody likes to admit that there is anything wrong with them. It is not enough, for instance, that a doctor diagnose a disease correctly. The patient must recognize, admit and accept the diagnosis. If not, he or she will refuse to take care of it. The proper medicine and treatment may be prescribed, but the person will not take it; or they will take only part of what has been prescribed; or they will take it a little while until they start feeling better, then stop until they feel worse, then take it again until they feel better, and so on. All of us could tell numerous stories of people who could never completely accept the diagnosis of their disease. If you asked them point-blank, they would say, "Yes, I have diabetes" (or whatever). Nevertheless, from time to time they stop taking care of it, as if something inside cannot finally accept the reality: "I have a disease, a sickness that must be taken care of continually."

Just so, every person who gets married discovers that resentment is a progressive and fatal disease that comes with marriage. If the diagnosis is not made and accepted by both partners and taken care of continually, it will kill their love. There are known ways to take care of resentment. Many people have discovered these ways and use them into long lives of being happily married. Others refuse the diagnosis, or cannot accept the rigors of taking care of it, or assume somehow that the disease can be allowed to run its course without having its inevitable outcome. Perhaps they contribute to the rest of us by proving one more time that it always does run its course, unless it is taken care of.

I have found my incurable disease. If you haven't found yours, it doesn't mean you don't have one. It just means you haven't found, admitted or accepted it yet. It is a wonderful thing to finally discover the diagnosis. Then you can start taking care of it.

In earlier times, the church talked about sin—alienation from God. That was the overall sickness from which the more specific diseases came. Separation from God is the big disease that covers all of us yet today. We are suffering and heading toward spiritual death from this disease, unless we take care of it. It is incurable. We never get free from the weakness. It activates or reactivates at any moment we pretend we don't have it and stop taking care of it. The sickness takes different forms, of course. We each have to make our own specific diagnosis under the general category. Some of us drink, some get high blood pressure, some cheat, or get angry, or lonely, or lazy, or fearful.

Nobody becomes really serious about taking care of their

disease until they are unalterably convinced that they have it. Nobody becomes really religious until they know for sure they have a sickness which is killing them. To be religious is to follow a specific spiritual path. You follow the path because you know you are sick and your soul will die if you don't. Never mind anything about God punishing you. Some people always put it that way. But if you don't follow the path, something inside the real you will weaken, will get bitter, shriveled and lonely, and will eventually die.

Every authentic spiritual path requires so much of us—makes so many changes in our way of living—that there is no way we will follow it for very long or with any consistency unless we are finally and fully convinced that we have an incurable disease. We have the sin—the alienation—and it will run its course unchecked within us until we realize we have it and decide we would rather do anything to take care of it than go on suffering with the increasing symptoms.

Then the great surprise comes. Having denied the disease, and been forced finally to change our ways in order to take care of it, we discover that the new way is a far better, happier, more satisfying way to live. It's a wonderful, joyful release and discovery to finally diagnose our disease and start taking care of it. In Christian language, it's called "conversion."

The Book of Acts records that when the people first started to recover from their alienation, they became so elated and so close to each other and so enthusiastic that they started pooling all their resources. Who *cared* who owned what—they loved each other! They felt such a bond of hope and caring and new possibilities that anyone was welcome to anything they had between them.

Then along came Ananias and Sapphira. They wanted the warmth and unity of the group, but they hadn't really admitted they had the disease in the first place. Naturally, they couldn't see giving up all their old ways of separation and fear when they couldn't admit they were sick. It was too rigorous and risky for them. So they tried to play it down the middle. Join the group, fake the spiritual path, but keep enough in reserve to be safe. Peter says to them, "Look, nobody *asked* you to do anything. So why did you try to pretend something you really didn't want to do and weren't ready to do yet?" Ananias and Sapphira couldn't face the full reality, or handle the diagnosis, so their sickness ran its full course, and rather quickly, according to the story.

Interestingly enough, Ananias and Sapphira were right, on a technicality. The early commune style of the church was impractical and soon abandoned. Though it was a beautiful idea, it was more efficient for each individual or family unit to take care of its own basic resources and share when there was special reason or a common project. The church still operates on that principle, usually on a very watered-down basis. Ananias and Sapphira weren't right for any right reason; they just couldn't get with the program. They never really felt what the others were feeling, so they never discovered what it was like to take care of their disease. They stayed outside the Faith and its Path. "Half-measures availed them nothing."

It has always confused the life of the church, has it not? There are always those who see the spiritual disciplines as something unfair, something to be avoided or pretended. Dangerous business. Better to honestly abstain from the Path than to pretend at it. If you see no sickness in your life, go on the way you are going until the diagnosis is clear, inescapable and accepted. Jesus came for the sick. Until we know we are sick, we do not need Him and will not like His Path.

You know, trying to recover from a disease always means making some changes. We don't usually have to change everything, of course. But it is the changes that make the difference. One thing we were all doing in the treatment program was working on a sobriety plan. What were we going to actually *do* to make a difference when we came out, so we could stay sober? The spirituality plan of the New Testament is also a sobriety plan, only written to cover all of us.

I've been noticing a few changes in myself this past week or so, but not all of the changes are very pleasing. I've noticed, for instance, that I don't seem to be as well-organized about details. I guess for years now I've been careful not to lose things or forget things for fear somebody would think I had been drinking. Now that I know I'm not drinking and don't have to prove it, it's getting harder to stay organized.

The other day, I walked into the store, bought some tobacco and was clear across the store and half out the door before I realized I had forgotten my change. That never would have happened in the old days. I went back to the counter, and the clerk was waiting patiently with a smile on his face and my change in his hand. I thanked him and took my change and started out again. Behind me I heard him say, "Hey Buddy, you came back for your change. You might as well take what you bought." Sure enough, I had come in, plunked down my money, and walked out without either the change or the tobacco. Some things just don't seem as important as they used to.

I started thinking about that phrase. "You forgot your change." Taking care of a disease means remembering to change. God, through all the circumstances of life, keeps trying to change us all the time. I had been forgetting my change in a lot of ways. What good is it to pray or read the Bible if you go off without your change? If you have a conversation with someone, anyone, and go off without your change, you might as well never have spoken. It's fun to be alive when we realize that everything we encounter brings with it an opportunity to learn, and grow, and change.

"All you have to do to live a long and fruitful life is just get yourself an incurable disease, and then take care of it." Admit you have it, and take care of it. Don't come to church and go off without your change. If you do, you were never really here. "They reject the road, and not the goal. But lo, he who rejects the road has rejected the goal already."

Luke 12:13-31

Week Five

SPIRITUAL BLACKOUTS

There are people, I am told—and I know some of them—who can take a drink or two and be content with that, leave it at that, and go on to live perfectly normal, healthy lives. I also know quite a few people who cannot do that. They may appear to manage it, on the surface. They may actually manage it for a while or at times. But if you knew them well, or followed them around for a while, you could see that it was not going to work out right. Drinking, for some, is a downhill road.

My daughter, it seems to me, has a very interesting quirk. She both likes and dislikes scary things. It has been that way since she was a little girl. Sometimes, for instance, she would want to see a scary movie. But then right in the middle of the most exciting scenes, she would cover her eyes and refuse to look. Now, that is a little crazy—to go to a scary movie on purpose and then hide from the very scenes that make it interesting. But to top it all off, afterward she would want to know what happened! I would say to her, "Willene, if you wanted to know what was happening, you would have watched!" But she would insist that she just couldn't bear to watch, yet she claimed to be eager (almost frantic) to learn what had happened. Sometimes people hide from what they want or need to know.

I know some people who can draw a paycheck for several months, even for several years, and go right on to live a perfectly normal, healthy life. I even know a few who can achieve a measure of success, or even inherit some money, and still go on to live sane and well-balanced lives. But I also know quite a few people who cannot do that. They may appear to for a while, on the surface. But if you knew them well, or followed them around for a while, you could see that they were severely addicted. The desire for

48

more and more material security, and the fear of some eventual future deprivation, rules and ruins their peace and their relationships. Eventually, it corrupts every area of their lives. The search for material security, for some, is a downhill road. The more drink some people get, the worse off they are. The more material security some people get, the worse off they are. They can't handle it. For them it's an allergy, a life-threatening disease. It turns into a compulsion. They want more and more and more.

One of the phenomenons of the alcoholic life is what is known as a "blackout." Obviously, if you put enough alcohol into any human system, it will lose consciousness. But a blackout is different. Normal people, and the people who occasionally over-celebrate, do not have blackouts. But after heavy drinking over time, people increasingly experience extended periods when they go on functioning but have no memory of it afterward. The person can walk, talk, argue and explain what they are doing and, while you could tell they had been drinking, in many cases you would not think them severely inebriated. Yet, afterward, they will have no memory of what has happened.

I have a friend, for instance, who frequently, after an evening of drinking, would wake up in a foreign city. He could never remember going to the airport, purchasing the ticket, boarding the plane, flying for hours. Eventually, he would "come out of it" in a strange hotel room, or walking an unfamiliar street. Then he would have to start figuring out where he was, how long it would take him to get back home, what sort of "explanations" he could make to his boss and wife, and how he could find some way to pay his growing Visa bill. That's a blackout.

My friend finally figured out that when he drank, he started fantasizing about moving to some place where nobody knew him, and starting his life over again. It is a perfectly normal fantasy. Most people enjoy daydreaming it from time to time. But in a blackout, this man would actually start to act it out. Of course, knowing all this didn't help anything. It kept right on happening, until he stopped drinking.

I have another friend who answered the doorbell one morning to find a police officer standing there. Up to that moment, he thought it was just another regular day. He had had a few drinks the night before, and had come home. That was all. Now, with a couple of aspirin and a few tricks-of-the-trade, he was up and as fresh as usual. But it turned out that he had been in an accident, had talked to the other driver, had left the scene in a huff, had driven the twenty miles back home—and he had absolutely no recollection of any of it. Nor did he have any idea why he had been over in that part of town. Now the front of his car was smashed in and he faced a hit-and-run charge, but couldn't remember any of it. And what else had he maybe done? Who would show up at the door next, and with what kind of news? That's called a blackout! If you've ever had one and you don't know what to do about it, I have good news for you! Come see me after the service.

Jesus often spoke of "eyes that do not see," of "ears that do not hear." It is hard to follow Jesus around for any time at all without getting the strong but eerie feeling that He is aware of many things that those around Him simply do not notice. It is as if Jesus is the only fully awake person, and those around Him are somewhere between partly asleep and almost totally oblivious. Jesus goes about, gently shaking people—sometimes not so gently—and saying, "Please wake up!"

Jesus knows and "sees" the Kingdom of God. He lives in it and for it fully on a daily basis. Around Him are people who are seeking it, people who are waiting and watching for it, people who are getting glimpses and moments of its glory, and also people who are completely unconscious of any of it. Jesus tells people that this Kingdom is in their very midst. He promises some that they will not die before they see the Kingdom. He reassures one man that he is not far from the Kingdom. He teaches that we must be born anew before we can see the Kingdom. What do you make of it?

A pattern does begin to emerge and connect things everywhere. Drinking is not the only problem in life. There is more than one kind of "blackout." One of the major problems in life is that we spend a lot of time in "spiritual blackout." We go through days, even years, and cannot remember who we are, why we are here, what this life is all about. Sometimes we live as if in a trance. Or we live as if we can no longer see or understand or remember which things are of true value. Occasionally, painfully, we awaken, or start to awaken, and begin to see the damage we have done—the things we truly love that we have neglected. If we are not very close to some strong support and affirmation, sometimes the sight is so upsetting that we head back into blackout just to get away from what we have started to "see."

A blackout is caused by sustained, excessive use of alcohol. What causes a spiritual blackout? Overdosing on security or survival concerns—trying to get a "fix" with material resources. In Biblical language, it is the Rich Young Ruler Syndrome. In ethical terminology, it is called "greed," but the judgmental sound of that word misleads some people. It is a disease. Some people have an insatiable craving for feeling "safe." They have a compulsion to survive. Normal desires for survival or safety go haywire, escalate off the normal chart. A normal, healthy person only wants a glass of wine or two with a meal. How much material security does a normal, healthy person want? (What percentage of the population are closet survive-aholics—people trapped in the fear and compulsions of a materialism run riot?)

As we mentioned, some people can get a paycheck or inherit money or achieve some success and still live a normal, healthy life. But those stricken with the disease can never get enough. The fear of deprivation drives them to acquire or achieve more and more. Behavior is distorted to a kind of insanity. Soon, other values don't matter, other people don't matter. The victim is driven by a need to control things, and by a compulsion to create a larger and larger buffer between himself and any kind of material want. If a person lives in this state for any extended period of time, spiritual blackout is inevitable.

Most of the time, it seems to me, when people get a taste of love, or a clear experience of God's presence, or a glimpse of the

Kingdom, they come out of it for a while—out of spiritual blackout. So we shake ourselves, make resolves, think it won't happen again. We start nurturing our relationships again, hearing music, seeing sunrises, training some of the skills we have for service and for accomplishment. And things go fine . . . for a while. Then one bill too many comes in, or there is a rumor at work, or something happens to trigger the disease again. Off we go on another binge. We start plotting, planning compulsively, drinking in anxieties, forgetting to trust in God. Weeks or months or years later, we come out of it, only to realize that we have been in spiritual blackout. And God knows what havoc has been done.

I never like to leave a worship service without some practical and helpful suggestions for people. It's beyond my comprehension, but some people never hear them. Can you believe that? I actually have people say to me that my approach may be theologically or theoretically brilliant (meaning, they don't know, maybe it is), but they don't get anything solid or practical that they can get their teeth into. Finally, one person summed it up for me when he said: "You just tell us to come to church, to tithe, and to pray, study the Bible, trust God, and religious stuff like that. But you don't tell us anything realistic that we can actually *do* something about." (Before you conclude that what I suggest is small or insignificant—try it.)

Is there any help for spiritual blackouts? If you have blackouts, there is only one way to stop them. Stop drinking. Stop the intake of the stuff that puts you under. It turns out to be the same with spiritual blackouts. Stop the intake of the stuff that puts you under.

If your values are material, you are "under the influence." The fear of survival will escalate to disease proportions. Stop and think about it. If you think you are in control, or if you think you must find a way to get in control, you are automatically in a state of terror. There is no way an individual human being can ever feel safe or secure in a world like this—if he is counting on himself, or she is counting on herself. It just plain, straight isn't possible.

Trick and try and pretend as we will, if we think it is up to us, we are in terror. The disease is rampant. There is no way we can acquire enough to give us any rest or peace. We must find a way to trust Another, a Higher, a Power beyond us . . . or there is no hope. If your values are material, you are "under the influence." You have the disease. Or as Scripture says, "we will die in our sins"—in our separation and alienation (lonely, self-righteous and terrified). Trust—or faith—is critical.

One quick aside. I have preached here long enough that you know I do not equate saintliness with poverty. I have shown you in passage after passage that it is a mistake—a misunderstanding of Jesus' message—to suppose that He wants His followers to be poor. Jesus really was not hung up on material things—meaning, He did not scorn or accept people on that basis. Some disciples were rich, some were poor. It didn't matter to Him, as long as they didn't have a problem with it. Neither poverty nor wealth was His measuring standard. It is important for us to keep that clear, unless we *want* to mis-hear.

There was a time when it came as a great revelation to me that if I didn't drink, I wouldn't have to be drunk anymore. Things had become so complex, had grown so convoluted, that simple equations like that no longer occurred to me. Finally, the simple word of mercy broke through. I didn't have to untangle all the knots, or make everything come out looking pretty or pleasing or well-explained. I *did* have to see that alcohol was no longer my friend. If I didn't take another drink, I wouldn't have to be drunk. It wouldn't solve most of my problems; it wouldn't make me rich or successful; it wouldn't make people like me; it wouldn't change my character defects. But I wouldn't have to be drunk anymore. And I wouldn't have to have any more blackouts.

If anyone wants to get rid of their spiritual blackouts, the logic is as simple. Stop trusting in material things—start trusting in God. If I don't have to survive, I don't have to be sick with fear anymore. If I do what the early Christians called "dying with Christ"—if I, finally and truly, turn my life over to God's mercy—then I am free of the terror at last.

We can stop expecting peace or joy or security from material benefits. Thousands have found and walked this Way before us. Being in control . . . managing our own lives . . . having all the things we want . . . keeping ourselves safe and secure—it is not "the friend" we thought it was. Moving back to God—getting close, learning to trust God, letting God have the management—that is what lifts the spiritual blackout. It isn't really mysterious or complex—we add that in because of our own panic. The closer we get to God, the more the peace and the power of God fill our lives. It's that simple. If you love God, you won't be lonely or afraid anymore.

Luke 11:2-4; Matthew 6:9-13

Week Six

THE LORD'S PRAYER

This message begins a series on the Lord's Prayer. No collection of words could possibly be more familiar to all of us than this one. I presume and assume that all of you have known and prayed the Lord's Prayer for as far back as you can remember. What could I possibly say on the subject that you do not already know?

However, and as usual, I keep discovering in my own life that passages of Scripture, and things very familiar in the Christian Life, keep taking on more and more meaning, keep bringing me exciting new surprises. Therefore, I expect the same thing also happens with you. We have discovered also that the most familiar things, the things closest to us, are often the greatest treasures of all. Yet we come to take them for granted. Occasionally, we have lost their true significance through casual familiarity. Such things can even happen with a spouse—the person we once thought to be the most wondrous person in the world. Many of us have discovered that, in some seasons of life together, we can lose this perspective for a while. In similar fashion, we can forget the very importance of the presence of the Holy Spirit. Even with a prayer of power and truth like the Lord's Prayer, we can sometimes fall into mere recitation—hearing and feeling nothing but the dull cadence of familiar noise.

Once, some years ago, for reasons and circumstances I have no time to go into here, the Lord withdrew presence and support from me for a few days. It was the most surprising and appalling experience of my life. Three times I have stood and watched my whole life crumble before my very eyes. That was nothing in comparison to this. This was something like having the wind knocked out of you, only on many layers and in many ways all at

once. It felt like I couldn't breathe. I couldn't feel. No thoughts
made any difference. Nothing mattered. It was like being alive,
only in the "void," in the abyss—no pain, no pleasure. Therefore
it was worse than pain—and yet even that didn't matter. I was
completely amazed! I had no idea, no comprehension, of how
much power, providence, affection and support were being put
forth to keep and sustain me in life every moment of every day. I
had taken it for granted. I thought some of that energy, some of
the caring, some of the thoughts and aspirations and
accomplishments were coming from me. I had never been without
the Lord's Presence before, and did not know what it was like to
have the hand of God withdrawn. I don't believe most people do
know, or they wouldn't feel the way they do about religion or
God.

I'm simply saying that sometimes we take things for granted.
And getting a fresh appreciation for what sustains us can be a
rare and great blessing. It is my hope that we can all get a fresh
appreciation for the Lord's Prayer.

There is no prayer in this world greater than the Lord's Prayer.
It can pick us up on any level of spiritual awareness, and carry
us as far as we are willing to go. It is timeless, in that ages come
and go, and circumstances change, but the prayer is undimmed.
We all have our own word preferences. I wish, for instance, we
would all switch from "debts" or "trespasses" to "sins." But such
things are minor. The prayer translates into any language, crosses
all cultural and economic barriers. As E.F. Scott has written:
"There has never been a time when it was not daily repeated by
all Christians, alike in their common worship and their private
devotion. It is the watchword by which they recognize each other,
whatever may be their race or calling or their plane of culture.
They learn it as children and hold fast to it, through all changing
experiences, until they die."

It is true, is it not? Nothing is more common, more shared,
more claimed between all Christians than this prayer. We have
some slightly different versions, and different groups add or
subtract a phrase—as one would expect of anything used so much

by so many. But there has been very little fighting over it. Rather, for a change, we accommodate each other's small differences, and feel no rancor. Creeds and doctrines divide us, but this prayer constantly draws and unites us—and it has down through the ages (with rare exceptions).

Already, just thinking of such things, being reminded of such things—and the tradition and heritage behind it all—sends chills up my spine. How many thousands of my fellow Christians, brothers and sisters of the Faith, have turned to this prayer for solace; have breathed it in their dying; have leaned on it in times of temptation; have turned to it when they needed inspiration or clarity? Some vast, if quiet, army of souls has continually marched through this life—carrying all their joys and sorrows, victories and defeats with them, just as I do mine—and this prayer has been both watchword and bulwark of their living. And they are my people, my heritage, my tradition . . . and yes, this is my prayer too. So I would love it also, and learn it, and pray it as they did. Each time I do, it reminds me that I am part of Jesus Christ, and part of His people. Sometimes that realization is delightful, and sometimes it is appalling—if I do not feel like I am living very well at the moment—but always it is wonderful to be reminded, to have it come clear again.

Perhaps I should confess that the Lord's Prayer has not always been this meaningful to me. I can even remember a period of time when the Lord's Prayer seemed like an empty and foolish ritual. It seemed to me that we had all said it so many times that none of us were still paying any attention. We mouthed it, but didn't *pray* it. We rattled it off whenever the bulletin said to, or whenever the situation punched the "ritual button." In a group this size, there are probably several people who feel approximately that way about it today. Well, take heart. The Lord doesn't seem to get especially angry about it. I remember other parts of my spiritual life that were very dynamic and deeply committed at the time. So please don't mistake me for trying to raise up some new guilt, or lay on some new obligation. The Lord's Prayer needs no defending, certainly not from me.

But I also learned, years ago, that not everyone was just going through the motions. The prayer has a way of winning us over, or winning us back, as life goes on. There are few gifts in life to match it. When once our minds finally open to it, familiarity only enhances what lies within. "Deep calleth unto deep . . . "

I also remember a certain scorn with which I once viewed the way Catholic priests would send their people from confession with instructions to say so many "Our Fathers." How unimaginative, how stupid—I thought. But I was the one who didn't understand. I thought the priests were sending their people to recite words, like our teachers used to make us write silly phrases on the blackboard fifty or a hundred times. But the priests were sending their people to contemplate who they really were—and to whom they belonged. They were sending their people to meditate on the primary precepts of the Christian Life, and to recall what their lives were dedicated to. If some of the people were too spiritually asleep to know what they were being asked to do . . . well, what can you do with people who are still asleep, anyway? You keep sending them to the drill, in the hope that one day they too will awaken.

Now, to some technicalities that are very important. The Lord's Prayer appears two different places in Scripture (Matthew 6:9-13 and Luke 11:2-4). Matthew's version is longer and more familiar. Most scholars suspect that Luke's shorter, crisper version is closer to the original. We will use them both and notice the contrast at times, but there's no reason for a fight between the two. Remember, for instance, that the longer versions of the prayer were developed and used—meaning, tested and found satisfying—for hundreds of generations, by thousands of people. They found the additions helpful to their understanding of what the prayer was calling them to. We defer to Jesus' authority, but in this case that is not at issue. Jesus did not carve these words in rock. He gave the prayer to the disciples to be used, and no prayer has ever been more used by a wider array of people over so long a time. The source is of great importance, but the usage by the church is also quite impressive. Perhaps most startling is that the variations are as minimal as they are.

Between Matthew and Luke, however, it seems clear that the giving of the prayer is more likely to be in the setting Luke gives us. Matthew puts it in the Sermon on the Mount, where he has collected all of Jesus' most impressive teachings. Luke says the disciples, after having watched Jesus pray—having finally discerned that prayer was the core and source of His inspiration and power—the disciples ask Jesus to teach them to pray. They also mention that John the Baptist had taught *his* disciples a prayer, and they now want a prayer from Jesus.

This brings us to two very important items that will have considerable impact on everything else we say or understand about this prayer. We would not pick them up without the help of the scholars.

First, scholars tell us that it was customary for prominent teachers in Jesus' day and time to teach their followers—their disciples—a prayer. This prayer embodied the special wisdom and approach of the teacher. This prayer was memorized by all disciples of the teacher. Knowing and reciting this prayer identified you as a disciple of your particular teacher. If you ceased being a disciple of that particular teacher, you ceased using the prayer. Also, you had no right to start using the prayer until the teacher deemed you worthy. That is to say, you were "given" the prayer by the teacher when he finally accepted you as a true disciple. Knowing and using the prayer was the mark of your discipleship—and a bond you shared with other disciples of the same master. So, we have an identity issue, a disciple thing and a bond between master and pupil that are inherent parts of this Lord's Prayer and that linger around its meaning, but not always with sufficient clarity in our day.

How can I say it? Even if we could—which we cannot, and don't want to—but even if we could forget everything about the content of the Lord's Prayer, the mere act of saying it has far-reaching and profound significance. Every time we say the Lord's Prayer, we are also saying: "You, Jesus, are my Master Teacher. I have put myself under your discipline. I will strive to learn what you teach me as quickly and thoroughly as I am able. I am under the yoke of your discipline. What you teach me by word, example or assignment, I will also obey to the best of my ability." To even speak this prayer is a reiteration of all these things.

You see, the relationship between teacher and disciple was one of great magnitude in the past. Our use of the word "teacher" (for the most part) is an anemic and insulting caricature by comparison. It was once like a complete apprenticeship—and the subject was Life. Right at the core of this bond between master and disciple (discipline = yoke = yogi) was the prayer, which was both identity (sign of belonging) and a summation of the way of Life that was being taught.

Second, we are told that Jesus' prayer was scandalously short, in comparison to the expectations of the day. That would seem typical of Jesus. We are also told that, at first blush, the prayer sounded terribly simple, common, "humble." Such a prayer was usually an attempt to point, at least, to the grandeur, the vision, the glory, the terrific commitment and high aspirations of the spiritual life and calling. Jesus plopped out this dirt-poor, three-sentence, incredibly unmagnificent thing about daily bread and forgiveness and temptation.

It was scandalous! It was appalling! It would be humiliating for every disciple of Jesus to have to come out with such a lame-duck prayer within anybody else's hearing. We're still working on "typical Jesus" aren't we? But we don't understand about the bond between master and disciple. You could quit, walk away, get another master. But you didn't do that lightly. A rabbi of any merit wouldn't take you on if you had shown yourself unteachable and undisciplined with others. Some people did eventually walk out on Jesus when the teachings got too tough. But not here. The disciples knew it might be a test, or a new teaching with a hidden point. So they started saying the prayer, swallowing their pride, claiming their identity. If the Master wanted to shame them, that was His business—theirs was to be disciples.

Eventually, of course, as they prayed, they began to get suspicious . . . then startled . . . then dumbfounded. Jesus had a little "Abe Lincoln flavor" about Him—a little Gettysburg Address Syndrome when He chose to use it. The prayer was dynamite. The prayer wasn't much to look at. It wasn't very impressive as a literary masterpiece. It didn't have any length, or flair, or brilliance, or flowery language. But if you started praying it—whammo! You can look at it . . . think about it . . . turn it around and around—and it isn't much. But the minute anybody takes it into God's presence and starts to *pray* it, starts to align to it, starts to let it nuzzle up to their motives and methods and inner being, then it becomes the very essence of prayer. Then its eloquence is unmatched, and it even flows as much in what it does not say as it does in what it does say.

Today I have tried to focus your attention on the Lord's Prayer. I have reminded you of the key place this prayer has held in Christian circles from the very beginning. I have tried to inform or remind you of the setting of Master and disciple out of which it comes, and of how that links this prayer to our identity as Christians, and to our belonging to Jesus. Finally, I have suggested that the prayer is more than it seems—that it is full of power and mystery, and may even hold a few surprises for those of us who have been using it faithfully every day for years.

I hope you will pray this prayer with renewed awareness and appreciation every day. The Didache (teaching of the twelve apostles, early second century A.D.) gives the prayer approximately as it is found in Matthew, and then adds, "Pray thus three times a day." That was the tradition for most Christians in our early history. I have only asked for once each day. So you see how reasonable and lenient I am with you, despite the rumors you sometimes hear from those who don't want you to live the Christian Life at all?

Luke 11:2-4

Week Seven

FATHER

Nobody can say everything at once. We are using Luke's shorter (and, most scholars agree, more authentic) version of the Lord's Prayer. The very first word is "Father." That raises issues alongside the issues of the prayer itself. I don't want you wondering if I have failed to notice them, or spending your time thinking about the sexist-language issues while I'm talking about the prayer itself. I simply want to talk about the prayer first.

We have established that the use of this prayer declares Jesus to be our Master—the teacher/guru under whose discipline we have freely chosen to place ourselves—that we might learn wisdom, and discover who we are, and find out how to live. That is the context, and the important and necessary introduction. It is somewhat futile to go on if that is not clear.

It is equally important to know that this prayer is not merely intended for corporate worship. It is not just an identification of our belonging to Jesus' group, and not just intended for us to recite together when we meet. It is also intended to be *prayed*. It is—and this is what many miss—it is also intended for our daily, private devotions. That is to say, each word or phrase within this prayer carries the message of what Jesus' WAY is. Let me keep repeating that several different ways . . .

The Lord's Prayer lines out the sort of attitude and approach toward life we are to have if we are Jesus' followers. The prayer is both a prayer and a compact summary of the Way of Life Jesus was teaching His disciples. This prayer contains the program for Life that Jesus was teaching. To pray or meditate on this prayer—in each of its parts, for long enough—aligns our lives with God in the correct manner. Are you hearing it yet? Perhaps you have known it already for a long time. Most people don't seem to, except in a very vague way. This prayer is not just a bedtime comfort or a Sunday-morning ritual—though neither of those are as unimportant as some people think. This prayer is THE WAY itself. Those who pray it with eager, willing, hungry souls— knowing or sensing why Jesus gave this prayer to them—find the Christian Path, and discover in this prayer the steps they must take to walk it.

One last reiteration, then. Picture the dynamic that is intended. Each and every individual Christian, knowing and naming Jesus as Master/Teacher, spends time at least once each day (remember that three times a day was the formula for the early church) thinking through each tenet contained in the Lord's Prayer . . . seeking to be and do what the prayer reveals . . . wanting to bring thoughts, words and deeds for that day into harmony with this prayer. Then these same people come together the first day of each week, and they say this prayer together, in each other's presence. Can you feel that? Do you sense the bonding that can take place in that? The comfort and power that can flow in such a community of believers? That is what is intended!

Can you imagine an early Christian saying, "But I don't know if I can pray this prayer because I'm not sure I believe everything I'm supposed to yet"? How silly that would have sounded in their mouths, not that it is any less so today. None of the creeds had been written yet. Many of the creeds that were later written came out of the meditations this prayer inspired—you couldn't hope to understand or believe them if you hadn't been praying this prayer, for years. First things first! If you want to follow Jesus, start praying the prayer He gives you. Let the rest come as it will.

When you pray, say: "Father." The first item—the first step, if you will—the first act or motion that we can and must make to get on the Christian Path or Way is to claim our relationship to God. This wasn't our idea. We didn't dream it up. We couldn't invent it if we wanted to. But it is offered, and we have to claim it or it does us no good.

This is the first item because it *has* to come first. This is the entryway into the entire Christian affair. In many ways, this is the major mission of Jesus on earth. That is to say, Jesus' life, death and resurrection are to open this way and to make it possible for us to claim this relationship. It isn't easy. The alienation between us and God is massive, and coated with fear, anger, pride and all the rest. "God was in Christ reconciling the world to himself." (II Corinthians 5:19) That is one of the great summations of the whole business. So there is a lot involved behind this first step. The prayer doesn't describe, teach or lay out any of the details. It leaves that to us, to our meditations and prayers, to our living and working and study and all the rest. The prayer just lines it out. The first step is to claim the relationship. We do this first because nothing else can happen until we do this. We are stymied until we can begin with at least some relationship, some association, with God.

You see what we are into? Are you starting to feel how Jesus works with us? He has such authority and power, yet He doesn't push or shove. He leaves so much of it to us. He trusts in our soul's desire to follow, so He merely calls and gives us a lead to follow, then leaves it to us. *When you pray, say: "FATHER."* One word, and we are into the whole thing. Who are we? Who is God? What is it like between us? All of it is instantly right there in our laps. Can we pray? Do we believe in God? How much? What kind?

Let us also note that this first step is not some kind of test we pass and then we have done it. This is not a first step and then we are on our way. This is a first step that is always and forever the first step. *When you pray, say: "Father."* Not just the first time you pray. *Whenever* you pray. This is always the primary thing: claim the relationship, reestablish your association. Many of us discover that we have to do this many times a day. Somebody gets displeased with me, makes me angry, hurts my feelings, threatens me . . . and what is my first and primary need? If I deal with the situation on my own, I will always mess up either myself or the other person. If I am awake enough to breathe that first word, "Father" (and if I have prayed and meditated enough over the years to know what that means), then I'm okay again. Then I know who I am, and where my help comes from, and where my true security lies. I have the primary relationship right. Then there is some chance to deal with the lesser relationships in some appropriate fashion.

So I never graduate from this first step. It never grows old or boring. And for the Christian, this one word stands for all the meaning of what Jesus taught, revealed and showed about the nature and love of God.

Again, the dimensions are endless, but a few comments about what Christians begin to contemplate: The relationship is very close! The relationship is very personal! We do not have enough time today, but it is most helpful to study the expected role of father and son as it existed in Jesus' day in Israel. It is important to know, for instance, that normally there was great affection between a father and his son. It is important to know that a son usually grew up as apprentice to his father, and that, most frequently, a son learned his father's skills and trade and then worked with the father, often for years, and then eventually took over the father's business. It was believed—and was true in a way we can barely imagine today—the old saying, "like father, like son." Unless something was badly amiss, you expected the same treatment from the son that you had received from the father. And if the son made an agreement with you, the father would honor it as if he himself had made it. Indeed, a son's identity was always connected to the father. Strictly speaking, there is no such thing as *just* King David. Israel knows that people don't just drop in out of nowhere. There is David son of Jesse, son of Obed, son of Boaz. (You probably don't remember Boaz, but he was the guy who married Ruth.) And Jesus, son of Joseph, is traced back through David's line.

All of this has a lot to do with the reasons early Christians called Jesus the Son of God. But it also has much to do with this prayer, and the shocking way in which Jesus goes to the core of our faith and/or our alienation, and instructs us: *When you pray, say: "Father."* It is startling. Few of us have the nerve for it, at first. None of us has the right to make such a high claim. "Dear God, this is me, your child, calling." At first, if there is a God, we expect either a disdainful and very total silence, or the roll of approaching thunder—and are not quite sure which would be worse.

That is the very point and the first point of this prayer we are given. The relationship is close. Very close! It is personal. Very personal! Nothing here about some vague "ground of being"; some ontological energy; some primal force; some cosmic principle in whose vast ebb and flow we find ourselves some tiny and insignificant speck. *When you pray, say: "Father."* Very close! Very personal!

This God you pray to cares about you—cares what you do, what happens to you, how you behave. But it's more than that—more than just what you do, achieve, accomplish. God cares about YOU as being, as person, as child of the heart.

Then also, it always followed in the Hebrew mind: "I must be about my father's business." What else, pray tell, *would* we be about? One word, the first word of the prayer, and we are called to claim our relationship with God—to know it as close and personal—and to realize that our lives are therefore dedicated to serve, honor and obey.

It is made clear in this prayer, then, that our destiny is totally linked with God, and that we must be about our Father's business. Eventually this will also remind us of the inheritance. It is a theme that Paul and other New Testament writers return to again and again. Of course! They have been meditating on this prayer.

This is only a few musings on the entryway into the Lord's Prayer. To find its true power and magic, we have to start praying it in unhurried, thoughtful devotion at least every day, knowing we will go on doing that—rain or shine, in season and out of season, through hell or high water—for the rest of our lives—because we are disciples of Jesus. In that frame of mind, in that fashion, with that intent, the prayer begins to truly speak within us.

I am sorry to now have to leave such high themes, but they have opened some wounds on another level. I cannot resolve the issue of sexist language because I do not believe a resolution yet exists. Nevertheless, the issue does exist and it does not seem possible or right to pass over the turmoil and pain involved without some acknowledgment. Precisely because this prayer is so central to our faith, and because it starts out with "Father," we all have necessary translations to make. This has always been the case, but for many, it is more poignant and more difficult than ever, and for many women we can quintuple that.

The issue is that some people are not men, and do not wish to think of God as male. Translating the implications of a relationship between a father and a son into a female experience can feel like a slap, a reduction, an insult—which, by the way, the God that Jesus revealed would not appreciate or tolerate for one of her daughters!

We know that God is not male or female by any definitions we know. Israel has known and taught that from the beginning, and built it into the Second Commandment: "You shall not make for yourself a graven image, or any likeness of anything that is in heaven above, or that is on the earth beneath." (Deuteronomy 5:8) We know that the Jesus who gave us this prayer did not think God was a male. "God is spirit," He said, "and those who worship must worship in spirit." (John 4:24) "That which is born of the flesh is flesh, and that which is born of the spirit is spirit." (John 3:6) "It is the spirit that gives life, the flesh is of no avail." (John 6:63) Jesus is not trying to define God in this prayer. Jesus is seeking the best analogy He can find to point to—to hint at—what the relationship is, or is supposed to be like, between us and God.

So every one of us has always had to do a lot of translating to get from our own experiences to the prayer's intended meaning. The more difficult our own relationship was with our own father, the more we have to wrestle with and translate the images that first come to mind. It is not a new problem. It is as old as language itself.

This is, I hope you realize, where some of the embellishments originated. From "Father" to "Our Father who art in heaven." It tells us nothing new, nothing we would not have come to by praying the prayer and meditating on it. The "Our Father" is even the name of the prayer for many, now. And often it is preached and taught that we cannot pray this prayer alone—that it is "Our Father," not just "My Father." That is an excellent point, and we will come to it later. But that isn't the most ancient form of the prayer. And this prayer is teaching you that even between just you and God, you are still the precious child.

More pertinent to our subject of the moment, some people couldn't wait for it to become clear to the novices and beginners that "Father" did not refer to any earthly father. From the beginning, it was clear that the prayer was not intended to be understood or to remain on any earth level or in literal symbolism. So the obvious—"who art in heaven"—was entered in the text. Fortunately, rather early on, people realized that if we didn't freeze the text, we would soon have a four-volume set of systematic theology rather than a prayer.

I am not trying to solve anything. I can't fix it for you. If you think this can be fixed, you are mistaken. This is a broken world. Things are not perfect here. Jesus would have chosen better words, and used clearer analogies, if we had developed a better language for Him to use, and if we were involved in better experiences that He could have compared with things of the Spirit. Hell was *Gehenna*, the garbage dump outside Jerusalem, because that was the closest thing Jesus could find to suggest to us what hell really means. The fact that we developed it into Dante's *INFERNO* is not really Jesus' fault. He had to use the language we were using (Aramaic), and He had to stick, in some form, to experiences we were having, or there would have been *no* communication, instead of merely imperfect communication.

Some of you think we should substitute "Mother" in the prayer. But that is not an improvement. Please don't misunderstand—it might be exactly right for you as an individual. And you might work with this prayer in your daily meditation using "Mother," and find the meanings and walk the disciple's WAY much better using "Mother." (And I'm not just talking to women.) If that is the case for you, it seems clear to me that is what Jesus would want and expect you to do. We are not literalists in this church—precisely because we do not find any evidence that Jesus was literalist in His approach.

But officially changing the wording to "Mother" for everyone is not an improvement. It takes us further from the context and meanings that Jesus was trying to point toward. And many people—if I need to remind you—did not have perfect mothers either! "Parent" is worse than either, for it is stale and contains little of the closeness and personal quality that are major to the message.

The fact is that we can lose this prayer for ourselves if we make it the ground on which to fight other battles or resentments. And this prayer has plenty of issues and battles of its own to bring you. So do what you have to—I can't fix it for you. But don't lose this prayer. Find the best, the strongest, the most nurturing, loving, caring, affectionate authority figure there is in your entire human experience. Start there! When you pray, begin by claiming the realization that God is in that kind of relationship with you . . . only far more than that . . . far better even, than that.

That is the first step, the most important step. Claim the relationship. Close! Personal! Caring! *When you pray, say: "Father."* And mean what Jesus was pointing toward with that word.

Romans 8:14-17; Galatians 4:1-7

Week Eight

DADDY

To say the Lord's Prayer means you have chosen Jesus as your Teacher, your Master, the One under whose discipline you have chosen to live and learn what life is about, what it means, and how to go about it. The Lord's Prayer is a prayer, but in this prayer is embodied the steps, the attitudes, the desires a disciple must "take on" to walk the Christian Way. We are not talking about perfection here. We are talking about a Way of Life—a pilgrimage, a journey.

That is a too-brief summary of where our study of the Lord's Prayer has taken us so far. Then we ran into the language barrier, and into a constant requirement: Each of us must always be translating all of the language of Scripture from earthbound words to inner truth—from mundane to spiritual understanding. This is one of the things we must learn. "The kingdom of heaven is like a merchant in search of fine pearls." (Matthew 13:45) That does not mean we all head into the jewelry business, does it? Learn this thing, please!

Around here, we are constantly grounding our spiritual precepts. If people start flapping their arms and soaring too high into mere theory or imagination, we say, "Where are you getting that? Are you just making that up? How is that attached and how does it square with what we know of actual 'messengers,' especially Jesus—born of the flesh, one of us . . . yet sent from God?" On the other hand, we are not literalist. Words are only symbols! Words are never perfect, and they are especially imperfect when used for spiritual purposes. That is to say, the heart and the soul can use mundane words to leap toward that which the words seek in vain to reveal. But the words themselves are never technically (or spiritually) right or accurate.

Jesus says, "The kingdom of heaven is like leaven which a woman took and hid in three measures of meal, until it was all leavened." (Matthew 13:33) Do you then go home, do that, bake bread, and say, "There, I guess I took care of that—now I have fulfilled the kingdom"???

Yet some of you were offended because I told you that you have to "translate" the words of the Lord's Prayer, inside your own soul, and seek their higher meaning within a heart that truly longs to pray as Jesus intended us to.

So you (and not just men) came to me and said, "Why tamper with the words? If they were good enough for Jesus, if these are the words Jesus gave us, then why don't we just accept it, and take it as it is given? Don't let's be so smart all the time and keep changing the meanings, lest we lose them." (Now, that may be a little better than how some of you put it, but that's essentially what I heard you saying.)

That is a beautiful and important point. We are disciples. We are supposed to be under discipline. We are supposed to be trusting, and humble, and teachable, and obedient to our Master. And this church hasn't always had that kind of attitude, and it is becoming a true church as quickly as its genuine humility and faithfulness grow. And with that attitude, I can hardly wait until the season brings us back to themes like tithing (some of you get enormously non-literalist when we get to that!) . . . or the requirement to forgive (even your pastor).

But back to the issue of translating, which seemed to bother some of you. The Scripture passage read: *When you pray, say: "Father."* And I suggested we all have to translate the word "Father" to the meanings Jesus was pointing toward. "No," some of you said. "Accept it just as Jesus said it." Let me ask you: How many of you speak Aramaic? You want it like Jesus said it, with no translation? How many of you promise to attend if we hire a person to come teach us Hebrew and Aramaic? If you are not translating all the time, you are understanding and comprehending nothing. The Word, our tradition has always said, is "a Living Word." If we lock it down to pre-set shapes so that we can feel secure and safe in our truth, then it cannot teach us anymore. Then it has become ritual, form, creed—and we have killed it, and it is no longer "the Word of God."

Once upon a time, at a summer camp in the 1940s, a young boy was leaping over a log and drove a spike deep into his foot. Soon he couldn't walk on it, but the camp was a week long. So he sat alone while the rest of the camp was alive with activities. That was okay. He was used to being alone. Then one of the camp staff noticed him. He was a big man with huge hands and calluses as tough as shoe leather. He threw the young boy over his shoulder as easily as a normal person would pick up a kitten, and he carried him everywhere, even on all the nature hikes.

The man wasn't much of a talker. He loved to move, to be in action, and mostly he tried to show what he wanted to say. One night at the campfire meeting, he seemed to get annoyed at the program. It was too canned, too dull, too pat, too boring. He strode forward to the bonfire, stooped and picked out a large, red-hot coal with his bare hands. Turning toward us, he juggled the coal, blowing on his hands, tossing the coal from hand to hand. Then, after a while, he slowly related to the group his thoughts.

The coal, he said, was very beautiful. It also gave much heat. He and his friends had often played with coals to amuse and warm themselves when logging in cold weather. He went on to say that, to him, the coal was like the Word of God. It was beautiful, and it had such power to heat and illuminate, to warm and inspire. But humans could not stand it in full strength. It would also burn them. Yet it was too beautiful to leave alone. So they must always juggle it. And if they took a little piece of this fire out of its context and played with it long enough . . . it would eventually get tame and safe. But it would also turn from fire to ash. "When you can hold it still in your hand and it doesn't burn you anymore, it is no longer the living Word of God," he said. And holding the now-black coal steady in his hand, he looked straight at me and said, "Do not forget."

When you pray, say: "Father." (blow, juggle, blow)

Some of you have also too quickly assumed that it is easy and nice for those of us who had essentially wonderful fathers, and who find ourselves male, at least this time around. I agree— that is much to be grateful for. But this too must be translated, and the danger is that sometimes we don't realize it. God is not just an overgrown manifestation of our good earthly fathers either! It's too easy to transfer individual characteristics and even personality flaws onto the relationship we have with the numinous, loving Being Christ was directing us to. Comfortable traps can be as deadly as wicked ones. They are sometimes even worse, because we don't struggle to get out of them.

Some of you are realizing by now that you are getting the same sermon today that you got last Sunday. Don't fret. If we get this first word right, the rest will come easy. None of us ever get and keep it clear enough. And we had the long, if necessary, interruption about sexist language. So it's not your fault, but you didn't fully "catch it" last Sunday. This prayer is power and magic, and it begins full force with the very first word. *When you pray, say: "Father."*

Okay, you don't like translations? Let's go back. *Abi* means "my father." It is the more formal, more polite, more respectful form of "father." ("James, I'm going to put you in charge of the sheep this month. Find the flock tomorrow at first light, and send Aaron back here to me." "Yes, my father . . . yes, *Abi.*") Nothing wrong with *Abi.* Some modern fathers I know could use a lot more of it. But it's more formal, respectful, emotionally distant.

Abinu means "our father." This is also formal, and even less intimate than *Abi.* Traditional Jewish prayers, in Jesus' day, began *Abinu.* And they almost invariably included a phrase about "in heaven." So it would appear that Matthew reverts to the more familiar, more traditional, safer form: *Abinu*—"Our Father, who art in heaven." It is as if the freshness and audacity of Jesus were too much, too stark, too surprising and upsetting. But (and some of you will say "of course") I am trying to persuade you to get your meaning from Luke.

This is a series on the Lord's Prayer. I won't suggest we change the way we say it together. I would, except that is likely to cause greater confusion, instead of greater worship. But we can try to comprehend as much as possible about what Jesus was giving to us, and put all the content of that into our praying, and let the Spirit take it from there.

When you pray, say: "Abba." Not *Abi.* Not *Abinu.* Say: *Abba.* What does *Abba* mean? Instead of a definition, or rather as a definition, get a picture in your mind. The picture is of a child, about age four or five. The child is running, arms outstretched. A look of pure delight is on the child's face. There is a man coming toward the child. His face is beaming too, and his arms are open also, and there is a gift hidden in his robe. The child's voice is filled with affection and expectation and a lot of things that won't ever quite fit into words. And as the child is running toward this man, the child is calling, *"Abba! Abba! . . .* Daddy! Daddy!" That is the definition of *Abba.*

Jesus taught us: *When you pray, say: "Abba."* Are you getting it? This is a step we have to take, if we are Jesus' people. This is a motion, an act, a leap of faith. Nobody had ever dared to address God with this sort of intimate, childlike trust and affection, until Jesus shocked His world by giving this prayer to His disciples. *When you pray, say:* [skip *Abinu,* cut behind it all, go straight to] *"Abba."* You don't have to try to revert back to your childhood. You only have to realize that with God, you are as a little child. But you do have to remember the trust, the delight, the affection and love, the open arms, the running toward.

What do you think of when you think of Daddy? When you think of the picture we have used to define "Daddy"? By the way, I didn't cheat with that definition. And I did read to you a couple of passages that show how early Christians (via Paul) were indeed meditating out of this Lord's Prayer, and were still stunned, however gratefully and happily, to be realizing what Jesus had suggested to them as their proper relationship with God.

But what do you think of, on the simplest levels, when you think of Daddy? Normally, Daddy is God to a young child. Daddy provides, protects, plays, tests, teases, disciplines, hugs, loves.

Daddy is often full of surprises, and you can never tell when Daddy will bring a gift. Daddy is the rules, and Daddy makes it work, and Daddy is sometimes stern—and precisely for these reasons, Daddy is what makes this big, scary world feel safe. Do you remember? What a feeling! When Daddy came home, all the wrongs would be righted—and maybe some of that would be hard, if you were attached to some of them. But afterward, it would be all right, and it would be safe again. If Daddy was close, then bogeymen and tigers and whatever . . . nothing was very scary if Daddy was near—except Daddy himself, if you got too far out of line. ("The fear of the Lord is the beginning of wisdom.")

I even remember, when I was old enough to know better, one time watching my father walking along the street below. I was seven stories up, in his office, looking out the window. He was coming down the far side of the street, back toward his office. It was the center of downtown Long Beach, California. He had to cross Pacific Coast Highway. He got to the crosswalk and stepped right out into the oncoming traffic. The cars were heading straight toward him. From up where I was, I couldn't see that the traffic light had changed. I remember thinking, "Oh dear, I hope that car doesn't hit him." I wasn't worried about my father—for just that split second, I knew that if the car hit him, it would split the car in two! I hoped the car could stop in time because I didn't want the people in the car to be hurt. *Nothing* could hurt Abba!

Why am I telling you this? Translate it somehow, some way, until you get into the meaning of the prayer. It seems to me that I know lots of people who do not have near as much regard, as much faith, as much trust and affection and respect and love for GOD . . . as I have for my earthly father! Taking trips with Jesus, trying to follow Jesus, is wonderful—the most exciting thing in the world—but not if you do not know how to call God *Abba*. That's part of the survival pack. Actually, that's the first item on the list. Fooling around with Jesus if we do not know God as *Abba*, we are dead meat, or dead spirit, or both.

Are you getting it this time? It doesn't matter how rich, or famous, or prominent, or successful you are—it doesn't matter how worried, or scared, or defeated, or ashamed you are . . . or whatever. *When you pray, every time you pray, say: "Abba!"* (Daddy! Daddy!)

If this is not the way you come to God, then maybe you haven't ever truly prayed yet. Or maybe you have been praying to the wrong god, if you do not come this way. Or maybe if we cannot come this way, we are not yet ready to pray. Or maybe delighting to come into God's presence in this way is more important than all of the other things we say or hear or do afterward.

One thing we do know: A man who had the spiritual power to calm storms, and transform lives, and make the lame to walk, and give sight to the blind—and before it was done, a man who changed the face of life itself by obeying His God through everything this world could do to stop Him . . . or any of us—this man, when He prayed, He went as a child, saying, *Abba.* If you follow Him, you will too.

Exodus 3:1-15

Week Nine

HALLOWED BE THY NAME

Sometimes the old gets so old that it is assumed, taken for granted, and finally neglected. In this way, things that are core principle, things that are cornerstone and foundational, can actually go unnoticed until a generation arises that no longer knows the foundation. It isn't taught or mentioned anymore. It has been assumed that everyone knows it, that it is obvious, for so many generations . . . that it is forgotten.

It would be interesting to gather our nominations for which central principles are most neglected and forgotten by our society at this present time. The fun, of course, is that forgotten truth can be rediscovered. The people who discover it afresh will be changed, converted, enthralled, transformed . . . and just as excited about it all as their ancient forebears were when they first encountered the same truth long ago.

With the first word of the Lord's Prayer, as we have seen, Jesus shocked His contemporaries, and required of His disciples a relationship and an approach to God that was scandalous in its intimacy, its affectionate trust, its presumptuousness on God's personal and individual love. Saying this prayer, every believer started out affirming: "I believe in God's personal, powerful, eternal love for me!" You see? The church's developing doctrines of grace, forgiveness, mercy—the very core of the Gospel—were not being invented by Paul. Rather, backed by the Cross and the Resurrection, and because the church was praying the Lord's Prayer individually and together day by day, these concepts were growing clearer all the time.

Today, of course, the theory of God's love—not its reality, not the experience of God's love—but the *theory* of God's love is so familiar, and has been for so many generations, that it actually

bores some people. What created the greatest spiritual revolution
in the history of mankind, and changed life on this globe on
every level of reality, is now, in terms of mere theory and concept,
so familiar that many people would rather garden or ski than
gather to talk about it. We "remember" that, for three hundred
years (and off and on since), countless people were literally willing
to risk their lives to come together to talk about this incredible
love of God and what was happening to them because they had
discovered it.

Not the experience, but the *theory* of God's love is old-hat
today. We do not always believe it inside ourselves where it
matters, but we take the outer intellectual concept so much for
granted that we even get angry if someone hints that there might
be anything left of God's judgment or wrath. What right has God
got to set standards, to require anything from us, to discipline or
correct us if we go astray? It is God's job to love—no matter what
we do to God, or to God's creation, or to each other, it is God's job
to love and forgive—and anything else is none of God's business!
If we wreck all the ecological systems and then starve to death—
is that not the wrath of God? That is exactly what the ancients
meant by the wrath of God. Get and stay in harmony with God's
ways, and the ways God does things . . . or perish.

So Jesus gives us the brand new, in the opening word of this
prayer, and that is now old to us. Then Jesus returns to the old—
the core tradition and heritage—for the second phrase. And that
is quite new to us. It was old, assumed, taken for granted in
Jesus' time, but it may seem like the newest dimension of the
prayer for us. *Hallowed be thy name.* What in the world does that
mean? Not only do we know it means something, but because it
is in this payer—this payer that is the distilled essence of
everything Jesus did and meant and came to reveal to us—we
know that it is one of the most important principles of life. It is
also more than words. It is an act, a motion we must make, a part
of the Way we are trying to walk because Jesus is our Master, our
Teacher/Guide. We are beginning to learn that a prayer is not
just a request tossed into the sky. A prayer is a way of being—a

way we align our lives to what we believe and what we expect, and to the God we trust.

Part of Jesus' genius is the way He mixed new and old— brought new out of old yet did not discard the old. Jesus loved and honored His Jewish tradition so well that the most powerful heresies could not break Christianity away from it. The Old Testament is still Christian Scripture, for instance, despite Marcionism. Jesus always built on the foundations others had laid. Let me take a few moments to illustrate.

In the synagogue service, there were three prayers that were solemnly recited at every meeting—the *Shema,* the *Kaddish,* and the *Shemone Esreh* (Eighteen Benedictions). The Shema even *we* know: "Hear, O Israel, the Lord is our God, the Lord is one." (Deuteronomy 6:4)

The Kaddish has two parts. The first said: "May his great name be magnified and hallowed in the world, which he has made according to his will, and may his kingly rule be established in your lifetime—in your time and in the time of the whole house of Israel. May the name of the Lord be praised from now on and forever. May the prayer and petition of all Israel find acceptance before our Father who is in heaven."

Put it into your mind, then, the picture of Jesus reciting this along with His friends and neighbors from the time He was a little boy—and of course, still doing so as we find Him attending synagogue in the Gospels. The affinities with the Lord's Prayer are instantly obvious.

Then followed the Eighteen Benedictions (the form of which changes over the years). Not only was it recited by the congregation at every service, but every pious person was supposed to say it individually three times a day—which is probably why the early church adopted the custom of saying the Lord's Prayer three times a day. Because of the length of the prayer, permission was sometimes given to use only two or three petitions at one service instead of all eighteen. While the later petitions vary more from age to age, the early petitions are ancient and quite standard. I will only read the first seven. Remember that Jesus would be praying these petitions probably three times a day through all His formative years.

1.) *Blessed be thou, O Lord, our God and God of our fathers; God of Abraham, Isaac and Jacob, a mighty and faithful God, a most high God, Creator of heaven and earth, our shield and shield of our fathers, our confidence in all generations. Blessed be thou, O Lord, the shield of Abraham.*

2.) *Thou art a mighty one who humbles the strong and judges the mighty, the ever-living God who raises the dead, who causes the wind to blow and the dew to fall, who cherishes the living and makes the dead to live. Blessed be thou, O Lord, who quickenest the dead.* (Somebody was explaining to me only the other day that Jesus was important because He told us about life after death. That is utter nonsense! Judaism had believed in life after death for at least a thousand years before Jesus, and probably for two thousand.)

3.) *Holy and fearful is thy name, and there is no God beside thee. Blessed be thou, O Lord, the holy God.*

4.) *Bestow on us, our Father, knowledge of thee and insight and understanding out of thy Law. Blessed be thou, O Lord, who givest knowledge.*

5.) *Bring us back to thee, O Lord, that we may return in repentance. Blessed be thou, O Lord, who has pleasure in repentance.*

6.) *Forgive us, our Father, for we have sinned against thee; blot out our transgressions from before thine eyes, for great is thy mercy. Blessed be thou, O Lord, who forgivest much.*

7.) *Look on our misery and prosper our cause, and deliver us for thy name's sake. Blessed be thou, O Lord, deliverer of Israel.*

Clearly Jesus' prayer, while new and startling in some ways, is also coming out of His heritage and tradition. Jesus has distilled and focused it all to amazing brevity for His followers. Yet if we do not feel the Jewish tradition behind it, we cannot fully grasp its content.

I would now refer you to familiar phrases coming from comic books and movies of only a few years ago. A policeman would bang on the door, saying, "Open up in the name of the law." Or instructions would come to the dashing hero in the movie, telling him to "Take this signet ring to the Duke of Cornwall, and bid him ride with all of his men to Devonshire, in the name of the king." Robin Hood was forever doing things in the name of King Richard, and his enemies were doing other things in the name of King John. And more than one fair knight fought and lived or died "For Arthur, and for England!"

It has only been a few generations since we forgot the meaning of names. Not all of us have forgotten, even yet, but through all prior history, everything was always done *in the name* of something, or someone. Certainly this is at the core of Judaism. I read to you about the incident of Moses meeting God, and finally requiring at least a piece of God's name. How could Moses go on—serve or call others to commit themselves to the impossible venture—if he could not do so in a NAME, if he could not call upon a NAME! "God," I remind you, is not a name. "God" is a title. "God" refers to a position, like Judge, or Doctor, or Reverend—only of course higher, whatever anybody may try to tell you. But "God" doesn't identify which god, any more than Judge identifies which judge.

Out of respect, Judaism almost never spoke the name of God given to Moses. The High Priest knew the name and used it in the Holy of Holies once a year. A name that high carries too much power, too much danger. It is not to be fooled around with. You go flinging it around, and there is no telling what might happen! So it is pointed to from afar with respect and reverence, and we use endless words merely pointing toward that Name and to the One behind it: Lord, Almighty, Higher Power, Great Spirit, Elohim, King of Heaven, Lord of Hosts, and on and on.

"Hallowed be thy name," within the Lord's Prayer, is a reiteration of sacred Jewish belief and the first three commandments. God is holy (different). Any effort to bring God into concrete form or image is idolatry. Judaism saw itself, properly, doing all things in the name of God, yet holding even this name in such awe and reverence that they would hardly dare to breathe even its partial form or sound out loud. *Hallowed*—sacred, holy—*be thy name.*

At the very apex of Jewish history, Moses says, "What is your name?" I have to know. I cannot go on this Mission Impossible and talk to the slaves in Egypt or defy Pharaoh without some name of power. Forgive me, but I have to ask. I have to know— what is your name?

The Covenant begins with the Commandments, and the Commandments start out with that name—written in such a way that neophytes don't even realize it is a name. Do you know how the Ten Commandments begin? By the way, the Ten Commandments are to Judaism what the Lord's Prayer is to Christianity.

So Jesus gives us His prayer. And the first word calls us to the most intimate, trusting, affectionate relationship with God. The numinous, almighty, eternal Spirit is to be approached as Daddy (Abba). And in the very next phrase, the prayer says, "Don't you dare forget who Abba really is!" This is one of the most incredible, powerful, paradoxical counterbalances there is: Daddy, of the hallowed name!!!

Ask for anything, for everything—but do not dare to presume anything. Trust, relax, play, enjoy every moment you get to spend with Abba. And never forget that this is nevertheless a Being beyond your comprehension; who speaks and it comes to be; who calls the worlds into being; who tracks the lives of every single individual in the L.A. basin all the time and simultaneously—and perhaps all those on a hundred thousand other worlds we do not even know about yet. And this same God has purpose, plan, destiny for all of it—for all of us—all of it coordinated, and interacting, and changing and growing all the time. Daddy, of the hallowed name!

Bring the tension to its peak and keep it there: The four-year-old running to the outstretched arms of Abba . . . and the numinous majesty before whom all human words recoil. Bring the paradox to full consciousness and keep it there. Pray with both awarenesses at full power. Do not be afraid. And do not be wiseacre. Know you are loved, and do not hold back your own affection. Do not play rebellious games either, or act disrespectful, or think you can live your own way by your own rules and never have to encounter or deal with the nameless ONE.

The concept of the hallowed name is behavior-oriented too, of course. All that we do, we do in the name of this God. All that we do, then, is to show our reverence and respect for this name . . . so that all others will also eventually come to honor and bless and revere this name. How can we honor God, our Creator, except by the way we live? The Presence is with us always—if we notice. But we know there will also come a clearer meeting—between this dimension and the next. We shall stand before our Creator, when we can more fully comprehend. And we shall say: This is what you made me—the gifts you gave me, the assignments you handed me, as nearly as I could understand— and this is what I have done with it all. *Hallowed be thy name.* This is how holy Your Name has been for me.

It brings us to the precept which is so old that, for many of us, it is now new again. There is a thing about life here in this world that tends to get and keep us self-centered. Even when we get "religious," it continues. We get focused on: What do I believe? Am I pleased and satisfied with God's performance? Do I like God's precepts and commandments, and which ones shall I obey? Which religion, which church, which theology, which descriptions of the meaning and purpose do I like . . . do I approve of . . . etc., etc.? It is all necessary, of course, to some degree. But what an attitude it also engenders. And if it is a stage we have to go through, nevertheless it is not where we can afford to stay. It is not worshipful!

What name is hallowed for you? That is, when do you stop asking questions, stop acting like judge and jury? When or where do you finally meet some God and submit . . . recognize holiness . . . realize superiority . . . begin to humble your own spirit . . . begin to worship? Before what God do you bow—in submission, and adoration, and praise? In respect, and reverence, and obedience?

It is an old thing—so old it is brand new for many moderns, who have never ever truly worshipped anything. Some even think it is a mark of strength and intelligence never to bow, instead of sure evidence of blindness and lostness.

The day we come to worship is the day life begins. The day we discover the real existence of a God greater than we are is the day when life starts to matter. Before what God do you bow—in submission? What God do you serve—in humility? What God do you worship—in adoration?

Abba, hallowed be thy name.

Week Ten

THY KINGDOM COME

The closer we get to truth, the more difficult it is to keep it clear, to stay focused, to remember, to build it into our way of living. Often, on the very verge of the greatest principles of life, we lose concentration, get bored, wander off, somehow forget why we came. Nobody expects it to be this way. Truth is exciting, dynamic, thrilling, soul-satisfying. From a distance, it attracts us with amazing force—like a bear to honey; like a child to Disneyland or Christmas; like a man to . . . well, you understand.

But then, as we get right at the edge of truth, or even into it— suddenly it is as if some spell were cast over us, or somebody put something in the drink, and we lose focus and concentration, forget why we came, and wander off again. It is rather like trying to find the North Pole with a compass. From a distance, it works fine, and the direction is exciting and compelling. But the closer you get, the more the compass floats uncertainly, and many a traveler wanders off to nowhere, or goes into the long sleep. *Thy Kingdom come.*

To try to understand what the faithful have believed about Jesus, and to try to understand what Jesus Himself believed— there ought to be a connection. But often they seem like two completely divergent subjects. If we were to make a list of Jesus' favorite themes or subjects, what would be on the list? What did Jesus talk about most, care about most, preach about most often? Prayer? He prayed a lot, but didn't talk about it much. Love? Not really. He implied it often, showed it frequently, but didn't talk about it much at all. Paul is the one who loved to talk about love, and after him, John. What Jesus really loved to talk about was God, and the Kingdom, and the Spirit.

If we were to pick Jesus' all-time favorite theme, I suspect we would end up choosing "the Kingdom." Weighing all the factors, Jesus was turned on about the Kingdom: God's Kingdom, the Kingdom of Heaven. He came to proclaim it; He talked about it endlessly; He told stories about it; and increasingly, it is clear that His whole life was about living in the Kingdom—now.

Some of you will perhaps wonder if I have this right. Let me show the contrast. In Matthew, for instance, Jesus speaks about love in chapters 5, 19 and 22. Two of those times, somebody else brings up the subject, and Jesus only recites an Old Testament verse in passing. But Jesus speaks about the Kingdom in every chapter from 3 through 13, in chapter 16, and in every chapter from 18 through 26. The Kingdom was ever on Jesus' lips. He was always discussing it, proclaiming it, describing its features, inviting people to come into it.

It is not terribly surprising, then, that "Thy Kingdom come" is the center and focal point of the prayer Jesus gives to His followers. I do not mean that the Kingdom is more important than God. But try to feel the motion of the prayer, the flow of it. The most important word is the first one. We tried to cover that. If we do not claim the right relationship with God, it won't do any good to talk about the Kingdom—God's or anybody else's. Granted. I promise not to forget if you won't.

But see how this prayer leads up to, and then away from, its central petition. "Thy Kingdom come" is the core petition, the cry, the passion of this prayer. This is where the action, the dynamic and the motion of the prayer come to apex. "Thy Kingdom come" is what the prayer wants to have happen! It is the relationship with Abba that sustains and nurtures Jesus— but for this very reason, it is the Kingdom that is His motive power. It is the Kingdom that brings His decisions into clarity, and it is His passion for God's Kingdom that organizes His love and loyalty toward God in daily behavior. So Jesus gets angry when Pharisees exclude sinners, because that doesn't match the Kingdom. When they get off onto all the regulations and details and seem to forget the reasons behind them, then they are missing the emotional connection to the Kingdom.

And Jesus gets—there is no word for it—some combination of annoyance, frustration, compassion and anger. Whatever the word, Jesus couldn't stand to see people maimed or diseased or blind—unwhole. It didn't match the pattern of the Kingdom. And He could take it for only so long, and then power would burst forth from Him, to heal.

It was the Kingdom that kept Jesus in that Garden—*not my will but thine be done.* It was the Kingdom that made His eyes sparkle. It was the Kingdom He wanted to share with His friends. And it was the love of that Kingdom that drove Him to the Cross. *Thy Kingdom come.*

It is no exaggeration to say that the Kingdom was the only thing Jesus really cared about here on earth. It was the only thing He worked for. Every decision was made according to how it would affect the Kingdom. That is why nobody has ever been able to come up with a Christian ethic that would stand on its own feet or make sense in its own right as a code of behavior. You have to pray three times a day, every day: "Thy Kingdom come." Then some of the behavioral precepts begin to make a certain sense, in that they have application to how we may live for the Kingdom. Praying for the Kingdom clarifies the ethic—studying the ethic cannot define the Kingdom! Did that lose you? Our behavior is supposed to come out of our prayer. Our prayer is not supposed to come along to bless or justify our behavior. Pray first, act second. Don't act first, and pray second!

Actually, one great sage did say, "Pray as men of action; act as men of prayer." But he was an idealist.

So far, I have suggested that the Kingdom was Jesus' favorite theme, and that it is also, therefore and logically, the central petition in the Lord's Prayer. The right relationship with God is established, and then we get to live for the Kingdom. Then this petition, "Thy Kingdom come," is to become the motivating and organizing theme around which our own lives revolve. The petitions that follow cover concerns we have about living for the Kingdom, but they are only there because "Thy Kingdom come" is now our central purpose. It is therefore assumed, obvious, established that followers of Jesus—those to whom Jesus gives this prayer—will also align their lives to this prayer and will themselves live for the Kingdom. This is not a tea party that Jesus is hosting. This is an invitation to a revolution. Only, it is an inside revolution first—a spiritual revolution. That means it is much greater, more far-reaching, more powerful than a mere political revolution.

The Kingdom was Jesus' favorite theme, and it stars as the focal petition in the Lord's Prayer. But there is still a question to ask: How do you mean that? As we reminded ourselves last week, many Jewish prayers included some sort of similar petition ("may his kingly rule be established in your lifetime"—Kaddish). Such prayers had been prayed for many generations and, for the last three hundred years before Jesus, they were coming with greater and greater fervency. Apocryphal books backed by Old Testament pseudepigrapha and Dead Sea and Nag Hammadi scrolls have made it ever clearer that many groups before, during and after Jesus were focusing on the Kingdom coming. But they meant the End of the Age. They meant the expectation that God would bring creation to some kind of just and final conclusion. Things would be resolved. God would bring life as we know it to an end, and set up the Kingdom as it was intended to be. "Thy Kingdom come" on the lips of many is a plea for God to close it out down here—to bring the last days and take us to heaven.

John the Baptist had much of this message in his movement. "Repent, for the kingdom of heaven is at hand." Superficially, that can mean: "Change your ways because God's mop-up operation is just around the corner." Jesus inherited that movement, but tried to change the meaning—with only partial success. So the question is: How do *you* mean it, when you pray, "Thy Kingdom come"? Do you mean you want the "second coming" (as Christians have often called it)? Many Christian groups do mean essentially or precisely that. "Get us out of here. We are tired of this veil of tears and injustice. Thy Kingdom come." Many Christians today half hope, or fully hope, that the nuclear holocaust will come—signaling the end of this world, and the beginning of God's Kingdom (as they see it). It isn't fun here, for many. When will the promises be fulfilled?

Many, many other Christians—often without great clarity as to what they mean or expect—pray "Thy Kingdom come" and mean, in some way, a passage from this realm to the next. It is a longing for heaven. Matthew's extended phrasing is very interesting here. "Thy kingdom come on earth as it is in heaven." That doesn't daunt the literalists, who say we are supposed to expect a physically reconstructed Jerusalem and eternal life right here on earth anyway—so "Thy Kingdom come" still refers to the end-time for them.

What Matthew's addition really shows is the eagerness of the early church to keep it clear that Jesus isn't just talking about a later time. No "pie in the sky, by and by" garbage. Thy Kingdom come *here*—on earth! And now! Whatever the end-time, that's God's problem; let us live in the Kingdom *now!* And that, of course, matches the Jesus I hear and know.

So the question is: How do *you* mean it? And the answer is: Jesus meant it like nobody else ever had. "The kingdom of God is in the midst of you." (Luke 17:21) "This thing you have been waiting for is fulfilled in your hearing." (Luke 4:21) Jesus was proclaiming, inviting into—and He Himself was living in—the Kingdom at the very time. He was waiting no longer. It was present and happening. And He kept revealing that anybody could be in on it—in it—if they would only choose to step into it. Is your compass starting to wander? Are you getting sleepy?

The Kingdom isn't in some other time zone, or some future eon. It isn't in some other place—some divine dimension. Wherever there is the KING and one loyal subject . . . there is the Kingdom! No power on earth can prevent it. Then Jesus says, in effect, "Watch me. I am loyal to the King. Therefore, wherever I am . . . there is the Kingdom. And if you believe me, trust me, follow me and thereby become a loyal subject also . . . the Kingdom will also be wherever *you* are!" No power on earth can prevent it, or take it away. Start praying "Thy Kingdom come," and you will be in the Kingdom immediately, and you will be

able to live for the Kingdom for the rest of your eternal life (which
has already begun). But you cannot serve two Masters. There
can only be one King. Stop living for any and all other kingdoms.
"Seek ye first the kingdom of heaven . . . " (Matthew 6:33)

You can imagine what was happening to the people of the
early church, as each day they meditated on "Thy Kingdom Come"
and tried to apply it in all their affairs.

It was a dimensional breakthrough—like Einstein's theories
were to physics—except a lot more important and far more
dynamic. Only a handful were able to follow Jesus into this new
way of being. Most kept right on thinking He was talking about a
Messiahship that would be a political and military coup. Or that
He was talking about later. Or that He was talking about some
other realm. But Jesus was talking about stepping into the
Kingdom here and now! Like He did. Nothing could stop Him.
Nothing can stop us either, if we choose to follow Him. *Abba, of
the hallowed name, Thy Kingdom come.*

Fortunately, we have Palm Sunday to illustrate this whole
thing. Jesus went on living in the real world—but according to
the way of the Kingdom, not according to the way of the world.
That is, He engineered, set up and carried out His coup as if
people believed what they claimed and wanted what they said
they wanted—and as if the world were not run by greed, power
and coercion. *Thy Kingdom come on earth.*

Put it the other way around: What sort of king would we have
to have, to truly test our religious beliefs? It would have to be a
king who would not rule by coercion, but by acclaim; who would
not abuse power, or use it to make himself rich or secure; who
would, in fact, trust the wisdom and justice of his subjects for
support, cooperation, effective rule—as well as provide
enlightened leadership himself. The citizens, in short, must be
given the freedom to choose to obey because they want prosperity
and peace for all.

Any other basis for the kingship must of necessity revert to
dominance, power struggles, coercion (however benevolent or
well-intentioned the verbiage). And then the old themes would

arise and increase, as they always do—until dissenters, competitors and any who did not side with the king would be ruthlessly dealt with to keep the kingdom secure. In short, and shortly, it would be back to the same old familiar principles that have always run our world: greed, fear, power, jealousy and all the rest.

So how did Jesus ride into Jerusalem on Palm Sunday? Just exactly like the new King would have to in all the essential ways. All that was necessary to bring God's rule on earth was for people to be citizens under this kind of Leader, in just the ways we have always said we wanted to be! And what happened? None of us, on any level, were anywhere near being able to handle it.

That taught some of us something. And all whom it taught, it converted. We awoke to our true condition. We call it "going to the Cross": watching Him die . . . being broken. And we can never live in this world by the old rules ever again.

So we start praying, "Thy Kingdom come." Try me again, Lord. I didn't catch it the first time . . . or even the first many times. Try me again, Lord. *Thy Kingdom come.* Now. It only takes the true King. And we've got You. It takes the King and one or more loyal, faithful subjects—and we're in . . . we're living in it. The Kingdom is here. Let me try again, Lord. *Thy Kingdom come.* Not mine. Not anybody else's. Thine.

What the world is waiting for is Palm Sunday done right—a Palm Sunday that will stick.

Luke 11:1:13; Matthew 6:25, 31-34

Week Eleven

THE BREAD FOR EXISTENCE

There are six "petitions" in the Lord's Prayer (as we have it from Luke). We have looked at the first three. The first one is but a single word. It tells us what our true and rightful relationship with God is. The second phrase takes us into the presence of the numinous, unfathomable God . . . whose name we only dimly and partly know, and if we know, hardly dare to utter. It is the old truth that, for many in our day, seems brand new. The prayer calls us to discern, according to our best capacity to do so, the grandeur and holiness of God. The third phrase takes us to the very core and purpose of the prayer itself. To pray this prayer establishes that it is God's rule and reign that is our highest allegiance and dearest purpose—the thing for which we gladly live . . . and, when called upon, the thing for which we will cheerfully die.

"Thy will be done on earth as it is in heaven" is probably a later addition, a further comment on the original "Thy will be done." It wanted to make sure people didn't think of God's Kingdom as something far away, or for some later time. The Kingdom is here, now, in our very midst. Live for it and in it now! Some scholars have pointed out that Jesus may have at first given this prayer in the short form, as Luke has it, and that Jesus Himself may have later added the phrases we find in Matthew, as He realized that many people were missing some of its intended meaning.

In any case, with the phrase "Thy kingdom come," the prayer reaches its apex and central focus. In the remaining three petitions, we come away from the prayer's heights to deal with some personal, mundane problems and concerns that we all have. The essence of the Lord's Prayer—and the Way of Life which it stands for and teaches us—is clear in the first three lines. But faced with such heights and called to such glory, we humans get very uncomfortable. There are fears and problems and realities, and we have some very real wonderments about whether or not we can live for such things the way we are—or for very long—with any consistency.

So the prayer descends to our fears and concerns. How do we survive if we try to live this way? What happens when—not if, but when—we make mistakes? And what about . . . you know . . . the unmentionable thing? Yeah—what about that? (Can we even whisper it? What about the dark side within us? What about Satan? What about the evil within? What about the shadow we all carry?) How can we pray such prayers before God when we have . . . that!?

So the prayer now goes on to deal with matters crucial to us on a pragmatic, daily basis: Trust. Forgiveness. Humility. It sounds so simple to say, and we find it wonderful to really pray this way. But many people do not realize the magnitude. It is true, for instance, that these last three petitions are appeals toward a lifetime's spiritual growth and labor. Every Christian, if you forgive the analogy, needs a Ph.D. in Trust, another Ph.D. in Forgiveness, and a third Ph.D. in Humility. There are no honorary degrees in this business. They all have to be earned—learned—in the daily rounds and trials of real life. If we flunk any of these three subjects, we can't go on into the Christian Life. Today we look at Trust. The basic, foundational, grassroots kind of Trust.

How many times in your life, so far, have you prayed to the Lord God (infinite in wisdom, goodness and love)—to the ONE who is able to do all things, and who also, we have learned from the Cross, finally and beyond question, happens to love you—how many times have you made your appeal, your personal request to God, saying, "Give us this day our daily bread"? What, exactly, do you mean by that? Does God answer this prayer? *Has* God answered this prayer? Will God always answer this prayer? Do you live by this petition? What, exactly, do you mean as you constantly beg God for "daily bread"?

There are some traditions, you know, which warn against praying thoughtlessly, or making careless requests, or invoking spiritual or divine powers without sincerity or devotion. But perhaps we should not get into that. Or maybe we should just a bit. One of the punishments for praying "Give us this day our daily bread" without meaning it, is to have a heart attack. (At the last official tally, I saw it was still the nation's number-one killer.) That's not the only punishment for mis-praying this petition, but it's one of them. Anyway, when I die of a heart attack tomorrow, I want you to know it wasn't because I prayed wrong, but because God has a sense of humor.

Never mind. I'm only saying that there are dramatic and immediate connections between this prayer and the lives we live. Stress is a killer. It takes the heart out of us. If I pray this part of the Lord's Prayer right, I do not live under stress. Daily bread is the end of stress! (At its very foundation.) Well, I do not always pray this prayer right. I'm not going to die of a heart attack tomorrow because writing this sermon has reminded me again how to pray this prayer rightly, and I can feel the difference! But for how long will I remember?

In praying this part of the prayer—this phrase, "Give us this day our daily bread"—we turn our survival, in all of its manifestations, over and into the hands of Almighty God. When we do that—when we mean it—we no longer live under stress. We trust God for our necessities. Three times a day . . . every day. If you believe in this Lord and receive and pray His prayer, it will change your life—no question! But even that, much as it is, is not all.

When we take a prayer like this, intended to be prayed every day (or three times a day) for years, then it is possible and important to discover and claim every implication we can find, every innuendo that seems intended. This prayer can stand that kind of scrutiny, and it blesses us with each new discovery we make.

Who are we saying this prayer to? Abba—of the hallowed name. That is to say, we are not asking for survival from the world around us anymore. We deal with the world, but that is not where we put our trust anymore. So we stop praying to the boss, the business, the country, the insurance company, the spouse, or whatever we used to count on for our security. We don't throw them away, or curse them, or get less appreciative when they are good to us. But that isn't where our trust lies anymore. We pray to God, "Give us this day our daily bread." And if we do that, the stress goes. It is in God's hands, and so it is all right with us. Even as we work to change the world, it is all right with us. Some people call it inner peace. But there is a direct connection between inner peace and being content with daily bread.

Notice then, also, that this is a request. It is not a demand. It is only a request. So many people miss this part, or get it wrong. (How do I know? Because I get it wrong so often.) It is a petition. If we know, at least in part, who Abba is and how much Abba cares for us, then destiny and our future belong to God. We are no longer in control or command. We are servants, citizens of the Kingdom, obedient under the King's rule and way. So we make request. *Give us this day our daily bread.* It is still up to God. The day will come when this prayer will fail on some level. It is not a matter of *if* the day comes—it is a matter of *when* the day comes in which we will no longer be sustained here. We know that day is coming. We simply do not know when. But we have accepted that, died with Christ, put our trust in God's hands. It is okay with us when our days run out, as long as it is okay with God. Still no stress. On this level, the trust is absolute.

Eventually, we all notice that the prayer says "us." Give *us* this day our daily bread. It is not greedy or self-centered. We expect to share bread—with family, with friends, with church. How big is the church? How big is Christ's church? This one word, "us," is about community and true friendship, about sharing and love. It keeps telling us new sermons and parables and possibilities as we find ourselves praying it . . . praying *give us*— not me, *us*—*give us . . . give us . . . give us . . .* day after day. If you believe this Lord, if you receive and pray His prayer, it will transform your life—no question!

The bread is daily bread. By the way, "daily" is a very rare Greek word. It only appears two places in the Bible, the other being in Matthew's version of the Lord's Prayer. And its use is not found in secular writings either, so there is little way to find comparisons for confident translation. It may mean "bread for today," or "bread for the morrow," or "the bread of sustenance," or "the bread of existence." It depends on which Greek root the word is coming from. My favorite, among the legitimate possibilities, is *eimi,* which means "to go." Give us the bread to go on with. That may not be right, but it *feels* right. *Give us this day the bread to go on with.* The scholars struggle, but the range of meaning is not wide. Any of these meanings still leave us with approximately the same message, just slightly different ways of coming at it.

The bread is daily bread. It is not a five-year plan. It is not a ten-year plan. I keep wanting to pray, "Lord, make me so rich that I will never need to worry or be anxious ever again. Then I will stop being stressed and start serving You." And of course, God says, "I have an even better idea. Why don't you learn to trust me now—just the way things are. Then you will have found the real truth, the real secret, and nothing will take it away from you ever again. As for your serving ME, that is the highest privilege in Life. You don't have to rush it to please ME! I have few needs and plenty of time. You're the one missing out. The reason for my invitation—well, I was thinking of you!"

Somewhere deep within, we know such truth. Nevertheless, Trust is a hard course to pass, isn't it? What do we really mean—what are we asking for—when we pray this prayer? Whatever we think we are asking for, we are asking for an end to stress and anxiety about earthly survival, and we are asking to be taught how to trust God day by day—one day at a time—NOW.

You do realize, I assume, that Mother Teresa and many others over the generations have prayed and do take this prayer to mean: divest yourself of earthly goods and depend totally on God's care (through the compassion of others) to keep you alive, to keep you eating—literally from day to day. And many of them believe that if you have two days' worth of bread, somebody else is starving because you have their share. If you have money in the bank, somebody else is starving because you have their share. And many suspect that Jesus was revealing a social gospel axiom in this prayer—that if we would all learn to trust and be content with enough bread for just one day at a time, then, and only then, there will be enough bread for everyone. If these people are right, then only those who take what we would call a vow of poverty have a right to pray this prayer. Everyone praying this prayer must end up, as the message sinks in, taking a vow of poverty—that is, living from meal to meal from the charity of others.

I mention this because we must be neither oblivious to nor afraid of this approach and interpretation. It bothers me that some of you think this is what God would like you to do and yet you won't do it. If this is what God is asking of you, then doing it will lead you into greater happiness than you have ever known before.

I am truly convinced, however, that this is not the intended message for most people. I sincerely believe that if most people took the prayer this way and lived by this kind of approach, starvation and poverty would decimate our species. There would be no one left to give. Jesus taught us better. He praised stewardship, and befriended many rich people, and taught that it is better to give than to receive. Beggars are not good givers! But we do need to keep remembering that it is not a matter of amount. Most of us have learned that the amount of bread or earthly goods a person has does not have very much at all to do with how much trust they live by. This prayer reminds us constantly to place the future in God's hands . . . to live and respond to all that comes in the "now," today . . . to be alive and to stay alive on a daily, one-day-at-a-time basis. If we try to deal with any more than that, it is too much for us. And it does not matter whether we have five, or five hundred, or five million dollars— the principle is the same: Trust God each day for the bread to go on with. (Except, of course, "Every one to whom much is given, of him much will be required." Luke 12:48)

This does not mean that I cannot plan for how to pay my taxes a year from now, if making that plan is part of today's legitimate agenda. But I cannot handle the anxiety of a year from now along with it. I can only handle today's task, or I start to overload and get caught in fear and wheel-spinning anxiety. No matter how weak or strong you are—the same is true of you. With God's help and presence, we can handle today. Nobody handles more than that very well, for very long. Daily bread is one of the greatest practical principles of the Christian Life. Naturally—or we wouldn't find it in the middle of the Lord's Prayer.

In this prayer, we request each day that we will receive the bread for going on. In this request, we assume that God has our survival in his hands, according to his plan for us. And so we stop worrying about it. If we are still worrying about it, we haven't learned to pray this prayer.

If we trust this Lord, if we receive and pray His prayer every day, it will change our lives—singly and together—no doubt about it. But daily bread is about living one day at a time.

Luke 11:1-4; 7:47b; Matthew 18:23-35

Week Twelve

FORGIVE US

The next-to-last petition in the Lord's Prayer is about forgiveness. "And forgive us our sins, for we too forgive all who have done us wrong." We do not always think we need forgiveness. But we all need forgiveness. This Lord's Prayer, at the core of the Christian Way because it was prayed by the faithful at least three times a day, suggests that we all need forgiveness at least three times a day. Some of us would up that quota considerably.

It is interesting that this series of sermons on the Lord's Prayer should have wended its way, through the weeks, to confront us with the theme of forgiveness at a time when some of us are struggling with that very thing. Since that is going to be in the back of a lot of minds, we might as well get it up front. This is not a prayer about life on the Moon, or on Venus. It is about here and now, and real life. Christians keep gathering to face the Word of God together. That is one way God heals and teaches us, if and when we allow it. If we stop doing that, we all keep getting more and more wrong.

Hopefully there are some people here today who don't feel embroiled in any unpleasantness anywhere in their lives at the moment. Sometimes we experience such seasons, and it's wonderful. But life keeps changing, and we seem to live with our problems until we outgrow them, work them out, or die with them. So this prayer is about real life. When we come to this part about forgiveness, there are usually issues and people somewhere in our lives that come to mind and bother us. We need to keep them in mind, and deal with them. But first we need to know and understand our prayer. If "forgiveness" were as simple a precept as some people try to claim, it wouldn't have remained such a major problem throughout all earth history. The truth of it is, it's easy to handle forgiveness if we are talking about somebody else forgiving or being forgiven. It is not always so easy when it is our turn. So let us each get back to our own forgiving and being forgiven.

The first thing we encounter is no longer a surprise. Forgiveness is important. We all need it constantly—coming and going. True forgiveness is not easy to give or to get, and the world shows this shortage in all of its ugliest parts. It is no surprise, then, that forgiveness is part of our most basic prayer—or that forgiveness is one of the greatest precepts of the Christian Life. This is not a kid's game. This is meant to transform us! Hit or miss—doing what comes naturally—is not going to make it.

We must, I think, add that Jesus seems to be more adamant on this subject of forgiveness than He is on just about any other subject. Self-righteousness and writing other people off are variations of "a failure to forgive" that also draw Jesus' fire with great consistency. But the precept that God forgives us on the condition that we also learn to forgive others is pretty point-blank. It comes across strongly enough in the Lord's Prayer, but also read Matthew 18:23-35.

God forgives us on the condition that we extend to others the same forgiveness that we receive from God. And how much forgiveness have we received from God? It depends on how close we have gotten to the Cross. Now, while that is absolutely true, such phrases can exist among us in our day without meaning what they really mean. We have to get it very clear—we have to search our memories for the actual experiences we have had of God's forgiving us. Pat phrases aren't enough when we come to hard realities.

I do not like to assign too much "homework," but sometimes there is no choice. I cannot do this for anybody else. It is hard enough for each of us to do this for ourselves. But this prayer cannot be well-prayed unless we are clear about how God has actually forgiven us in our own lives and experiences. This is the forgiveness we are required to extend to others.

We are still only summing up the framework of forgiveness,

the centrality of the precept. We are forgiven on the condition that we extend the same forgiveness to others. We are unable to forgive—meaning, we are flat-out incapable of forgiving—anybody beyond the level of forgiveness we ourselves have received. Large portions of humanity are incapable of very much forgiveness because they have been too proud to receive very much forgiveness from God. People who focus a lot on being "good"—on chalking up good deeds—frequently find it hard to admit that they need very much forgiveness.

By the way, there is still a lot of talk about "unconditional love" in our day. I keep reminding you that God has lots of conditions on real love. If that were not true, we would all be rolling in it—only it wouldn't be worth anything. We are forgiven on the condition that we will also forgive. How much love is there without forgiveness? Jesus was much more poignant: "He who is forgiven little, loves little." Perhaps you would like a different translation? "But he loves little who has been forgiven little." (NIV) Now *there's* a meditation for a Sunday afternoon! It is one of Jesus' most basic precepts. And no matter what the popular slogans say, those who discover God's love know that they had better start learning how to love others.

Now we come to the hard part. Everything I have said thus far should be fairly familiar if you have been around the Christian Church for very long. How may I now gently suggest that what we have boiled this all down to—in terms of a working "rule of thumb"—is not correct? What most often goes under the name of "forgiveness" today is not true forgiveness, nor does it work very well. Rephrase even that: it works to some degree, and we would be worse off without it, but it usually falls far short of, or even gets in the way of, true forgiveness.

What am I talking about? We think of forgiveness mostly in terms of our getting rid of anger or resentments that we are carrying toward others. If you hurt me, I think the Christian Faith requires me to forgive you. It may have nothing to do with you. You may not be in any way involved. I am just supposed to get loose, to get free from whatever anger or resentment I have toward you. That is what many, many people think this is all about.

It is an important point. Will you remember that I said so? We do all have to struggle with cleansing ourselves from past wrongs, injustices, resentments. If we do not find some way to let go of that material, it makes us sick. You don't have to read the Bible to find this out. Any psychologist deals with such issues constantly. There are all kinds of articles and folk-wisdom dealing with this very important subject all the time. And it *is* very important, okay? So I have been fair, and acknowledged that this familiar idea of forgiveness is very important. So will you now leave that subject for a while, and come consider with me the Biblical concept of forgiveness?

It comes clearest fastest, maybe, if we think of the purpose or function of real forgiveness. The purpose of forgiveness is to *restore a relationship*. After genuine forgiveness has occurred, a relationship is at least as strong, whole, affectionate, trusting as it was before whatever trouble came along. If the relationship is not totally restored, true forgiveness has not taken place! All genuine forgiveness is a two-way street.

If you forgive me but I do not receive the forgiveness, then you have unloaded the poison from your own soul, but our relationship is not restored. There will still be no trust between us. Our relationship can bear no weight. Are you beginning to see my concern? We have people talking about "I forgave so-and-so," but they don't really want to have any more to do with that so-and-so. That isn't forgiveness. That is not what the Lord's Prayer is about—not what the Biblical precept is talking about. Any person you have truly forgiven, you have invited back into your life with at least as much commitment and caring and love as you ever had before.

Think about it the other way around. What do you think Jesus means with the claim that we are forgiven—by Christ, by God? Does it thrill you a lot to think of God sitting up in heaven saying, "I really forgive you, but I sure don't want any more to do with you"? Who would get excited enough to live or die for a forgiveness like that? The purpose of forgiveness is not just to give you peace of mind—it is to restore relationship. Forgiveness is not just against stress and tension—it is for community.

When Jesus says "I forgive you," that means: "You and me, kid, back together and all the way . . . without any double-mindedness or subterfuge in me whatsoever . . . clear to the Cross again, if that's what it takes."

If the debt is money and it is forgiven, how much is still owed on the account? Nothing! That's the clearest illustration. Would you loan money to the same person again? Gets tougher, doesn't it? If you wouldn't loan money to them again, then the debt is forgiven, but the person is not. Do you see the difference? If the person is forgiven, you would loan them money again just as fast as you would have the first time. (But no faster!)

You remember the Biblical precepts about sin washed white as snow? (Isaiah 1:1; Psalm 51:7) See? No piddling around. If you are forgiven, you are back IN! We have to get beyond this modern notion that as long as I can keep my own mental balance, keep from getting ulcers, keep a little serenity . . . well, that's what it is all about. Well, that's *not* what it is all about. The Bible is talking about community, about love, about a constant and continuing total restoration of relationships.

Forgiveness therefore requires a restoration process between two people. You cannot forgive alone. We badly need another word for letting go of our own resentments when another person will in no way enter into the restoration of true forgiveness. If you offer forgiveness and the other person will not receive the forgiveness, you have saved yourself from ulcers, but no forgiveness has taken place.

There are necessary parts to forgiveness. They have traditional names, but we need not be wooden. It is the process that matters. Some of the traditional names are good for reminding us. First, a person must feel sorrow, regret, remorse—so much so that they are repentant (penitent). Very often, this does not happen until or unless the injured party complains, confronts—says what is hurting them, and how.

I am particularly poor at this. I don't like to tell people when I think they are abusing me. Maybe I'm wrong; or maybe it will pass; or maybe it was my imagination or paranoia; or maybe it will make things worse . . . and all the rest. So I let it go until it's huge within me. That isn't Christian, like I try to tell myself. It's just chicken. (Silence isn't always golden; sometimes it's just yellow.) Some of you are almost as poor at confronting as I am. Maybe we deserve each other. In any case, if there is little confronting, there is little chance of forgiveness. Occasionally a person will see their error and feel remorse without being confronted. But ninety percent of the time, without confrontation the situation will get way out of hand before anybody begins to deal with it. Most of us don't intend any evil, and so we don't see it unless somebody complains.

For forgiveness to take place, there must first be remorse or penitence. Secondly, a person *asks* for forgiveness. That is what we are doing in the Lord's Prayer, at least one or more times a day. Do you keep dubbing-in the specific things you are asking forgiveness for? If not, this part of the prayer is just rote—noise without meaning.

This second step is where the wrath of Christendom really comes down. It is terribly hard to ask for forgiveness. But if a person asks for forgiveness and we deny it, then we are truly in trouble with Christ. If a person asks for restoration into our friendship and love, and we say "sure" but only intend to be civil and keep them at arms-length, that is when we are in trouble with Jesus. Christianity is *not* running around pretending we love and forgive people no matter what they do, no matter what their attitude. But if somebody does repent—does ask for restoration and reconciliation—and we won't grant it, then we are the ones who are OUT! And they are the ones who are IN, so far as God in Christ is concerned.

Thirdly, after forgiveness is asked for (and most often, *both* parties need to request and to receive forgiveness), there is still one step of great importance. The old language called it "penance." So thirdly, penance must be set. It is best if both parties work out the penance together. If one person sets penance, it is at least necessary that the other person agree to it. Penance is not punishment! (Though often it is construed as such.) Penance is a genuine effort to repair whatever damage is repairable—to make amends—sometimes to do alternative good where restoration is not possible.

If I break your chair and you forgive me, I must still make every effort to repair the chair or replace it. Otherwise the whole basis of forgiveness is phony. And so often today it is! No self-respecting, caring person wants you to sustain damage on their account. If you will not receive penance, it is a scornful and degrading put-down. If they do not want to do penance, then their request for forgiveness is just hot air. (And that needs to be made clear.)

Fourthly, after the penance is set and agreed to (though not completed), forgiveness is declared. Restoration and reconciliation are pronounced and lived by from that moment on. This needs to be clearly stated by both parties, so both can return to trust and cooperation again.

Some of you have been trying to forgive people who haven't asked for your forgiveness—who have no intention of remorse, repentance, penance or a true relationship. And you have blamed yourself, and thought you were somehow wrong or not quite Christian. Stop feeling badly. It is a misunderstanding of the concept of forgiveness—a misunderstanding of what Jesus is asking. Jesus says we must forgive seventy times seven. But that assumes somebody means business—that somebody is asking for our forgiveness, asking for a restored relationship with us. But if somebody wants real forgiveness and we give them the anemic, trustless truce so common today—that is when we are in trouble with our Lord!

So we can still get clear of our own resentments, and stay on "watch" (if appropriate) in case there is a change of heart. But we are not required to pretend anything, or to risk or trust or get involved with a person who is not willing to enter into a true process of forgiveness with us. (Never mind the exact language, we seek the intent.)

Sometimes we have unwittingly turned off people seeking our forgiveness because we have wanted to be "nice." We won't allow others to do penance for us. Or we give the impression that we are too self-contained or self-sufficient to be concerned about the foibles or failures of others: We can handle it. We can sustain the damage. "It's no big deal for a strong saint like me." We may not intend it, but if someone has wronged you, it is a big deal to them. There is no restoration of a relationship where damage is neither acknowledged nor healed.

So I have suggested that our generation is distracted by a shallow forgiveness, or at least a one-dimensional second cousin to true forgiveness. And we have lost touch with the Biblical precept that requires a full restoration of relationship with anyone who wishes that with us—as we wish it with God.

Which reminds me: To pray the Lord's Prayer means we get willing to go into this process and through the steps of genuine forgiveness with God, on a daily basis. New life—restored relationship with God—every day. Is that marvelous or is that marvelous?! We never have to be even one whole day away from forgiveness with God. We never have to live with more than one day's guilt. Isn't that something? HE came to free us!

Luke 11:1-4; 3:21-22; 4:1-2, 13

Week Thirteen

INTO TEMPTATION

A few of you have been waiting a long time for this sermon, not so much because you need it as because you want to see if I've got it right. "Lead us not into temptation," or the more cryptic "Do not bring us to the test," is one of the most puzzling comments in the New Testament.

It is often our first reaction that there must be some mistake. Jesus would not put a hidden, complex, mysterious, almost-beyond-comprehension phrase in the core and central prayer He was giving to His followers. That would be unkind, to confuse generations of believers trying to pray this prayer on a daily basis. No Christian can really miss or duck this prayer. So eventually, every Christian would run into the riddle. Jesus wouldn't do such a thing! There must be some mistake, some mistranslation, or some simple explanation.

Because this prayer was so important to the Christian community—that is, because it was used so quickly and widely by so many—Matthew's lengthier version, "Lead us not into temptation, but deliver us from evil," is understandable. But a mistranslation that changes the essential meaning is even less likely than with most passages. In other words, Jesus *would* do such a thing, and did!

When we stop to think about it, it is one of Jesus' trademarks. A seemingly spiritual *non sequitur* . . . a Sphinx-like one-liner . . . a homey little parable that suddenly drops us into the lap of paradox— these go with Jesus like Z goes with Zorro. "Render unto Caesar the things that are Caesar's, and unto God the things that are God's." (Matthew 22:21) And boy, does that sound beautiful and seem right! And it got Jesus out of a jam. But nobody has been able to figure out what it means for two thousand years!

I do not mean to imply that Jesus doesn't make sense. But it is true that our minds struggle hard with His perspective, and often fight it. And Jesus constantly hits us with teasers—friendly invitations to transcend our normal ways of awareness, of seeing and believing. Nobody can follow Jesus for very long or very far without giving Him quality time, and undivided attention. So it is not surprising to find a strange petition in the Lord's Prayer. If we did not, we would have to wonder if it really came from Jesus. We should know Him well enough by now to know He would never leave us bored, and never leave our minds untouched, or our souls on the same level where He found us.

Study group people know that this is one passage I never try to help them with. I just tell them to keep pondering and praying it for themselves. That seems to be what Jesus intended. And you can imagine the abuse I take, for weeks, until they slowly forget about it. So why would I be willing to preach about it today? It is probably a mistake to do so. On the other hand, I am learning that when people are not ready for something, they either miss it entirely or forget it very quickly. Thus God safeguards wisdom, and its dangers, even from the gabbers.

There are probably some people here who have prayed this prayer all their lives without realizing that this last petition has endless strange dimensions. Don't feel ashamed. A high percentage of Christendom recites the prayer as a ritual of identity and loyalty, and the content is never really considered. It is simply recited as it was taught, without question. And there *is* value here other than the content. Furthermore, most of us learn this prayer when we are young, and give it a content that is comforting and generalized. It may not occur to us to analyze it from then on. And so, for many, "Lead us not into temptation" means, if I understand it, a sort of general petition to "protect us from evil," to "keep us safe." People leave it at that, and find comfort in it. I doubt if Jesus would be very angry. It may be better, however, to take comfort from Jesus where He offers it, rather than to take His most challenging precepts too restfully.

Eventually, most folk in our wing of Christendom *do* notice the paradox. Why are we begging a loving God not to lead us into temptation? Satan is supposed to be the tempter, not God! Why, in the petitions of our most important prayer, must we ask God to desist from doing us such damage? Surely Jesus was careless in the way He put this. Doubtless Jesus meant to say it another way. Only, Jesus apparently *didn't* put it another way. Almost never careless, Jesus would certainly be even less likely to be so in giving His followers this prayer.

We won't ever close down or close out the mystery of this prayer. But we can stop taking it for granted. *Lead us not into temptation.* The first reaction—not for all of us, but for many of us—is: God would never do such a thing! Almighty God, God of grace and mercy, forgiveness and love—God would never do such a thing!

I remember, as a troubled young pastor in New England, taking this question to the mentors/saints whom I had, by that time, fortunately run into. (There were three of them, none of whom knew each other—Frank Weiskel, Lee Whiston and Winn Hall.) One said, "Have you never been on the stormy, north-side of God?" I said I had been in dark places but assumed it was my fault, or encounters with Satan. He said, "I'm sure that's true also, but God is even tougher than Satan. God is not always tame, or safe, or nice—like you have been taught or like we all want to believe. There is more at stake here than we want to think. Stop being so self-centered. It isn't all your fault. Sometimes God hands us some of Creation's trouble. It may even be a compliment."

I struggled with what he told me, and got only a little bit of it. Some time later, when I had a chance to see the second saint, I posed the same question, saying I couldn't believe God would ever lead us into temptation. This man had a smiling face with piercing, dark eyes, so you were always getting sort of healed and wounded at the same time. He looked at me with that gentle, rapier smile and said, "You were born, weren't you?" It was three weeks before I began to realize what a wondrous and helpful response that was.

The third man told me, without insult, that I wasn't "old"

enough to understand yet. He also told me to read the third and fourth chapters of Luke, and that when I was old enough, that was where I would find it.

The first big problem we have with this last petition of the Lord's Prayer is that we don't think God would lead us into temptation. But God would, and God does! It finally comes clear, in fact, that if God loves us—and *because* God loves us—God has no choice. Satan tempts us with counterfeit goodies. Satan tries to mess up or counteract the good with seemingly appealing shortcuts, with corruptions and aberrations of the truth. But God leads us into the places of temptation. We have an earth saying: "Power corrupts, and absolute power corrupts absolutely." This is always true, unless God is in charge. But it is God who keeps giving us power, hoping we will stay humble and leave God in charge. But we *are* given power—we *are* led into temptation. There is no possibility of power, growth or purpose apart from temptation. Light casts shadows. God's only other choice is to leave us undeveloped—to leave us asleep, or dead.

Last Sunday was Mother's Day. What could be more beautiful than parenthood, participation in creation? And yet, to be given such absolute power over infant human beings is indeed being led into temptation! Every ability we discover, every gift we are given, every opportunity that comes our way . . . is backsided with the temptation to abuse the power; to gain control for ourselves; to use things, events and people for our own ends instead of for God. The most dangerous place of all is after God has called us, commissioned us, sent us . . . and we are on the job (the mission), doing what we believe or know God has called us to . . . and then we take over and start running it ourselves, but in the name of God. Sure, God is on our side because it was all God's idea in the first place—but we have taken over. That is the most dangerous place of all. God leads us all into that kind of temptation, if we will go with God at all in the first place. What is God's alternative? Never to deal with us at all.

What happened immediately after Jesus was baptized and received the Holy Spirit? He was led by the Spirit for forty days into the wilderness. There in the wilderness, Jesus also encountered Satan. There was no help for that! The mission had to be planned, strategized, understood. God knew the wilderness experience would be fraught with the toughest temptations Satan could devise. There was no help for it. Jesus had to go there. God sent Jesus into that wilderness of temptation. And it is Jesus who gives us this prayer.

So we would like to believe that God would never do such a thing as lead us into temptation. But God would, and God does. There is no choice, except to abandon us, or leave us as we are.

Now the second problem arises. Seeing the necessity—realizing God *must* lead us into temptation—why would we pray not to be so led? Well, we can imagine ourselves praying for escape, but why would Jesus instruct us to pray against what God is trying to do with us?

This is a prayer of great faith—the most personal, dynamic faith the world has ever known: *Abba—Daddy of the hallowed name.* It ends with a humility to match. This last petition does not ask for the highest Christian virtue directly; rather, it embodies the *attitude* of humility. It is not logically or theologically correct to ask God *not* to lead us into the hard places—into the temptations and testings—knowing that God must do that for our development. But the reality is that this is still our proper and rightful attitude, and any other attitude will cost us dearly.

As always, the fastest clarity comes in the analogy Jesus gives us—the relationship between a loving, wise parent and a trusting, exuberant child. It is the first day of school. The parent has tried to explain it all, and the child has tried to get used to the idea, but the day finally arrives. The parent takes the child to school and says, "This is your wonderful new teacher, and this is your exciting new classroom, have a wonderful day." And the child says. "I don't want to do this. I want to go home with you." And the parent says, "You can't come home with me, school is important. You're going to love it. It means you're growing up. You'll be safe. It will be all right. Trust me." And the child says, in one way or another, "I don't want to do this. I want to come

home with you." Do not lead me into temptation. Do not bring me
to this test. I'm afraid. I don't think I can handle this. "Come on,
Abba—if you love me, you won't do this to me."

Whether it is walking into a classroom at age five, or a new
job at age forty-five, or the last hospital room at age eighty-five,
the dynamics are much the same. Theologically, it isn't correct to
fight God's plans for us. But honesty is more important to the
relationship than acting correct. No matter how much you believe
and trust God's love, and no matter how much you love God
back—if you aren't afraid in God's presence, you aren't in God's
presence! God always has an agenda that is scary for us. We are
afraid we will fail, or disappoint, or make fools of ourselves, or
die. No matter how many times God says, "Don't worry, I'll catch
you," we still wonder: Will God catch us? Can God catch us?
What if something distracts God at the crucial moment? What if
we're slippery? What if . . . What if . . .

There is another side to this same attitude. We are never to
be wiseacres in the face of evil or temptation. Putting it more
clearly: In God's Kingdom, never volunteer! Never buck for
promotion. Be grateful for everything, and be content with
whatever level you find yourself on. But never volunteer.

This does not signify shirking or lack of enthusiasm. In human
organizations, we sometimes have to do extra to get noticed, and
have to get noticed to get any real opportunities. In God's
Kingdom, we are always noticed. The right opportunities will
always be offered to us. Each new test will come just as soon as
we are ready for it, and, from our perspective, always a little
sooner. If we get cocky, get ambitious, try to speed things up, or
think we can take on greater temptation than we are ready for, we
only end up defeated, resentful and rebellious children. It is
right for us to hold back—to be alarmed at the power of temptation
and evil.

From Noah to Abraham to Moses and down to now, every
saint's first reaction to God's leading has been: Don't send me!
I'm not good enough. I'll blow it! I can't do this for You. Send
somebody else. Send my brother, Aaron. Surely there are others

with better qualifications. "Depart from me, for I am a sinful man, O Lord." (Peter, in Luke 5:8)

So, in our right minds, we would really rather not have the money, the power, the position, the prestige—knowing what comes with it, and how many others have been defeated so badly by such things. We would rather enjoy our friends and loved ones, and the fellowship of the church, and sit around talking and praying and learning and growing for as long as possible. And please, God, leave it this way. Do not give us any new assignments. We are not at all sure we could handle them.

And do you see how this prayer ends without an ending? It does not expect to have the last word. It ends with unfinished thoughts hanging in the silence . . . waiting for Another to speak.

P.S. One cannot pray this prayer consciously for very long without realizing that Jesus was giving to His followers the principles of prayer that He Himself used. Knowing that He was headed for a cross, Jesus must have been closing His own prayers for months (at least) with this plea that He would not have to go there. *Do not bring us to the test.* It is the Gethsemane clause. Jesus both does not want to face the ordeal of this death, and does not want to fail the test by deserting God in that Garden.

The Gethsemane clause is never left out of the Christian contract. The covenant each obedient servant has with God includes the testing and the temptation. Will you make it through your life here without having the clause activated? Will I? We don't want to be interrupted—again. Please let us go on living here in, hopefully, an ever-greater security. And hopefully some of what we do here also serves You. But please do not bring us to the test. Can you pray such a thing with a little heartfelt sentiment?

Nevertheless, we know it can come—a new challenge, a new test, a new temptation, a new assignment—any day at all, it can come. We do not want to fail or betray or let down our Lord. But against real temptation, we feel weak and uncertain and undependable. God has big business, and we would certainly rather die serving God than die some of the other ways we know about. But if God brings us to the test, will we respond as true believers should?

Lead us not into temptation. We pray it humbly every day—knowing that some days, despite our requests, God will. Is it very clear in your mind which times in your life God was leading you into temptation? In my case, they are directly connected to all my most dramatic spiritual breakthroughs. I wouldn't wonder if it is the same with you.

SECTION TWO

SPRING

Mark 7:14-23; Proverbs 6:16-19;
Deuteronomy 30:6-15, 19

Week Fourteen

SEVEN BY SEVEN

Sometimes one thing comes clear by comparing and contrasting it to another. That sort of thing has kept happening to me in a particularly interesting way, and with great frequency, for over three years now. I keep seeing comparisons and contrasts between the church and twelve-step recovery. Even when I don't mean to draw comparisons, the church (you might be surprised) is a subject that comes up for frequent mention in twelve-step meetings. My ears prick up whenever that happens. I can't help it.

Many twelve-step recovery members don't realize it, but their organization is intentionally patterned after the basic concepts of the Christian Faith, and specifically tailored from the Christian path of spiritual growth as developed by the Oxford Group Movement. All the ingredients are the same. Only the language has been changed to protect the innocent—well, to protect against exclusiveness, and to give folk a chance who either misunderstand or have learned to hate the concepts as they have been taught by the traditional church.

So they talk about "sobriety," and we talk about "salvation." They say "serenity," and we say "peace." They talk about being "on the program," and we talk about "commitment" or "dedication" to Christ. They say "twelve-stepping," we say "evangelism." We say "penance," they say "amends." And so forth.

But it doesn't stop there. The parallels are more profound than that. They talk about going to meetings and what happens if you don't. We talk about going to church but no longer remember what happens if you don't. They know it's essential to confess you are an alcoholic, and only some of us know it is essential to confess that we are sinners. In one way or another, a twelve-step recovery group and a congregation face all the same problems and promises. A twelve-step recovery group is not a church, except by a correct definition almost never used anymore. The spirit of Jesus Christ, as we would understand and define it, is sought and understood as the core and hope of the program. But our words for that are not used because there are still Buddhists, Muslims, Jews, atheists, agnostics and others who need to get sober and find a new life.

So it is fascinating to have one foot in both camps, so to speak, and to watch the two compare and contrast. Often I feel that one makes it clearer to me what the other is trying to do. Often the twelve-step recovery program reminds me of what a church is supposed to be about, and I have a great urge to share that with you. It happens in reverse too! So I hope I'm not stepping on any toes as I make these comments.

We were talking about the Gospel a few weeks back—salvation by faith and not by works, and the way in which the love of God changes us from within, when we come to believe in it. Everything changes when that happens. We go at things differently. It occurred to me that a twelve-step recovery group illustrates this in a way that clarifies our own purposes.

Imagine, if you will, a person who is in the advanced stages of the disease of alcoholism. Some of us don't have to use imagination. Almost anything can happen at that stage: stealing, murder (especially drunk driving), assault, and so on. Not everyone in a twelve-step recovery program has done all of these things, but everyone in such a group knows friends who have done all of these things and who are now living productive, caring, exemplary lives. How does that happen?

Go back to the beginning of the change—the first days on the program. People come into the program with incredible problems, with unbelievable wreckage surrounding their lives. But when they walk through those AA doors, they are greeted, applauded, accepted as valuable and important human beings, no matter what they have done. That's gospel. That's what the church is supposed to be about. That's what the church is supposed to be like. If that didn't happen, the many sane and lovely people—some almost "normal"—who attend most twelve-step recovery meetings (four and a half million of them) wouldn't be alive today. The few who were would be into even greater wreckage and would not last much longer either.

Now, imagine that a policeman who is also a recovering alcoholic (such things happen) is the one to arrest a drunk for, let's say, breaking and entering. A few weeks later, perhaps on probation, the same officer sees the apprehended crook at a twelve-step meeting. In that meeting, it is still gospel! In the meeting, those two may become dear friends. And from the beginning, that policeman will be assuring the arrested person, "Hey, if you keep coming here and work the program— everything's going to be fine." Maybe the next day, on the outside, the policeman will be testifying in court against this same person. That's the law—not the gospel. Both things have their place. And the person will have to live under the law, serve the term, pay the fine, be on probation or whatever the court decides. What is going to "save" that person and bring him into a whole new way of life? It isn't the law! It will be the gospel, acted out in that twelve-step group. If that person keeps coming to the meetings, he will soon be helping others and finding a way of life he didn't even know existed. That's the gospel. That's what the church is all about.

For me, at least, that really clarifies some of the issues between "Law" and "Gospel." Sometimes it helps to see what the church is—and is supposed to be about—from a different vantage point. Please don't think I'm saying twelve-step groups are perfect, or better churches than churches are. Lots of twelve-steppers take potshots at the church without having any notion what they are talking about. Lots of twelve-step folk are fond of saying that they believe in the spiritual life but don't like religion (especially organized religion). That's like saying the twelve-step program is wonderful, but there shouldn't be any twelve-step meetings.

Interestingly, it doesn't bother me much that some of them haven't thought it through, and that they make dumb remarks about the church. What bothers me is that some of you say things just as strange. But that's another topic.

In twelve-step programs, we also have people who come, stop drinking, but don't work the program. They are called dry drunks. They stop the worst of the old life, but they don't start a new one. They aren't drunk anymore, but there's no joy in their lives either—a sad place to get stuck, and most of us find ourselves stuck there at times. The same thing happens in the church—dry Christians. Every organization, I suppose, has people who talk the talk, but don't walk the walk. This is sad for the people who do that. It also tends to kill whatever organization they pretend to be a part of.

What would it be like if a twelve-step group went on a "membership drive" the way a lot of churches do? Can you imagine? All the members would be out saying to people: "Hey, it doesn't matter if you drink or not; it doesn't make any difference if you want to go on drinking; it doesn't matter if you work the program—you don't have to care about sobriety—just come and join our group. You'll find a lot of nice people there, and we serve refreshments after the meeting." Can you imagine what would happen to a twelve-step group if it started caring about attendance records, instead of about sobriety? How very bizarre!

Actually, a twelve-step group puts tremendous emphasis on attending meetings. Even an old-time traditional church looks flabby by comparison. Twelve-step people tell each other, "If you stop coming around, you'll be drinking again." That's twelve-step language for, "If you don't come to church regularly, you're going to go to hell." It makes me nervous how so many of us ministers take poor church attendance as an inevitable reality we can do nothing about. In twelve-step recovery, however, the point is never that "we wanted a big turnout" or "we hoped fifty people would show up and only thirty-five came out." People don't think or talk like that until they have absolutely lost sight of their purpose and no longer know what they are doing, or why they are doing it.

Lent is a time of special spiritual stock-taking—a time to take some new step on the spiritual path. During each Lent, it is the opportunity of every Christian to get ready to "die" to something in their life, in order that something new may come to life within them. Crucifixion/Resurrection is not just our belief, it is our "way," our expectation, our principle. The power of the Christian Faith is not just in the big death that separates this realm from the next. It is also in all the lesser and even little crucifixions and resurrections that move us from one awareness to the next, from one task to another, from one attitude to a better one.

So we begin Lent by asking questions like: Am I just talking the talk, or am I walking the walk? Am I on the program, or just putting in time? Am I really finding peace and learning love— that is to say, am I a recovering sinner, or am I still a practicing "sin-aholic"? And if I really am a sinner, caught in the disease, how many meetings can I miss, how long can I stay off the program or put off working the steps—before I run out of time, or end up getting evil? (For those of you in twelve-step recovery programs, that is the church's word for getting "drunk.")

According to our tradition, there are seven sins which summarize and epitomize all that holds us back from the good life, from communion with God, from faithful and loving service in the grace of Jesus Christ. They are called the Seven Deadly Sins—deadly because they lead toward death, because they take all the fun out of life, because they ruin us and leave us in despair.

Though I have stumbled across them again and again from seminary days on, it came clear to me not so long ago that I had never really studied or meditated much on the Seven Deadly Sins. They were part of my vocabulary, but not part of my awareness.

So I started asking people, including some of you. I discovered that none of us could even name the Seven straight out. Clearly, they are no longer part of our daily or working awareness.

Suddenly that seemed a bit strange—as if it didn't matter; as if we didn't care if the enemy took us over; as if we were so cocky we didn't have to worry about that which has devastated the saints in every generation before us. Of course, this isn't our real attitude. At least I don't think so. We have simply never thought to take them seriously. As John Loudon says, "At first the Seven Deadly Sins seem mere relics of the medieval past. They remind us of life-denying asceticism—a vengeful God who tempts, then damns." To our ears, the Seven Deadly Sins seem a quaint list, more suitable for marketing perfumes than for serious study or contemplation. In fact, our society has refined the Seven Deadly Sins into the most acceptable character traits of a healthy American way of life! Self-gratification is a national goal. Thinking positively, especially about being rich and successful, is every American's solemn duty. You are supposed to think that way, whether you want to or not, because it is good for you and good for the country. Retiring early, or as soon as possible, with lots of money is a standard and normal goal. The only thing wrong with anger is repressing it. And so forth. How incredible that the standards have not merely changed or developed or moved into a different emphasis. They have literally reversed! We want what the saints before us feared. We fear what the saints before us wanted. Is that not fascinating, and maybe just a bit disturbing? Were they really so far off course . . . or are we? Or is it just that we are using an opposite language to try and mean the same thing?

To match the Seven Deadly Sins, there are also the Seven Lively Virtues. They lead toward life, put joy back into our hearts, and make it possible for us to live faithful and obedient lives in the grace of Jesus Christ. I have been wondering if the virtues "match" or countermand the sins. That is: Is each one of the virtues, though good and appropriate in their own right, also specifically designed to counteract one of the sins? I find no lists that seem to match them up this way, so it must not be the case. Yet I find it interesting to play with the list that way, and I hope to get you doing it with me.

One of the greatest fascinations of all is the realization that each of the Seven Deadly Sins is also a trait or instinct specifically designed to ensure our physical survival. Within balance, the Seven Deadly Sins are necessary here—in this realm. I suppose that means we will never be entirely free of them. We can only look for ways to keep them from taking us over.

Likewise, the Seven Lively Virtues are designed to ensure our spiritual survival. If the tension between virtue and sin ever came to complete resolution—that is, if one or the other "won" us over entirely—we could not survive here . . . at either end of the spectrum. If the virtue wins, we only die physically. If the sin wins, we die both physically *and* spiritually. One suspects, or at least I do, that God does not expect us to entirely resolve the issues in one lifetime here. That, I suspect, is no reason for us not to try.

In Christian Faith and comprehension, we are not saved by being virtuous, and neither are we abandoned for being sinners. We are saved by the grace and love of God in Jesus Christ our Lord. To study sins and virtues is not the core of our Faith. But it can help us to see "where we are" on the road—how well we are cooperating with God, and where and how we are struggling hardest still.

Lent may not be known as a particularly joyful time, from a secular or agnostic point of view. But it is a joyful and exciting time from a spiritual point of view. We get to move closer to the Way of Jesus Christ our Lord. That is bound to draw us toward everything we truly want and desire in our lives.

In His name, may it ever be so.

Leviticus 19:15-18; Luke 10:25-28; I John 2:15-17

Week Fifteen

LUST

We begin a survey of the Seven Deadly Sins. Let us be wary, from the beginning, of a natural tendency to try and "make it" through this discussion with the hope of skirting as much blame as possible. My first reaction to any accusation is to defend against it. Everyone is guilty of all Seven of the Deadly Sins to some degree. We have been guilty in the past, we are at present, and we will be in the future. Moreover, none of us would be living, without some portion of each of the Seven, because they are necessary to our survival. The question is not, "Can we get rid of them?" The question is, "Can we stay aware of them, so they do not take us over?" Each of the Seven does the most damage when we are unaware of its presence—when we cannot see that it is at work within us.

So do not try to make it through these sermons with a verdict of "not guilty." The verdict is "guilty," and you are loved anyway. The verdict has been there all along, so there is nothing new to fear. If these meditations increase our awareness, put things in better balance—if in any way they strengthen the virtues or weaken the sins—then our lives will be better, happier, more productive, more joyful for it. The sins really are deadly. The virtues really are lively.

I am taking my order of the Seven Deadly Sins from the list of Gregory the Great, who lived from 540 to 604 A.D., and who is considered by many to be the greatest pope ever. I am taking them from the bottom to the top, meaning from the least important to the most important. Do not emphasize that distinction very much, however, or we will be into one of those childish games of "Would you rather be killed by a python or a tiger?" To make it into the list of the Top Seven, you have to be good—that is, good at what you do. Sin kills. Sin makes people unhappy, morose, despairing and, finally, dead. To make it into the list of the Top Seven, a sin must be exceedingly effective.

Let us be clear then: Lust is at the bottom of the list, but that doesn't make it a pushover. Lust is still an ace at ruining life and killing the spirit within. Its position just means there are sins even more powerful or tougher to deal with. Frankly, that's the only reason I bring its position to your attention. I find it intriguing, to put it mildly, that the saints and pilgrims before us put lust in seventh place.

When I asked people to name the Seven Deadly Sins, nobody knew them all, but most people knew a few. Everybody who named any included lust on the list, even people you would think had never thought of it. Trying not to muse about what that says about our society, I would guess that if we were making the list today, we would put lust as number one or two. I'm not sure we would call it a sin, however, and I'm fairly certain we wouldn't consider it deadly.

So here we go, into a search to comprehend the meaning of lust. Remember, we are not trying for a verdict of "not guilty." We are trying to understand so that we can see the ways lust is still affecting our lives, holding them back, weighing them down.

Two men are driving home from work. Each is alone in his own car. It is bumper-to-bumper traffic at about 1.2 miles per hour. Both begin thinking, "If I could just win the lottery, I wouldn't have to spend time in this commuter traffic anymore." Then each one begins a "harmless fantasy" about what he would do with the money if he won the lottery.

The first man dreams of an island and a boat, of leisure time, of never having to worry about work, or bills, or providing food ever again.

The second man dreams of being able to buy a controlling interest in the company he works for, of being able to make the changes he would like to make. He dreams of being able to run the company successfully, in his own way, without anybody telling him how or when.

One of these men is having a fantasy of almost pure lust. This is not going to be a very sexy sermon. I hope you aren't too disappointed. Lust is not about sex, it is about power. Lust is famous for playing in the arena of sex, but the issue is still about power.

Listen to the words we use when we apply lust to the area of sexuality: ravish, prowess, conquest. Lust turns sex into a power play instead of a relationship. In lust, sex is something to be taken or stolen, instead of something to be shared. The line is not fine, but sometimes it sounds like it. If two people who love each other decide to make love with a lustful theme in mind because they enjoy it, and their trust for each other makes it truly safe, that is not deadly but delightful.

Back to the two men in bumper-to-bumper traffic. As you have figured out, the second man is indulging in a lustful fantasy. He is dreaming about having more power—power over his company, power to produce and accomplish things his own way. I chose what seems a very mild if not commendable illustration because it is clarifying. The first man illustrates greed and sloth. The second man is a picture of lust.

If the fantasies are light-hearted and infrequent, they will do only minor damage. If, by the time they arrive home, the two men shake the fantasies, smile at their foolishness, and return to the realities of their families, responsibilities and real opportunities with gratitude and joy, then the daydreams will have done small damage indeed. Even if the men allow their fantasies to linger, so that they ruin the evening with dour attitudes and discontent, even that will be small harm in comparison to letting one of the Seven Deadly Sins have any real authority or room to maneuver in one's life.

Lust is about power, especially illegitimate power: power we claim for our own purposes; power we go after instead of waiting for it to be granted; power that is not assigned together with a clear task; power we hunger for so that we may be in control. I wish to be great, and to have my own way, and so I lust after power.

It is never completely clear to me, at the time, that I am being lustful. There is always something sneaky or slightly hidden about lust. The motive can look almost authentic. The purpose can be mistaken for something worthy. I only want to own the company so I can do a better job, do more good, clean up the waste or injustice that now exists. I only want to possess the woman because we would both enjoy it so much; it would make her happy too. Lust always tells its servants (and slaves) little lies like that.

Horace, in 20 B.C., had a list of seven major sins. His word for lust was *amator:* to be in love with love, rather than with a person. What happens then to the people? The partners are "taken in" and think the love has something to do with them. When the truth comes out, it is devastating for everyone.

Evagrios of Pontus taught that women and bishops constituted the greatest temptation to monks (desert ascetics), and that both should be avoided as much as possible. Impurity was the problem. To mix women—sexual pleasure or thoughts of a family life—with the way of a monk was an impossible corruption of both; it must be one or the other, but the two together would ruin both. The bishop was just as dangerous because he was in the political structure of an organization. A monk had no business playing politics, seeking power, climbing the ladder of ecclesiastical authority. Pontus taught that it was an impurity to mix that life with the one of an ascetic who prayed and meditated only to be in God's presence, only to see and know the glory of Christ.

It is easy in our day to come across such comments and come away with very distorted views about the attitude of the ascetic saints toward conjugal love or family life, or about their attitude toward work and responsibility in the world.

One of Jesus' most famous statements is: "You have heard that it was said, 'You shall not commit adultery.' But I say to you that every one who looks at a woman lustfully has already committed adultery with her in his heart." (Matthew 5:27)

I used to raise and train and show purebred collies. When Sandra, my pride and joy, was in heat, I always had plans for the puppies. Long and careful study went into deciding what dog should be the sire, what bloodlines would be the most outstanding. I went to great lengths to make sure no mongrel got to her to spoil all my plans. It would have seemed to me a great disaster, and it nearly happened a couple of times. You see, impurity or adultery was the issue. I wasn't concerned about her pleasure; just don't mix the bloodlines! That is where the ancient morals were coming from: should a man spend fifteen years raising a child not of his own blood? Lust is a power play; sex is only one of the many arenas it plays in.

To look at a woman lustfully is to want power over her, to dehumanize her. To treat a living person, a child of God, as if she were an object of desire to be used or possessed is deadly. That is what lust always does to whatever it touches—it reduces it to something less than it is intended and created to be. That is what makes it so deadly! And therein lies the terrible awakening. Anything that I want for myself too much is reduced, ruined, corrupted, spoiled. To want power or dominion over something or someone will lead toward death, especially my own. It will begin to kill my soul, because my soul is built to be in community, to share, to be creature. If I go for power over things or people, it will ruin them, if I get away with it—and will kill me spiritually, whether I get away with it or not.

Is there any way in which you still seek power over anything or anyone—instead of seeking relatedness, understanding, sharing? Is there any way in which you still seek power over things, over the environment, over nature—instead of being one with nature, in tune with things, a natural part of your environment? Contemplating such things, we can each see clearly where we are struggling with lust in our lives. At those places, we are unhappy . . . we are not ourselves . . . we are not as in tune with God as we would like to be.

The corresponding virtue in this case is easy to identify. Love is the counterpart of lust. Be careful, however, not to jump it to the full-blown eternal verity. Here, we are merely talking on the level of a virtue, not about the eternal gift of God's love. So reduce it down to the level of something you can choose, something you can decide to do—caring, affection—"I like him, I really like him." That is quite powerful enough. We don't lust after people when we see and perceive them as true persons. They become too important in their own right to be mere objects of our lust for power. To care about your neighbor as much as you care about yourself is the great axiom by which we try to stay reminded.

Love cures lust. It is important to be clear, however, about what is going on. That woman or man you look at with lust in your heart: is it really lust? I have known some people, over many years, who have fallen in love with somebody and it wasn't appropriate for the love to go anywhere. So they take a careless glance at Scripture and jump to the conclusion that they are in trouble because of lust, and it's a terrible sin. They do some of the things you are supposed to do to counteract lust, like care more, concentrate on the person's real value, focus on spiritual values. Of course, they only make it all worse, harder to deal with.

If it isn't lust in the first place, it needs different treatment. If it is lust, love will cure it. But what if it is already love? Nothing will cure it, and only "distance," over time, will prevent disaster. Lots of severe harm comes from misplaced or misused virtue.

At the bottom of it, lust, like other sins, presumes that God is not enough. I must find some other power, some inappropriate or counterfeit power, so I can get in control, have things I want, move things around to my liking. It is not the way of faith, or trust, or humility—not the way of worshipping the God who is higher and greater than I am. So it leads to death because it separates us more and more from God, who is the source of life.

The Seven Deadly Sins are diseases of the soul. Like a mold or mildew, without constant surveillance and strong measures, they tend to grow, to take over and ruin everything. The sins become more difficult with age. If they get a strong hold, they become more and more difficult to root out, and their results become more and more obvious to everyone except the host,

who struggles under the familiar patterns of denial that plague so
many diseases.

Just so with lust. It is hard to imagine what chance any of us
could have without strong confidence in God—without the love
and power of Jesus Christ to set us free.

Matthew 6:11; Philippians 3:8-4:1

Week Sixteen

GLUTTONY

"The boa constrictor, when he has had an adequate meal, goes to sleep, and does not wake until he needs another meal. Human beings, for the most part, are not like this." Thus adroitly does Bertrand Russell set the scene for our second of the Seven Deadly Sins.

Gluttony is for many of us a surprise. While we can understand that it is an indiscretion or lack of wisdom to be gluttonous, it seems rather extreme to list it among the Seven Deadly Sins. So from time to time we take a bite too many, or enjoy a Thanksgiving Dinner, or weigh a few pounds more than we would like . . . but really, one of the top and most dangerous sins? Come on! Only two days ago, a person asked me if any of the Seven Deadly Sins had to do with eating or drinking habits. They didn't imagine so, and were surprised to learn that it was so. Many of us start off surprised that gluttony has such stature among the sins. But often, after more careful consideration, we wonder that it is not closer to the top of the list.

Likewise, I am startled, at first, to find gluttony one step above lust. Having meditated on the lust for power, having gained a little insight on the incredible damage it does in the world, and having re-identified some of the ways lust still operates in my own life, it is staggering to think that gluttony could be a graver problem than lust. Surely going off our diets cannot create the havoc that our power plays do. Even if eating too much is bad for me, surely it doesn't do damage like trying to control things and people, and like using others for my own self-centered ends.

What is this "gluttony" that it should be so feared by the saints of old and considered so potentially satanic? Let us try for some perspective before continuing.

As many have pointed out, none of the Seven Deadly Sins is an act. Some of you have already gotten frustrated trying to correlate the Seven Deadly Sins with the Ten Commandments. There is a correlation, but they speak from different levels. The two lists do not match up. The Ten Commandments turn quickly to listing specific deeds that are forbidden: you shall not lie, you shall not steal, you shall not murder, etc. The list of the Seven Deadly Sins mentions no specific deed. Some of you have already wondered about it. Why isn't rape or kidnapping on there, or war, or torture . . . or whatever we most fear or dread? But the Seven Deadly Sins list only the *sources* of evil deeds. They speak of the life patterns (the attitudes) that will make us the sort of people who do evil things.

You remember the story of the conscientious jury? They were sitting on a complicated case. The man had been accused of crimes both despicable and loathsome, which we will not go into. The trial dragged on for more than a week. The jury was out for only a few hours. At the judge's question, the foreman rose and said, "Your honor, we find the defendant not guilty. The defense has proven to our satisfaction that the defendant could not have committed these crimes because he was not on or anywhere near the premises at the time of the crimes. But this jury would like to add that, because of the evidence brought forth in this court, we are all convinced that had the defendant been there, he would have done it."

Somehow that brings up the more important question: What kind of people are we? If we aren't just afraid of being caught—if we are "there" and the opportunity presents itself—what would we do? If we can come to awareness and learn to handle the Seven Deadly Sins, then there is no way that we will commit any of the evil deeds. That is one of the main reasons why the list of the Seven gained such prominence and spoke with such power to so many generations. There was the realization that if a society could learn to manage these seven sources of evil, all the evil deeds that plague mankind would cease.

So the Seven Deadly Sins remind us that our real problem is

within, that whatever we do on the outside—and however we strive to improve the quality of life through law and politics and education and economics and farming and science—the quality of life will not truly improve unless we also walk a spiritual path within. Unless virtue replaces sin at the core of the soul—at the source—evil will continue to undo all our outer achievements and improvements. The change at the source is called "conversion." The presence of God, the power and love of the Christ, allowed within, make that change. That is the real subject of Lent, and of Maundy Thursday, Good Friday and Easter. We are only trying to comprehend the Seven Deadly Sins—the sources of all evil—in the hope that such meditations will enable us to cooperate a little more with what God in Christ is doing for us.

Back to gluttony, with our new perspective. We aren't looking at a deed—one bite too many, overeating, or any other specific deed. Like the other seven, gluttony can take many, even endless, forms. We are looking at one of the sources of great evil. What is gluttony?

Glut = to fill beyond capacity (especially with food). Gluttony is the principle of excess. Thomas Aquinas taught that at the center of gluttony was the word "too." Too soon . . . too expensively . . . too much . . . too eager. Enough is not enough. There must always be more than enough.

Gluttony is the principle of "more than is necessary." I don't really need it, but I take it because I can. More is better. If one mouthful tastes good, never just eat it and be thankful—two must be better, and four better than that. We come eventually to the image of the insatiable, sucking child. Only, a nursing baby is adorable. A grownup or a business or a nation that is like that is not so adorable. Once we go into the mode of intake without restraint or balance, the appetites become voracious, then deadly.

Gluttony has always been associated specifically with too much food and drink. What today we call alcoholism was categorized by the ancients under gluttony. That alone begins to change the seriousness of the concept. And amount is not the only issue. Excess is the real issue. One puff of marijuana, one sniff of cocaine is excess—too much!

Gluttony is about wanting pleasure—sensual gratification—especially food or drink. So we come to the semantics problem. The bottom three sins are easily confused. In a way, they seem to be three expressions of something very similar. And yet they each deserve a place of their own, for there is a different principle working. So let us play word games, and then see if they can also stand apart.

The last, or lesser, three sins of the Seven are lust, gluttony and greed. Gluttony, we could say, is simply lust applied to food. Or gluttony is greed for food or drink. Lust is only a form of greed—greed for power. In fact, that is exactly how one dictionary defines it: lust is greed for power. And so the three seem interchangeable. A lusty person is a glutton for power, and so forth.

Only, lust is about power, not really about sex. And gluttony is about pleasure, personal gratification. And greed is about fear—which we will come to next week. And so the three really need and deserve separate categories. Fear, power and pleasure have lots of connections. But on the inside, we must learn to recognize, know and deal with each one in its own right. I don't really lust for food, unless I want to use it as a political tool, or a military weapon. Or maybe I try to use good food to get my way with a person. Then that is lust. If I want the food for myself, for my own pleasure, then I am a glutton.

Today, I suspect, we can see the problems of gluttony more clearly than ever before in history. We have graphic and terrible knowledge of what happens when people who can "afford it" live to excess, and when some nations gut the world's resources to satisfy their own pleasures. I don't claim to be a world economist, but I hear rumors that pure luxuries—like coffee, chocolate, sugar, tobacco—are taking up enough land and human resources to be depriving increasing thousands of the necessities of life. More and more, "colonialism" shows itself as a terrible crossfire between lust and gluttony—the need to have power and control over undeveloped nations in order to keep supplying the home nation with luxuries it is willing to buy. A little greed mixed in there also, no doubt.

Suddenly gluttony does not seem like such a harmless or simple little sin. Maybe there is more to the Lord's Prayer—the part about "daily bread" (instead of five days' bread, or six months' bread)—than we have realized. What are a few more bites, or a love of chocolate or coffee, or a diet filled with sugar? Well, it is increasingly clear that it means sickness for me, and starvation for the world. Clearly if a thing brings destruction all around, it is a source of evil, and this one is looking deadlier and deadlier with each passing year.

I am no world economist, and neither am I a dietitian. But what I hear, from those who are, is that it is increasingly clear that simple, indigenous, peasant-type diets are conducive to health, stamina, long life and good emotions—happiness, a positive attitude, a sense of well-being. And concurrently, rich, refined, expensive luxury foods make us more prone to disease, depression, anxiety, stress and anger. They decrease our pleasure and shorten our lives.

Why would a whole nation go on with its eating habits and support a food industry that is sending it to the hospitals at ever-increasing rates? For the same reason I keep returning to that dish of ice cream even though I know better. I'm a glutton. I want my gratification, my pleasure. I can always rationalize that I'm only one person, and one more time won't matter. I can remember saying the same thing about one more drink—that it wouldn't matter. And that it wasn't anybody's business but my own, anyway.

But the saints down through the ages have thought it *was* somebody else's business. It was God's business. And gluttony was one of the greatest foes to peace with God. So they fought it, and by grace a lot of them found a way out of it. Interesting, isn't it, that Paul the Apostle already knew that appetite could be such a problem? "Their God is the belly . . . . " (Philippians 3:19) Who would have thought that people would have been aware of our problem so long ago? But that isn't really what's strange. What is strange is that we are still having so much trouble realizing that we should be taking it seriously.

Of all the Seven Deadly Sins, it seems to me that gluttony

most clearly illustrates the fact that the sins are a necessary part of life. I have mentioned several times already that none of us would be here if we did not have a propensity for each of the Seven. We must eat to live. And since that is true, every day we are exposed to the possibility of eating too much, liking something too much, wanting more than is good for us. There is no escaping the possibility and potential for gluttony in this life. Every single day will be a day of renewed temptation. Coming to terms with that is part of what we must do to become aware of the way gluttony works in our lives.

In my own case, I am having a very revealing time of it as I realize afresh how I have always loved excess. The golden mean has always seemed boring to me. I do most things with passion and intensity. I rarely buy one of anything. A strange shock, after thinking of myself as more disciplined than most, to suddenly realize that gluttony (some call it "compulsiveness") is a huge theme in my life. I hope you are faring better with this one than I am. On the other hand, it is quite fascinating, and I am looking forward to some exciting changes. In my old age, I am learning to wait at least six months before I call changes "improvements."

Before we go to the corresponding virtue, please note that gluttony kills the pleasure it seeks. Lust kills relationship, which is what it thinks it wants. It is the real truth of all the Seven Deadly Sins. They are deadly! And more than that, they specifically kill what they seem to promise. (And some of you still think there is no Satan?) There is no pleasure in overeating, or overdrinking. The gratification of the moment leads to an ever-increasing nightmare. In the case of gluttony, the nightmare threatens to engulf the whole world.

Today's virtue is obvious. In modern times, we think of temperance more in connection with drink, and gluttony more in connection with food, but that is a recent aberration. The two clearly go together. I quote: "We must take infinite pains not to do anything from mere impulse or at random without due consideration and care. For nature has not brought us into the world to act as if we were created for play or jest but rather for earnestness and for some more serious and important pursuits."

That is a father writing to his son. Do fathers still speak that way to their sons? I have known some who did, and one who I hope smiles when he reads this sermon. But this sounds more like the 1930s and '40s than it does like today. This particular father, whose name was Cicero, lived from 106 to 43 B.C. It is a classic concept of temperance that he reveals. Consideration, self-control, moderation, seeing the larger picture, keeping one's own pleasure in proper perspective (meaning, not very important) is the aim. Elimination of the impulses and appetites is not the aim, but keeping them in due bounds, keeping them subordinate to higher purposes, keeping them under discipline so that they do not rule one's life—that is the goal.

In Plato's THE REPUBLIC, temperance is that rational ordering of the animal vitalities which leaves the soul free. Temperance has often been told and interpreted in Christendom as a joyless abstinence. And it often *has* been, at the hands of those who have grown desperate to avoid some temptation that has beaten them again and again, until they dare not compromise with it any longer. But classical Greek thought wanted to be temperate because it led to a better life. And classical Christendom wanted to be temperate because it left room for Christ (God) to be the reason and focus for living.

Clement, one of the greatest of the early Church Fathers, wrote: "Our mode of life is not to accustom us to voluptuousness and licentiousness or to the opposite extreme, but to the medium between these, that which is harmonious and temperate, and free of either evil—luxury or parsimony." So it is the harmony with God—the being in tune with the Spirit—that is sought.

Of Christ, Paul wrote: " . . . who for the joy that was set before him, endured the cross." (If Jesus had gone for it out of any other attitude, would it have worked?) Early Christians, and many since, have limited their appetites because of a quality of life they wanted, out of gratitude to Christ for gifts greater than what the appetites could offer, and because they came to see that appetites

run riot would destroy the very peace and serenity they sought—
including their closeness with the Holy Spirit.

Karl Olsson wrote: "To love Christ is to be shy toward other
loves. To love Christ is to be content with what life gives, to sit
loose in the saddle, to be ready to depart. To love Christ is to be,
in the best sense, playful."

Temperance kills gluttony, and creates room for better things.
We do not have to have more, or have things our own way, or
have always the same things and always everything in excess.
"Man shall not live by bread alone." If each day we require only
"daily bread"—that which is necessary and not to excess—then
there is time and room left over for other things: time for God, for
the belly is no longer god; time for play; time for gratitude.
Gluttony never leads to gratitude—have you noticed? And
temperance is about freedom, not about deprivation.

Proverbs 19:17; Job 20:20-22;
I Corinthians 5:9-13; II Peter 2:1-3

Week Seventeen

GREED

"The wicked borrows, and cannot pay back, but the righteous
is generous and gives." (Psalm 37:21)

Two sermons ago, two men were driving home from work. The
traffic was bumper-to-bumper at 1.2 miles per hour. Seeing it would
take awhile to get anywhere, each man turned to daydreaming about
winning the lottery. The first man dreamed of retiring to a lovely
island, a boat, a position of leisure and plenty, where he would
never have to worry about earning a living again. The second man
dreamed of gaining a controlling interest in his company so he could
build and shape it according to his own designs.

The second man, I told you, was enjoying a temptation of
lust. The first man was caught in a spell of greed. Today our
subject is greed, the top of the bottom three of the Seven Deadly
Sins.

By the way, the second man, as he reached the far end of the
bridge, began to think of all the people who worked in his
company. He realized that he was quite fond of each of them, in
his own way. They were not perfect, but they were very important
people, so he concluded that when he won the lottery and bought
out the business, he would call together all the employees, and
they would decide together what improvements to make and how
to share the profits justly between them. As the man arrived home
in a wonderful mood, the whole family felt close and life seemed
good that evening, for love kills lust. In caring and affection, we
lose the drive for power and control over others.

Maybe six months from now, when the man learns that lust is
often more efficient and effective in this world than affection and
caring, you may need to worry about him again. After all, lust

would not have survived so heartily through all these millennia if it did not work, if it did not help with survival. Lust exacts a terrible price (loss of relationship, isolation, loneliness), but we are afraid to give it up because we are fairly certain that if we do, we will not survive. Lust is about power. We always want more, and rarely give up any if we can help it.

Gluttony is about the desire for gratification, the effort to satisfy the senses with quantity—excess. Once we hit that mode, there is never enough. On a world scale, it means tragedy and unspeakable suffering. Fortunately, the contemplation of other Deadly Sins removes it further from our consciousness.

Can you imagine what it would be like if we had only one major sin to worry about? There just wouldn't be any relief! How would we ever get that one glaring fault out of our minds? We never would get to sleep. Be grateful there are seven.

Carol Matthau, wife of Walter Matthau, worried herself into a state of deep depression over her husband's health. She wrote a letter to her dear friend, Oona O'Neill, daughter of Eugene O'Neill, and child bride of Charlie Chaplin. By return mail, she received a thick envelope from Oona, which she saved until she got into bed that night so she could savor the comfort and advice of her friend.

When she opened the envelope that night, all but one of the pages were blank, and something fell onto the bed, wrapped in a clump of tissue paper. When she opened the paper, her eyes could scarcely perform their duty. It was an old, exquisite diamond bracelet, obviously priceless and exceedingly beautiful.

On the page that wasn't blank, Oona had written: "Darling, I couldn't bear you sounding depressed, so I'm sending you this to cheer you up."

Now Carol had a new problem. How do you respond when somebody does something so completely out-of-bounds for you? So Carol was telling Felicia Lemmon, her closest California friend, about it the next day. She was still in a state of shock, she said, and searching for some appropriate response, if possible, to such an extravagant gift.

"I mean, what do you say, Felicia? What can you say?" she asked over lunch at the Swiss Cafe on Rodeo Drive in Beverly Hills.

Felicia was up to it. She shrugged and said, "Send her a wire. Say, 'Still depressed. Keep 'em coming.'"

Greed, like lust and gluttony, is insatiable. Once activated, it can quickly overwhelm everything in the territory. Many stories and fairytales are built around the theme of greed overwhelming a person once it is let loose. Most famous, perhaps, is the story of King Midas, and how everything he touched turned to gold, and how quickly that destroyed everything, including his most precious relationships.

What is greed? What kind of mindset would send a diamond bracelet to a friend who is worried about her husband's heart? Surely the Matthaus were rich enough that Carol didn't have to worry about financial survival if Walter died. Yet the implication is that a costly gift would reassure Carol, so she didn't have to worry so much about the loss of her provider. Of course, that isn't stated out loud, but the symbolism is clear enough.

Felicia is scathingly humorous in suggesting, "Give the greed its head!" The two friends probably managed to jolt Carol out of her depression by their antics. I presume there was real caring underneath. At first it all sounds like "typical Hollywood," but we recognize the themes well enough to laugh.

Lust is about power. Gluttony is about personal gratification. Greed is about fear.

The motivating force behind greed is the fear of deprivation. I must have more clothes, more money, more insurance, more of everything because maybe I will run out. Greed, like the other sins, is not usually aware of its own rationalizations. The most exploited rationalization is the one that works best, and the one that reveals the real motives best: "You should buy this item because it is a good deal."

You cannot walk into any shopping mall in the country today without discovering that almost every store is having a sale. The fact that the lie works, despite its obvious and ludicrous character, shows that we need the lie. Our culture is desperate to find sufficient rationalizations to go on with its greed. So we have built a national myth that everything we buy must be at a super price, so we are really saving money. I know one young couple who saved so much money in their first year of marriage that they are now $12,000 in debt and trying to pay it off at credit-card interest rates.

We have endless other rationalizations as backups, of course, but the super deal illustrates it well enough. There are no honest prices left. You cannot walk into a car dealership anywhere and get a straight answer to a simple question, "How much is that car?" The salesman knows he must convince you that you got the world's best deal and that he would go out of business if others bought at the same low price. He knows that I, the customer, will not be happy unless I believe myself to be a crook and a thief. Greed is rampant in our society. We do not need half of what we buy. We do not even *want* a quarter of what we buy, but buy we must.

Twenty-eight years ago, when I first entered the ministry, I discovered that unless I took strong measures to prevent it, about twenty-five percent of my conversations with one member or another of my parish was about why they were not in church the previous Sunday. By the end of the first month, I had heard it all. By the end of the second month, I was sick of it. By the end of the third month, I was giving prizes for creative new excuses, just so I wouldn't go stark, raving mad. Then, mercifully, came the revolution. People stopped feeling like they needed to come to church out of custom and duty, and slowly the excuses became irrelevant and faded away.

Today if somebody tells me why they weren't in church last Sunday, it's just informative. They are catching me up with what's going on with them. How pleasant! But guess what took the place of the old rationalizations? Now if I'm not adamant, I spend twenty-five percent of my conversations listening to what super deals my friends made on all their recent purchases: super lifetime memberships in health spas; curtains cheaper than the cloth they are made of; houses bankrupting the banks that are selling them.

Greed is about fear: the fear that we won't have enough to live, to be important to our family and friends, to retire with, to take care of ourselves with. Fear can always imagine endless scenarios of disaster, so enough is never enough. Kahlil Gibran says, "Is not dread of thirst when your well is full, the thirst that is unquenchable?" What a picture of greed!

In Buddhism, greed is one of three hurdles of ego inflation that must be overcome before a person can attain liberation. Spirituality is utterly incompatible with greed. All the religions of the world know that. Why doesn't our society know that?

I'm not sure, but I suspect that most of us want to be greedy for our friends and loved ones, not just for ourselves. We dream of being generous (and being loved for it). We dream of putting our children through college, or helping them buy their home, or coming through if they lose their job for a time, or getting them started in business. I bet that ninety percent of the daydreams across the country about winning the lottery are about what we want to do to impress or help those we care about. We know our hearts are in the right place, so sin can't be a problem. We haven't learned that Satan uses the best in our hearts to tempt us—that Satan uses love to kill love, uses intellect to cloud the truth, uses our best motives to undo us.

Evagrios, a contemporary of Augustine (400 A.D.), says, "Greed suggests to the mind a lengthy old age, inability to perform manual labor (at some future date), famines that are sure to come, sickness that will visit us, the pinch of poverty, the great shame that comes from accepting the necessities of life from others." Hence, in our fear of these eventualities, we become more and more greedy. Interesting, again, that one who lived so long ago could speak as if he had been eavesdropping in our minds. The issues we face are not as new as we would like to suppose—and neither are their solutions.

I caught the tail end of a marvelous program on television about how values have changed from a striving for excellence to a striving for the success that used to be a byproduct of excellence. Unfortunately, the program ended trying to prove that you are more likely to succeed if you go for excellence rather than success—a little telltale reminder of the real perspective.

Generosity is the counterpart virtue to greed. All of us are already rich. Greed makes us want to be filthy rich, to have an endless supply of everything, like God, so we can give without any fear of running out. Generosity—sometimes thought of as compassion or mercy—is the antidote to greed. If we are as rich as we want to be, generosity won't be possible. Generosity implies a giving away of something we value or need or could benefit from keeping for ourselves. Nobody has to wait to be generous. It is a choice, an act of will—it comes from the heart.

Of course, if we start trusting in God for all outcomes, then the fear begins to shrivel and the generosity flourishes. That is not an act of will—that is the Gospel in action. That is mercy and grace taking over and beginning to heal the sin at its source.

But we are cheating. That is what God in Christ does for us, beyond anything we can choose or supply or manage for ourselves. We are merely trying to locate the Seven Deadly Sins and come to clearer awareness of how they operate in our own lives on a daily basis.

We can choose to be greedy. As with each of the sins, every time we let ourselves go into the pattern strongly, the temptation to do so is greatly strengthened and will be ten times more likely to continue. Each time we are temperate, that pattern is also strengthened, and we are much more likely to resist the temptation the next time it comes around. All the sins and virtues work on that principle.

Have I mentioned that greed is higher on the list than lust and gluttony? Fear is an even greater killer than power or excess.

Lust, gluttony and greed are all concerned with our relationship to the outer world, the physical realities. Each of these three sins is deadly because each causes us to relate to our environment in a way that makes us miserable, unhappy and alienated from our surroundings. The lust for power, the desire to gratify our senses, the avaricious hunger for so much wealth we can never run out—each of the three makes us alien and antagonistic to our surroundings. Moreover, the first three sins all kill relationships with other human beings and leave us isolated and alone. More subtle and devastating than that, they alienate us from God.

On the other hand, generosity, temperance and love build up relationships, put us more in tune with our environment, and bring us toward greater peace with God. Some of this we can do something about. Some of this we can see and understand and cooperate with. But we cannot get rid of lust, gluttony and greed just by deciding to. If it were that simple, the world would have solved all its problems a long time ago. It takes a Cross and a response—a rebirth and an Easter morning—to get any real release or freedom from the Seven Deadly Sins.

Next time, we head into the second group of three—sins that are more powerful, more subtle, and far more deadly than the first three. Isn't it good to know there is still no reason to be afraid?

Proverbs 19:15; Matthew 25:26;
Romans 8:22-25; II Thessalonians 3:6-13

Week Eighteen

SLOTH

It's getting harder and harder to preach these sermons on the Seven Deadly Sins because I keep wanting to stop and tell you all the interesting conversations I'm having because of them. For instance, a young person who missed the sermon on lust, but read it later, came to me and said, "You say lust is about power, not about sex, and that lust kills sex. But I don't think that's right. When I think about having complete control over a woman, it gets me sexy as hell."

Think being a preacher is a piece of cake? Every Sunday you open your mouth—ready or not—and each week you only make more trouble for yourself. Aren't kids great?! Nobody was going to put some idiot theory over on this young man. Plus he *wanted* to know—honest, open and straight to the point. (I would love to stop and ask how each of you would have replied . . .)

So I said to him: You are right, of course, but it is an aberration, like a mirage. You imagine the situation in your mind, and it seems very sexy. That is the power of lust's temptation. And if you were actually to experience what you imagine, it would be a tremendously exhilarating and sexual experience. But lust is a Deadly Sin. It kills sexuality. When you kill something, it generally puts up quite a fuss for a little while. For a brief period, lust seems to enhance sexuality. But if you actually gain control over a woman and use her as a thing, the potential for real relationship will shrivel almost instantly. The sexual appeal itself will not only die very quickly, it will actually reverse. You will feel loathing or repulsion for the very person who once attracted you so strongly.

My young friend then said to me, "How do you know these

things?" I know he recognized that I was telling him the truth. I could see it in his eyes. We are born knowing more than we let on—especially to ourselves. But now he wanted to play games. So I said, "My mommy told me."

I also told him he could find out in two ways. He could watch and listen to others, or he could find out for himself. And that whichever way he chose, he could know with equal certainty, but the second way would cause him and a lot of others great pain. And I told him that, among other things, I read the Scriptures and the saints and the fathers of the church—like St. Augustine. And I made him promise to read the 13th chapter of II Samuel. And I hope you will too, because some of you had the same questions and reactions as my young friend, but you haven't had an opportunity to mention it to me yet.

After that conversation, we got to talking about the rest of the Seven Deadly Sins. When we came to sloth, he said, "Sloth? Yuck! What's that?" Since then, I have talked to many people who literally couldn't recall ever having heard the word "sloth," and who didn't have any kind of definition in mind. Starting with people in their late forties, the incidence of familiarity with the word increased, taking a dramatic jump from those in their sixties on up. Apparently three generations of people haven't even heard of one of the Seven Deadly Sins.

Moreover, those who had heard of sloth were not much closer to its real meaning than those who hadn't. They all identified it with laziness. When pressed for an explanation, they said sloth referred to people who were too lazy to work for a living, like people on welfare who shouldn't be. Pressing further, I got nowhere. Why was it deadly? Because it was bad for the economy. Were retired people or wealthy people slothful? No, retired people had already done their work and earned their keep. Rich people couldn't be slothful because they couldn't be a burden on the state.

In summary, sloth seemed to be a vague sort of sin, applied to nobody we knew personally, but "a lot of shiftless people out there somewhere aren't carrying their fair share of the load, and it's making it really hard on the rest of us honest, hard-working folk." I gathered that sloth is the basic insult to the so-called Protestant work ethic. So I really have tried to get an understanding of what the concept means in our day. My dictionary says: "Aversion to work or exertion; laziness; indolence; sluggishness" (also, "a flock of bears").

Sloth (which means "slow" in Old English) is actually a rather lazy and inadequate translation of a much more powerful concept. Two different words appear in this slot, depending on whose list of the Seven Deadly Sins you are using. Gregory the Great calls it "melancholy"—Latin, from the Greek *melankholia*. It means an excess of black bile—sadness, gloom.

Sloth does not mean lazy, it means depressed! At least that's the word in today's language that comes closest to what the ancients were talking about. Depression is one of the Seven Deadly Sins, and anybody who has ever messed with it knows how deadly it can be.

Oh, but you say that's not fair—depression is a disease. Ain't it the truth! Aren't they all! "I know," you say, "but if I'm depressed, I cannot help it." Then I can't help it if I'm lustful either, and the gluttonous say they can't help it, and the greedy say they can't help it.

They are all diseases, the very worst, and none of us feels we can help it or extricate ourselves if we ever get very deep into any of them. That's the way it is with the Seven Deadly Sins, and that's what they are about. Funny how the depressed can look at the lustful and say, "But you could do something about your behavior if you really wanted to." The greedy look at the gluttonous and say the same, and so on.

An even more famous name for sloth appears on many lists. Thomas Aquinas uses *acedia* instead of melancholy. A = not, plus *kedos* = care. I not care! The most devastating and inhuman sentiment in any language: I don't care. Depression, aimlessness, purposelessness, boredom, listlessness, loss of meaning. The slothful become slow and lazy and stop striving or producing because they have too much black bile—because they become depressed, or lose their way, or lose their purpose. No human being is ever lazy, but we can lose our incentive, our purpose, our aim, and begin to wonder if there is anything left worth striving for. "Lazy" is only a lazy word for the deeper problems of depression and loss of incentive. Sloth means to stop caring.

T.S. Eliot describes it in *Ash Wednesday:* "Because I do not hope to turn again. Because I do not hope. Because I do not hope to turn."

And in *Choruses from "The Rock":* "There is no beginning, no movement, no peace and no end but noise without speech, food without taste. . . . And the wind shall say: 'Here were decent godless people: their only monument the asphalt road and a thousand lost golf balls.'"

In ancient writings, sloth is a sin of terrible magnitude. Sloth is the cause of ignorance. The ancients perceived that human beings do not spend sufficient time and conscious effort to become spiritually aware—to come awake to true identity or to discover purpose under God. Ignorance is considered no excuse. We are ignorant because we have not cared enough to spend our "forty days in the wilderness," our "nights in prayer," our Sabbath days in studying the Scriptures.

The Buddha puts tremendous emphasis on strenuousness— meaning, the strenuousness of spiritual discipline and development. In all the great spiritual paths of the world, there is a strange mixture of calm and patience together with urgency. "It is necessary for us as Christians to pray every day, to study some portion of the Scriptures each day, seeking in grace and praise to discover God's will for our own lives on a daily basis." Some of us get tired of hearing that, especially if we don't do it. If we don't do it, we corrupt or trivialize whatever contribution we are supposed to be making to the church, to the people of God, to life.

The very core of the concept of sloth is spiritual indifference. It can take many forms. Helen Luke puts her finger on the real concept rather than on a rigid definition, as she comments on Dante's *PURGATORIO:* "Always the suffering is precisely the sin itself known in the perception of its true effect on the individual (or collective) psyche. The envious, for example, sit with sealed eyes unable to see anything, for envy kills all true discrimination of values; the wrathful are choked and blinded by the smoke from their burning fires of resentment; the slothful never stop running and that is particularly obvious in the driven busyness which is the bane of our society and which is, fundamentally, a slothful escape from the hard work of the journey within."

Depression and workaholism, two of the greatest banes of our time, are both synonyms for sloth. If you are hoping I am making this all up and you want to chide me for always changing the meanings of our words, what are you going to do with Dante? Or let me quote from Thomas Aquinas: "We might say that all the sins which are due to ignorance can be reduced to sloth, to which pertains the negligence by which a man refuses to acquire spiritual goods because of the attendant labor; for the ignorance that can cause sin is due to negligence . . . . " (Question 84, Article 4, Reply to Objection 5)

Aquinas put *acedia* at the bottom of his list because, as he imagined it, we sink down through the sins to a lower and lower state. Finally we sink into ignorance and depression—we lose sight of God's will and purpose, feel despair, and no longer see any reason for striving to extricate ourselves from the black hole. Sloth is at the bottom because it is most death-like—nearest to death. So sloth means avoidance of the thought, study and discipline necessary to make spiritual progress.

It makes me wonder more and more about what sort of values I have mindlessly taken in from the society I live in. Ease is better than effort. Great strenuousness takes place in the hope of gaining a place of ease. Leisure is the goal of life, is it not? How many days have I spent daydreaming of one day getting to a place where I will have no more hard challenges? If I can just make it through this one more big problem or struggle or issue, then maybe the road ahead will smooth out and I can have a calm, peaceful and prosperous future.

Is that really what we want from life? From God? From our

friends? From the church? To be put out to pasture—to be told nothing more is required of us? The Kingdom moves on, and the battle is surely continuing, and so many people still have so many needs—including our affection, respect and encouragement—and we don't want to be part of it?! Sometimes I think our whole culture is in the throes of some kind of low-grade depression.

Maybe another word for sloth is exhaustion. It is indeed a Deadly Sin to be so out of touch with our Lord that we work ourselves into a state of exhaustion: "I not care."

"I am ashes where once I was fire, and the bard in my bosom is dead. What I loved I now merely admire, and my heart is as gray as my head." (Lord Byron) I used to love that poem. Self-pity plays a very big part in sloth, alias depression. Some dirty so-and-so finally pointed out to me that the reason I get burnt out is because I don't bank the fires. I try to do it all alone, without God, or my friends—no trust in God, no faith. So what else could I expect, except to end up exhausted, depressed and burnt out?

The matching virtue has to be hope. Hope is vision—an awareness of the Kingdom in our midst, always growing, something to be part of, something apart from which no effort or labor seems worthwhile for very long. In the presence of God, we have hope, and our hope is continually renewed. Without that presence, it is only a matter of time before we sink into *acedia*. "I not care."

This time the Holy Spirit has buried a hook in Satan's schemes. Exhausted, depressed, burnt-out people come eventually to a standstill, to a place where they do nothing, or do as little as possible. If it gets severe enough, they even turn off the television and just stare into space. And then sometimes, they sink into the secret: "They that wait upon the Lord shall renew their strength. They shall mount up with wings as eagles . . . . " (Isaiah 40:31) Poor Satan has to start all over again.

Sloth is the first of a new category within the Seven Deadly Sins. Lust, gluttony and greed have focused us on the external affairs. They are terrible enough, and we can see how they are the sources for deeds and behavior that corrupt and foul the earth.

The second three sins are more devastating still. They move to interior battles: Why bother? Who cares? Who am I? Many saints who learn to handle lust, gluttony and greed are still picked off by sloth. Likewise, hope is a much higher virtue than temperance. (I'm not talking about optimism, which couldn't survive for ten seconds against an enemy as powerful as sloth.)

As we consider the second three, we are surveying the field of the enemy against us, checking the terrain through which we must travel. Some people think it is weak or cheating to look for or need a companion for the way. Against the Seven Deadly Sins, no human has a chance—if the choice is to walk alone. So far in human history, those who have claimed it otherwise, have proved it most.

If you don't want to go with Jesus, find someone you trust more, but try not to pick someone who is already an agent for one of the Seven Deadly Sins. If we try it alone, that is how we end up—an agent for one of the Seven.

Matthew 5:21-24; Ephesians 4:22-32; I John 4:13-21

Week Nineteen

ANGER

PRIDE

    ENVY
    ANGER
    SLOTH—HOPE

        GREED—GENEROSITY
        GLUTTONY—TEMPERANCE
        LUST—LOVE

You see the bottom three sins grouped together. They are the chief sources of our external problems—the sources of our errors and acts against our environment. When we are not in tune with our physical realities, not in harmony with God's Creation and its rightful principles, we move into lust, gluttony and greed. Each one is quite literally deadly. If we get very deeply into any of these three, we begin to die physically, mentally and spiritually. The deeper we get into any of the Seven Deadly Sins, the more rapidly we move toward death.

The Seven Deadly Sins represent secular power, and the Seven Lively Virtues represent spiritual power. But language, as ever, is troublesome. Love is the counterpart to lust. But it is not the high *agape*, or "charity," of the King James Bible. (My, haven't we wrecked that word, "charity"?) This love we are using as the counterpoint virtue to lust is deep and affectionate caring. We do not use those we truly care about as objects for our own gratification, or as tools in our striving for power.

Temperance may be a cut-down version of a higher spiritual virtue called patience. But few remember anymore what that word once implied. Likewise, generosity is a bit anemic for the "righteousness," almsgiving, *tsedaqah* that stood opposite greed for the ancients. We neither like nor understand the word "sacrifice" in our time, but that brings the contrast into clear relief: to be greedy, or to be a "living sacrifice."

The middle cluster of sins is the source of our most grievous internal problems. The focus has changed from that which we want, or think we want—from the environment outside of us—to that which is going on inside of us, in the interior life. In one sense, of course, all our battles are interior battles. But if I am caught in lust, my attention is focused on some outer object I want control over.

I spend too little time talking about the Seven Lively Virtues. You can't do everything at once, at least I can't. So I mention them, and I even thought it would be fun for you to try to figure out which virtue matches which sin. Like, who ever would have thought that hope was the counterpart to sloth? (Remember also that there is a variation of depression that is ignorance, especially spiritual ignorance. And the classic counterpart virtue is wisdom— *sophia*.)

Up at the top, stands pride. It is the chief and king of all the sins. And its counterpart is queen of all the virtues. But we still have a few surprises coming before we get to them.

We come today to anger (*ira,* ire). Frequently, we think of anger as being directed at something outside of us. Why isn't it listed among the three sins in the bottom group? We know, even as we start to argue, that this is not the crux of it. Anger is an inside job. Outside things trigger anger, but it is always there, waiting to be triggered. Some of us have put locks and shields and alarms all around our anger, shutting down our energy to almost zero, just to protect against a possible outbreak of anger. Nevertheless, it smolders beneath the surface.

What can we say about a subject so vast? First of all, anger is a Deadly Sin. Violence destroys, and the more violent it becomes, the more destructive it becomes. The destructiveness of outer-directed anger is plain enough. Whether physical damage or verbal damage is done, the intent of anger is to kill something— to bring something to an end. Usually, of course, we don't want to kill a whole person; we just want to kill part of them—some way they are thinking, or some way they are talking, or some way they are behaving. The same is true of groups or nations. But where is the anger coming from?

As I have mentioned several times, each of the Seven Deadly Sins is connected to our survival patterns. With anger, that connection reaches its apex. It is hard to imagine that our species would or could have survived apart from its capacity for anger. We are a violent and aggressive species. If we worry now that our violence may destroy us, surely we can see that without violence, we would have perished long, long ago, before we even got started. If we lost all our violence, say, this afternoon, how long would we survive as a species? A few months at the most!

We go about in explosion machines. We eat things that have been killed or reaped. Even in the quiet delicacy of our dining rooms, we spear and cut our food. More-gentle cultures are appalled by the savagery of our eating customs. Our schedules are violent, speedy, rushing everything too fast for digestion, or comprehension, or compassion. Everything we touch we try to change, usually by force, fire pressure or violence. We are a violent people, and we survive by means of violence.

What is the dividing line, then, between a reasonable aggressiveness and the anger we call a Deadly Sin? Nobody has ever been able to figure it out. There are no clear, neat definitions or descriptions. Some violent acts are against the law most of the time in most circumstances, except, of course, when the law of the country requires that we perform them. It is hard to talk about anger for very long without starting to get angry. Anger breeds anger. Anger is catching. All of us have mountains of it we don't know what to do with, and it just sits around inside of us waiting to get hooked.

Moreover, the familiar principle applies: The more we allow our anger to surface, the more it grows and the more often it surfaces—until pretty soon we have no control over it. It runs and rules us, coming and going at will.

In times of danger, our survival patterns boil down to variations on two themes: fight or flight. If either one doesn't work, we can sometimes try submission. Each of us retains whatever methods have worked best in the past. If angry behavior works for us, we tend to keep using it. But I suspect all of us have a considerable store of anger within us that we do not want and do not find useful. More than that, we know it is eating away at important parts of our souls. We wish we could get rid of it or learn to handle it better. Even if sometimes it has served us well, we do not trust it or like it. We feel miserable and unhappy when it grows, and wonderful when it begins to dissipate.

In the endless struggle to understand words, it is interesting that "temper" means to strengthen or toughen. Temper was once used to mean calmness, composure. More accurately, it was, in medieval times, the mixture within a person of the four humors (sanguine, phlegmatic, choleric and melancholy). To temper something was to add a substance or agent to alter or modify it—to strengthen it, or to bring it into better balance. To get rid of anger was not an option. To temper it was the aim and hope. Temper was seen to be something like character. Temper was the way we controlled our anger, from which came folk-sayings like: "Your temper is one of your most valuable possessions; don't lose it."

Jesus was often angry, not just the time in the temple with the whip. Some of the exchanges between Jesus and the Pharisees were scorching and unsurpassed for verbal violence (Matthew 23). Jesus was sometimes angry with His disciples, not just impatient or frustrated. "Get thee behind me, Satan" (Mark 8:33) is no term of endearment in any language.

As the Scripture readings have already pointed out, Christianity has never assumed we could live without anger. It has assumed that we must constantly reconcile, continually looking for ways to forgive and renew. Nevertheless, did Jesus ever capitulate before the authorities of His time? Did any of His disciples stop all the trouble and consternation they were causing, by deserting their beliefs or their efforts to spread them? Did Paul back away from the disputes and terrible anger he was causing?

Anger is found in, from and between Christians all throughout the New Testament. Isn't it eerie to realize that Mark, who wrote our Gospel, and Paul, the great apostle, could hardly stand the sight of each other through most of the formative years of the church? Clearly both loved Jesus, loved His church, and lived as well as they could for Him, but they couldn't stand each other's company. Eventually, it appears, they did learn to speak to each other.

Anger is a killer, but we can't avoid it. We can't survive without it, and none of our best heroes, not even Jesus, show us a life without it. You might remind me that, on the Cross, Jesus lived beyond His anger and forgave the very people who were killing Him. I would tell you that truly impresses me—in ways, it even breaks my heart, breaks it open to let a little light and love in. Eventually, that action gets to us on another level, too. Aware of the way Jesus puts up with me and does not give up on me, I am sometimes moved to put up with others and not give up on them. Truly that is part of the dynamism and beauty of our Faith. It does not change the fact, however, that Jesus was angry enough to stand His ground, to force the issue, and to leave His opponents with no option except to acknowledge His leadership or destroy Him.

So what can we do with anger? We *don't* try to get rid of it! We do try to temper it, to be in control, to let the energy of our anger burn to serve God rather than burn to destroy our enemies.

What can be said about anger that is helpful on a practical level? The Seven Deadly Sins are the toughest enemies we encounter, and we are getting up toward the top of the list. So if I, or anybody else, make it sound simple, as if you can learn one trick and have it down pat for life, well, just walk on by.

What are some of the things we do know, large and small, about anger?

The easiest way to get rid of anger is to stop caring. If I don't care who wins the basketball game, I don't get upset, no matter what happens. In fact, I don't *know* what happens, because I don't care and so I don't watch. That works on any level. The easiest way to avoid anger is to stop caring. The trouble is, that's the definition of sloth. All we have to do is let the Fourth Deadly Sin kill our souls, and we don't have to worry about the Fifth Sin. Terrific . . .

Notice the hidden hint: Anger comes from caring. We want to preserve something, we want something to happen, we want to bring some benefit to somebody, somewhere—and so we start caring. Then if anything threatens the good we wanted or hoped for, we get angry. All anger comes from caring.

Getting enough sleep helps us to have a better temper. Our anger is in better balance.

Exercise is also helpful. The anger level is not so close to the surface if we work out on a regular basis. In fact, even in the midst of anger, a good run can often be very beneficial.

Food makes a big difference in our anger level. Peaceful food, prepared lovingly and eaten without haste, does much to help us with anger, especially if we eat in this fashion on a regular basis.

Time each morning to pray, meditate, get our bearings, remember who we are and what we are about—time to reestablish our submission to God, and our desire for the presence of the Holy Spirit—is tremendously helpful with anger. In fact, it cuts out the part of anger that we think of as sin.

Becoming overextended, too busy, saying yes when we should have said no, feeling guilty, not standing up for ourselves—all these and many more like them raise our anger level and make us increasingly violent.

The most helpful thing I know about dealing with anger is the realization that it comes when something or someone is threatening me. Usually I am not conscious of what the threat is at the time. It may be quite subtle. If you don't like something I am saying from the pulpit, my psyche can track that pretty quickly to starvation. Maybe you only wanted to add an interesting thought or experience; I'm angry because you have threatened to kill me.

It sounds as silly to me as it does to you, but the mechanisms of anger are firing all around us and in us every day, in just this fashion. If I want to do something about my anger, I have the hard task of tracking down the threat that is causing my anger. If I can discover what is being threatened and admit what I am afraid of, then I can take my fear in to confront my faith. If I can get that far, I've got it! The anger is under control without being repressed. The sin part—the deadly part—is gone.

In the presence of God, in the awareness of Christ's love, all fears melt down to size. Trust in God brings it back into balance. I still may not like what's happening or what I am thinking might happen, but trust takes the fear back down to size. When the fear is reduced, the anger automatically drops with it.

On the practical level, that's the best I know, so far. Track the anger to the threat: What am I afraid of? Then take the fear back to faith, to trust in God. That is why the counterpart virtue for anger is faith. Faith is trust. I trust God, in Jesus Christ, to love me forever. Why such love from such a ONE, God only knows; I surely don't. What I do know is that no anger can stand against that faith, because no threat is very serious in the light of God's love. I·also suspect there is no other kind of help for true anger.

Ecclesiastes 4:1-6; Matthew 27:15-18;
Luke 17:11-19; I Thessalonians 5:16-18

Week Twenty

ENVY

Why is it so high up on the list of the Seven Deadly Sins, this envy, this green-eyed monster? Something terribly malevolent is implied and intended in this concept of envy. Why would the ancient saints fear it even more than lust or greed, or sloth, or even anger? This sixth of the Seven Deadly Sins is the worst or deepest source of all sins except for pride itself, which defies God straight out. What is it, then, that comes to mind at the sound of the word "envy"?

There are no big surprises this time. Envy is defined as "resentment aroused by the contemplation of another's desirable possessions or qualities"—to covet, to be jealous, to begrudge. That doesn't sound nice or mature or friendly, or very Christian, but neither does it sound nearly as serious as gluttony or lust or sloth. What is going on?!

We are playing around the pastel edges of what envy is really about. We have modern definitions that sort of clean it up and make envy sound like a fairly civilized, understandable, ordinary, tame and almost harmless sort of sin. I mean, we would be better off without it and all, but why get all excited?

Further on, in the dictionary entry, are some hints from a bygone age. Under obsolete meanings for envy it says: malevolence, from the Latin *invidia,* from *invidere,* to look at with malice. Going further back, to the Greek word that is translated as envy in the New Testament, we come to *phthonos:* ill-will, detraction, spite. *Phthonos* is from *phthio:* shrivel, wither, spoil, ruin, especially by moral influences; to deprave, corrupt, defile, destroy. So, to envy someone is to try to deprave, corrupt, defile them.

The meaning has not been changed so much as trivialized, which is perhaps the most dangerous change of all. Today, for instance, if you say to a young woman, "So-and-so envies you," she thinks that's nice, that it is a compliment, that it is pleasant to have someone look at her and see that she has a lot going for her.

Remember, however, the wicked witch in the story of Snow White. Not so cute! Not to be toyed or fooled with. If five hundred years ago someone had said, "So-and-so envies you," it would have been cause for grave and immediate alarm.

Envy is not as open and honest as anger, but it is more deadly, more bent on destruction. Envy is not just wanting what others have. It is a great desire to destroy those who look good, who have it good, who seem to be better or smarter or richer or more lovely or kinder or more effective or more influential or wiser than we are.

So envy is not just a backhanded compliment—it is a deadly killer. It kills both ways: it destroys the envied person, if possible, and for certain it kills the person who bears the envy.

King Saul loved David until one day when the two were returning from a victory over the Philistines. The women came out to meet and greet the returning army, and they sang, "Saul has slain his thousands, and David his ten thousands." The account of that day ends, "And Saul eyed David from that day on." (I Samuel 18:9) The New English version says, "From that day forward, Saul kept a jealous eye on David." The origins of the evil eye.

This is one of the classic stories of envy. The next day an evil spirit began to take over Saul's life. First the envy, then the evil spirit. Or in our language, first Saul allowed envy to settle unchallenged within him, and from that day on, he began to go mad.

Clearly David was Saul's greatest commander, his close friend, the court poet and bard, his son's best friend, husband to his daughter, favored of God, immensely loyal to Israel and to Saul himself. All these wonderful credentials made it worse and worse. David was *too* much!

The hallmark of envy is that it hates goodness—it hates people not for their bad or evil qualities, but for their best qualities. Most people react to rejection, displeasure and rebuke from those they care about by trying harder to be better, to please. With the envious, we would have to see what we were doing right, and then stop it. With envy, all good efforts and good intentions backfire, and make it worse. Envy hates for people to look good, to do well, to perform well. If it can, envy will destroy those who are in any way succeeding, those who are accomplishing things, those who are making a contribution, those who are caring, those who are liked.

So Saul envied David, and David sensed the displeasure and worked to do more and more for Saul, which only made Saul's envy grow. Saul began to do cute little things, like trying to pin David to a wall with his spear while David was playing the harp and singing to comfort him. Eventually the envy killed Saul, destroyed all that he had worked for, killed his son and his relatives, and put the whole kingdom in grave jeopardy.

I mention this to show that envy is not for fun and games— it's not the friendly little sin our society seems to take it for. Something within us hates it when others do well or look good. In envy we turn against the good, and try to destroy the very blessing and benefit that are on our side.

Do we really love the good? Do we love it when others excel? Do we truly rejoice whenever goodness flows, even for those we know and care about? Would it please you just as much if your spouse or your best friend won the lottery instead of you? Do we recognize ourselves as a family of God's children so that we are all on the same team, so that goodness or achievement that comes for any one enriches and blesses us all?

Envy doesn't like any of it. Better for nobody to win than for somebody besides me to win. Envy says that even if I don't care— even if I don't want it—nobody else should have it either. Anyone who has it good probably cheated. In all likelihood, they deserve to be punished.

The Tenth Commandment is "Thou shall not covet." (Exodus

19:17) Covetousness is often used as a synonym for envy. I'm not trying to minimize covetousness, but it's more on the level of the bottom trio with lust, gluttony or greed. Covetousness does not have the depth of evil, the twisted power or the hidden agenda of envy. The rule on covetousness is straightforward: You shall not covet your neighbor's house, or wife, or golf score; you shall go get one of your own. So if I get my own, my covetousness stops. If my neighbor has a car he wants and I have a car I want, then we're both fine.

Not so with envy. Envy is much deeper and blacker on the inside. Envy needs to destroy, to put down. The truly envious do not work to succeed or accomplish much themselves. They work, expend energy, and think and plan with incredible energy and dedication to make sure nothing goes very right or very well for anybody around them. Groups, churches, whole nations get caught in envy—they stop doing very much for themselves and just want to make sure nobody else has it very good.

In some of the ancient traditions, envy, rather than pride, causes the fall of Satan. Rather than falling because of rebelliousness due to pride, Satan gets upset by the news of God's plan to create a new kind of being. Humans will have the potential to exceed the glories of the angels, goes the myth. At this thought, Satan rebels, because of envy. "Through the devil's envy came death into the world." (Wisdom of Solomon 2:24)

John Milton says, "The infernal serpent; he it was, whose guile, stirred up with envy and revenge, deceived the mother of mankind . . . . " (*PARADISE LOST*, book 1, lines 34-36)

One of the most chilling verses in the entire Bible is Matthew 27:18: "For he knew that it was out of envy." Is it possible that Jesus is delivered up to be crucified because of envy? That tells us the nature and magnitude of the Sixth Deadly Sin! We cannot abide to have the Son of God in our midst because we cannot stand the comparison.

This second group of sins shows us our greatest struggles with the internal, interior life, as the first three show our greatest struggles with our environment. So what is the interior mechanism of this envy that is so quiet, subtle and low-key, yet so incredibly malevolent and deadly?

First, comparison. Pride says we are better than others. Envy believes others are better than we are. Those are the top two on this hit parade, the two gravest errors of humankind: to think we are better than others or to think others are better than we are. To talk about one without the other is like training a child to handle all the dangers of heat but never mentioning anything about the cold; like teaching someone all about math and science, but never teaching them anything about feelings or relationships.

Envy is the mark of those who believe they are no good. The envious have not discovered that God loves them. They do not know or trust that the Great Creator has designed and made them. Deep within, they feel, "I am not enough; I am not good enough; I never shall be enough to be worthwhile, or valuable, or acceptable, or cherished." Therefore, with a growing urge, an increasing need, a passionate driving demand, such people must bring others down to what they perceive to be their own level or, to be safe, a little lower. We, the envious, must take away, from all those who have luster, whatever light they are shining, so that all will be as gloomy and depraved and dark as we feel within.

Thus, envy drives off all love, all affection and approval, all of the very things it most needs. It ceases to believe in those things—they do not exist; they are all counterfeit, all a charade, all pretend. Envy finds it unbearable to contemplate the existence of genuine love, or a God of grace and love.

Where envy has a hold on us, it is so very hard to change. We are certain that, at those places, we have only been more honest, more courageous, more realistic than those around us. We were only trying to bring people down from falsehoods and impossible dreams and meaningless hopes, so we could all get on the same plane and start out even. At least that is the way it feels from envy's side. Don't ask me how I know. I know for the same reasons you do . . .

As with each of the Seven Deadly Sins, what we really need is conversion: to be born anew, to discover the love and caring and forgiveness of Almighty God for us personally. Pride says we are good enough to take over. Envy says we are no good and never will be. The Cross says to pride: "Then why are you killing the Messiah of God?" To envy, this same Cross says: "But I forgive you, and I, God's Messiah, think you are worth dying for, and you need to know that I and the Father love you." Meanwhile, we look at the counterpart virtue, gratitude. Think about thanksgiving, praise, appreciation. Most important of all is gratitude for what we are, for how we have been designed, for the gifts and abilities we have been given. Envy cannot survive in an atmosphere of grateful awareness of the blessings and possibilities that are ours.

Be grateful for your own life. Trust your Creator. Be thankful for your true name, for your own unique identity. Rejoice in the gifts you have been given, for the talents, wisdom, caring and perspective you have to share.

Envy's entire perspective and method and purpose are destroyed in the presence of gratitude. To insult yourself is to insult your Creator. To be envious is to lose sight of Who made you. If you know who you are and what you are worth in the eyes of God, it absolutely flat-out does not matter how great or good anybody else may be. In fact, how good they are is wonderful too. And that's the Gospel truth!

Luke 1:46-55; Philippians 2:5-11;
Exodus 33:1-5; Acts 7:44-53

Week Twenty-One

PRIDE

So we come at last to the seventh spectrum, the deadliest source of sin and evil known to humankind—and the highest source of light and joy, the most life-giving virtue possible for humankind. We also come to the parting of the ways for many people, a parting of the way from Christianity.

We have seemed, at times, to be merely playing word games, trying to hunt down and comprehend concepts as they were used and meant by the saints. Maybe it is possible to come away from this list simply remembering that sloth is a flock of bears or, for that matter, that pride is a company of lions. With pride, however, we are also at the very core of the concepts—at the core of the Christian understanding of what is conducive to life and what leads to death. The conclusion is disturbing in the extreme.

It takes only a moment to focus. Would you rather have your children proud, self-confident, with a proper sense of their own dignity and value—or would you like your children to be meek, lowly, submissive, humiliated? I pick on the children because that allows us to be somewhat objective and totally involved at the same time. We want the very best for our children. Do we want humility or pride to be the standard and hallmark of our children's lives? Do we want powerful, strong, self-assured winners—or lowly, humble, sensitive receivers?

Between these two there is no neutral ground, no happy medium. Pride and humility represent two very different ways of life, two enormously contradictory value systems, two opposite ways of understanding everything. Nor have I cheated or slanted the issue by the synonyms I used. *Pride:* a sense of one's own proper dignity or value, self-respect; pleasure or satisfaction taken from one's work, achievements, or possessions; the most successful or thriving condition, as in "the pride of youth."

That sounds good to us, proper, like something every human being should have, and the more the better. Yes we want our children to have that kind of pride in themselves, their family, their community, their nation. Someday we hope they will be able to take pride in their own homes, children, work and accomplishments.

Humility: modesty, submission or self-abasement; lack of pride. *Humble:* meek, modest; showing deferential respect; lacking high station; lowly, unpretentious. *Humbled:* to destroy the pride of; to abase, degrade. *Humiliate:* to lower the pride, dignity or status of, to disgrace. (Interesting! I Peter 5:5 says, "God opposes the proud, but gives grace to the humble"; the dictionary says to be humbled is to be disgraced, to have your grace taken away. Somebody is obviously confused!) *Humiliation:* degradation, disgrace (again), shame, mortification. This is clearly not what we want for ourselves or our children.

Yet John Donne, English poet and theologian (1573-1631) says, "Humiliation is the beginning of sanctification." Sanctification is something we very much do want, at least for our children. Among other things, it means to be made fit for heaven, fit for relationship with God and with the whole company of saints. The saints of old say that humility is not just a nice virtue to keep hidden away somewhere, to be used in small doses. Humility is the queen of all the virtues—the one without which the others will do us no good. Humility is the setting in which all other virtues thrive and grow.

Something or someone is confused! I remember the first time I got into this crossfire between pride and humility. All Christian writings honor and extol the virtues of humility. Yet everything I had been taught by the environment and psychology of my culture pointed to pride. I thought at first it was just a semantic puzzle, but pride carried to the point of arrogance, or humility carried to the extreme of self-deprecation, isn't just a misunderstanding. "The meek shall inherit the earth. Blessed are the meek." The

Bible talks one way, recommending humility; our culture recommends the other way, the way of pride.

At first I tried to check the earlier usages. Sometimes it was fun. *Tuphoo*, one of the New Testament words for pride, means to make a big smoke, to inflate with self-conceit. *Ga'own*, one of the Hebrew words for pride, means to swell up (hence haughtiness), to mount up, to rise, to be majestic, to triumph. *Humilis*, the Latin root for humble, comes from *humus*—earth, ground, soil, "Dust you were, and to dust you shall return"—hence low, lowly, base, of the earth, earthy. A few still associate humility with the notion of simplicity—being in tune or in harmony with nature, with the primary life forces.

None of these usages help, however. They only confirm the great gulf between the two concepts of what humans should be like. At least the concepts are consistent through time. The pride side says it is good for people to be proud, self-sufficient, self-confident, independent. It is good to be powerful, to be able to control things, to know what we want and to go after it with self-assurance. If sometimes this borders on arrogance, insolence or feelings of superiority, it needs to be toned down a bit. On the other hand, maybe we really are superior, deserve more than most, have a right to power and privilege *because* of what we accomplish and the positions to which we have risen. In any case, it is clearly the American Way, and has the sanction of nearly all American wisdom, experience, expectation and approval.

You don't get many points in our society for being humble. You do get points for acting humble after important victories or achievements or awards, but that's just for show, and it fools nobody. You do not get points for being humble.

The Christian side actually encourages humility and warns against pride. Jesus says many times that those who humble themselves will be exalted (Luke 14:11; 18:14; Matthew 18:14; 23:12). There is a parable about two men who go to pray; God hears the humble one. This sermon's readings are astounding passages about the place and importance of humility. It is a steady theme throughout the Scriptures: "Pride goes before destruction" (Proverbs 16:18); "serving the Lord with all humility" (Acts 20:19); "be clothed with humility" (I Peter 5:5).

The light didn't break for me while thinking about humility, but while working with its greatest synonym, meekness. The two are used interchangeably. When I tried to be what I thought of as meek, I always became ineffective at best and, more often, phony or passively manipulative. I couldn't get anything to connect in real life with "the meek shall inherit the earth." Nobody I identified as meek was going to inherit anything, at least not for very long. Then I stumbled onto that line in Scripture: "Now the man Moses was very meek, more than all men that were on the face of the earth." (Numbers 12:3)

I knew enough about Moses to know that if he was taking blue ribbons and high honors for being meek, I sure didn't know what the word meant! I tracked it down again and, sure enough, it meant submissive, obedient, subservient. Who? Moses? That was a laugh! But there was a catch: Moses wasn't obedient, subservient or submissive to Pharaoh, or even to Aaron or Miriam, or to Caleb or Joshua, or to any human being on the face of the earth. Moses was submissive *to God alone!* Meek has that special definition: subservient to God alone. If you are meek toward God, you haven't time to be meek toward anything or anyone else. To be meek toward anything except God is idolatry! Suddenly, for me at least, everything started clicking into place.

Humility carries the same significance. The lowliness, submission, modesty, self-abasement, unpretentiousness . . . is in relationship to God, in awareness of God's greatness and sovereignty . . . and is not to be applied or practiced in any other context or relationship.

Then people say to me, "Now it comes together. We use pride language in our relationship to the people and things of this world, but if we are talking about God, then we must switch to the words of humility."

It isn't that easy. There is no place for pride with God's children. Why do we have to switch from language to language?

To stay humble and meek—subservient and obedient to God—
is the only stance we have time for, isn't it? Let the rest fall where
it will. If we keep switching to pride's language, we also keep
switching to its attitudes and methods.

That brings us to the crux of the concept of pride. Pride is
not about true confidence, and is never about joy. True confidence
comes from God, rests upon God's authority, depends upon God's
purposes and power. Listen to pride's language: self-confidence,
self-assurance, self-sufficient. *I'm* going to do this. I have the
capabilities. I believe in myself. I have faith in myself. Isn't that
incredible?! Is the language just terribly twisted, or do we really
mean what we sound like?

Pride is about being independent and self-sufficient. Pride
must have power, must be in control, must make sure that it has
its own way. It is unteachable, refuses help, is ever aloof and
increasingly alone. Pride is the denial of finiteness, mortality,
imperfection, incompleteness. It is always the greatest spiritual
sickness of humankind.

Pride energizes and leads the other six Deadly Sins. It
empowers lust, gluttony and greed. With sloth (depression), pride
says, "I was not honored, promoted, supported like I should have
been. I would have made such great contributions, but nobody
helped, nobody recognized my worth. To hell with the world, and
especially with all those who should have supported me and didn't.
I quit! That will teach them. I don't care anymore."

The teamsmanship is also clear with anger. Anger comes from
fear, and fear is the backside of pride. And finally, pride is at the
other end of the spectrum of evil from envy. The envious want to
be in control but cannot manage it, so they fight all those they
think are making it. So pride is king and organizer of the Seven
Deadly Sins. Adding it to any of the others takes it to the max,
heightens it many times over.

One other thing must be said. Pride is just as deadly when it
goes after the good as when it goes after power or evil. If pride
claims that it wants to rule and control for good motives, to
accomplish wonderful things, it is still pride and ever the king of

the Seven Deadly Sins. Wherever in our lives we want power, wherever we want to be in control, we are in competition against God, and are moving into deadly ways. Coming to realize this, I come to know how much I need the Savior.

If we want to do any good, we must become humble. Pride is the killer, no matter what its motives! By definition and content, pride does not desire to worship God. It desires to be *like* God, to act like a god, to have others treat it like a god. That is why pride is so afraid of faith, trust, love, fellowship and anything that requires letting go of power, of control. Clearly, pride keeps us away from God, and keeps us in animosity toward God.

"If God does not exist," said Dostoevsky, "everything is permissible." Then pride is the proper and only sensible approach. If God does exist, then humility is the only stance that makes sense or has a hope of letting God lead us into truth and love and light. Humility is the rejection of all power for one's own purposes, whether it be the power of knowledge, affection, physical prowess, technology or whatever. Humility is knowing that God is greater than we are; that God has wisdom we don't; that our rightful stance is to be teachable, subservient, obedient, aware of our great need, and eager to receive in gratitude, trust and joy.

Pride is the ultimate alienator (sin-bearer, sin source) because it says to God: I do not want or need you. "I am the master of my fate: I am the captain of my soul." (William Ernest Henley, "Invictus")

Humility says the opposite. Humility admits its need, its weakness, its desire for communion. Therefore, humility is the greatest of the virtues because, more than all the others, it constantly invites God to come, to be in charge, to take the lead, to reconcile us and put us back on the rightful path. And there is nothing God cannot fix if we come to God in humility. There is no way God can help us in our pride, because no matter what God does or offers, we turn away and reject the gift.

To sum it up: Pride is the ultimate stance of the true atheist. Humility is the opposite. Whenever we wish to know where we truly are on the faith journey, we have only to check our position on the spectrum between pride and humility. This is where belief and unbelief are truly measured.

Mark 7:14-23; Deuteronomy 30:15, 19;
Romans 8:31-39

Week Twenty-Two

BEYOND THE SEVEN DEADLY SINS

How does a person become aware of the Seven Deadly Sins without becoming grim and negative? What was the purpose of going into such a topic in the first place? Suppose we actually do realize the intricate web of the Seven as they weave their way through every day and every activity of our lives. Is there anything we can do about it, anything that will make a real difference? Does knowing about the Seven Lively Virtues mean we can claim and use them?

Somehow, the more we tune in to the meanings and machinations of the Seven, the more we recognize the demons that really do trouble our living. As Lorraine Kisly has said, "Perhaps they interest us because they are names for our suffering, for the psychic pain of our isolation, frustration and fear."

What are we up against? What is life for? What is life like? To some degree, we give and find different answers to such questions. From culture to culture, from religion to religion, from one age to another, the answers might be quite divergent. No human ever lived, however, who did not wrestle with greed and lust and the rest of the Seven.

To talk about sin is not to be negative. To talk about sin without any hope of redemption is to be negative. To talk about joy, prosperity, promise and success without any acknowledgment of the barriers and pitfalls may be the most profoundly negative stance of all.

In Mark's passage, Jesus reminds us where our real struggles lie: blaming it on the externals. It was Adam; no it was Eve; no it was the serpent. Who made me worried and anxious the last time I was worried and anxious? The trouble is, I can answer that question! It really wasn't my fault. You see, I had these four appointments to keep, and the first person showed up fifteen minutes late with this incredible problem . . . it goes on almost forever, doesn't it? Nothing can happen to my finances, my health, my popularity, my attitude or my performance without my finding some external cause to explain it, justify it, carry the blame for it.

"No," Jesus reminds us. All of our real problems come from within our own hearts. That's the very first lesson when it comes to sin and learning to deal with it. We blame the externals to try to escape the conviction of sin. Then we won't have to deal with it. Whoever it was, it wasn't me!

It's a whole new world, a whole new game, a whole new life . . . when we come awake to the inner life, to the spiritual dimensions all around us. The awareness begins with the realization that the externals are not the causes, but are only their symptoms. The interior—the heart, the soul—is either alienated from or in harmony with God. That is our true condition. The externals tend to reflect the inner condition. Sometimes there is a time lag, but the externals are not the source. Is that not what Jesus is trying to tell us in this teaching?

J.C. Penney was well-advanced in years before he began to realize this truth. He was a "good" man, as we say—an honest, hard-working man—but he was primarily interested in externals like success and making money. When he worked at Joslin's Dry Goods Store in Denver for six dollars a week, his ambition was to be worth one hundred dollars. By the time he reached that goal, he wanted to be worth a million dollars. Nothing wrong with that— no evil implied or intended—just limited and narrow-minded.

Business was everything until Mrs. Penney caught cold, developed pneumonia, and died. "When she died," said Penney, "my world crashed around me. To build a business, to make a success in the eyes of men, to accumulate money—what was the purpose of life? What had money meant for my wife? I felt mocked by life, by God Himself." Yes, well—who mocked whom?

After several more fiery trials, J.C. Penney was financially ruined. Only then could God break through for real, to stay.

Afterward, Penney said: "It is not enough for men to be upright and moral. When I was brought to humility and to the knowledge of my dependence upon God, sincerely and earnestly seeking God's aid, then it was forthcoming, and a light illumined my being. I cannot otherwise describe it than to say that it changed me."

Augustine wrote in his Confessions: "I inquired what iniquity was, and ascertained it not to be a substance, but a perversion of the will, bent aside from Thee, O God, the Supreme Substance, towards these lower things . . . . "

Maybe God never threw us out of The Garden. Maybe we are still in The Garden, only lost, so we have no sight of God, and worry that God is no longer there. It would come to the same thing, in any case. There is no Paradise without the conscious awareness of God's presence. Hell, by definition, is merely the absence of God. We have only to shut the eyes of our souls . . . lose the contact . . . go spiritually to sleep—to find hell anywhere, to make a hell out of any place.

The choice is there. We try to blind ourselves when we blame things on externals. That means we have no choice—it's not our fault. But the choice is there! "Behold I set before you life and death . . . . Choose life . . . . " (Deuteronomy 30:19)

How I wish I could remember that, in the grim times as much as in the lilt and laughter. My head believes it. My heart knows it's true. It is possible to choose life in the very teeth of death. We have seen Jesus do it. We have seen many people do it, even on their deathbeds. Death could not hold them . . . the sting was already gone . . . they were too close to their Lord.

Life and good. Death and evil. They are synonyms, are they not? To find the good is to find life. To find evil is to find death. The sins are deadly. The virtues are lively. We are not punished for our sins. We are punished by our sins—not by God, but by *our sins*—by separating ourselves from God, by trying to go it alone. Paul isn't making it up that "the wages of sin is death." He's just remembering Deuteronomy 30.

The first principle is to not blame the externals. If I do, I'm trying to pretend there is no source of sin in me. That means fix everybody else, and don't mess with me. It also means there is no hope for me.

The second principle is to remember that the choice is before me—it is mine to make. When I do see or admit any of the Seven Deadly from within, I am overwhelmed. I do not move or even twitch without seeing at least one of the Seven at work.

All the saints attest to this horrendous side of awakening. The first time the young preacher realizes that preaching is a lust for power . . . that counseling is the ego trying to act superior . . . that doing unselfish deeds is the most selfish deed there is . . . that the "call" to the ministry itself is backsided by the hope of getting an inside track with God . . . well, it is horrible. Every motive is a two-sided coin: virtue on one side, sin on the other. So it is necessary to realize that the choice is set before us. God sets it there. Nobody can take it away.

We cannot, however, decide to wipe away one side of the coin. That's what most people think religion is about—an act of will whereby we decide to wipe off the sin side and keep the virtue side of our coins. That's "theory religion" made up by people who have never tried it! The choice is whether to spend the coins for God or for ourselves, or maybe in some cases for some third party who we think is God or who we think is a better us. People cannot wipe off the sin side of the coins—they cannot redeem their motives just by wanting to or trying to. To choose life is to choose God, to want God with us, to want to be with God.

Of course! Everybody wants that! The reason the Seven Deadly Sins devastate us, however, is because there is so much distance between us and God. In our culture and society, it is obvious that most people do not want very much to do with God, not directly or personally or for very much of their time. Checking my own inner being, I understand why.

Contemplating the Seven Deadly Sins shows us more and more clearly what we are up against. The more we awaken spiritually, the more powerful and all-pervading the Seven become to our consciousness. Trying to make rules against the Seven Deadly Sins only shows the hopelessness of our condition in ever-starker terms. There simply is no way to make sufficient rules, no way to make sufficient vows, no way to enforce enough of our good intentions, no way to keep enough New Year's resolutions. Willpower is simply not adequate to cope with the Seven Deadly Sins (the proverbial squirt gun in hell).

We need help! I preached the series on the Seven Deadly Sins because I know that anyone who contemplates them with any earnestness, with any honesty, for very long, will come into the clear, simple, soul-splitting truth of how much we need Jesus.

Yes, I know that name bothers some of you. Use Holy Spirit, or God, or Higher Power, or Eternal Mother, but Jesus is the one we could *see*—the One who loved enough to die for us, who cared enough to come among us in the first place. The truth is, we don't know very much at all about God or the Eternal Mother or the Holy Spirit or the Higher Power . . . unless it is like Jesus. We don't know about the magnitude of love and mercy, of grace and personal salvation, except for what Jesus showed us.

Without Jesus, we go back to trying to wipe off the sin from one side of our motives. Jesus says: "You'll not make it that way. It sticks too close. You can't do it on your own. This is not a do-it-yourself religion. Come with me and I will show you how to spend the coins and live the motives according to the pattern and design God made and intended for you. We need a new covenant here, a new understanding between us. Never mind getting perfect first and then making an application for employment."

He says: "Come with me now, just like you are. What we need is time together, time to talk and practice and do things together, and just be together. It isn't going to work with rules— it takes relationship. I love you. Try to love me back, as much as you can. You'll get the hang of it, but most of all you have to be with me, spend time with me. Start rearranging your life so you can spend all your time with me, until you don't do anything without me. You will start knowing yourself better and better, and you will find out who you really are."

1.) Stop blaming the externals.

2.) Know that the choice is always there, always possible, no matter how closed up or closed off everything may seem.

3.) Know that the choice is between being with God or going it alone. The choice is not about being right or keeping all the rules.

Matthew 18:15-35

Week Twenty-Three

KEEP CLEARING IT UP

What do you do if somebody important to you sins against you? The question behind that question is: How do you live in the church, how do you stay a part of God's Kingdom? We are in some mystical way a part of one Body, for we partake of one loaf, but we are also splintered endlessly because we cannot figure out how to live by the precepts of this Scripture passage.

"If your brother sins against you . . . . " I assume the intention is broader than male sibling—someone important to you, more than an acquaintance. It also implies "equal" or peer—someone in authority over you does not apply.

If your brother sins against you, what do you do? Well, standard procedure is to go around to all your other friends and tell them the whole story, slanted from your point of view, and see how many people you can get on your side before the offending brother realizes what you are doing. By that time, you are embroiled in a reeking mess, and reconciliation is twenty times more difficult.

The first thing you *should* do when sinned against, or when you think you are sinned against, is go to the person alone. The first response, and the one with the best chance, is for you two to work it out together before anybody else knows, before embarrassment or pride escalates. That is the best hope for regaining the brother.

If that doesn't work—if there is no headway, no softening on either side—then what? Do you call in the police, threaten to sue, resign from the committee, stop coming to church, or get bitter and criticize most everything you can think of every chance you get? I've tried most of these ways at one time or another, and some of you have too. Go back to the principles Jesus teaches us.

The mandate of the message is: Keep clearing it up. Keep getting the miscommunications and the misunderstandings taken care of—get it healed, forgiven, forgotten, or something—but keep clearing it up! It kills not just the individuals, but the community too, if we do not keep clearing it up. Remember Matthew 5:23-24? "If you are offering your gift at the altar, and there remember that your brother has something against you, leave your gift there before the altar and go; first be reconciled to your brother, and then come and offer your gift."

If the two of you are stymied, Jesus says bring in two or three others. Two or three less-involved peers listening to both sides can frequently find a way to unstop the blocks. The goal is not just to decide a dispute, but that the two quarreling "brothers" will start hearing each other again and be able to open the channels between them again.

But sometimes one or the other feels that the witnesses are biased. And sometimes they may well be. In those cases, you call the whole church together, each of the disputers puts the case before the church, and the church decides what it thinks is fair. Everything has to stop somewhere. This time both parties are expected to abide by the church's decision—the church being the whole community of friends around these two individuals—and the church is only "church" insofar as it tries to discern and be obedient to the guidance of God.

What if either party is unwilling to abide by this final decision? "Let two stout monks in the name of God explain the matter to him." Lost sheep are one thing; contentious wolves are another. Jesus is compassionate, not soft. If a person does not believe in the importance or authority of the community, he or she is not a part of that community.

Then Jesus moves the matter to another level. He makes it clear that when it comes to the church, "Whatever you bind on earth shall be bound in heaven, and whatever you loose on earth shall be loosed in heaven." I have searched and searched for alternate meanings, but to no avail. It seems terribly clear that Jesus is promising that our stumbling and inadequate attempts to be His church here in this world will nevertheless be honored in heaven. And any time two or more people set out to form a Christian community—to become a faithful band of followers—their efforts shall be known and confirmed in the realm to come.

So now I have to go back and redefine "brother" a little. It is a peer, a covenant-bound person who is engaged with me in some effort to be the church here on earth. It isn't just someone important to me, but someone important who is also part of my faith family.

The practical impact, though, is the importance of the church to my life, if I am serious about following Jesus. That is to say, I must be part of some church, and I must live under the authority of that faith community, and I must take that so seriously that I expect my behavior and progress within the church to be a reflection of my status in heaven.

This passage teaches us that we cannot make it without a church (a community of faith that we live in and are part of), and that we must live under the authority of that church (or move to a faith community we will be obedient under), and that our future destiny depends on the learning and growing we do within the context of some church here on earth. If this community becomes primarily a political or economic enterprise, then living under its authority is almost certainly doomed to power plays and a competitive spirit that does not seek the truth above greed or self-interest. But if the community remains a fellowship of friends who seek spiritual awakening, then living under that authority has some chance of discovering order without losing compassion.

The truth is, we need order and structure under which we freely choose to be accountable. Sometimes our own opinions are too narrow, and we know that. We need community—a people to whom we belong and for whom we care and strive as much as we do for ourselves. We cannot make it alone. The universe is too vast, and life too large, for us to find our way into truth and life and love all alone, even in eighty or ninety short years. So we also need allegiance and love for God as revealed by Jesus.

Now, what is it that so frequently stops our spiritual progress, and that delays, corrupts or sidetracks the spiritual pilgrimage? "If your brother sins against you . . . . " That's right—the relationships within the spiritual fellowship that mean so much, that bless us and affirm us, inspire us and encourage us. Therefore, we are all the more upset when they turn difficult. They do that from time to time, and they shall go on doing that. It is part of the meaning of being the church. You don't think the Holy Spirit would be foolish enough to let us into heaven without some trials and experiences of getting along together, do you?

"If your brother sins against you"—somebody you care about, somebody you thought you could or should be able to trust, somebody inside the spiritual fellowship—then that is a trial indeed! This, Jesus knows. And so He tries to instruct us, if we can hear it.

Now comes Jesus' illustration: A man owes the equivalent of, say, five hundred thousand dollars. He isn't rich. We aren't told what went wrong. But we can imagine how it would feel. How long does it take a normal wage-earner to save five hundred thousand dollars? If you can imagine it at all, it is a life-long task. It means that every spare dollar for as long as you live goes to pay off the debt. The feeling is: "What's the use?" Even if you pay it off, there is no time or life left. It is the way some of us feel about the national debt, only this is more personal, gnawing at you every morning, sapping your strength through the day, and staring bleakly at you each evening.

The lender calls for the debt to be paid. Apparently it is overdue. This man's equity, whatever it is, will be turned over to the lender (king, or whatever), and the man will become his slave until it is deemed that he has worked off the debt, which in this case is clearly for the rest of his life. Furthermore, his wife and children will also be slaves until the debt is worked off.

You think *you* have problems? Do you sometimes feel like a failure? How would you like to come home to the wife some night and say, "By the way, honey, I have a bit of bad news for you . . . "

So the man is called in, and this is his fate as far as he knows. To have such a thing happen is so appalling that, despite its uselessness, he falls to his knees and implores his new master to give him more time. "Please do not thus destroy my family, bring my wife to such shame, undo any chance for my children to have decent lives of their own. Surely I can make more money for you each year if you leave me free than if you enslave all of us."

The lord, in this story, does not do what the man asks—not anywhere close. "Out of pity for him," the story says, "he released him and forgave him the debt." How much does he now owe? Nothing! Two moments ago, his life and the lives of his whole family were ruined and enslaved, utterly and without recourse. The highest hope he could think of was to be allowed to work out the rest of his life to pay off his debt, but as a free man, without destroying his family along with him. That was the biggest ray of hope he could imagine, and even that was far-fetched. Now, not only is he free, but his whole life is back in his own hands. He owes nothing! The richest of us here cannot imagine how wealthy he felt, just to owe nothing.

Only, this is a very sad story, probably the saddest story Jesus ever told. This man was so frightened, so sick with fear and shame and worry, that he never heard what the lord said. He only heard what he himself had asked for—more time to pay off the debt. The concept of being forgiven couldn't break through to him. It was too enormous. It was beyond his imagining. He had been hopeless and helpless against his fate for so long that his brainwaves could not comprehend it. He was forgiven. He owed nothing. But he couldn't believe it. In his heart, he still lived under the weight of the impossible debt.

And so when a friend comes by who owes him a hundred bucks, he grabs him by the collar and says, "Jake, you gotta give me the hundred you owe me. I have to have it. I'm desperate. You gotta give it to me today."

You see, he's obviously still terrified. He's gotta get the hundred, gotta get every dime he can scrape together, because in his mind he still owes the five hundred thousand, and it's going to be collected any day. His terror still rules him. Can you possibly understand?

So the forgiveness is repealed, and the man ends up in worse shape than if he had been enslaved. He is turned over to the torturers. The story runs out of words with which to describe his pitiable condition. There is no forgiveness for those who cannot receive or give or believe in forgiveness. Even though they are free, they live as if they were in prison, under torture.

The illustration reminds us that when we are sinned against, or when one who feels wronged comes to us to get it straightened out, we should remember first the bonds of the friendship itself. If that does not help us, we should go to the friends we have in common, and try to gain perspective through the interlinking friendships. And if that does not help, we must remember that we live under the discipline and vows of the church, as followers of Jesus Christ, and so we turn to the whole church.

If that does not help, we must remember that we live under God, to whom we owe all of life and everything we have or ever shall have. And we think of a Cross, where we have each been forgiven far more than five hundred thousand dollars—and we think of the ways in which we are loved and accepted, without any way on earth or in heaven of our ever deserving it, or earning it, or paying it back. And then we can proceed to our choices and responses and attitudes.

Each time even a glimmer of it comes clear again, we are ready to take communion and rejoin the Christian Church. For as long as we are the church, the mandate remains: keep clearing it up!

Mark 2:1-12

Week Twenty-Four

WHAT ARE FRIENDS FOUR?

Sometimes we learn as much from Jesus' stories as we do from the story of Jesus. Because of Jesus' integrity and wisdom, His parables carry truth and reveal the inner principles of life. But from our vantage point, it is all written in the Book. And pretty soon, we take it all on the same level. The Prodigal Son, and the Rich Young Ruler, and the Good Samaritan, and the Faithful Centurion, and the Gerasene Demoniac . . . they are all equally real to us. I have to stop and make myself concentrate before I can remember which ones are parables, and which ones are real-life encounters.

It is early in the ministry of Jesus. We are in Capernaum, a town at the northern end of the Sea of Galilee. It is conveniently close to the border, where Jesus can escape from the jurisdiction of Herod Antipas. It is where Jesus lives, and this story takes place at His house in Capernaum.

Jesus is apparently holding a class or discussion group in His home, and more people have come than were expected. People keep gathering until they fill the doorways, and perhaps Jesus does not even realize how many people are gathered outside, beyond His sight. He goes on teaching.

The rest of this account is pure, wild, spontaneous verve. The thing is delightfully outrageous. Do these friends know Jesus? How do they think He is going to react to their tearing His roof off? How many neighbors do *you* have that you could tear their roof off and still ask them for a favor? Did anybody repair Jesus' roof afterward? Do you ever imagine Jesus grumbling and mumbling that night, and muttering, "It's not enough I have to preach and teach and heal all day. Now I have to go fix the blinkin' roof." So He's a carpenter . . . He knows how. But I do

note that there is no further mention of Jesus ever teaching out of
His own house again. Just because He's the Savior doesn't mean
He can't learn.

Well, I'm not onto the main issues yet, am I? I imagine the
four friends are in one of those "devil-may-care" moods that we
usually associate with high school or college students on an
outing. It has been known to affect people of all ages, at times.
People take dares, drop their fears for a while, act and respond
in the moment with single-minded enthusiasm, as if the present
moment is the only reality that exists. If there is no anger or
greed in it, such moments are magic and wonderful.

So here comes this noise and racket on the roof. Dust and
debris start falling down on the people trying to listen to Jesus,
and no doubt on Jesus too. People can't get out because there is
too much crowd on the outside. Then down comes this pallet
with the paralytic on it. The four friends, presumably still up on
the roof, stick their heads in and say, "Oh, hi there, Jesus. We
couldn't get through the door, so we thought we would tear your
roof up, drop in, and ask you if you could help our friend."

And Jesus did not say, "You know, it would have been nice if
you could have waited a few more minutes. You might even have
sent a note in, or asked the people to pass the word into me."
There is no further mention of the roof. There is no comment
about rudeness, no complaint about interrupting the class, no
teaching about "patience is a virtue." The Scripture merely says,
"When Jesus saw their faith, He said to the paralytic, 'My son,
your sins are forgiven.'" Talk about knowing your priorities!

Bible Study groups often spend two or three whole evenings
working at this correlation between forgiveness and healing. It is
clearly the most important principle in the passage, and it is one
of the pivotal teachings of Jesus. If we begin to perceive things
as He does, it changes our way of understanding everything. In
this one passage, we are confronted with the meaning of our
distance from God—of our alienation from our Creator as a
condition of life on this planet. And we are tantalized by the
prospect of what we would be like if we were truly forgiven and

reconciled to God. And we are presented with wonderments about Jesus. Who is He? God alone can forgive sins. God alone has such authority. But Jesus does it! The paralyzed man walks out carrying his pallet. Who, then, is Jesus?

This is an incredible passage. It is not a parable. It is a real-life encounter with Jesus. And what comes from it—for those who have eyes to see and ears to hear and hearts to believe—is amazing indeed. I remind you of that because we aren't going to talk about any of that this morning. I want to fool around out on the edge of this passage. Sometimes it's a little safer farther from the center.

So let's forget all about this story of the paralytic for a little while, okay? I was thinking the other day about times in my life when I have tried to do without God. Have you ever done that on purpose? Some people try to get along without God most of the time. Don't misunderstand—I know there are very few true atheists. Most people believe in God in some fashion or manner. Lots of people believe in God, but still want nothing to do with him. Lots of people believe in God—believe he exists somewhere in some form or other—but they still try to do without God insofar as their own lives and decisions and purposes are concerned. People can believe in God and still want no friendship with him, no real or active relationship.

That, we would say, from the Christian perspective at least, is the biggest mistake a person can make in this life. It isn't the worst crime, from a social or political point of view, but it is the worst mistake a person can make. It robs us of more love, joy, meaning, purpose and power than any other single mistake we can make. Nevertheless, sometimes we try to get along without God.

I want to talk this morning about the second biggest mistake we can make: trying to get along without friends. It isn't a surprising new insight. "You shall love the Lord your God, and your neighbor as yourself." It is the First Commandment, and

another like unto it. The biggest mistake is to decide to get along
without God. Another mistake, like unto it, is to decide to get
along without friends.

It becomes increasingly clear, after we have been here for a
while, that there is no religion, no theology, no love, no meaning
to life . . . outside of community. And there is no community
without individual friendships. The church has taught us this
again and again. Where there are strong friendships, the church
thrives. Where friendships are shallow, the church becomes
lifeless form and ritual. There is no theology, no commitment, no
dedication or joy or zeal . . . where there are no friendships. The
first thing God does, at every authentic conversion, is give a
person a mission for the sake of the community. Moses is sent to
free the Israelites from Egypt, and to bring them back to the
mountain to become a covenant community. Jesus is sent to the
lost sheep of the house of Israel, and to establish them as a new
covenant community. Paul is sent to be an apostle to the Gentiles.
Check the conversion stories of Abraham, Jacob, Isaiah, Samuel,
Jeremiah, Peter, Augustine, Luther, Wesley, George Fox, your
next door neighbor. It is always the case! Conversion always comes
with an assignment, and that assignment is always for the benefit
of a community.

The second thing God does is start bringing friends. Moses
gets Aaron, Caleb, Joshua, Jethro, Miriam. Jesus gets Peter,
Andrew, James, John and the others. Paul gets Ananias, then
Barnabas, Silas, Luke, Timothy, Priscilla and the others. First
the vocatio, and then, like unto it, the friends. There is no
Christendom without community.

The first thing we think of, when we think of Jesus, is that He
reconciles us to God. The second is like unto it, only we don't
always remember it. Jesus embodies the very principle of
friendship. It is the substance of His ministry. If you try to follow
Jesus—if you turn your life over, try to walk in His WAY—the
Holy Spirit of Jesus Christ will send you friends. You may turn
them away, but they will come and keep coming as long as you
try to walk in the WAY. And nothing will work right or feel right

until you notice this, and begin to receive the friendships that are sent to you.

Do you remember yourself back in grammar school? What was the difference between the kids who had friends and the kids who didn't? It was the difference between day and night, wasn't it? It was the difference between confidence and insecurity, between happiness and misery. Some things don't change very much over the years.

Our age and culture tend to turn off friendship. The pressure to succeed, the way we view marriage, the frequency with which we change jobs and homes—even our attitudes and values— work against friendship. We wish to be self-sufficient. We are too busy for God or friends. Friends and God interfere with our plans—they get in the way when we get willful or start to self-destruct.

It is also true that true friends mean too much to us. Inevitably, we lose some of our friends to time, or distance, or misunderstanding, or accident, or jealousy, or death. And sometimes we feel that our friends let us down, or they feel we let them down. It's hard to be perfect in a world like this. For a while, we may be able to handle it pretty well. But it hurts! Some of us, after it has happened enough times, begin to withdraw. We do not want to hurt or be hurt that badly. We begin to shield, to guard, to keep our distance. It doesn't happen all at once, or with great consistency. But we begin to withdraw and shrivel. We prefer loneliness to pain. We try to get along without God, and then without friends. Love is the purpose of life. But love hurts. Sometimes, through some seasons of life, we decide it isn't worth the price.

Of course, that isn't the reason we give. We dedicate ourselves to our work. We decide we are marching to a different drummer. (Have you ever noticed how many different drummers there are?) We consider that we have a different destiny, or we commit ourselves to being ourselves with new vigor and ferocity. In Ibsen's play, *PEER GYNT,* the hero commits himself to "be myself." He visits the lunatic asylum, where he assumes people are "outside themselves." Begriffenfeldt, the director, corrects him: "Outside themselves? Oh no, you're wrong. It's here that men are most themselves—themselves and nothing but themselves—sailing with outspread sails of self. Each shuts himself in a cask of self, the cask stopped with a bung of self, and seasoned in a well of self. None has a tear for others' woes, or cares what any other thinks. We are ourselves in thought and voice—ourselves up to the very limit." To be an individual without a community is madness.

Suddenly I want to come back to the story of the paralytic. How many different kinds of paralysis are there? It doesn't matter. I have no trouble identifying. What a crazy, beautiful, outlandish, humorous, tear-jerking story. This paralyzed man has four friends. And what friends they are! Where do they come from? What has this man done to make such friends? We are never told. But they are beautiful indeed. They do not like it that their friend is paralyzed. They will go to any lengths, go through any antics, suffer embarrassment, risk danger. Was the paralytic begging them to put him down and leave things alone? Probably. But his friends are "merry"—undaunted.

What are friends for? We think friends should be for us, but friendship is bigger than that. Courageous and caring as these friends are, they still cannot heal the paralytic. The wound we all carry is deeper than that.

But these friends also have faith. That is one of the most startling twists to this story. The paralytic does not have to have faith—his friends have faith for him. The four friends carry this man to Jesus. It is the New Testament principle of intervention. Sometimes we aren't supposed to mind our own business. Sometimes letting people do their own thing is cruel. It doesn't make a bit of difference to this paralytic that Jesus embodies love, and has authority over demons, and can call upon the power of God to reconcile and to heal. It doesn't make any difference to him if he never sees or meets Jesus. So these four friends carry him. They drop whatever else they are doing, and neglect whatever else they care about. They carry him through the heat of the day, and past the crowds, and up to and through the roof! They do whatever they have to do to get him to Jesus.

Have you got four friends like that? Are you one of the four for anybody else? I would like to be a good friend to some people. I guess all of us would. I used to think it meant I should be strong and able to help or save my friends. But it doesn't. I am not strong enough, or wise enough, or good enough, or faithful enough to help my friends. Oh, sometimes I can listen, or loan money, or get lucky with an important contact. I can encourage my friends, and believe in them. It's not that such things don't count. But they are not enough. Eventually, inevitably—just like with me— my friends need more than I have to give. In the long run, the only hope is to get them to Jesus. If I can get them to Jesus, I know they will be all right. Even *that* I cannot do very well by myself. We need each other. It's hard to carry anybody very far, all by yourself. It takes at least four. Do you have at least three other friends who know what friends are for? If not, the Holy Spirit is trying to introduce you, if you will just watch and cooperate.

Sometimes we try to get along without God. That is our biggest mistake. A second mistake is like unto it—we try to get along without friends. If you are converted, trying to walk the Christian WAY, the Holy Spirit will send you friends. You don't *have* to make them. You don't even have to know how. You just have to stop turning them away. But it is a promise as certain as the sunrise: If you are converted, the Holy Spirit will send you friends. The Holy Spirit will also send you as a friend. It is the very core of the Christian Life.

Matthew 18:15-22; Luke 9:1-6; 10:1-12

Week Twenty-Five

ON TURNING YOUR BACK

I have never known any person very well, or for very long, who did not eventually run into the hard problem of having to turn away from some things—from some people. We call it "prioritizing" today. That sounds less personal and painful, but it is not.

An old saint in Worcester, Massachusetts, used to say to me, "Remember, Bruce, elimination is as necessary to the health of the body as ingestion." Transcendence, growth, change, conversion of every kind and degree always require a certain amount of reordering of our lives. New things come, but some things must go. If nothing goes, there is no room for the new.

As Christians, we are particularly troubled by this reality. It is right that we put most of the emphasis on reconciliation, acceptance, forgiveness, restoration. But it has come to the place where we almost never hear about the other side of the coin. And so I keep running into folk who are deeply troubled and who assume themselves to be wrong and unchristian when faced with the necessity of eliminating some things or some people from their lives. They say to me, "But I never heard in church that such things could ever be right."

Come to think of it, I don't know that I ever did either. And that is a very grave omission.

One of the clearest themes and thrusts of the Christian Faith is the whole area of reconciliation: opening closed relationships; forgiveness; reversing and redeeming, by the power of love, the evil and resentment and animosity that divide God's children from God, and from one another. The resulting loneliness and pain and destroyed peace are the source behind most of the familiar mayhem on our planet. In short, one of the things we ought to expect—and probably one of the strongest motives that drew us to the Christian Life in the first place—is the possibility that we ourselves can become more loving, and the hope that we would meet other people who would share with us and deal with us according to the ways of reconciliation. It does happen, but we also discover that it is not all instantaneous, or simple, or automatic.

Now, it is neither appropriate nor possible for us to deal much with those who have walked out on us. We believe in freedom—it is their choice—and most of us cannot "afford" to do more than accept the rejection on as simple and practical a level as possible. Otherwise we get into vindictiveness and judgments and resentments that shrivel the soul. So we put the matter in God's hands, accept it for the time being, and move on.

But there is another issue that troubles every person who takes the Christian Life to heart: Is it ever right for us, as Christians, to leave, to say goodbye, to disassociate ourselves from some person? And what if that person comes back and says to us, "Let's be friends again"? Are we required to forgive and to take that person back into our space and time no matter what?

I presume the subject is clear, that you know what I am talking about, that you are even able to relate to it personally. Most of us have lost people out of our lives (not by death or distance, but by some bitter stress or misunderstanding) and we regret it, and the empty place is still a wound within us that throbs afresh each time we touch it.

But our subject today is the other side of the coin. What about the people we want or need or think we need to get out of our lives? If we have done it, must we always feel guilty about it? If we have only thought about it, is it ever right to go ahead and do it? I am presuming that we have no interest in coming at this from a merely human or legal or pragmatic point of view. Seeing the issue from the Christian perspective—wanting our lives to be under the discipline and guidance of the Holy Spirit—is it ever permissible to turn your back on somebody?

I entered the Christian ministry convinced that love (as I

understood it) was always the answer, and that turning away from a person on purpose was never the Christian choice. Well, one area of exception seemed to be the area of romance. Nobody could marry more than one person. So turning away in that category was sometimes unavoidable. But short of that, I believed that the Christian should always hang in when it came to caring about and relating to other people.

As if he knew that this was my conviction and belief, he was waiting for me on the very first day we moved into the parsonage of my very first church: a young man dressed in the full armor of needs and problems. I, of course, knew it was because he had never been fully accepted, truly understood, cared about, really loved. Fifteen years later, three churches later, three thousand miles from where we met, I finally said to him, "Get out of my house. I don't want to see you anymore. I don't want you in my life." That was the first time in my life I ever did such a thing. It was no accident or whim, but it seemed a very strange thing to do, all the same.

That was just over ten years ago. I must say, not having him in my life has been a big improvement. I heard not long ago that he was still alive and doing quite well. Both things were hard to believe. I was surprised at how good that news made me feel. (But it didn't make me feel good enough to invite him back into my life.) Nevertheless, I was finally convinced that it had been necessary and "right" for me to turn my back on that person. I wasn't doing him any good. And I felt he was doing me, my family, and the churches I served a lot of harm, and harming himself in the process.

Psychologically speaking, it still opens "Pandora's box," doesn't it? If in some circumstances it is right for me to turn my back on another, then there must be some circumstances in which it would be right for others to turn their backs on me. And if that is the case, perhaps one day it might even be right and necessary for God to turn away from me. That is the spectre which is raised. That is what makes the subject so important, and interesting, and emotional. Somehow, in this category more than in most, we recognize that in some fascinating way, the little acts and scenes of our daily lives are reflections of vast and mighty cosmic issues.

So we keep reading the Scriptures, and we keep watching what Jesus was actually like. Surprisingly, Jesus gives instructions on the very subject (Matthew 18). He outlines procedures for people having trouble with each other. It ends with the person being rejected! That is to say, the instructions continue to the point where turning your back is the appropriate choice. I don't remember being told about that in my Sunday School, church, youth group or even in seminary. Somehow, I was always left with the impression that it could/should never come to that.

Of course, a Christian is supposed to read the Scriptures for herself. I finally learned that. I keep trying to teach you too. It isn't about niceness—it's about truth. It turns out that Jesus was adamant about going His own direction, living for the Kingdom. Nobody could put emotional, national, spiritual or physical ties on Him strong enough to divert Him from His course. He taught His followers to live much the same way. We ourselves can be compromised; not such a big deal. But the Kingdom is too great for us to knowingly compromise it. Sometimes we must turn away from things or people who want to require us to do that.

The pressures of scribes, Pharisees, even the Sanhedrin—and Jesus' turning His back on them—should be obvious! Why isn't it? Challenger after challenger comes to debate with Him. Sometimes we get interesting conversations. Sometimes Jesus simply shuts them off and walks on by. With some, like the rich young ruler, it is hard to know who turns his back first. It is clear that Jesus feels no compulsion to have the conversation work out "nicely" or to have everybody leave feeling friendly. (The man at the Pool of Bethesda is another incredible example.) It is not Satan but Jesus who says, "Do not give dogs what is holy; do not cast your pearls before swine." (Matthew 7:6) Instructions about shaking the dust from your feet and about letting your peace return to you are explicit. (Luke 9:5) "He who is not with me is against me, and he who does not gather with me, scatters." (Luke 11:23) There are times to turn your back

on people. It isn't a matter of being unchristian unless you continue
to act friendly and attempt reconciliation when you are not supposed
to. It isn't something to feel guilty about unless we fail to turn away
when we should.

Yes, in the same passage Jesus teaches that we must forgive
seventy times seven. But that kind of forgiveness assumes and
depends upon the person having repented, and we have lots of
people talking about forgiveness today who don't seem to know
that repentance is an essential part of it.

Christian love is not physically injurious to any person for
any reason. That does *not* mean it is soft! I remind you that the
only reason Jesus made any impact on the world with His kindness
and compassion and love was because He was not soft! It wasn't
because He was afraid, or because He wanted something for
Himself, or because He couldn't stand strife or was trying to avoid
unpleasant scenes. He was kind and compassionate and loving
because He chose to be. He forgave because He had forgiveness
to give and chose to give it. That is what made the impact. He
didn't have to—He chose to!

The church is frequently too soft for that kind of love today. It
forgives because it is afraid not to, rather than because, in love, it
chooses to. And so, when the forgiveness is granted, we cannot tell
whether the person has been appeased, or tolerated, or redeemed,
or merely ignored. Half the time, even the forgiven person doesn't
know if he or she has repented! Softly, quietly, we drift off into the
dusk, where even love is so soft we cannot tell if we are being loved,
or just tolerated, or maybe we just go unnoticed.

So consider the following:

1.) Christianity has always been in conflict (battle) with those
who reject its basic message. A Kingdom based on love is still in
opposition to, and at odds with, every kingdom based on any
other premise. Of course, a Kingdom of love must stay with love's
methods, or lose the war. The only other thing we can be sure of
is that Jesus' definition of love is not what most people mean by
that word today.

2.) The application of love's principles must be appropriate to the person being loved. Trying to find one precept or one rule for all people or all situations will always result in a soft, counterfeit (uncaring) love. Many of the teachings of the New Testament apply specifically to relationships between people inside the fellowship of the church. There is a different code for those outside the church, and still another code for those who are known enemies. We might expect that every Christian would be very interested and instructed and aware of these three different, appropriate approaches.

And every Christian is required to forgive. But there are two basic categories of forgiveness, if you are on the forgiving end:

a.) If the person you need to forgive is unrepentant, getting the poison out of your own soul is all that is required. Nothing happens to the relationship, and reconciliation is not expected.

b.) If the person is repentant, forgiveness is mandatory and means the complete restoring of the relationship, with no holding back on your part.

It remains clear, however, that there are times when Christians will be required to turn their backs on specific relationships, which means turning your back on a specific person. Let us be careful! It is never right to turn your back on a person simply because of an error, a blunder, a mistake, a failure, an inadequacy on their part—no matter how much injury this may have inflicted, from your point of view. Closing out a relationship does not mean that we are angry, vindictive, jealous or resentful. In fact, if these emotions are still the dominant factor, we probably still belong in the relationship, with much unfinished business to attend to. God puts up with our sin and errors all the time, and expects us to be willing to put up with the growth pains of our brothers and sisters too.

However, some relationships are themselves off track, and keep heading in the wrong direction. Often we try to decide who is the good guy and who is the bad guy, but that is not always relevant. Sometimes one person is clearly the opposition, but sometimes two people simply stymie each other. Every time they get together, forward motion stops, strange issues come to the fore, progress for both of them is blocked. There are, likewise, certain situations that close us down. Some people can work at great heights with no bad reactions, for instance, while others cannot. Some people can work well in mental institutions, while others feel quickly unnerved or depressed.

It is clear that there are certain situations, certain issues and, on occasion (at least for a while), certain people we do not belong with, should not stay around, should not keep trying to resolve things with. It is not merely that we are then permitted to turn our backs—we are *required* by the Holy Spirit to leave, to turn away, to get out. Specifically, when anyone or anything consistently and persistently interferes with our knowing and following the guidance of the Holy Spirit, we are required to break it off, to leave. The Pilgrimage is always top priority.

Christians need to be aware that such dilemmas will come. Again and again, I have watched sincere Christians struggling with situations they should be turning their backs on. But they will not or cannot do it—sometimes for years—because they have it in mind that the Christian Faith (God) does not permit it. I have preached this sermon to remind you, via Jesus' own teachings and example, that sometimes the Christian Faith (God) not only permits it, but requires it.

Now, a couple of comments to make sure you know you heard me right. The toughest category, in my opinion, is the children. On rare occasion, children get into a negative relationship with their parents wherein the child continually fails and/or gets into trouble as a way to punish or control the parent. It is a terrible pattern from which there is no relief for parent or child until the parents finally awaken and turn away completely (for a while).

That is the most difficult of all, but close seconds are when we are required to turn away from a spouse, close friends, or relatives. Some jobs or organizations become very painful partings at times, for some of us. If, in the situations where we are required to turn away, we hang in and hang on, the eventual result is idolatry. God is displaced from first place in our lives, and these other values (real or imagined) move into first place.

In any case, Jesus, Scripture and the Christian Faith do not always instruct us to keep, maintain, restore or reconcile every relationship. Sometimes (and they are never fun times) we are required to let go, to turn our backs, to make no move to reconcile. Jesus refused to restore or heal the relationship between Himself and Herod, or Pilate, or the priests, or most of the Pharisees. He even broke the ties between Himself and many of His own former disciples. Love does not require us to forsake or betray the Author of Love himself! Jesus seems to have been one of the few human beings who ever figured that out. Perhaps that is why He was able to go on believing in love's power so totally, and in the very places where we are most tempted to quit on it.

Fortunately, it never has to be left looking grim. After we shake the dust, or excommunicate a brother or sister, or turn our backs, there is still the surprising power of the Gospel that is beyond our control. And that means hope. Be ready for reunion—always. Sometimes it comes best when we stop trying to control it. Who knows on what day a Saul will walk a Damascus Road? And wherever real repentance strikes, it is always a whole new ball game. The only way we can be ready for any of it—the detachment or the reunion—is to stay very close to Jesus Christ, very constant in our prayers. And we need to remember that the love of Jesus Christ is not soft! Not soft for you, or me, or anybody else. That may be partly why you can bet your life on it.

Luke 4:1-13

Week Twenty-Six

HELPING PEOPLE

I have been trying to recall and count up all the people I have run into in my lifetime who do not believe in helping other people. So far, I haven't been able to get a single name on my list. A few names went down at first, but in each case, a moment's reflection made it clear that they had to be erased. Certainly I have run into individuals who had what seemed to me rather bizarre notions of how to go about helping people. The variety of convictions and methods on the subject is staggering. But truly, I cannot recall knowing anyone thus far who didn't think a lot about and care a lot about helping people.

The common assumption is that most people do not believe in trying to help others. The problem with life, we tend to think, is that most folk are greedy, self-centered, too busy to be bothered with the plight of others. Therefore, one of the great missions in life is to educate people out of their "natural" lack of caring, and to inspire them to try to help their neighbors. We tell ourselves that if we could only find a way to get people to care about each other, the world would be such a wonderful place. The trouble, we think, is that most people just don't care very much about others, aside from me and a few of my friends, that is.

This whole line of reasoning makes perfect sense, and seems to match my experience with reality, until or unless I make one fatal mistake and start looking for the individuals who match this description of how almost everybody is. I can't actually recall a single one. Some people come a little closer than others, perhaps, but nobody in my experience seems very close at all to the way "most everybody" is. It is very hard to remember that nobody is really like almost everybody is supposed to be!

In reality, we live in a world where everybody believes in helping people. Nobody has to talk anybody into it—we already really want to help people. In fact, if you try to encourage somebody to be caring about others, you are merely being arrogant and irritating. But caring and wanting to help is not the issue. Something else is. If people already care and want to help people, then what is the problem in our world that keeps making it look like there isn't enough caring or help going on?

Helping people is not easy! I think that's the answer. I think that's what throws everything off. We have all inherited the myth that helping people is easy. All you have to do is want to. The assumption is that we can all help people any time we want to, as much as we are willing to. Therefore, since there is still so much need—since so many people are not getting help—it must mean that we and almost all others are still mostly selfish, mostly uncaring, mostly unwilling to put ourselves out to help others. What other conclusion could there be?

The only other conclusion is one that is unbearable. That is why the myth persists, and why we go on assuming the worst. It isn't easy to help people. It may not even be possible. Who has moxie enough to face that? If we are merely selfish or uncaring, there may be some hope for us—maybe we will change, even at the zero hour, and make the world all right. But if we are helpless, or even if helping people is one of the most difficult and complex tasks in all the world, then what hope is there for us? It is so much easier to live with the notion that I can but I don't want to . . . than to face the stark reality that I want to but cannot.

The greatest and deepest pathos in life is wanting to help and not being able to. Any time a loved one is suffering or dying and we stand by helpless, we know again the worst of life. We will do almost anything to avoid such intolerable situations. Much better to see ourselves as greedy or selfish or sinful—at least that way maybe we can be punished and maybe things will be okay again. But if we are helpless, then what? It isn't easy to help people. It may be almost impossible. The myth that we can do it any time we want to, any old way we like, and whenever we get kindhearted enough and generous enough to want to . . . well, it just isn't true. But we perpetuate the myth, reinforce it for each other, and teach it to our children because it hurts less than facing the truth: it isn't easy to help people!

May I remind you of a few of the side issues and complexities? I know one church leader who says the big problem is not in *convincing* people to do good, but handling the jealousy if somebody actually *does* good. Paul certainly had that problem at Corinth (I Corinthians 12-14). He kept saying that all the gifts, all the leadership, all the efforts and energies were needed and valuable. But at Corinth, they kept wanting to stop and quarrel about who was doing the most good. I guess it never has stopped from that day to this, both in churches and between churches. We are so desperately hungry to see ourselves as people who help people that we claw at any evidence or possibility like ten lions over a morsel of meat.

Some individuals see the church's primary purpose as an outlet for the urge to help people. That way they can feel good about their giving and good intentions without having to deal with the real-life failures and struggles of a personal effort to help people.

James Breech, in his book *THE SILENCE OF JESUS*, points out the complexity that surrounds our efforts to help. He says that humanitarianism focuses on the suffering of mankind in order to avoid caring about actual people as real people. Altruism, on the other hand, affirms another in order to escape from self. Actually, Dr. Breech puts it more strongly: "Altruism is a form of self-hatred posing as love [for another]."

It is obvious that helping people is a topic surrounded by strong opinions, even violent passions. No human, to my knowledge, is uninterested or unbiased about the subject. And distributing Thanksgiving or Christmas baskets, no matter how big or how many, is really not going to cover the subject. Neither are the old individualism statements, which seem to be coming back in some quarters today: "If everyone would sweep in front of his own door, tomorrow the whole world would be clean." Or,

"If everyone would help his next-door neighbor, tomorrow nobody would be in need." The logic is lovely, and such sayings have real merit, but they hardly help us with our border wars—physical, emotional or spiritual.

So we live in a world where everybody wants to help people. But how, when, where and whom? It isn't easy to help people. If we are talking about significant help, it may not even be possible.

Jesus knew all of this, and struggled with it mightily. He knew it a lot more clearly than we will probably allow ourselves to know it. The Crucifixion and Jesus' refusal to avoid it make this quite clear. Trying to help people requires a Savior, a rebirth of mind and heart, the descent or infusion of the Holy Spirit, a new purpose, and a new way of living to go with it. That's what the New Testament thinks. And we're going to help people with a little food, or a little money, or some information, or some extra kindness and attention?! Isn't that interesting. It cost Jesus everything.

Well, but Jesus seemed to agree with the Old Testament dictum, "You shall love your neighbor as yourself." Why do people think that means Christmas baskets, or helping somebody change a tire? Maybe it means, "If you're not going to go all the way, stay out of it. At least keep out of the way."

The forty days in the wilderness were when Jesus had to wrestle with the question, "How do you help people?" Satan said, "Feed them." Jesus said, "That isn't going to make it." For the most part, the church is still pretty sure Satan had the right idea. Satan suggested that Jesus use political organization and power to help the people. Again, Jesus realized He would fail if He built His ministry on such terms. Again, for the most part, the church suspects that Satan had the right idea. And there was the third temptation. But if we can't even see through the first two, you can imagine what chance we would have with the third! Nevertheless, Jesus rejected the temptations to build His ministry on any of the traditional ways of helping people. Clearly, Jesus knew that helping people was not easy. He seemed to know that only God's power could help anyone, that He Himself would have to stay surrendered, humble, obedient—not the genius in command of salvaging other people, but the servant of God—or Satan would corrupt the entire mission so swiftly and subtly that few would ever even notice. At least that seems to be Jesus' realization and conclusion from His prayer and fasting. Only God can help people. Everything must be done by God's timing, and patience, and guidance.

So we watch Jesus after the wilderness. What mighty new power and method will He call upon and depend upon to accomplish His purpose, having rejected all the normal, familiar approaches? He does a lot of things . . . here and there . . . off and on. But the real power is so low-key, so strange and unlikely, that at first we don't see anything. Jesus just wanders around talking. He performs miracles here and there. There doesn't seem to be any thrust, any plan, any forward motion. Mostly Jesus is making twelve friends, shaping and forming a "community," and slowly inviting others into the community.

It took time. Nothing seemed to happen. But you have to *be* a community in order to invite others into the community. Each individual, of course, was dedicated to God even more than to the community. But the community was the rallying point, the power, the source of healing and support and inspiration that carried the Message. People found both the Word and the Spirit by finding and becoming part of the community of Jesus.

I am hopeful that this year, our Board of Outreach will continue to seek and present us with concepts of ministry until this congregation finds the area where the Holy Spirit wants this particular church to be truly engaged. In the meantime, I get a little weary of the animosity I keep feeling from some of the social-action enthusiasts in this congregation. My plea has never been that we should have no concern for helping people. Everybody wants to help people—even me. My plea has been that we try to figure out what we are really trying to do, and whether or not we are doing it as the community of Jesus Christ.

In the early church, as nearly as can be pieced together, the communion meal was also like a bread line. The Christians gathered to eat, and they brought with them whomever they had encountered who was willing to come. Eating, talking, feeding the hungry, telling about Jesus, praying, and finding a group of loving and accepting friends were all intertwined and happening at the same time. Doesn't such a communion sound alive and wonderful? The early Christians would have found it hard to understand how you could care about somebody and leave them out of the community. Today, we mostly try to help without inviting people into the faith community.

We live in a world where everybody believes in helping people—where everybody wants to help—if they can only figure out how, or agree with a few others about when and where. We aren't going to do that very well if we do it casually or according to our own whims or moods. It needs to be intentional, and with the whole community aware and involved. And we have to invite people in, and expect them to help because they have been helped. Receiving help without learning to give help means you haven't been helped yet.

SECTION THREE

SUMMER

I John 4:7-21

Week Twenty-Seven

WHERE DOES LOVE COME FROM?

I don't usually talk much about love. Next to "God," "love" is the most abused word in the English language. Frequently in the church, it is used when we have run out of anything important to say. At other times, we use it to confuse the issue, or to produce guilt, or to sidetrack a project that is heading in a direction we don't like.

On the other hand, love is supposed to be the product and the eventual goal of the Christian Church. Nobody anywhere ever gets too much of it. Nor do any of us give too much of it. We may give or get too much of other products trying to masquerade as love, but love itself is still the most valued item in the world.

It isn't news to anybody, but we do find ourselves in this predicament of needing and wanting to talk about a concept we cannot define. In fact, we are not always sure when we are being loved. And sometimes we are not certain about when we are giving it, either. We can't define it, and we aren't sure when it's coming or going. Nevertheless, it is our second-greatest interest, and everything depends upon it.

Read I John 4:7-21, but whenever the Scripture says "love," read "mush." That is to remind us of how soft and imprecise the word really is, and how few of us mean the same thing by it.

The question is not, "What is love?" Strangely, with this subject, we have to save that question for last. The question today is, "Where does love come from?"

God is love. God is the source of love. God is where love comes from. Any religious person can tell you that, if you don't tell them first. It is still the proper answer, and I believe the true answer. An answer can be true and right, and still only turn itself back into more questions.

Take for instance: "Love the Lord your God with all your heart . . . and your neighbor as yourself." That answers all of the most important questions that humans ever ask. But even though we do not doubt its truth, we still recognize that it hasn't answered anything. It has only focused and deepened all the other questions: What is God? How can I best love God? Who is my neighbor? Who am I? How do I love myself? How can I love my neighbor in the way I love myself? What is love?

You see? Seven questions where before there was one. Each one of them is worthy of a lifetime, and indeed we are in the ongoing process of responding to them.

I have three rule-of-thumb axioms to present to you.

I.) NO PERSON CAN CONTAIN OR GIVE AWAY MORE LOVE THAN HE OR SHE HAS RECEIVED

Consider the contrasting principle. Most people believe that we are all born with an unlimited capacity to love. We are all, then, able to love anybody as much or as little as we want to. Therefore, whenever and whomever we do not love, it is because we have decided not to.

A lot of guilt and pain come from this assumption. If somebody does not love us, we automatically assume that there must be something terribly wrong with us, or the person would not have chosen to reject us so. It makes us either very sad or very angry.

If the axiom is closer to the truth, it means that if a person does not love you, it is because that person has run out of love to give. If that person has no more love to give, then you would logically feel compassion for them because it means that no one has loved them enough. Hardly a reason for you to feel hurt or angry. In fact, if you yourself have some extra love handy, that's what is called for.

The normal assumption about our native ability to love simply does not match our experience. Over and over, people choose not to love someone, yet discover themselves doing it anyway. It is there and they cannot stop it. Or people consciously decide they ought to love someone, and despite every effort, they fail to do so. Of and by ourselves, we are unable and completely incapable of producing or manufacturing love. We are all living with whatever amount of love we have received from beyond ourselves.

If this is true, everyone has a different capacity to love, and it changes from moment to moment. One of the reasons we need to be a church together is precisely so we can fill in each other's blank places and create together a loving community. If a stranger walked through our door at this very moment, obviously hurt, and stumbled and fell with the cry, "Help me!"—you would respond to that cry. Every person here has had the experience of being helped when hurt.

If the stranger was not hurt, but was instead disheveled, unshaven, poorly dressed and obviously drunk, people's responses would begin to show a wider range. Some of us have never known what it was like to be loved when we were that socially unacceptable. All of us would be struggling with an inner awareness of how we would expect to be treated if we were in this stranger's place. We tend to judge as we have been judged, or as we would expect to be judged.

If, however, the stranger burst through our door, shouted "I hate you!" and shot someone sitting next to you, then that stranger's need might fail to bring a single loving response.

Truly, not many people have known what it feels like to be loved when their own hearts were as wrong and evil as that. That is why the church is supposed to start out from the grace of point zero, and why entrance is symbolized by baptism. Only if we have visited a Cross that we have helped to raise—and discovered what it is like to hear Him say, "Father forgive them"—only then is love available when people need it most. That is why the church is for sinners only. Our product is not morals. Our product is not goodness. Our product is forgiveness. "Those who have been forgiven little, love little." That's where love comes from. That's what The MAN said. (Luke 7:47)

No person can contain or give away to others more love than they themselves have received. It's only an axiom, but it is freeing.

See if it doesn't match what you see and feel going on around you.

II.) NO PERSON EVER DOES, OR EVER CAN, EARN OR DESERVE LOVE

Again the counter-principle: Most people operate on the theory that there are certain things they can do which make them lovable, which give them the right to be loved, or which give them some claim on the love of another. (After all I have done for you . . .) Perhaps they are thinking of one of love's alternatives or counterfeits: approval, acceptance, tolerance, or the like.

Back to our subject. Nobody earns the right to be loved. Nobody can stake a claim on another person's heart. If someone dies for me, how do I repay that? How do I earn the right to have a person do that for me? Yet that is love's nature, should the circumstances require it. If someone loves you, that reveals a lot about them—and nothing about you. The Gospel is not about how good *we* are. It is about how loving God is. We can never get that really said, can we? Going to heaven is not about how good we do. It is about how loving God is. Bill Coffin says it: "You are not loved because you are valuable. You are valuable because you are loved."

By the way, if another person does not love you, that also reveals something about them, not about you. Love is a gift that is freely given. If it is not that, it is not love. So the church often "slips"—especially when it wants more time or money with which to help—and it says or implies: "You should be more loving (give more, do more)." That is a contradiction in terms. It is the church forgetting its fundamental truth: Love is a gift, not a duty. God does not *have* to love us. We do not *have* to love each other. When we get loved, it is because somebody wanted to. That's what makes it great!

Yes, Jesus says it a number of ways. If we follow Him . . . love Him . . . obey Him—we will love each other. But the printed page forgets to show His smile. If we get close to Him, He will fill us with love, and then who is going to stop it? We read it grim, and hear a rule or a duty. Why don't we hear Him laughing and saying, "I dare you to take some and then try to hold it back!"

If a person has love to give, it will be given, and nothing can hold it back. If a person has not been loved, there is none there to give, and nothing can draw it out. It would behoove us, then, never to expect to be loved, never to feel we had any complaint coming when we are not, and always to be surprised, delighted and grateful when we discover that we are loved. The axiom is: no person ever does or ever can earn or deserve to be loved.

III.) PEOPLE HAVE THE FREEDOM TO ACCEPT OR REJECT LOVE

The counterpart to this is that we mostly assume we accept all the love that comes our way. The truth seems to be that we are very persnickety about receiving love. Just as "charity begins at home," so does its rejection. When parents mix two parts of love with four or ten parts of "don't touch that . . . you have to swallow this . . . you can't go there and you must go here"—well, baby gets a lesson in love versus freedom, and that means love must often be rejected. It isn't the parents' fault either! Where do you think we are, Eden?

Love is full of "impurities" in our world, and we have all learned to fear the lover and reject the love. Hopefully we also learn, in time, that receiving love, even from humans, is worth the risk and doesn't have to steal our freedom like it did when we were children. Nevertheless, the reason we are not more loving is because we have rejected so much of the love that has been offered to us—from humans and from God. We wouldn't receive it, and so we haven't got it to give.

We have rejected a lot of love because it takes time and experience to learn to recognize it—which is next Sunday's question. Like fool's gold, there is a lot of fool's love in our world. (All that glitters is not gold; all that acts nice, or affectionate, isn't love.) Most of us have some bitter memories of times when what we thought was priceless treasure turned out to be fool's love.

But that isn't the whole story either. The reason we are not more loving is because we have refused and rejected the love that is offered by God. And here is where I would like to cut out and remain silent, but that isn't fair. We know instinctively, from a seventh sense, that though love is a gift with no strings attached, receiving love does affect us with the power of love itself. And even though I cannot define love—whatever it is, it is a lot stronger than I am. I know instinctively that if I accept very much of it, I will lose my freedom to be my own person in my own way—meaning, in the way I am now.

If I receive love, I will cease to be separated off from God and other people. I will feel a unity that will begin to affect and control my living. A true "lover" (agent of love) makes no demands, but love itself is the most demanding force in the world. Therefore, I try to accept just enough love to survive on—and maybe, in my best moments, just a tiny bit more. The minute I begin to feel the effects of it, there comes this great urge to save my freedom, to back off lest I lose control, to guard my security. So I cut off the offered gift. And you know what? It is precisely at those times—right after I have turned away from offered love (especially from God)—that I scream the loudest about how there isn't enough love in the world. It's like I'm trying to distract attention from what I have just done. And you know what else? I've started to realize that other people do this too. Just when they have turned away from love that is offered, they start talking loudly about how scarce love is.

Do you ever wonder why great miracles happen in times of crisis, and we are more like what we wish we were like all the time? In times of crisis or tragedy, the need for love is so great that we fling the doors wide open. At such times, our self-centered freedom doesn't mean much, so we get careless—we start praying passionately and earnestly—and then open our hearts! The Holy Spirit is always right there, waiting and offering, delighted to be invited. So we get magic moments. Miracles happen.

We can only hope that, on some such occasion, we will get such an overdose that we will forget to shut down the doors afterward. It happens! All through history, it keeps happening. People lose all sense of reality. They become fearless, joyful, hopeful, enthusiastic participants in LIFE, in the great Pilgrimage. They begin to find value in all manner and types of people. Nothing seems to affect their sense of personal well-being, or calls them back to counting up the injustices and sufferings and hardships they must endure. Instead, they start talking about a New Kingdom that is secret, yet all around us—in our very midst.

The first axiom is: No person can contain or give away more love than he or she has received.

The second axiom is: No person ever does, or ever can, earn or deserve love.

The third axiom is: People have the freedom to accept or reject the love that is offered.

If you cannot remember all of that, remember this: "You are not loved because you have value. You have value because you are loved." (Bill Coffin)

I Corinthians 13

Week Twenty-Eight

LOVE IS A SPENDTHRIFT

For those of you just tuning in, we are asking three questions about love. That is not to imply that we are answering the questions, only that we are asking them: Where does love come from? What is love? What is love good for? Today we are on the second question: What is love?

Webster says that love is "a feeling of strong personal attachment induced by sympathetic understanding; ardent affection." A valiant try. We could hardly expect more from a definition. And yet it is hopelessly inadequate. It hardly explains two people standing hand-in-hand and saying, "Until death do us part." It really doesn't cover spending your life making music, or working in a hospital in Africa, or teaching children, or dying on a cross.

What then is love? When that question hits the brain-circuits, it blows all the fuses. Something twitches, expands, explodes. A winsome look, a shrug of the shoulders, a foolish laugh—and the one who asked the question smiles and nods in agreement. Love has no definition. To define something is to set boundaries, to find limits. Love breaks boundaries. Some are not sure it even has any limits. Other things are often judged and clarified by the light of love. Earth has no light bright enough to bring love into clear relief.

Love "calls the worlds into being; creates us in its own image; sets before us the ways of life and death; reconciles the world to itself." We just can't put that sort of thing into neat little packages of definition. Only God knows, and even God could find no word of definition—except a Word made flesh.

It is recorded in the Old Testament that Moses once asked God to define and identify God's self. "What is your name?"

Moses asked. (In those days, to name was to define.) God must have smiled. What innocent effrontery—with a brain so small to ask a question so large! Finally God replied, "I am that I am." If you must have a name, call me "I AM." It is enough that you know I exist. (Yahweh, Jehovah = the One who IS.)

Just so with the life-force—the expression of God's existence, the nature of the power of the One who IS—that we call "love." It is enough to know it exists. Hard enough to know that, to remember it, to believe it. We do not have to define it to feel it . . . to know it uses us . . . to realize it calls us into life, and ever into greater, more abundant Life.

Knowing we cannot define, and knowing we must keep trying to comprehend, we go on checking our ways against what seem to be love's ways. In our case, that sends us to the study of Scripture, and especially to the information about Jesus. From this we still get no final definitions. But we learn that "love is sometimes like this . . . " and "love is on occasion like that . . . " and "love has been known to conduct itself in the following manner . . . "

From the Scriptures we also learn that love is not often like what we want it to be like. Love is rarely even close to what popular concepts picture it to be. It was a great shock, to me at least, years ago when I got out of seminary and into some of my first Bible Study groups in the parish. It was a shock to begin to discover that Jesus was not a very good "Christian." Jesus did not live by the codes or expectations of love, at least not by any understanding of love that I had been taught. I and most of the people I knew were far more loving than Jesus. That is, we tried to please each other, tried to be "nice," acted considerate and polite, tried to be thoughtful and helpful, and we also tried to be fair—to keep a pretty close balance of favors between us.

No matter how we tried, in those early study groups, we just couldn't get the records about Jesus to match our expectations. He was supposed to make us more "loving." He was supposed to make us even nicer, more thoughtful and considerate. But by our understandings, we were already far more loving than He was. He was not nice. He was a bear-cat! He didn't seem to try to please anybody, and often He displeased many. He took shamelessly from His friends, and did immense favors for people He didn't know and would never see again—even at the expense or embarrassment of His friends. We could go on and on. The plain fact is that Jesus was supposed to be the source and example of love, and Jesus wasn't doing it like any of us thought we were supposed to be doing it.

The confusion at this point is stunning, staggering, dumbfounding! The majority of people in our society have a general set of expectations, pictures and understandings about love. A much smaller but still influential group tries to understand love from what they consider to be the source—God, as revealed in Jesus Christ. And these two groups have completely different concepts in mind?!

If I tell you "God loves you," and you think I mean "God will be nice to you," we might talk for days and make all kinds of agreements assuming we understand each other, and yet we couldn't be further apart. I don't know of anything in the Scriptures that suggests love is soft, easy, polite, pleasant, undemanding, unconditional or even reasonable. Love in the Scriptures seems instead to be dynamic, transforming, uncompromising, unyielding. It comes more often as an imperative rather than as a pat on the head. Some people still think the good news of the Gospel is that God loves us, and therefore life will go our way. The Good News of the Gospel is that God loves us! But what in the world is love? What do we expect from it?

We are still trying to get oriented to our question, "What is love?" What do we expect from knowing that God loves us? There is not and cannot be a clear definition because love is too large for us. Nevertheless, there are widely divergent impressions about the very nature of love. We all use the word carelessly as well as very intentionally—and either way, we are frequently saying the word without any clear notion of what others are "hearing," and vice versa.

Let me suggest next that part of our confusion about love is caused by our intense need to claim that we ourselves are loving people. If each definition must end up making us look good, or recommending us to God as good illustrations of love—then, you see, the subject is hopelessly prejudiced. If love is so high I cannot define it, then in all probability I have not lived up to its full potential in my daily life either. To comprehend where love is trying to lead me, I must be willing to let go of my need to see myself as already a very loving person.

By the way, which one among us is the most loving person? Is it the most popular? Is it the most self-effacing? Is it the gentlest, or the kindest? Is it the one with the least opinions? Whatever, we would each be highly insulted if somebody said to us, "You are not a very loving person."

What a terrible indictment! How guilty that would make us feel. How judged and rejected we would feel. And yet, the truth is that all day, every day, we are going about our business in the midst of people we do not love, and we remain completely unaware of thousands of people who very much need to be loved. On a good day, we may become aware again of a few people we do love, and maybe even we will have a small chance to act or respond according to that love. But in truth, we are not very loving people—that is, not by any absolute standard. We are barely awake, barely getting started on our careers of becoming beings—people—of love. It is important for us to be able to accept that, or we will always be pretending, play-acting, trying to make it look good—instead of seeking the truth.

Love may not be limited, but we are. Think of the criterion. We should be cautious about claiming love for any person we would not (potentially) die for. Or who we at least would be willing to get into serious trouble to defend or support, if circumstances required it. There is not much they could do to turn away our affection, not many mistakes possible that would devalue them in our eyes. How many people did you say you loved? You say you thought a Thanksgiving basket qualified? You're not reading the same Book I am!

We aren't very loving people. Becoming loving is not something we have accomplished—it is something we are here to learn, to test out, to try on, to grow into. To learn to love is the purpose of life (in case you've ever wondered). We don't get many graduates—never mind Phi Beta Kappas, or summa cum laudes. So it's very freeing to come down off the pedestals and say, "Help me, Lord. This love thing is a lot more than I had it figured for. I can't even get it right three nights running in my own home, never mind all the time for the whole world."

I'm not trying to distress anybody, but love is not unconditional. Love is not nice, and we aren't very loving people . . . yet. Some of you are very loving in comparison to other people I have known. And that's wonderful. (Of course, you're not sure what I mean by that yet, are you?) But comparing ourselves to the standard of New Testament love? It is simply true—we are beginners.

To recuperate from such insight, many people revert to the Greek language. That's called "divide and conquer." The Greeks used several words for love, and that takes some of the heat off. So we use *agape* to refer to a spiritual, self-sacrificing love, like we often associate with St. Francis or Albert Schweitzer or Gandhi. And *philos* refers to friendship, like between David and Jonathan, or people who play golf together, or philosophize together. And *eros* is reserved for moonlit nights and honeymoons and passion between a man and a woman, etc.

Sometimes it *is* helpful to dissect something, if we do not forget that the pieces still belong together when we are talking about real life. The dissection of love has many people believing that there is little passion or excitement or emotion in agape. Or that there is little nobility or spirituality or self-sacrifice in eros. Both assumptions are dead wrong, and lead to great misunderstanding.

Hebrew, like English, has one word for love. Translating it into the Greek *agape* is not an improvement, in this case, but an inescapable error. There are not three different kinds of love, but many ingredients to true love. A person can experience the ingredients separately, but that is not yet love. For instance, a person can feel pity without passion, but if they feel no passion, then they have not felt love yet either. A person can feel agape without eros, but if there is no eros in it, it is not yet love.

Have you ever been in one of those conversations where people are talking about how hard it is to love some people? Somebody always comes up with Old Faithful: "Well, you can love them, but you don't have to like them."

That's what comes from dissection. Christians feel obliged to pretend that they have agape toward everyone, but they will keep philos and eros for those they really care about. Doesn't that make agape the least valuable of the three? It certainly does from any receiver's point of view! It merely turns things so upside down that people would prefer to be "liked" rather than "loved." But in truth, if we cannot come up with a little thing like "liking," it is some kind of monumental spiritual snobbery to claim that we can nevertheless keep in step with the passionate caring of the God who goes all the way to the Cross for us.

Quite frankly, if you don't have any liking for me, you can keep your love. I can't use it, don't need it, and will be considerably better off without it. I might still appreciate some justice, or at least fair play, even if you *don't* like me. But if there isn't any affection in your love, forget it. Which is just a way of saying: That's not really love! That is only a word game we play so we can go on pretending that we love everybody—like we're supposed to, or think we are supposed to. "Nothing personal, you understand, but I do love you—it is my duty." Yuuuuckkk!!

Love is an empty word, a meaningless theory—unless there is an "I" on one side of it, and a "you" on the other. When we talk about only physical affection, or only intellectual interest, or only spiritual compassion—we do not reveal different levels of love. We only reveal that our love is not yet whole.

In the 13th chapter of I Corinthians, Paul is attempting an answer to the question, "What is love?" He answers it in the proper way, by pointing not to a straight definition but to the quality and nature of love as he understands it. Literally, he resorts to poetry, and the heart (right brain) more than the mind (left-brain logic) has to discern his meaning. But do not get entirely lost in the beauty of his words. It is a checklist. Where we claim to love, is it patient (uncompromising and enduring), and kind? Is it jealous or envious? Does what we call "love" in ourselves keep score on wrongs and slights we have received? Does our love set up our own conditions and expectations, or look for God's? Is it willing to face anything with faith, hope and endurance?

Another Paul, whose last name is Scherer (1892-1969), puts the same theme in different words. What is love? He answers, "Love is a spendthrift." Love goes out on a limb. Love spends the whole wad. Love goes for it all. Love burns bridges, kills the fatted calf, sells all it has for the pearl of great price. Love is a risky, daring, caution-to-the-wind sort of thing. Think of any experience, any illustration that moves you, any picture or example of love that you like. Isn't there always this one common note or quality present? Love goes for it all, dares the loss of all, puts all of its weight on what it cares about and believes in—not life ignorant of realities or in scorn of consequences.

Scherer's full comment is: "Love is a spendthrift, leaves its arithmetic at home, is always in the 'red.' And God is love."

Today I have tried to say more about what love is not . . . in preparation for next week, and what love is. For myself, not just for you, I need to reawaken my curiosity. If I want to be loving as Jesus meant it—as the early church understood it— I must break from today's understandings and assumptions, and so must you. Jesus started a world religion, a following of highly disciplined, highly committed, enormously motivated individuals gathered around faith and loyalty to God as Jesus had revealed God. But the principle that gave it power and inspiration—the principle that taught and corrected and restrained and freed—was love: the love of God, and what that kind of love means here on earth to individuals like us. That is what Christianity was and is about. If we want to be part of it, we have to ponder in wonder and seek again the content and meaning and flavor of Christian Love.

Meanwhile, sometime this week, make a list of the people you really love. Would you give up your life for them? Would you give up your money for them? Would you give up your property for them? How many people do you really love? Are you more loving or less loving than you would like to be? In short, how is your love life?

Leviticus 19:17-18; Deuteronomy 7:4-9;
Mark 12:28-34

Week Twenty-Nine

WHAT IS LOVE?

Where does love come from? It comes from God. We don't make it up. We can't manufacture it. We have to get it—receive it—in order to have it to give. And if it is true love, if we are at all whole, it comes body, mind and soul—with passion, intellect and eternal perspective . . . at least awareness beyond mere temporal affairs.

Some of you made lists this week, like I asked you to, of the people you truly love. Some of you were surprised at how quickly the list diminished, but gratified at who and how many stayed on the list despite the high qualifications. Some of you told me there were a few other surprises: people you cared about more than you realized; others who . . . well, we won't go into that. Some of you made two or three lists. One list for people you would die for. A second for people you would give all your material possessions to help. A third list for those you would be willing to get into serious trouble to support or defend. It's fun to preach to creative people.

In any case, last week we made the concept of love very high. And it *is* high! We do need to step apart from the evaluation of our own performance sometimes, and see the depth and breadth and height of love. It helps us to get teachable and humble again. We realize that we have not arrived, have not finished the course. Love has a great deal more to teach and reveal to us. It can still transform us if we let it touch us anew.

Having made love so high last week, it is also fair now to bring it back to where we live. Love is also incredibly versatile, and it does invite us and include us. So we also legitimately claim that we do love, and are sometimes loving. While we do not

224

love perfectly, the love we do receive and give again is still wonderful, and sometimes amazing and inspiring. People we may not love all the time, we still love some times. If they do not belong on last week's lists, neither do they belong off all our lists. So hopefully, this afternoon you will put all the people back on your list that I tried to get you to take off last week.

We cannot define or contain love, not in any whole or absolute sense. But we can participate anyway. Let me suggest, then, some rule-of-thumb indicators of the presence of love, things we have learned are earmarks, signs, common denominators of the presence of love—no matter what form it happens to be taking at the time. These are helpful for checking what we think is outgoing love. They can also help to clarify incoming love. It is true, you know, that we sometimes hand out that which we call love—and it really isn't. Also, we sometimes accept from others what is called love—and it isn't either. When that happens, somebody will always get messed up, until clarity is found.

I.) TO SEE (PERCEIVE) THE HIGHER IDENTITY OF ANOTHER is the first indicator of love.

Love has the strange, almost eerie capacity to behold another from a special vantage point. Unbelievers would say that love idealizes the other person. We might almost agree. Love sees, partially, "through the eyes of God." Love sees the other person as he or she is intended to be. Love knows or senses what the person will be like when fully developed, when "grown up," spiritually speaking.

The difference between love and idealization is small, but important. Love is not deluded—it knows the gap between the reality of now and the possibility of becoming. This clarity is possible because love does not see the other as primarily existing for its own gratification, security, reputation or advancement.

Romantic love and neurotic love (is there a difference?) idealize the other into what the "lover" needs or wants—whether it fits the reality of the other person or not. When we are young spiritually, we also do that to God. Eventually, we have to trade this god we want, this god we make up, for the GOD who is. It turns out better in the end, but we don't know that during the rebellious, struggling days (years) in which we keep trying to make God deal with us like the little god we have made up in our heads. Real people turn out better too, better than the ones we try to make up to please us or take care of our needs. It is far better to know and love people than to keep trying to warp them into what we need or want from them. That is a lot of what marriage is about. That is why we marry Rachel, and keep waking up with Leah. Only after years of struggle, and finally learning a little something of love, do we discover that it really was Rachel after all.

Remember that strange phrase in II Corinthians 5? "From now on, therefore, we regard no one from a human point of view." (verse 16) Love is always looking for the hidden identity, the image of God, the signature of the Creator. Without ulterior motive, without some prior plan, love is eager to know: "Who is this? What has God come up with this time? What is the destiny, or at least a trace of it?" Love sees (perceives) the higher identity of the other. If somebody does that to you fairly regularly, you can be sure they have some kind of love for you. If you find yourself seeing another person in that way, you can be sure you have some love for them.

II.) TO HAVE ANOTHER'S BEST INTERESTS AT HEART is the second indicator of love.

I suspect this is familiar to all of us as the action side of genuine love. And how marvelous it is to watch love in action! The stories go forever, not that there are too many of them. Most impressive to each of us are the times somebody else has acted for our best interests, especially when there seemed to be no ulterior motive on their part—except, of course, to see us more like our true selves.

But there are certain quirks about love that are hard to get used to. For instance, love does not necessarily do what the loved person wants, or thinks they want. Love does not always comply with what is asked for. That is hard to get used to—whether with love we are giving, or love we are receiving.

We have run into the fact of it time and again. Sometimes the teacher who was hardest on us, loved most. Most of us can look back on certain occasions when our parents seemed most severe, and realize that it was the rigors of love that produced moments of stern discipline. Punishment does not always come from love, to be sure. And it is terrible and futile when it does not. But where there is no discipline, there is no love either.

What happens, of course, is that love tends to treat us according to that higher identity which it perceives within us. Therefore, it does not always operate according to the present moment, or according to what we want or like, or according to what may seem most sensible to the majority of people standing around.

For that reason, love is famous for being "salty." Genuine love does not make others weak or dependent. Love is not willing to trade excuses so everybody can stay lame. You know how it goes: I won't tell on you, if you won't tell on me. I won't expect anything of you, if you won't expect anything of me. Let's agree to be totally accepting of each other, and then we won't have any trouble.

Love cares too much to agree to such rules. It does know the Silver Rule, however: "Do not do unto others what they should be doing for themselves." It also knows a Golden Rule, but that is a very high and dangerous precept, and only a few saints can use it without doing more damage than good.

In any case, love does not pander or please or "accept" another, like the more normal and human levels of cooperation, justice, compromise and influence. Love often stretches or breaks most of the expected rules of relationship. That is because love has another's best interests at heart. That is precisely why love is such a troublemaker in our world. Nothing causes more trouble than love—except maybe the evil and fear that try to stop it. Even so, it is usually love that starts the fight.

Now it comes clear—at least the possibility does—that we

can love an enemy or a friend, an employer or an employee . . . even a relative. That is to say, the principles can apply, if we have the love to give. Love will look very different depending on whom we are loving, and what the circumstances are. But it is possible in any situation, if we have the love to give. And see how much it depends on the first principle? We cannot have another person's best interests at heart if we do not have some inkling about their true identity and destiny.

As always—especially in our busy, over-stressed, over-rushed society—we get in a hurry. We want to do the loving deeds without first allowing the love perspective to enlighten us. We end up giving jackhammers to poets, and property to pilgrims, and slide-rules to butterflies.

III.) TO APPRECIATE, RESPECT, REGARD THE CONTRIBUTIONS OF ANOTHER is the third indicator of love.

"Love is not jealous," the Scripture reading said last Sunday. How marvelous it is to genuinely rejoice and feel pleasure at the good fortune, the accomplishments, the victories, the applause that go to another. How wonderful it is when some award or reward or recognition comes our way, and we become aware that somebody near to us is as delighted about it as we are.

We are not strangers to such a thing, but we are not inundated with it either! If we were going back to last Sunday, we could add this to the list: How many people could win the lottery, and you would be as happy about it as if it had happened to you? Would that tell you who you love? It wouldn't work for all of us. Some of us don't care about the lottery. But if you want to win it, that would tell you!

If Russia orbits a manned space station (or a womanned one), or finds a wonder-cure for diabetes . . . would we rejoice at the progress and potential benefit? That gets complex. We are better off down on our own familiar levels. In areas where we compete or feel threatened or try to excel . . . only love is able to delight in the gifts and accomplishments of another. It is the goodness, the excellence, the blessing in others that trouble us even more than their evil. It isn't really true, we know, but we act as if it were true that the success of others threatens us more than their failures; that the faith of others threatens us more than their doubts; that the beauty of others threatens us more than their flaws.

So we do not love perfectly. But there are times when love flows in and fills us. And we find ourselves, at least for a time, living by these rule-of-thumb indicators:

- To see (perceive) the higher identity of another.
- To have another's best interests at heart.
- To appreciate, respect, regard the contributions of another.

That doesn't confine, define or explain love. But it helps to clarify some important items. And it means we get to put a lot of people back on our lists. We do occasionally get glimmers of how wonderful they truly are; and sometimes we do actually do loving things for them; and sometimes when they do well or get real recognition, we are at least as delighted as we would be if we had been in their place. Besides, love has a tendency to grow . . . I know!!! That can be a mixed blessing. But we haven't got time to talk about everything on one Sunday.

Now listen if you can—this is the real point of the sermon: Does it not come clear—is it not easy to see, when we get it lined out like this—how impossible it is to love very much, or very often, if we have not first given our own lives over to God . . . put their management into the guiding hands of the Holy Spirit? And what chance has our love to grow or last in a world like this, if we have not decided to trust God for all final outcomes?

Therefore—and this is why the First Commandment comes first, and why it *is* the first—"You shall love the Lord your God . . . . "

From the Christian perspective, this takes on incredible meaning. You shall love the Lord your God—who first and always loves you. Or how will you be able to love those who partially and imperfectly and only sometimes love you?

So yes, it must come to the neighbor too. And we all know that, and want it, and long for the day when it can be more complete. But we cannot do that willy-nilly, or by our own power, or according to our own whims or notions. If we like love, want more of it, believe in its power to transform the world—then we first pay attention to loving the God who first and always loves us.

Do you perceive God's higher identity?

Do you have God's best interests at heart?

Do you rejoice when things on earth go more like God would want them to?

Do you perceive Jesus' higher identity?

Do you have Jesus' best interests at heart?

Do you rejoice when things on earth go more like Jesus would want them to?

Romans 12:9-21; 13:7-10; Ephesians 3:7-19

Week Thirty

LOVE IS NOT A THING

There is something nice about a trilogy of sermons about love. But as you have discovered, I never learned how to quit when I was ahead. We must not leave our present question— What is love?—without a parting insight. It changes my perspective quite a bit. It helps me to understand some of my struggles, and to be a little more understanding of some of your struggles. Sometimes it even helps me to make decisions and set directions.

There is, then, one further reason for the difficulty we have in defining and grasping the concept of love: LOVE IS NOT A THING.

Let us go back to the basic phrase that makes love matter. That phrase is, "I love you." Love isn't worth anything unless there is an "I" on one side of it, and a "you" on the other. Even the love of God has little impact until we realize that God is the "I" on one side of it, and we are the "you" on the other. Love is intensely personal. It is also specific. If your lover says, "I love you, but then, I love everybody," somehow that doesn't have the same impact. It even bothers us, if we are being honest, that God loves everybody. Somehow, a generalized love like that is no longer inspiring. Not until or unless we are reminded that God's love for us is unique and tailored to us specifically— not until that realization breaks through—do we become religious.

From the first sermon in this series, we have said that love isn't very powerful—doesn't do much for us—unless there is an "I" on one side of it, and a "you" on the other. "I love you" can change everything. Take away the "I" or the "you," and we end up with gibberish. As a matter of fact, we have done that a lot, in the Christian institutions. We have tried to take away the "I" and the "you" and let love stand as a generalized concept. We have tried to engender a "loving" style of life that has no personal contact inherent within it; that has no personal feeling driving it; that has no personal motive correcting or inspiring it. And sure enough, it ends up gibberish! Creeds don't love—people do. Institutions don't love—people do. Rules and morals and manners and a good upbringing don't love—people do!

So take away the "I" and the "you," and what is left of that magic phrase, "I love you"? Nothing! Nothing is left. Love is not a thing. Love is nothing . . . nothing without a subject and an object. Real love always hopes to complete the loop. Whoever says "I love you" hopes the object will turn into a subject and love back. That is the great opposite of the vicious circle. It is love circling, empowering, inspiring, caring . . . giving and receiving in an endless, spiraling, connecting loop. But love by itself is nothing. It is the person on either side of that concept that makes it meaningful. Love is only the channel between the two. Love is the name we use for a special kind of corridor, a link, a way of connecting.

So love is nothing. If I say "I love you," it does not mean that I offer love. What is love? Love has no content. If I say "I love you," it means I offer myself—me—whatever that is at this moment. Every person who loves you offers a different thing, because they are a different self. Have you ever gotten the same love from different people? Why doesn't love get boring? Even the same person is somewhat different each new day you see them. If they love you, you get who they are, and what they are. Love simply means we take down the barriers—we risk the pain of being known and knowing. Love means the channel is open, the shield is down—whatever I am or have is available to you. And of course, I risk the vulnerability of letting whatever you are or have come flowing back through the channel to me. Love is nothing—and yet love is everything, because it alone allows us beyond the isolation of our own borders.

Love is so dangerous! When will we ever stop pretending that love is always nice, or that we always want it? Nobody is ever really seriously or severely hurt, until they allow themselves to love. And nobody ever truly loves without getting seriously hurt. As someone said: It is a lot like being reborn. To love is to come out of a relatively safe, or at least familiar, world. There is no way to do that without some shock, and surprise, and trauma . . . like a newborn infant finding itself out of the womb, where things are hard as well as soft, and other people are there and making noise, and there are also great and endless opportunities.

To discover that God loves us is to discover that God offers us what God is. We receive the gift of God's presence with us. What more could we possibly want, once we begin to fathom what this gift is? In any case, that is where love's reputation got started, I suppose. God gives us what God is—and the nature of that contact has become the standard for what we call "love": forgiveness, mercy, grace, peace, constant guidance and caring. "God is love" means that we have come to associate "love" with what we receive from God. That is only a way of saying that God reveals God to us, and what we experience of what God is like with us, we end up calling "love."

Somehow we still allow it to surprise us when we receive love from a mere mortal, and discover that they do not live up to what we have come to expect from God. You would think we would have more respect for what it takes to develop the qualities of true love. But, you see, we get stuck on the word "love," and forget that it simply means we will get what the person is, not what some predefined formula says "love" is supposed to be like. We get what the loving person is. We do not get a person carrying some canned commodity called "love."

Most of us have learned that hate and love can trade places with each other very quickly. They have in common the openness—the taking away of restrictions and controls. Hatred also tends to complete a loop, and bring back hate from the one we are hating. But with hate, we give the destructive side of who we are. With love, we give the constructive side. Either way, we open ourselves to relate and communicate and deal dramatically with another. Therefore, hate and love shade back and forth in many relationships, depending on how things are going, and on how spiritually developed the people involved are.

From such musings, I find a great many things readjusting and refocusing. Three things in particular stand out. The first one has to do with how people can become more loving.

I.) We have already said that love comes from God, and that we are able to love only as much as we ourselves have been loved. That matches. When we experience another giving of themselves to and/or for us, that gives us courage, gives us the desire and the capacity to try giving ourselves—both back to the one who "loved" us, and also forth, to others. Love in motion sets up this back-and-forth principle. Is that not true in your experience? Have you not seen it operate with others?

But here in this strange place called earth, it is also clear that our love is not whole. We not only wish to be more loving— more willing to give of ourselves and risk knowing and being known—we would also like our love to keep improving in quality. You know what I mean: less ego in it, less manipulation, a more open-ended trust and freedom. I'm not trying to sell it; I believe we all greatly desire to be people with a greater quality of and capacity for love than we have now—no matter how loving we may consider ourselves to be.

So how do we improve our love? It is suddenly very clear that the quality of our love is precisely the quality of our inner being. In other words, I must look to my own purpose, my vocatio, the focus and discipline of my life. What do I know? How much do I care? What am I trying to accomplish? What do I appreciate? What is my true vocatio? If at any time, in any way, I myself increase, then automatically the quality of my love increases. I have more to give.

So that is the first axiom: To increase myself is to improve my love. To take love seriously, then, means I must spend time paying attention to some of my needs; filling some of my empty places;

training some of my gifts and skills. In short, I must learn to love myself, learn to be more selfish—in order to have more of a self to give. I am not talking about becoming irresponsible. Just talking about being responsible to myself—or really, to God who made me—in order that when I love my neighbor as myself, that will be a better experience for my neighbor (as well as for me). Therefore, the first teaching, the first priority, the top concern of the Church is that each individual member seek first his or her own conversion—give first priority to her or his own relationship to God in Christ, and make sure that he or she is on an authentic spiritual WAY of Life.

Some people do not yet know that this is the first business and concern of the Christian Church. Others do not like it, or do not understand why it is. *You* must both know it and understand why. There is no Outreach unless there is somebody to reach out. And that somebody must have something to offer, and know where it comes from.

Did Jesus do this? We know nothing of Him for the first thirty years. When He finally emerges, He knows the Scriptures cold. He has thought more deeply and more creatively than anyone else we have ever seen. He knows His identity and His powers, and they are better developed in Him than in anyone else we have ever seen. After His ministry begins, Jesus gathers around Him the people He needs. He limits His mission to territory He can cover—and ruthlessly eliminates the rest. Always He goes apart to pray, to rest, to keep centered. Yes, Jesus did this— Jesus had so much to give to others that the world is still spinning with the tales. But indeed, He did start with His God and Himself. You must be a self to be able to love. You cannot love if you do not know something of who you are and what you have to give. At least be fair—do not try any kind of love on another that you have not first tried on yourself.

So, firstly, we need to know that just because somebody loves us (opens the channel from their end), it doesn't mean we are going to like everything coming through. We must stop assuming and expecting that. Probably the more mature we become, the

more often we *will* like it—and the more we will want to know
another for who they are, not merely to get ourselves pleased, or
to fill our own needs.

II.) Secondly, we must stop assuming that because we love
somebody, they will like what we have to give. Even more important,
we must not assume that this "loving," as we think of it, means that
none of our destructive, jealous, fearful, threatened side will be
coming through to the other. If you love somebody and open the
channel at your end, and if they respond and open the channel at
their end, then they are in far more jeopardy from you than ever
before! We need and want to know that, if we really care.

It's good news and bad news. The good news is: I really like
you, want the best for you, want to know you, associate with you,
do many things together. The bad news is: Everything I have left
unresolved about my self—my dark side, my shadow, the fears
and guilts I have not yet dealt with—will sometimes sneak across
the channel of love too. Only, I won't know it, won't realize it.
And if you mention it, I will deny it and blame you. You will do
the same with me. Literally, we won't realize it.

So love is a paradox. It means we take down the shields and
barriers. It also means we are vulnerable and in jeopardy from
each other like never before. So trust and be open . . . and be
warned . . . but go open anyway. That is love.

You see? Impossible paradox. Yet it works if two people want
it to, if they keep accepting both realities, and keep growing. We
aren't really destroyed; it just feels that way at times. We are
smelted, uplifted, tested, increased, transformed—by loving and
being loved.

III.) Thirdly, if you want to love, you need Jesus Christ. I'm not
trying to be partisan. It simply is true. Not everybody does want
love. I guess none of us do all of the time. We are very good at
withdrawing, going silent, leaving, finding somebody else—going
the first two or three rounds of relationship over again, and again,
and again.

No other religion in the world wants love. Eastern religions abhor it. Islam and Judaism think it might be okay as a byproduct, or a reward—after all the other important issues are taken care of. Only Christendom truly wants love, and thinks of it as the core of the WAY itself, as the goal as well as the process that leads to it.

If we want love, we end up needing Jesus, who alone helps us with the evil, the shadow, the kind of salvation that leads us back into loving—always back into relationship—with God, with ourselves, with others.

Jesus leaves the channel open. We see His love more and more clearly, as He gets at our evil more and more adamantly. Until, seeing the end of it . . . sometimes . . . some of us . . . well, it changes our minds . . . and then our hearts . . . and then our lives. We love Him back, open it up again, try to keep the channel open to Him, with ourselves, with each other.

Love is not a thing. Love is the channel by which two beings lower the barriers, take away the shields, and give of who they are to each other.

Matthew 6:1-18; 5:11-12; 10:37-42

Week Thirty-One

IN IT FOR MYSELF

There is a strange thought-pattern that has grown into the proportions of a tradition in many wings of Christendom. It is the assumption and expectation that Christians are, or should be, "selfless"—that Christianity is always about being and doing "for others." By my perceptions, and in my experience, this attitude does enormous damage to individuals, and considerable damage to the Christian Church.

We have spoken of this before, and some of you see the flaw and try to move out of it. But we have also discovered that it returns like some mystic boomerang. Not too strange, I suppose, when we have built the other picture into our attitudes and images and definitions for so long. Saints are selfless, we think. The lives of true Christians are marked with great acts of self-sacrifice. One of the most frequent remarks we make about people we admire is that they had no personal motives, and sought no personal gain.

Clearly this does not match the reality. The saints go after different goals. That is the only thing that makes them different. It is like the Taoist story:

In the south, there is a bird. It is called *yuan-ch'u.* Have you heard of it? (It is related to the wild geese.) This *yuan-ch'u* starts from the southern ocean and flies to the northern ocean. During its whole journey, it perches on no tree save the sacred Wo-tung, eats no fruit save that of the Persian Lilac, drinks only at the Magic Well. It happened that an owl which had gotten hold of the rotting carcass of a rat looked up as this *yuan-ch'u* flew over, and, terrified lest the great bird should stop and snatch at the succulent morsel, it screamed, "Shoo! Shoo!" And thus afterward, the owl congratulated itself on being so fierce, or, in a more thoughtful mood, it exclaimed,

"What a selfless and self-sacrificing bird this *yuan-ch'u,* that it did not try to rob me of my piece of rat!"

So it is not that Christians are selfless, but that they go after different goals. It is not that they make great sacrifices, but that they cease to want some things that most people want. And they go after other things with a fire and a passion that many people in our society do not "see" or want.

There is a principle of emptying one's self in order to be filled, of surrendering in order to come into one's own, of dying in order to truly live. The cross/crucifixion is a life principle that must be applied to an almost endless array of our common, daily experiences. That is core truth for us, and we do catch a lot of flak for it from those who have not yet understood it. That is the way true life works, and we do not apologize to anybody for this incredible truth that we have been shown.

But for us, it is neither grim nor selfless in the larger picture. Jesus, in our tradition, "sitteth at the right hand of God the Father almighty" and "liveth and reigneth with Him forevermore." I use the old language to remind you that this is not some new perspective, not some new twist I have tried to put onto it. Part of the basic Christian message is that this sort of thing is worth a few days of pain here on earth!

Our enemies and adversaries rib us a lot about this kind of thinking. They talk about "pie in the sky, by and by," and sometimes try to make it look like we have caused pain and injustice on earth by believing that this world's rewards are not the highest goal humans can live for. It should not surprise us that those who love the world better than God's Kingdom would say such things. It is still *our* truth, however, and we claim it or lose it. They aren't being nasty—it's just that if they do not really believe there is a life beyond this one, naturally they wouldn't want to sacrifice much in the here and now to prepare for it. Without the belief, they cannot follow the logic. For them, "here and now" is all there is.

The point is, we are not being selfless or sacrificial except in the eyes of those who don't realize why or what we are really after. Why would Frank Laubach rather spend time praying than making money? Why would Mother Teresa rather care for the sick than be an executive in some large corporation? They aren't being selfless, they are "onto something" that has become enormously important and valuable in their eyes. And don't you know that there are some business executives who are as saintly as Mother Teresa and who do at least as much "good," also?

It is not true, by the way, that Christians are only after "long-term" rewards. We all want rewards, and we look for, dream about and plan for them . . . unless we have lost all hope. Only, we never know when the rewards will come. We choose our goals, go after them, try to match our lives to patterns and truth and action that will eventually bring us to our chosen ends. We are open and willing for the rewards—the "return"—to come any time. Whatever the goals, some return will begin to come almost immediately. Sometimes we don't like the return, and have to change goals. But if the goals are good, the return keeps increasing the longer we stay faithful to the quest.

Again, the difference is not in whether we want rewards, but in what rewards we want. The difference is not in being selfless or selfish, but in what goals we have chosen. However, some people do seem to exist, during some periods of their lives, in a kind of Twilight Zone. They are not quite alive, and not quite dead either. They have no recognizable goals for themselves, at least none they can identify. They have not chosen any path with zeal or commitment. They seem afraid of risks, yet they long for excitement. They seem lonely, but do not trust themselves or anyone else for real relationship. They are often found on the fringes of various organizations, including the church, and they do, sometimes, go into selfless and sacrificial modes with no awareness of the goals or purposes that justify such expenditures. That is sad indeed. They pay the price, but get no reward. They walk the path, but see none of the glory. They burn out in a few years, or move from organization to organization. They spread sadness and negation wherever they go. They always do more harm than good, no matter how hard they try. The rightful motive is missing. The energy source is lacking. They run on their own batteries, and those are bound to run down if they do not get recharged from the source that is beyond us.

Coming down to it: When it comes to the church, some people are not in it for themselves. I don't want you to be among them.

Let's get off all the theory and theology and Scripture for just a moment, and talk straight experience. I think back of the people over the years who have told me they were not in it for themselves. Within this category, and rated in order of both frequency and amount of problems created, they said:

• "I'm in it for my children . . . " I don't need the church myself. I'm busy and fulfilled, but I want my children to have a Christian upbringing. (Well, children don't have a Christian upbringing with unchristian parents raising them—no matter how you cut it.)

• "I'm in it for my wife (husband/spouse) . . . " She likes it. I just come along to keep her happy. (Once, years ago, I made the mistake of replying, "Have you ever noticed how happy she really is?" Both of them stopped coming—for a while.)

• "I'm in it because it contributes to morality in our society . . . "

• "I'm in it for the business or political contacts it can provide . . . "

• "I'm in it to get help for a social cause I am in favor of . . . "

• "I'm in it because I hope it will help others . . . "

To state the obvious, some of these people get involved with the church and then come in contact with Scripture, with faithful people, with the Holy Spirit. Some of them get converted— meaning, they start to comprehend what Christianity is really about—and they start to want it for themselves, and then they begin to pay back for all the trouble they caused. They don't maybe *know* all the trouble they caused, or mean to pay back for it, but they do. So the church is supposedly willing to put up with all of us—waiting and hoping this sort of thing will happen, and we will start to wake up and grow and improve.

Nevertheless, these people do cause enormous problems. They do not believe in the Word. They do not believe in any of it, for themselves. (And this is not a potshot at them; this is what they say of themselves.) So they are constantly an influence for sidetracking, for slowing things down, for getting in the way, for diluting the commitment, for confusing newcomers, for turning attention away from Jesus Christ, and so forth.

If we take this issue to its core, it gets big: What is the purpose and function of the Church of Jesus Christ? Are you in it to save somebody else? Are you in it to save the world? Or are you in it for yourself? Let's get it starker still: Is the purpose of the Church to perfect the world, or is the purpose of the Church to perfect you? (Hint: The world is ending; you aren't!) Put it yet another way: Is Christianity an authentic Way of Life, or is it just a means to other ends? Is the Christian Way intrinsically valuable in its own right, or is it just a gimmick, a tool to be used as or when we choose?

How we understand and comprehend such matters changes the way we approach and decide everything. Are we building a parking lot so community groups will find us more attractive? Or so more people can gather and have a greater impact on society? Or so more people will come here and dedicate their lives to loving God and following Jesus Christ?

It shoots through everything. Do we study and learn and love the Scriptures because we think it will "work"? That is, because we think it will help us to be successful in the world, by our preconceived definitions of success? Or because it speaks of God, helps us to get closer to Jesus, reminds us of that which we honor and love and long to be part of? Both are fine motives, strong and clear—but what a difference!

The Scripture passages this morning were chosen to remind us that Jesus did make His own appeal to His early followers on the basis of their highest self-interest. It seems also clear to me that the first generation or two of Christians were dramatically and obviously excited about what they had been told, had been invited into, and were looking forward to. One picks up no hint from Peter or Paul or any of them that they were doing their duty but expected nothing for themselves, or that they had discerned the proper moral course and were impersonally and stoically following it out of a sense of selfless obligation. They were afire with what they believed and expected for themselves and their friends. That was the astounding mark of the early Christian community—that it was so enthusiastic, and so terribly pleased by what Jesus Christ had opened up for them. They were in it for themselves! They loved sharing it with each other, and with anybody who was interested, but what they had found and what they had been promised so far-outweighed everything else they had ever heard about, they were uninterested in other pursuits. You cannot tempt with coins those who have rooms full of gold. Peter was no saint for any of the motives we usually try to lay on the saints. He just thought life with Jesus was the cat's meow— no matter what it cost him—and nothing else looked nearly as good to him, in comparison. Because that was the way he really felt, and really believed, more and more his life looks "saintly" to the rest of us.

In any case, without apology or subtlety, Jesus speaks to us directly of rewards. He consciously and purposefully compares the rewards of the world with the rewards of His own Kingdom. There are trade-offs, He makes clear, and suffering to go through, and many principles He tries to explain for us. But the message is loud and clear: "Great is your reward in heaven." Heaven does not wait for later. It begins when we enter the Kingdom. It is far from completion in any of our experiences here, but its reality and rewards do begin immediately. As Jesus tells us: "There is no one who has left house or wife or brother or parents or children, for the sake of the kingdom of God, who will not receive manyfold more in this time and, in the age to come, eternal life." (Luke 18:28-30)

So Jesus stresses rewards that we want for ourselves as the motive for listening and following. God is the highest value. To know God . . . to be in God's presence . . . to experience God's *shalom* . . . are the greatest of riches, the highest value—and worth forsaking anything and everything to obtain. The saints are not selfless—they want the highest and best they know about. It is just higher than most people perceive as real. And like most of the rest of us, they live for and prepare for that which they most love. When Jesus hawks His wares, He talks about "joy complete" (John 15:11) and "life abundant" (John 10:10). He talks about getting rid of hatred and finding love, discovering our true selves, and learning about God's power and plans—and having it all keep unfolding forever. Nothing and no one else comes anywhere close to offering what Jesus offers. Most of us don't really believe He can deliver. *That's* the issue—not whether we are selfish or selfless.

If you are not yet in it for yourself, I hope you will reconsider your goals and motives. Is God . . . God's Kingdom . . . God's church on earth—worth anything to you personally? It is an insult to Christ, you realize, to be in it for any lesser reason. How would you like to discover that your spouse married you for your mother, or for security, or because you would be good with the children? You think it pleases Jesus, or God, for you to be in it for others, but not for yourself? Guess again! When it comes down to it, you are all you have to offer. If you yourself do not care yourself—it is worth nothing!

We must learn to say: It is because I am sold . . . because I believe . . . because I love what I see of the Kingdom, and it draws me, and I want to live for it. It is because I believe it . . . and I need it . . . and I want it . . . and because I am the one who is learning to love back the One who has shown such love for me. That is why I'm in it.

Stop all the altruism. Be done with fake motives, and false ones too. Stop being religious, and let yourself hear and love Jesus for who Jesus really is. Only after God is really important to you, do you have any chance of knowing your importance to God.

Be in it for yourself.

Matthew 13:45-46

Week Thirty-Two

A DESIRE TO BE CLOSER TO GOD

Sometimes, about midsummer, I get this need to forget all the details and trappings and prepositional phrases of the life of the church, and get back to what the Christian Faith is about. When I start asking, "What am I doing here?"—I need summations, not details. I don't mean theological summations. I mean summations of Jesus' story, and how we are still part of it.

In the wake of Jesus' ministry on earth, amazing and profound things took place in the lives of those who believed in Him. For two or three years, Jesus taught and healed and made friends, and spoke of life's true purposes in ways that seemed both old and new, yet compelling. The growing response of the common people brought Jesus into increasing conflict with the religious and political structures of the time. Jesus would neither cooperate with the existing leadership nor sidestep the growing issues between His Way and the way of the establishment. Since He would neither run nor fight, it ended in His crucifixion. Stunned and staggered for a short time, His followers quickly recovered and became dynamic witnesses and bearers of His new Way of Life.

When asked how it was possible for them to do all that they were doing, they invariably said it was because Jesus had appeared to them after His death, and that He was with them, guiding and upholding them all the time. They always added that He would do the same for anyone who really wanted such an arrangement with Him.

And that's it—the summation! The rest is history—history unfolding . . . and all the fascinating details that go with it.

The life of Jesus of Nazareth is incredible and endlessly fascinating. But the reason the world remembers Him is because of what happened to His followers. You know how it is: You grow up in this world, full of enthusiasm and curiosity. The possibilities seem endless, and the variety of experiences calls us to come taste and succeed and amount to something. Of course, there are warnings and rules running through it all, but that doesn't kill our enthusiasm when we are young.

After thirty or forty years, however, most people notice that there are set patterns underneath the variety of events. Most people find their niche or rut and pretty much stay there. New names and faces appear in the news, but the story gets more and more familiar. Nations rise and fall, but the problems remain the same. After the first three hundred times we watch a love triangle working its way through to its inevitable conclusion, somehow the plot doesn't seem as riveting as it did the first time. We end up suspecting that things don't change very much. We keep hoping, for a while. We keep longing for growth and change in ourselves. But it gets harder to think we will ever really change very much after the first few hundred tries. The second verse is the same as the first, and so is the two hundredth. Things go on and events keep happening, but nothing really changes. Not until or unless God comes into the picture.

The followers of Jesus—followers of all ages and both sexes— were really changing. And they liked it! The people who became their friends began to change, too. That's why we remember Jesus. What was He? What was there about Him that could have such an incredible impact on people? How did that happen, and why?

My own suspicion is that a lot of the people of the early church did not have any very clear explanation for what was happening to them. They knew that they loved and trusted Jesus. They knew He was present with them—guiding and inspiring them—in the guise of what they increasingly called "The Holy Spirit." This was long before any doctrine of the Trinity had been thought about. Most of the early followers, I suspect, were content to respond to what they experienced within, and to what they were finding in fellowship with each other. So their lives changed, and they became humble, forgiving, loving people—and most of all, perhaps, a people of hope. They didn't have many explanations for how it was happening, except they knew they were accepted and cared about—truly and deeply—by Jesus. They believed that also meant they were accepted and loved by God. So that came out in the way they did everything. It showed up in their attitudes toward everything. Those who knew them, often felt the warmth and joy and wanted to be part of it, too. So the Christian Faith literally spread like wildfire through the Roman Empire, and beyond.

Here we sit, all these many years later, still wondering what it is all about. It is miraculous that we do sit here—that there are still congregations of people all over this island and the nation and the world who still gather to honor and celebrate what Jesus has opened up for us, and to find some way, if possible, to get in on the excitement. But lots of times it isn't very exciting anymore. Many people are as excited about the Christian Faith and helping to bring or build the Kingdom of God as they are about brushing their teeth or paying their taxes, or doing any of the things we categorize as necessary or "good for us."

Another way of saying it is that we don't change easily anymore. The patterns of discipline and devotion that once characterized the joy and hope of the Christian Faith, now often survive as mere obligations—obligations that are never enforced. We try to make ourselves pray—you couldn't stop the early Christians from praying! We try to make ourselves forgive—that isn't the same as being filled with such acceptance and grace that it just spills over. We try to make ourselves be generous— there have been those who have given to the church because the *ecclesia* (the people of God) was so wondrous to them and they wanted everybody to have the experience of being part of it.

No, we don't change so easily anymore. We are more "mature" than our early-church counterparts. No matter how good any message is, when it becomes known and familiar, we all develop resistance to it. We guard ourselves against its enthusiasm and exuberance, and sort of "dare it" to sweep us off our feet like it did Peter or Paul or Silas. And if somebody tells us the story of the Prodigal Son or the Waiting Father or the Self-Righteous Brother, we say, "Yes, I already heard that one," like it was some kind of joke for our amusement or entertainment. It doesn't always occur to us that we are still prodigal, or waiting, or self-righteous . . . even if we did already hear it.

So the early Christians were *experiencing* their faith. They were losing their jobs, and finding new ones. They were risking their lives, and finding new ones. They were losing old relationships, and finding new ones. They were far more vulnerable in the world, and worrying about it a lot less. They had something to share and to say because of what was happening as they prayed and as they "heard" that Spirit Being talking to them within—giving them suggestions, making requests, sending them on all kinds of errands. And they dropped whatever they had to, to respond to that Inner Voice: money, father, mother, wife—whatever they had to. They were *experiencing* their faith, and if and when they found time, they tried to explain to themselves and to each other what was happening. But the explanations didn't much matter, because it was *happening*. They found that life with God was so much fun that it was worth any price on earth it might cost them. The explanations were only for fun, for sharing in their spare time. The explanations didn't really matter. The experience was what mattered—the reality of Life in God's presence.

Today we have a tendency to think about it and think about it and not really try it on very much. If we think about it long enough, maybe it will sink in enough and we will suddenly want to try it all the way. At least that seems to be the theory. And maybe on occasion that does happen to an individual here or there. But not for most. For most people, the experience comes first, then the explanation. How do you describe the value of friendship to someone who has never had a true friend, and who suspects there is no such thing? It is always the human dilemma: We can't find out unless we try something. But trying things is dangerous. If they don't work out, then where are we? And life is neither long enough nor strong enough to try everything, or to survive everything. Maybe that is why they call it a "leap of faith." Somewhere along the line, if we want to know about the Kingdom Jesus is talking about, we have to want to know badly enough to risk everything to go find out by trying it on. Maybe it will end in disaster, but there is only one way to really find out. Was it any different for Peter, or James, or Luther . . . or anybody?

I think it was G.K. Chesterton who said that Christianity "has not been tried and found wanting; it has been found difficult and left untried." That may be all right for some people. But how will *we* explain it to our God, if we make it all the way through this life and never really "try" the Christian Way with wholehearted enthusiasm, as if it were our highest and most important concern?

What am I accusing you of now? I am not accusing you—I am accusing us. And I am accusing us of the same thing I always accuse us of: cheating ourselves out of some of the best joy and peace and love that there is. We aren't cheating ourselves out of *all* of it, of course—some of us have found and are still finding some of it. But it's nowhere near what the Christ is sitting here waiting and hoping to give to us!

So, yes, I am accusing us of trying the Christian Faith only tentatively, and piecemeal, and skimpily, and fearfully, and partially . . . on purpose. I am accusing us of trying to think our way into Christendom, trying to talk ourselves into it . . . and getting into endless arguments with ourselves that prevent us from trying it. "O taste and see that the Lord is good." (Psalm 34:8) If your spiritual life is not dynamic and exciting, don't just assume that there is something wrong with the church, or with the Faith, or with God, or even with you. All you need to do is choose one of the disciplines of the Christian Life that you have never seriously tried before . . . and start doing it. (That's point number one in this sermon.)

There are members among us who have never really committed themselves to worship with us. They come to evaluate, or to criticize, or to encourage. Sometimes they like it, sometimes they don't. Sometimes they don't come for a while, sometimes

they do. But they have never really committed themselves to
worship with us. Yet it is one of the requirements. You can't try
the Christian Life alone. You have to join with a congregation
somewhere, know yourself a part of it, care about it, pray over it,
work for it, want its love to grow and spread . . . and all of it
"under God's mercy and will." Some of our members have thought
about Christianity, but they haven't tried it at this level because
they have never committed themselves to worship with us (or
with any congregation).

    You may think it unfair, but I do know that we have some
members who do not go each morning to their prayers, and there
dedicate themselves anew each morning to do God's will insofar
as they can understand it. Some of us say we are lazy, and others
that we are too busy to give God our precious time. But those are
not the issues. We have areas and categories of our lives that we
wish to stay in control of—that we are not willing to turn over to
the light and guidance of the Holy Spirit. Talking about it is
minor; experiencing the Holy Spirit is everything. But the Spirit
won't talk to us very often unless we turn our lives over. There is
no way we can be the church or know what Christianity is about
if we do not try it on!

    We have members who do not study the Scriptures. We have
members who do not tithe. We have members who have never
tried forgiving their enemies. We have members who have never
tried to accept or receive the sacrifice of Christ on the Cross. We
have members who have never turned their vocations over to
God. We have members who have never turned their fears over
to Christ. None of these ways of behaving are incidental. These
are all major, basic steps of the Christian Way. Christ comes to us
most often and most clearly when we are struggling to do what
His Way requires of us. That is how we become the church. We
cannot give what we do not have. We cannot tell others of things
we have not experienced. We cannot be what we have not done.
The reverse of these is also true. We have members who are trying
and experiencing one or another of each of these steps of the
Christian Path. Some of us are getting excited, and finding

miracles, and experiencing amazing changes going on in our lives. Others of us are changing, but only a little bit . . . in a few areas. And then we all get together—those of us changing not at all, and those of us changing a little, and those of us in dramatic new love affairs with the Christ—and guess what happens?

Of course! Those who are not growing tend to discourage or discredit those who are. (Why do you think Jesus got so angry with the Pharisees?) And those who are pretty new at it can sometimes be discouraged if they think the negative (cynical) attitudes or remarks are coming from veterans of the Christian Life who know what they are talking about. (Instead of from spectators who maybe have been around for a long time and talk about it, but never try it.)

Once I was sitting in a twelve-step meeting and listening to one of the brethren expounding on the great virtues of twelve-step programs in comparison to the hypocrisy and ineptitude of the church. That happens rather frequently. You would be surprised at how many alcoholics believe they have, during some period of their lives, "tried the church" and found no help there. No reason to limit the category to alcoholics. It is a strange phenomenon. We get familiar with this place, and with each other, we get busy with our activities and normal programs—and forget that people are dropping in from time to time, looking for a spiritual Way, for the Faith we represent. Isn't that why we are here?

Anyway, this fellow didn't know I was a minister. He wasn't after me. He was just telling it like he saw it. And how he saw it was really skewed. Nevertheless, it got me to thinking what it would be like if twelve-step groups someday evolved to an approach similar to what we now have in the church.

I tried to picture an AA group that invited everybody who was interested in alcohol, on any level and for whatever reason, to come and participate. People would gather around the tables, and some would bring their booze, and be drinking it. Others would be talking about how it had ruined their lives. And quite a few folk would be there for no defined reason yet—thinking of giving it up, or thinking of going back to it, but not really certain it mattered one way or the other . . . but they "liked the people." Frequently there would be big discussions about whether people should or shouldn't drink, and whether people should or shouldn't work the program if they wanted to stop drinking. And there would always be a contingent of those who claimed to have tried sobriety for a while and found it didn't do anything for them. So from every twelve-step meeting, some of the members would go home roaring drunk, and some only tipsy, and some sober. Some people would go to the meetings to drink, and some to study the twelve steps. But it would be hard to study the steps with drinkers interrupting. And every time a discussion started, it would turn into an argument about whether the steps were important or necessary in the first place—instead of being a time for explorations of what the step itself was about, and how to actually take it.

I wonder how many people would get help by going to twelve-step groups if they were run like that? If you had a friend or a loved one who really needed help, how encouraged would you feel about sending them into a mess like that?

In the AA twelve-step recovery program, there is one requirement for membership: "A desire to stop drinking." What is the requirement for membership in the Christian Church? A desire to stop sinning. In our language: A desire to stop being alienated from God. A desire to be close to God. A desire to do God's Will.

Do you have any idea what would happen around here if every single one of us—every member of this church—had a desire to get closer to God? What would happen to us, and between us, if we all knew, for positive sure, that each and every one of us had a sincere and burning desire to be closer to God, to do God's Will?

Point number two in this sermon: From now on, ASSUME IT! From now on, from this very moment, assume that everyone you know or meet here has a sincere and burning desire to be closer to God, to do God's Will.

Matthew 7:13-14; Luke 13:22-30; John 10:7-10

Week Thirty-Three

THE NUMBER-ONE CONSIDERATION

"Enter by the narrow gate; for the gate is wide and the way is easy, that leads to destruction, and those who enter by it are many. For the gate is narrow and the way is hard, that leads to life, and those who find it are few."

There was a blacksmith show at the fair. The blacksmith had just finished making a horseshoe, and had dropped it on the ground to cool, when a few teenagers came strolling in to look around. Acting like he'd been in blacksmith shops all his life, one boy nonchalantly picked up the cooling horseshoe. He dropped it rather quickly. The blacksmith, watching out of the corner of his eye, commented, "Kind of hot, isn't it son?" But the youth was undaunted. He rejoined, "It doesn't take me long to look at a horseshoe."

I think that's a perfect picture of the way we often look at the Scriptures, and especially of the way we treat this passage. This one hasn't had time to cool off yet since Jesus dropped it in front of us. Even if we pick it up, we have a tendency to put it down rather quickly.

"Enter by the narrow gate; for the gate is wide and the way is easy, that leads to destruction, and those who enter by it are many. For the gate is narrow and the way is hard, that leads to life, and those who find it are few." Ouch!

I don't much like thinking that a lot of my living is a wide and easy way. But it is hard to shake the thought altogether. I look around and ask myself how many of the people around me are living wide and easy lives? The backdrop of the passage forces the contrast. How many people are really living for God's Kingdom with purity of heart, with full dedication because they love it, with purposeful dedication because it is their highest aim? Ouch! Still pretty hot, isn't it?

Was Jesus being nasty or friendly when He said this thing to us? We almost invariably conclude that He was scolding us. The mind goes instantly to punishment. We feel abused, put down, threatened. Something in us wants to cry "Unfair!" We either want to conclude that Jesus was wrong, or we want to make it very clear that He was talking about all those other people—not about us. Straight and narrow, or wide and easy? Doesn't take us long to look at that!

As best as I can tell, the passage in Greek is contrasting wide and broad with small and narrow. Translations are not wrong, but they have begun to interpret, as I suppose is inevitable. We assume narrow is hard, and broad is easy. But that is a corruption. Broad ways are often hardest in the long run. They sometimes lead to the hardest consequences. And narrow may be very pleasant—the easiest, softest way in reality . . . in the long run. I'm just interested to see how the passage has been made to accent our fear of God's hard discipline, when that maybe isn't implied at all.

How do we get ourselves to remember that Jesus is on our side? Jesus has gone to a lot of trouble to come to us. He is expending incredible time and power to heal and teach and love. He is about to do a great deal more—because, and only because, He cares for us! When we pick up His teachings and they burn us at first, we need to remember that. Look at the twin passage in John 10:7-10. It makes it clear that Jesus is the door. The purpose is that we may have life, and have it abundantly. That is the meaning and message. Somehow, with some of these teachings, we lose sight of Jesus' real agenda.

A group of Ivy League college students was taking a field trip for its sociology class. Most of them had never been face-to-face with life in the slums before. Seeing a little girl playing in the dirt, one of them asked, "Why doesn't her mother clean her up?"

The teacher replied, "That little girl's mother loves her, but she doesn't hate dirt. And she hasn't got any way to prevent the dirt even if she did. We, on the other hand, hate dirt, but we don't love the little girl, so we are content to leave her here. Meanwhile, we can hardly wait to get out of here and wash up. Until hate for the dirt and love for the child exist together in the same person, she is likely to remain here."

Suddenly we begin to remember: Until hatred of sin and love for the sinner come together in a people, there will be no help for the lost.

If Jesus tells us about a narrow door, it doesn't mean He hates us. It means we live in a place of alienation from God and each other, and it isn't easy to get out. We keep wanting Jesus to be "nice." By that we mean that we want Jesus to approve of us as we are—to tell us that where we are is just fine. But somehow we don't look fine to Jesus. He sees all the fear and pain and resentment and anger and loneliness and quarreling, and says, "Poor things! Nobody ought to have to live in all this dirt."

"Enter by the narrow gate." Eventually, if we do not drop it too fast, it will occur to us that Jesus doesn't think we should stay where we are, or have to live like we do. If we are going to "enter" some gate, we can't stay where we are. First and foremost, this passage is an invitation—an invitation to move to a new place. As usual, we are being invited into the Kingdom. Our normal reaction is, "It doesn't seem fair or right that so many of us should be condemned." Okay, call it whatever you like. But then ask yourself: How many people do you know who ought to stay just the way they are? How many people do you know who are really happy, fulfilled illustrations of realized potential? You don't really like the world the way it is, either! So why get upset with Jesus that He notices it, too?

Jesus sees the anxieties, the injustice, the fear and depression, the malice and divorce. And He says: You need to come out of here. This is no fit place for little girls . . . or anyone made by God. But come out of here by the narrow gate ("I am the gate"), or you will only end up in another place just like this one.

"The gate is narrow and the way is hard, that leads to life, and those who find it are few." Our perspective is that we already have life, and somebody may try to take it away from us. Or that God might say we didn't use it right and punish us, or take life away as a punishment. Somehow we get it all worked around to sounding that way when we deal with this passage. We can't hear Jesus at all from such a stance.

Jesus doesn't think we have life yet! Like Geppetto, God is a great craftsman, and physically most of us move around quite well without the strings—although lots of us can still remember the strings, almost like they were still there. But the life-giving Spirit is far from finished with the new creation. The Spirit has only barely touched us, so to speak. And we must still choose whether to stay here as we are, or move into the Kingdom.

Jesus doesn't think we have Life yet. He is talking about something we have yet to find, trust, claim, walk into. And most of us, He says, will not do that. Most of us prefer to stay where we are—as we are. Most of us still want to find an easier, softer way—a gate that is wide and easy. Most people are not interested in Life. They are interested in comfort—in security. They think success means safety.

Jesus is simply telling it true—telling us the way it is—so we can see it clearly and make up our minds. The way is narrow. Most people will not follow Him into it. Most churches and communities will not even make a very good start.

We must re-order our schedules to have time for prayer. We don't do that. We try to crowd it in, or we keep it a week or two and go right back to our old ways—running our own lives. The way is narrow, focused. We don't all choose to go.

The road is narrow. We are asked to give ten percent. We give five, or two. It is symbolic. It is the way we always respond—changing the narrow way that works, back into a wide and easy way that does not—making sure that we are still in charge, still doing it our way. So most churches merely limp along, and the way we live is only barely different from how we lived before we met Jesus, and our souls are always gasping for enough air to barely survive. I told you about spiritual blackouts. How do you feel about spiritual emphysema?

At other times, we go overboard. God asks us to love our neighbor—we try to love and save the whole world, and wear ourselves into uselessness trying to prove how special we are. All it proves is that we still think we are in charge. The gate is narrow. We are not supposed to go to the right or to the left of it. No fancy footwork. No grandstand plays. Just humbly follow Jesus through the gate that leads us into the Kingdom.

We must see ourselves as part of Christ's body, the church. We will want to discover our spiritual gifts and use them to build up the "body." But instead we get to seeing our little efforts as unimportant, or we get sidetracked back into building some other kingdom.

The poet and musician Sidney Lanier was a flutist of extraordinary skill. He played in the Symphony Orchestra of Baltimore. One day, as the orchestra was rehearsing and the symphony was building to the grand crescendo with drums, clappers, horns, trumpets and a full organ all blazing away, a whimsical thought occurred to the young Lanier. To himself he said, "Nobody could possibly hear my little flute in the midst of this thundering roar." At this impish thought, still holding the flute to his lips, he ceased to play his part. Instantly, the conductor rapped his baton angrily, stopped the orchestra, pointed directly at Lanier and demanded, "Where is the flute?"

Why do we think the Holy Spirit is hard of hearing? Where is your flute? Where is your time, your money, your caring, your love? *So what* if it doesn't seem like very much to you? It is because it is *yours* that the Holy Spirit wants it. It is also because you really *are* part of the music. Naturally, we cannot hear very well from where we are. Who do we think we are, God? But out front, where God listens, it makes a difference. Where is your flute?!

I don't know if any of these thoughts lead you where I hope they do. I really have only one thing on my mind today. It is to ask you this: What is the number-one consideration in your life?

That isn't exactly correct. Rather, I want to suggest that you try an experiment with me, for at least a week. During this coming week, will you make it your number-one consideration to ask: What would be best for my soul? What would be most helpful for my spiritual condition? (If there is somebody here who cannot yet deal with such language, ask instead: What would be best for my character development?)

Let us be as clear as possible. The experiment requires that each time we become conscious of any choice—each time we find ourselves making any decision of any kind, large or small— the number-one consideration is: What would be most beneficial for my soul? Naturally, the experiment requires that you proceed to act and choose according to whatever matches this number-one consideration.

Just to get on the same wavelength, be reminded of some contrasts. The question is not: What would be good for somebody else? That is a very interesting question. So interesting, in fact, that we ask it all the time. You are begged to discard it during this experiment. Ask only after your own spiritual condition.

I have it in mind, for instance, that very often I view choices and make decisions according to what will further my position here. The big three considerations are: money, reputation and other people's approval. It occurs to me that I often do what I do and decide what I decide because of the impact I think it will have on my finances. If I see an item in the store that attracts me, I sometimes ask myself if I can afford it, or if it would favorably affect somebody I care about, or if it would do something to enhance my work or reputation. None of these will do, you see. During this experiment, I may only ask what will be good for my spiritual condition. I must shop or not shop, buy or not buy, on that basis alone.

If somebody asks me for a favor this week, I must consult the number-one consideration before I can reply. If I do this favor, will it improve my spiritual condition? If not, I must refuse the favor.

Money, reputation, other people's approval—these are the big three. Sometimes they are subtle, and ingrained, so watch them carefully. In my profession, for instance, it enhances my

reputation if people think I am humble. It doesn't always help if
I actually *am* humble. But it is important for people to *think* I am
humble. There are lots of ways to act humble that are irrelevant,
or even detrimental, to my soul. You get caught in many similar
binds, too. I'm just saying this is a serious experiment. No matter
how much fun you start to have, take it seriously.

In normal decision-making, money, reputation and other
people's approval are the big three considerations. The little three
are: Will it make me comfortable? Will it entertain me? Will it
gratify some desire? Of course, the big three for some are the
little three for others, and vice versa. But the easiest way to keep
it all clear is to just throw everything else out and keep only the
number-one consideration: Is it good for my own soul? What will
be best for my own spiritual condition?

Jesus was always looking at what would be good for us
spiritually. We *want* Him to pay attention to what will be good
for us in our earthly circumstances. That is why it is so hard
to comprehend what He says. "Teacher, bid my brother divide
the inheritance with me." A sane and practical request to our
ears—a matter of justice, and fair play, and practical reality.
But Jesus says, "Who made me a judge or divider over you?
Beware of all covetousness." How can we understand such
double-talk, such evasions? It's easy once we finally realize
that Jesus really cares about our souls—what we are becoming
on the inside. What we think is important is only "the props"
for the real drama—the growth of souls. (What used to be
called "character.")

Start looking for what will be best for your spiritual growth.
That is the number-one consideration. Nothing else matters.
Nothing else counts. Try to make it for just one week. Let us
discover for real and for sure, at least once in our lives, whether,
after such an experiment, we are happier, or sadder, or what.

The gate is narrow. To us it looks small. How do we know
from this side that it opens up into a Kingdom so vast? The gate
is Christ. The gate is an invitation into a new kind of life. Are you
going to be one of the few who find it? Nothing bad happens to

you if you do not go through the narrow gate. Read the passage again. Nothing bad happens to us if we do not go through the narrow gate—except we get to stay where we are . . . and like we are.

Mark 4:1-9

Week Thirty-Four

SOME SEED

In Jesus' attempt to communicate with us about spiritual matters, He ends up endowing all sorts of very familiar, ordinary things with extraordinary meanings. *Sheep* and *shepherds . . . rocks* and *lilies . . . vines* and *wine . . .* even *bread* and *water*—have all taken on incredible levels of significance. Everything takes on freshness, and new dimensions and meaning, in Christ's presence.

So it is with the *seed.* Already a natural marvel and key to many life-support systems, the seed in Jesus' stories and illustrations becomes a symbol for the life-force of the Kingdom of Heaven itself. Who could fathom the power of faith as Jesus means it, and as He tries to tell us about it—as a seed, a mustard seed? Or, to get onto our own theme for the day: what an incredible word-picture, this portrait of a world in which the seed of God's Word—God's truth and love and purpose, the very design of what God is bringing into being—this seed is being spread everywhere . . . is falling upon the world in all places at all times . . . is seeking a place to take hold, a place to be welcomed and nurtured, a place where it can take root, and grow, and bring forth life as God intends it to be.

We are far removed from the land by now. It isn't clear to us, as it was to Jesus' listeners, that seed must be sown, and that if it doesn't take root and produce a crop, there is death and starvation for the whole community. We know it, but it isn't clear to us, like it was to Jesus' listeners, that the seed falling on good ground and bringing forth thirty to a hundredfold—that wasn't just a pleasantry. That was food! That was survival. The seed must produce enough new seed for the next sowing. Anything beyond that, you could eat. Beyond that, you could sell it for others to eat, and use the proceeds for a plow, some repairs, or whatever. (After you tithed, of course.)

It takes us hours to think and imagine our way back into all the subtle and obvious symbol meanings of a simple phrase like, "A sower went out to sow." Of course he did! And some of the simple, profound power of the story is muted for us because we haven't been out sowing lately. Or rather, the ways we have been out sowing lately we don't think of in those terms.

I remember the rage for mustard-seed jewelry back in the late fifties. There were pendants, earrings and tie clasps, desk sets, charms and all sorts of knick-knacks made from a mustard seed embedded in a globule of clear plastic. It was to remind everyone to have faith as a grain of mustard seed. Sometimes symbols get away from us, and carry meaning we never intended. Any farmer could have told us that seeds do not do well embedded in plastic. More prophetically than we knew, we symbolized a generation that had isolated its faith into a sterile, inert showpiece. We didn't let it out into the real atmosphere, or put it into real ground where it could grow or affect anything. It was just to look at.

Even that, maybe, was better than the symbolic experience of a person who received a greeting card with some mustard seed enclosed. The card urged the receiver to plant the seed and let their faith grow as the mustard plant grew. I suppose hundreds of people received such cards, and maybe were encouraged and inspired by the message. But one unfortunate person actually planted the seeds as instructed, and was rewarded with several fine tomatoes.

I like tomatoes. But for some things, there is no substitute— and faith is one of them. Some of us have spent a lot of time and life trying to get along with substitutes—optimism, positive thinking, self-confidence, bravado and countless others. Growing tomatoes may be no disaster, but the shifted symbolism is much too accurate for comfort.

So we can ruin the symbols, but let's try not to. The seed stands for the dynamism of God's Kingdom ready to break forth—

full of enormous power and potential, full of the very essence of the life principle—yet carried and scattered very conveniently in seed form, looking for a place to settle in and grow.

We are not the seed, we are the soil. It is very hard for most of us to keep that straight. Our minds have a tendency to change the symbolism right before our very eyes. Soon we are thinking and talking as if *we* fall on thorny ground, or *we* get carried away by the birds, or *we* are the rich harvest (or are supposed to be).

We are not the seed, we are the soil. Maybe you could try to remember that as the first point for today. We are the hard-packed path, or we are the rocky ground, or we are full of thorns, or we are good ground. The seed doesn't come from us. We do not control the seed, and we are not responsible for its presence. The parable is about how we receive the seed—about what happens to the seed when it lands on us.

Some soil is hard-packed. There is no penetration, so the birds get the seed. The schedule is too tight, the opinions are too set, life is already spoken for—already used up—there's no room for God's seed. Interesting that this is the only kind of soil Jesus links with Satan. It offends some people to have birds linked with Satan. Birds are nice. Birds sing. Birds are pretty. Birds should be protected. Well, Jesus liked birds too, in other contexts. But be fair: This is about sowing and seeds. Have you ever planted a row of corn and had the crows undo all your labor—over and over? It is one of the original scenarios of total frustration. Birds that like seeds are no joke to a farmer. If you sow your crop and pay no attention to the birds, you will starve. And how like Satan—to steal the seed, the kernel, the life-force. We think all is well—the sun shines, the rains come, the land is full of promise—but then, with a sickening feeling, we begin to realize that no grain is coming up, or only a little in scattered patches. And by now, the season is so late—maybe too late. Disaster! *That's* Satanic.

The rocky ground seems to represent people who are fear-oriented. Unlike those in the first category, who think they have no needs—boy, does the rocky ground have needs! "How would *you* feel if you had to have all these rocks I carry in *your* field?"

So rocky-ground people are instantly delighted by the falling seed, like they are always delighted by every new quick cure or easy answer that comes along. But the soil is shallow, and the enthusiasm for the new truth is quickly overcome—first by all the old problems returning, and then by the next new fad or "teacher" coming along. Rocky soil doesn't like the cost of commitment . . . at any level. It would rather focus on the problems, or the pain.

Thorns represent the cares and worries of physical survival that crowd out the growth of the seed: money, position, popularity. Everyone seems to understand this one easily, quickly and clearly. Maybe it's because we don't want anybody to feel they have to go on talking about this one for very long. "Thank you very much, yes, this one is quite clear to me. (So shut up about it.)"

The point and purpose of the parable is the good soil, of course. The other kinds of soil are only mentioned to highlight the good soil by contrast. Fascinated with thorns and rocks and birds, we sometimes forget the good soil. What is it like?

Good soil is full of nutrients, easily watered, relatively level, cultivated, plowed and ready to receive the seed. That is a whole new sermon, isn't it? We need to get a real farmer in here to tell us all the analogies of good soil that would have been obvious to Jesus' listeners. Sometimes we forget that at one time the whole civilization lived pretty close to the land. In any case, good soil is ready to receive the seed. It is freshly plowed (which it may or may not have considered to be a harrowing experience). Above all, it is not otherwise occupied. It is ready and waiting for the seed, having nothing better to do.

To reiterate: It is not hard like the path, but freshly turned. It is not full of rocks—that is, it may go through harrowing experiences, and know the testing, but it is not concentrated on the negative. It does not live focused on the problems, nor is it frightened by whatever disciplines or challenges may lie ahead. And it is not full of thorns. It needs sun and rain and food like everything else, but it is not hung up on the symbols or realities of such "possessions."

Soil is no good if it is used up, but it is also no good if otherwise occupied. It is one of Jesus' most frequent points, and most frequently missed. Indeed, it seems rather unjust to us. What if a good field is busy bearing another crop when the seed of God's Word falls? We come up with all sorts of justifications, and honestly do not think God would want us sitting around.

But Jesus constantly offers a different perspective: Why are we fooling around with crops God did not sow in the first place? And if we are and the Word of God comes to us, then we must instantly drop whatever other crops we are working on (no matter how good)—or miss the real reason for our being . . . and for our being here.

How do we get to be receptive soil? By knowing ourselves, knowing our need of God, knowing we have nothing better to do than wait and watch in order to serve when we are called. Maybe most of all, we are receptive soil when we simply remember that we are not the seed, we are the soil.

If God's seed is growing in us, then we will see lots of seed being sown, and indeed we will feel part of it, as we watch it at work in so many places in and around us. But that is dangerous too, if we start to think we are the seed—start to get into the center of things, try to push it, control it, make it happen, take credit for it. We are not the seed, we are the soil. When we consciously step into the sower's role, we only end up throwing dirt.

"A sower went out to sow." Indeed, yes! You have felt the seed falling on your soil . . . for as long as you have been alive. Something at the core, some partly conscious inner "self," keeps wanting to respond to the urge to care, to love, to be "good," to seek truth, to do justice. We are plagued from the beginning with a hunger to be open, to share, to know and be known, to be forgiving and to accept forgiveness. Nobody "taught us." We long to be whole, to strive for excellence, to live "clean" and what we sometimes call "childlike." Oh, to be rid of all the lies and games and power plays! To leave behind the cruelty and fear and all the divisions—all the residue of resentments, animosities, deep-burning angers . . .

Yes, we long with a great yearning to come out into the light and joy of Life. But who can believe it is truly possible in our world—except in special moments with very special people . . . and even that is tenuous and fragile. Has it not always been so? Every marriage we make . . . every partnership we form . . . every friendship that grows—it awakens the hope. And how often, in our world, the hope is partial, or it backfires entirely—until we are tempted to close out the hope for good, to stop responding to it. We cannot stop the yearning, but we can stop responding—stop putting ourselves in such vulnerable positions.

Why should the soil keep receiving the seed when we know there is fire; when sometimes others steal the harvest; when enemies keep sowing weeds; when there is blight, and hail, and drought, and storm, and gophers? And yet somehow, despite it all—all over the world for a million years—good soil has been bringing forth the harvest. (Not always well. Not every year. Never perfectly. But nevertheless!)

The sower still goes out to sow. The seed is incredible—full of life and power and potential beyond our dreams. And we feel the seed falling around us and on us—begging to be claimed and nourished and grown. Has it not always been so? You have known and felt the seed from your earliest memories. There has always been a great urge to live for the seed—instead of for the birds, or the rocks, or the thorns. That great possibility dogs our steps, and nibbles at the edge of our consciousness, all of our days.

How gently the sower sows. No week goes by without our having to shake it off to get back to "real" life. No day goes by without our having to make choices against such ideals in order to do what we think of as "survival." And often the seed does take root, and we rejoice to feel it growing—and looking back, those are the only times and experiences that really matter.

Likewise, we never get angry or hurt or discouraged or depressed but what some inner voice calls us to turn away from it, to come out of it, to rise above it. How we fight, thrash about and argue within ourselves to pretend that we do not hear the inner urging—that we do not know anything about any seed! And we tell ourselves we cannot afford to trust these urgings that are too soft, too beautiful, too unrealistic, too unnatural, too spiritual.

A sower went out to sow . . . patiently, unceasingly—every waking day of our lives, the seeds of God's Word fall gently, quietly . . . seeking our receptivity . . . trying to find some response, some nurture . . . hoping to find a place in us to take root and grow.

Only that which comes from these seeds brings any real or lasting joy, gives our lives any true meaning or purpose, makes our experience in this life worth any of the striving. So Jesus asks: How are you doing? What kind of soil are you, right now? Are you learning to trust the seed that keeps falling? Are you learning to relax in the knowledge that it is not up to you, and that it will keep falling? Do you love it, and let it grow in you—no matter how much your natural fears may warn you against it?

A sower went out to sow. We are not the sower. We are not the seed. We are the soil. It is our proper, rightful, "easy," delightful function to let the seed grow within us. That is what we are designed for. It takes tremendous effort to harden ourselves against it, to reject the seed, to turn away, to stay alone, to be busy with other things, to make the choices that keep us in control. That is why we feel so heroic and courageous and tired and tragic so much of the time. It is anguish for the soil to reject the seed. It requires enormous energy and contortion and stress for the soil to keep pretending that it is the seed, or the sower.

II Corinthians 1:2-11

Week Thirty-Five

DARKNESS IS ALSO A FRIEND

Many months ago, I was in a committee meeting and the point came up, as it does again and again, that we need always to be positive in our approaches, and stress the happy, successful possibilities in life. I didn't say anything for a while, but apparently my face reflected something less than serenity. Somebody finally asked if I didn't agree that we should always think positively, assuming success and satisfaction as the outcome. I do not remember the exact conversation, but I suspect I replied to the effect that I was glad I was not that emotionally retarded.

God has given us the capacity to weep as well as to smile, to repent as well as to rejoice, to feel great sorrow as well as high elation. To program myself to be cut off from all but a tiny portion of this rich spectrum of awareness in order to wear a happy smile all the time is a severe loss. Moreover, I am much impressed by the Christian religion, its founder, its teachings and its heroes, who declared a faith that was unafraid of suffering, failure, loss or death. Having spent a good portion of my life enamored of the crucified One and His friends, who even dared to head into death to find life, I was not about to exchange it all for what seemed a crass and shallow posturing—that we should always act happy and positive, whether we mean it or not.

Of course, there is power in positive approaches. Christendom itself is always positive, if we take the long view and if we are talking about God's Kingdom. I only become uneasy when people want to be positive on the short view too, and about all matters having to do with success in this world. What I want to lift up for your consideration is the surprising, outlandish, incredible discovery of Christianity: that darkness is also a friend, that failure is often a great blessing. In fact, God's clearest and most powerful

268

blessings may come more often through our dark moments than they do through our success, contentment and satisfaction. Only those who have experienced failure, no longer fear it.

Dr. Leslie Weatherhead, one of England's great religious seers, said: "I can only write down this simple testimony. Like all men, I prefer the sunny uplands of experience when health, happiness and success abound; but I have learned more about God, life and myself in the darkness of fear and failure than I have ever learned in sunshine. There are such things as the treasures of darkness. The darkness, thank God, passes, but what one learns in the darkness he possesses forever."

Despite his great reputation, I don't think Weatherhead's words would ring so clear and true if they did not remind us of themes we have heard and read and felt through the years. A friend of mine whose son had committed suicide told me that he would have given anything to prevent that tragedy, but he wonders if he ever would have found the Lord or the church if it had not happened. I have friends who are actually grateful to be alcoholics, because the path to recovery led them into the spiritual life they had hungered for but did not know how to find. From accidents, cancer, strokes, losing jobs, broken relationships and shattered dreams, the saints awaken and begin their journey toward God. That is what I have seen and watched and experienced.

I read THE POWER OF POSITIVE THINKING by Norman Vincent Peale for the first time back in the seventh grade. In the eighth grade, I was given Dale Carnegie's HOW TO WIN FRIENDS AND INFLUENCE PEOPLE. Over the years, I have read a lot of the progeny of those books, taken courses, and listened to hours of tapes. Each time, I try to get into it for a while. It always turns out too shallow or too false, and I am reminded of the statement, "When I became a man, I put away childish things." If Jesus had gone that way, He would never have been crucified. Paul would never have converted. Peter would never have heard the rooster crow. Would I really want to trade their darkness for positive thinking's light? Not likely!

Next to Christendom, I am drawn to Buddhism. Have you ever contemplated the Four Noble Truths (on which all Buddhism is based) and compared them with psycho-cybernetics, or Robert Schuller, or any of the recently pictured roles of the successful American male? I just can't help but suspect that some folk haven't thought about it very much, beyond a temporary and shallow desire to be acceptable or well off in the next few years or so, as if there were nothing more to life than that.

Aeschylus, one of the greatest playwright-philosophers of all time, *had* thought about it some, and he said: "God, whose law it is that he who learns must suffer. And even in our sleep—pain that cannot forget falls drop by drop upon the heart, and in our own despite, against our will, comes wisdom to us by the awful [awe-filled] grace of God."

What can we say, then, about darkness? There is truth to the saying, "It is always darkest before the dawn." It also seems true of life that there is no growth without pain, no conversion without some form of despair.

Sometimes we look around and see the sunsets, hear the birds, see the moonlight playing on the ocean, and we are in awe of the loveliness of nature, the incredible beauty and order that exist all around us. We say it brings us closer to God. Sometimes we see a newscast and wonder what it would be like to be caught in the maelstrom of Lebanon, or fleeing as refugees from Cambodia with nothing left but a sack of cloth and one relative. Sometimes we also cut in for a moment on the anguish of people out of work, or the helplessness of people in wards in large hospitals everywhere. Does that also bring us closer to our Creator, closer to God? Is it more spiritual to hike the trails of Mount Rainier than to walk the wards of County General Hospital in Los Angeles? Are they not both revealers of Nature—part of God's creation? I wonder if we don't need to do both—to face both—to be afraid of neither.

Sometimes darkness is a friend, albeit in disguise at first. I worry very much about people who are afraid of the dark—who insist on acting positive, successful and happy all the time, as if it were some creed one dares not transgress. Do we really want to become people who cannot cry for the pain of this world—who have no compassion, even for ourselves? Is it not a relief and a rejoicing to discover we are not always pleased with some things (or some people) the way they presently are?! Rather, we have hopes, and dreams, and goals—and faith in God, who is bringing all things to what they are intended to be.

On a more personal level, it is dangerous to operate on the premise that we should always act positive and happy, that there is something wrong with us if we feel discouraged. Then soon we avoid awareness of our own inner condition. We start pretending, which is a form of denial and self-deception.

"The attempt to avoid legitimate suffering lies at the root of all emotional illness," according to psychiatrist M. Scott Peck in THE ROAD LESS TRAVELED.

"Neurosis is always a substitute for legitimate suffering," said Carl Jung.

Underneath both statements is the realization that our pain and despair are trying to alert us to both the crises and the opportunities of the spiritual life. The darkness we encounter most frequently bears the message of change and healing that we desperately need.

Scott Peck again: "The illness exists long before the symptoms. Rather than being the illness, the symptoms are the beginning of the cure. The fact that they are unwanted makes them all the more a phenomenon of grace—a gift of God, a message from the unconscious, if you will, to initiate self-examination and repair." Darkness is often our friend, though we never think so until later.

Peck continues: "Only those few who accept responsibility for their symptoms, who realize that their symptoms are a manifestation of a disorder in their own soul, heed the message of their unconscious and accept its grace. They accept their own inadequacy and the pain of the work necessary to heal themselves. . . . It was of them that Christ spoke in the first of the Beatitudes: 'Blessed are the poor in spirit, for theirs is the Kingdom of Heaven.'" Blessed are those who do not run from their darkness.

What does it do to us as a people if we think that we must always be positive, always act successful, always put on the face of confident achievers who have neither qualms nor doubts nor any hidden weaknesses or fears? If we have no self-pity, we can have no compassion for others. "You shall love your neighbor as yourself."

What do we do when it gets dark? We do not have to run, or hide, or pretend, or be afraid of life's dark times. After all, we begin the Christian life by accepting death. Baptism is a drowning. When dark times come, we assume it is another form of the spiritual path we follow, another time in which we will learn and grow and eventually discover new wonders about God's plan and purpose for us.

In order to let that happen, the first requirement is to accept and feel the darkness for what it is. If it is sorrow, let it flood in. If it is remorse, let it voice its worst accusations. If it is loneliness, let it tear the heart. If it is fear, let it howl until its warning is clear. What good is it to know Jesus, if that knowing doesn't allow us to face the darkness?

The saints tell us, "Surrender to the worst." Whatever form the darkness takes, imagine it turning out as bleak and dark as possible. If you are caught in the dark, never play it light. Never comfort yourself with "Oh well, it isn't so bad," or "It probably won't happen," or "It could be worse." Picture the outcome as darkly as you can. Surrender to the worst.

Then bring your faith to bear. Can you handle the worst outcome if God stays close and helps you? Once you know that, the fear is back in proper perspective. If it comes to the worst, it will be okay. Together, you and God can handle anything! Then you are free to see and cope with the situation as it really is.

Secondly, assume there is a reason for what you are feeling—sorrow, discouragement, depression, shame, frustration. Don't try to talk yourself out of it. Let the darkness speak to you. It has a message for you. Behind that message is God with some important prospects and the power to accomplish them, but first the darkness has to speak. Welcome it . . . listen to it . . . learn from it.

Remember that it is not wrong to "feel this way." Indeed, you may not be in the wrong. Sometimes dark times are the result of staying faithful in a separated and broken world. Sorrow, sadness and discouragement are not always the mark of *your* deficiency. Read the Bible: Joseph, Moses, Elijah, David, Jeremiah, all the great prophets, Jesus, Peter, Paul . . . all the greatest we know had such moments. Very often it was when they had been most faithful. Even so, out of their darkness came new marching orders. ("What are you doing here, Elijah?")

Face the darkness when it comes. Surrender to the worst. Then listen for the message the darkness is bringing. Finally, double the watch. Count on it: Out of darkness, God will show a new path, a new purpose. When it comes, you will realize without a doubt that there was no other way to get to this new place except through the dark time.

We worship a God of death and resurrection. In Christendom, we do not move from light to light. We move through death to life . . . through sorrow to joy . . . through pain to love. The glory is not in the suffering—but suffering must not be allowed to turn us aside.

Good days are wonderful, and light is what we seek, but darkness is also a friend, if we keep walking with Jesus Christ our Lord.

Romans 8:12-28 (NEB)

Week Thirty-Six

TOGETHER FOR GOOD

Choosing a very simple, straightforward sermon title can sometimes have surprising results. It didn't cross my mind, until later, to think of other implications. This could be a sermon about marriage, and that phrase "together for good" comes with terror or delight, depending on how that subject is going for us at present. Or maybe it could be me announcing that I love our new house and I'm never going to leave this parish. "You are stuck with me. We're together for good." But I am not that audacious or presumptuous in categories so far beyond my authority and control.

There are a couple of really good sermon possibilities in the title as well. The title might imply that we come together to do good, and/or that good comes from our being together. I like that topic a lot. Finally, the title reminded me that we are on an eternal journey. We seem to come and go, meet and part, lose track of each other and find each other—here in this realm. But we are together for good. All separations are temporary. (God says, "In your realm, divorce is a sin. In my realm, divorce is an impossibility.") Remembering that has its sobering side. Sometimes we think we would like to break a relationship once and for all. Eventually time or life or eternity will bring us back to face it, to repent, to reconcile and heal. We are stuck with a God of love, who builds all things to operate according to love's principles, and that ain't always fun.

Nevertheless, when I am reminded that we are together for good—despite the inherent problems—my heart soars. All the hope and faith and reason for striving connect to the soaring. "Jesus came to cancel out the concept of goodbye." One more sentence on this subject and I will be hooked, and off and running, and this will end up being the subject for today's sermon after all. So back to the passage for today.

The Scripture reading was from the New English translation. The Great Apostle is revealing both his faith and his experience with how God, through the Holy Spirit (when we believe and allow it), draws all the threads of our lives together, and integrates and coordinates everything we are doing and even what is going on around us—and we find ourselves living way beyond our normal capacity. We feel carried, blessed, effective, energized, amazed at what is getting accomplished, humble in the realization that God has deigned to use us . . . and I now start to pour forth a barrage of words, as everyone does who tries to describe this incredible possibility. Indeed, Paul is growing elated just writing about it, and he is about to break forth, as he sometimes does, with prose that competes with angel choirs. (You remember: "If God is for us, who is against? . . . Who can separate us from the love of Christ? . . . I am sure that neither death, nor life, nor angels, nor principalities, nor things present, nor things to come, nor powers, nor height, nor depth . . . " You remember?)

Sometimes it's fun to go back and see what it was that got Paul so excited, that set him off, that inspired him to such utterance. He's writing a letter to some Christian friends he hopes to visit soon. And so he talks about his own experience with the Holy Spirit, knowing that will resonate with their experience too. And he starts describing and trying to explain how it feels to be conscious of the Spirit's presence helping with your life.

He starts off pretty reasonable, talking about the choices we face between natural life and spiritual life—about some of the chaos of trying to live for God in a world not yet at peace with God. But quickly his gratitude for the Spirit's presence and guidance and help ascends. The Spirit organizes, coordinates, plans, oversees everything, and keeps moving everything toward its rightful goal, no matter how it may look to us at any particular moment along the way. The Spirit even reworks, or translates, our very prayers into what they ought to be—into what our deepest souls would truly pray. That's the kind of awareness and experience that sets Paul off. If we choose to live for God—if we turn our wills and our lives over to God—that is what awaits us.

I quote to you from Frank Laubach. He is with the Mohammedan Moros on Mindanao in 1930. He makes what I think is an absolute parallel comment to what Paul is saying: "I feel simply carried along each hour, doing my part in a plan which is far beyond myself. This sense of cooperation with God in little things is what so astonishes me, for I never have felt it this way before. I need something, and turn round to find it waiting for me. I must work, to be sure, but there is God working along with me. To know this gives a sense of security and assurance for the future which is also new to my life. I seem to have to make sure of only one thing now, and every other thing 'takes care of itself,' or I prefer to say what is more true, God takes care of all the rest. My part is to live this hour in continuous inner conversation with God and in perfect responsiveness to his will. To make this hour gloriously rich. This seems to be all I need think about." (*LETTERS BY A MODERN MYSTIC*)

Rather uncanny, don't you think, to find two such completely similar descriptions of what it is like—one from Corinth, about A.D. 57, and the other from the Philippines in 1930? It means the option of living this way is really open. The Holy Spirit is alive and well, and is faithful throughout time. We are discovering that the Spirit will still be present with us, will still act in this fashion if we want it to—today. I cannot imagine more exciting news.

Sometimes I find it helpful to have a shorter phrase or statement to remind me of all the richness of such promises and possibilities. In this particular case, while the translation we read is superb, the familiar phrase that represents this concept comes from the King James Version. The words sound good to our ears: *All things work together for good for those who love God.* I'm going to request that you memorize that sentence, if it isn't a favorite already. And then it is my hope that all of us will quietly promise, right now—alone, and together as a church—that we will repeat this phrase to ourselves at least twenty times a day for the next three weeks. If the car breaks down, if the parking lot comes to a standstill, if you inherit a million (dollars or bills)—whatever happens, repeat the phrase, twenty times a day, for three weeks.

I hope you can start off believing the statement as truth, because then it has power. But that is a tall order. If your faith isn't at that point, you can still memorize the phrase and repeat it twenty times a day as a genuine experiment in faith. You then repeat it as a possibility you want to believe in. And that repetition will be an invitation for the Spirit to get into conversation with you about whether or not it really is true. The Spirit is not above getting into "show and tell" games with us, if we bring our honest doubts. I'm not talking about belligerence or defiance—the Spirit just waits patiently for that stuff to pass.

The phrase, again, is: *All things work together for good for those who love God.*

Take it slow. *All things work together.* Most of us do see this at least on some level. There is pattern and order. There is far more pattern and order than we notice or realize, but we do notice some of it. Some notice it best in the stars, some in music, some in the seasons or plants, or the intertwining of life—bee and flower, sun and rain, and on to endless musings. We have sayings like, "No man is an island." We know that the saints of every religion and culture have slowly come to the realization of a greater and greater unity of all things. To identify, to see one's self in another, to recognize that one person's fate inevitably affects us all . . . in some fashion, we are all aware of such principles. Sometimes, to be sure, we try to "beat the system." We spend some time trying to ignore such truth, to "live and let live" (in the negative sense). Sometimes we try to make it through a whole day without prayer, and pretend it won't hurt anything. But when we are sane, we know better. *All things work together.* Everything is affected by everything else.

Shalom Aleichem tells about an old man standing on a crowded bus. A young man standing next to him asked, "What time is it?" The old man refused to reply. The young man moved on. The old man's friend was shocked at such rude behavior from this normally kind and generous person. "Why were you so discourteous?" he asked. The old man blushed, and answered, "If I had given him the time, next he would want to know where I'm going. Then we might talk about our interests. If we did that, he might invite himself to my house for dinner. If he did, he would meet my lovely daughter. He is handsome. They might fall in love. I don't want my daughter to marry someone who can't afford a watch."

Everything is intertwined. *All things work together.* To believe in a Creator is to know this must be the case. Certain principles are established, and that which flies in the face of these principles will meet greater and greater resistance, and inevitably fail.

All things work together . . . for good. That is a quantum leap of faith. The Creator is good. Therefore, all things work together for good. Most of the actual "faith" of the nineteenth and twentieth centuries has believed that things are neutral. That which is created is neutral—having the possibility for good or evil according to how we use it. But we are in charge. We decide. God is either uninterested (directly) or non-personal, or God appears in a later scene in the drama. Much of the most religious devotion of the last two centuries is still irreligious in this fashion. It masks an incredible pride. "It is up to us. We are in charge." There's a categorical difference between that and what Paul and Laubach were claiming—finding themselves in a daily, moment-by-moment experience where they were less and less in charge, while more and more kept happening. And we do notice that both of them did indeed seem to accomplish unbelievable things. (In seven years, Laubach was able to inspire half of the 90,000 illiterate Moros to learn to read and write!)

All things work together for good. Some still suspect a lot of things work for evil. Most think this place is neutral and it's up to us. And yet, we need to add, there is a rather significant number of people, especially in churches, who make the jump, claim the positive, and try to live and believe that *all things work together for good.*

All things work together for good . . . for those who love God.
The New Testament is more cautious than the positive/optimist.
Sometimes we do not want to believe what Scripture says.
Sometimes we try to make it say more than it does, or we try to
make it say what we want to hear. This world is not obedient to its
Creator. There is spiritual warfare here. There is alienation and
separation here. Things don't work together for good when we
stay apart from God, when we try to get safe or secure in our own
little kingdoms instead of reporting for duty under a Leader higher
than ourselves.

J. Paul Getty, land investor and oil magnate, was said to be,
at one time, America's richest man. When I read about him, I am
not inspired. I do not feel the tremendous drawing power I feel
when I read about Jesus, or Paul, or Frank Laubach. I think,
rather, how much I hope I am not too much like him already (and
know that I am). Better to lose the house I love, or the job I
love—anything—rather than be like him. His biographer, James
K. Glassman, says, "He changed his will 21 times, using it as a
weapon to punish what he saw as disloyalty. He drove one son to
suicide and missed the funeral of another who died at the age of
twelve." Then Glassman quotes Getty's diary entry from the week
of his twelve-year-old son's funeral—the funeral he didn't attend.
It says very little, and yet it is one of the saddest comments one
can imagine. The entry says: "Funeral for Darling Timmy. A sad
day. Send cable to Zone that Aminoil can have 50 percent of
Eocenle by giving us 50 percent of Burgan and paying 10 cents
per barrel handling." Doesn't that bring tears to your eyes?

What a contrast—what a huge difference—between Paul and
J. Paul. Can there be any doubt which one we would rather be
like? Unbelievably, we know there can be! On some crazy days,
in crazy moments, we still dream more of being rich or powerful.
Things do not work together for good when we are still in charge
of our own lives, separated from our Creator, living with values
that are all twisted up and screwy as hell.

The promise is high and incredible, but it carries a warning—
and huge chunks of modern Christendom have been ignoring it.

All things work together for good for those who love God. Not otherwise. Not if we are off doing our own thing. Then we set up waves of resistance; we create static in the channels; we swim against the flow of God's plans and exhaust ourselves, at the very least ending up needing help that should never have been necessary in the first place. It's okay! God loves to bring the help when we really want it—no matter how little we deserve it. But it cannot work until we turn to be with and go with God.

All things work together for good for those who love God. Twenty times a day, every day, for three weeks. No matter what is happening . . . no matter whether you think things will be good or troublesome or terrible for you . . . every time you can think of it, say the phrase. Try to claim it . . . until you discover what Paul meant, and what Frank Laubach was talking about. We are going to want this so much that we will either find it, or close this place down and forget it.

Psalm 23; Hebrews 3:1-6

Week Thirty-Seven

FEAR NO EVIL

Norman Cousins tells us of an incident at a high school football game in Monterey Park. Several people left their seats because they became nauseated. They reported to the physician in attendance that they felt queasy after drinking cola. He, in turn, asked that a public announcement be made to request people not to drink any cola beverage because of the danger of contamination.

"At that point," Cousins noted, "about two hundred people became instantly ill and had to be hospitalized." Their recovery was subsequently enhanced by the news that there was nothing wrong with the cola after all.

If you had been there, and if you had been one of the two hundred people who got sick, would you have been mortified when it turned out that there was nothing wrong with the cola after all? I vividly remember a Saturday morning when I was in the fourth grade. Saturday morning was big-chore time. In my case, it meant cleaning all the pens and stalls. It seemed like a big job to me. And every week, it was there to do over again, and looking bigger. On this particular Saturday morning, I just wasn't feeling well at all. My stomach hurt, I felt sore all over, it was like my head was in some kind of a vise, and everything felt weighted down.

I hadn't been in bed very long when my friend Travis called to invite me to go riding. My parents shrugged and said I probably wasn't well, but if my illness should pass and I got my chores done, I could go. Well, I felt much better in no time—about three seconds. In fact, I so over-recovered that I got all the pens and corrals cleaned in two hours instead of the normal four, and they were cleaned better than usual, just to make sure there would be no reason to keep me home.

That memory haunts me. It does because I wasn't kidding about feeling rotten that morning. I still wonder if I wasn't really coming down with the flu. And I doubt that any of those two hundred people wanted to miss the game and go visit the hospital. They really did feel sick, and were no doubt anxious, wondering if they had been severely poisoned.

Back in October and November of 1983, at least half of the people in this country were seriously frightened, and truly wondering if they would ever see the beginning of 1984. The situation hasn't changed much. No great conversion has swept over the nations of the world. There is no real reason for more confidence now than there was then—maybe even for a little less. But somehow the worst of that particular wave of fear has washed over us, and passed on. Isn't it strange how fear comes and goes like that?

I'm only pointing to the obvious fact that fear cripples us. There is always a lot to fear. No human has ever lived a five-minute span of time on this earth in which it was not possible to reasonably imagine great disasters occurring. The potential for fear is always with us, always all around us. And each and every time we become fearful, it is disastrous. It isn't always easy to recover and go clean the corral, or to sheepishly get out of the hospital and go home. Sometimes the fear sticks, and cripples us for life. Sometimes the fear destroys things hard to replace.

A scuba diver, for instance, is not likely to panic twice. Down under, most anything she does in fear will kill her. But the scuba diver knows that. That's a great advantage. A diver simulates, and thinks, and imagines, and constantly trains herself not to panic.

Sometimes in the course of normal days, we forget to stay in training. Then fear catches us unaware, and we run in front of cars, or we ruin a relationship, or we don't recover in time and somebody has to operate. (Or we blow the deal, or the job, or the marriage, or the life.)

I'm not likely to end up in the hospital over a cola scare. You may not be likely to get the flu to avoid cleaning the corral. But all of us have our own vulnerable places. And fear cripples us all—cuts our power, corrupts our perspective, warps the patterns of our love and our life.

One of the things the Christian Faith is best at is freeing people from fear. Faith in Jesus Christ is a giant fear-killer. There is a lot of verbiage floating around, and we all know that talking about faith isn't always the same as having it, but any person who actually starts walking the Christian Path also starts losing fear after fear.

Reason doesn't help against fear unless it is backed by authentic conviction, experience and emotion, but it can still line it out for us so we can see where we are and what to do.

First of all, it is not possible for us to believe in the love of a personal, almighty God . . . without starting to lose our fears. "Who shall separate us? Shall tribulation, or distress, or persecution, or famine, or nakedness, or peril, or sword?" (Romans 8:35) We don't start out with full-blown faith like that, but we also can't touch the love of Jesus without getting onto the theme. Slowly, relentlessly—sometimes not so slowly—it grabs our fears by the scruff of the neck and throws them out of our lives. In our day, the sword is nuclear war, the peril is overpopulation, the nakedness is depleted resources, and the famine is everything from losing a promotion to actual starvation. Even then, it's the persecution that frightens some of us—the not being liked, or accepted, or approved of. Nevertheless, with any of these things, the plan is simple: You fix it if you can. If you can't fix it, you try to improve it, make it better than it was. If you can't improve it, you try to cut the losses, minimize the damage as much as possible. Fear begins with that last step. If you can't improve things, how bad will the damage get? But fear comes heaviest with the next level. What if you can't minimize it, stop it, delay it? What if it comes down to the bottom end—like the bumper sticker says: "Cancer cures smoking"? What if the headlines read: "Chemists announce abortion no longer an issue—Secret chemical leaked into waterways in recent experiment leaves all males sterile"? Or: "Pentagon announces there will be no more population problem after tomorrow"? What do you do if things really *are* beyond your control? Funny that it takes some of us so long to realize that they really always have been. Nevertheless, if they blow up the world, that is serious, but it is not like some final disaster. It's not like some irreparable or incontrovertible loss. People who think so either do not know God, or do not understand the definition of "almighty."

In the second place, you cannot get into the Christian experience without facing and coming to terms with death. We don't save that until last, or hide it in some secret mystery known only to 32nd-degree saints or something. The crucifixion of Jesus is right at the front door of the Faith. That's why, in so many ways, the first step is the hardest. You don't come in here and then find out you don't have to die. You have to die to get in here! Baptism is drowning. Every communion meal, we remember: take death unto ourselves again and come through it. Paul says we "die every day." (I Corinthians 15:31) Jesus says, "Take up your cross daily and follow me." (Luke 9:23) The whole concept of dying with Christ is not saved for the veteran saints. It's for openers— for the novices, and initiates, and beginners.

Again and again we stumble onto the mystery and miracle of it. I don't mean just in the past, or in Scripture—I mean we experience it for ourselves, and we discover it in people all around us. Again and again, story after story, we hear the great note of freedom that comes to people who surrender to their own death and go beyond it. A hospital, an accident, a near accident, a crisis, a suicidal depression . . . and then the familiar but incredible thread: "I felt like my life should have ended right there. It was like it was finished and over. And now each day is like a bonus, an unexpected gift, a special extension I have no rights to or claims on. It belongs to God, and so I try to let it be any way God wants it. But I died back there at that last fork in the road."

And not only do we hear it again and again, but is it not also from the very people who seem most alive, most fearless, most full of love and peace and joy? Of course! That is the doorway into the Christian Faith. (And not all who come through it call it "Christian.") This life is borrowed time in an impermanent realm. There is no security here—there is no reason for us to expect resolutions, solutions, vindication or final satisfaction here. Knowing that is a great release, and so the fears begin to crumble.

In the third place, when things get rough, we do have Christ's presence with us. Strangely enough, this really is more for the seasoned saints. Not that the Holy Spirit is not present with each of us always, but it takes most of us quite some time to learn how true and powerful and perfect is our shepherding. That's a whole beautiful subject of its own. Fortunately, in times of trial and crisis, we tend to re-order priorities and clear channels almost automatically, and often become much more aware of the Spirit's presence. So this also belongs with the ways in which faith in Jesus Christ is a giant fear-killer.

How do I do the opposite of pounding the pulpit? I need to say this—not quietly, because it's very important, yet it needs to come softly, light on its feet: Fear is the greatest of sins. It shares this position with pride. It is the backside of pride. Fear, then, separates us from God, from our true selves, from each other, from the truth. The point is, if we want to know where we are being faithless, apostate, sinful, rebellious . . . we have only to look to our fears. If we want to know where we are doing the most damage . . . we can look to our fears. If we want to discover where we most need to apply our faith and invite Christ into our conscious living . . . we can look to our fears. The reason I need to put it lightly is because if you hear it at all, it still comes crashing down like all the prophets of the past were pounding pulpits. After all, losing our fears is one way to summarize the whole Christian drama. It is our fears that keep us from loving, from healing, from knowing our identity, from knowing each other, from being able to do the miracles which Jesus tried to teach us—within and without.

So the book of Hebrews reminds us that we are the household of God (another way of saying "citizens of God's Kingdom"). Moses was a great servant in that household. Christ is the Son, set over the household. But *we* are the household—"if only we are fearless and keep our hope high." If not—if we are not a people shedding fear, and helping each other and anyone who comes here to shed their fears—well, we may have a sign out front and our name in the paper, but we aren't really what we say we are. Where Christ is, people lose fear and come to life. If that isn't happening, Christ isn't present. (Well, isn't being acknowledged or followed.)

So if you aren't in training, get back into training. Be like the scuba diver, or the soldier, or whatever your favorite image is of a person who cannot afford to react in fear. Simulate, imagine, take yourself into the places and situations you know are fearful to you. Then bring the power of your faith to bear: the love of Almighty God . . . the death you have already died in Christ . . . the presence of the Holy Spirit with you. And sometimes when you meditate, bring that best phrase of the 23rd Psalm before you: "I will fear no evil." Just that one phrase. Let it sit there in your consciousness until everything else has ebbed away. "I will fear no evil." Then let it talk: NO evil? No EVIL? Do you mean it? Stay with the meditation until you mean it!

Does evil have any power? Is not all evil—all of Satan's tricks—merely a corruption of the good? Only God has true power. Satan is a liar. Evil cannot last—it has no patience. It isn't that well-organized. It hasn't got vision or commitment or love enough to keep it going for long enough. If you have decided to trust, what do you trust? God? "I will fear no evil!" I'm not trying to do the meditation for you, just hinting enough to hope some of you will get into it. Of course, some of you are afraid to pray or meditate. You fear it, not knowing what might happen to you if you get into the clutches of the Divine Power. It's okay to fear the good. That makes sense. Goodness and God have real power. That kind of fear is the beginning of wisdom. And for some odd reason, people who truly fear God do not stay apart from God for very long.

In the seventeenth year of his work as a missionary, he had never been in more peril. Surrounded by hostile and infuriated tribes, and strongly tempted to flee, he wrote in his journal: "January 14, 1856. Evening. Felt much turmoil of spirit in prospect of having all my plans for the welfare of this great region and this teeming population knocked on the head by savages to-morrow. But I read that Jesus said: 'All power is given unto Me in heaven and in earth. Go ye therefore, and teach all nations, and lo, I am with you always, even unto the end of the world.' It is the word of a gentleman of the most strict and sacred honour, so there's an end of it! I will not cross furtively tonight as I intended. Should such a man as I flee? Nay, verily, I shall take observations for latitude and longitude to-night, though they may be the last. I feel quite calm now, thank God!'"

Later, upon receiving an honorary doctorate from the University of Glasgow, he recalls it: "Would you like me to tell you what supported me through all the years of exile among people whose language I could not understand, and whose attitude towards me was always uncertain and often hostile? It was this: 'Lo, I am with you always, even unto the end of the world!' On those words I staked everything." And as you know, David Livingston went back to Africa, and went right on staking everything on those words, until time and life ran out.

The question is not: Will time and life run out? The question is: Will we live it in fear . . . or faith?

Matthew 18:1-14; Hebrews 1:10-14

Week Thirty-Eight

GUARDIAN ANGELS

"For I tell you that in heaven their angels always behold the face of my Father who is in heaven." It isn't the part of the passage that normally jumps out at us. In fact, it is possible to read this portion of Scripture many times and not even notice that angels are mentioned. But the statement seems pretty clear, when we stop to look at it. Jesus does seem to be telling us that there are angels assigned to each and every child, and that these angels have direct access to God.

In context, the statement is clearly a warning: See that you do not despise one of these little ones because (if you need a "because") they have angels watching over them! I hadn't really thought about it much for years, but it caught my eye a few months back and I have been wondering ever since: Whatever happened to the angels?

"Are not all angels ministering spirits sent forth to serve, for the sake of those who are to obtain salvation?" Hebrews makes it sound like a question, and it sounds to my ears like a very good question. So I think at first, "Oh, goody—he's going to answer this interesting question." But then the text moves right on, making it clear that it was a rhetorical question. He means the question like, "For pity's sake, doesn't everybody know this?" And I think, "Oh, whew—glad I didn't raise my hand."

You know what happens when a subject like that gets your attention after a period of not noticing. You don't notice angels at all for years, and then suddenly they are everywhere you look. Well, angels are mentioned 180 times in the New Testament alone. (And 114 times in the Old Testament.) If your eye stops deleting them out, if the mind stops ignoring them—and if you read the Book very much—you start running into angels every place you look. So I started wondering: Whatever happened to the angels? We don't talk about the angels anymore. You could follow the members of this church around everywhere they go for months and never hear the word mentioned—unless somebody happened to be talking about baseball, or it was Christmas time and somebody was working on a pageant.

Is there any such thing as an angel? Has anybody here ever encountered an angel? Does anybody here know of an instance in the last hundred years or so when an angel did anything important, significant or even interesting? Does anybody here actually and truly believe that angels exist? Whatever happened to the angels?

To get technical for a minute, there are supposedly many ranks or levels of Celestial Beings—nine actually. Though we lump them all into the category of angels, the lowest and least powerful level is made up of the Angels. Mostly this is the level that humans encounter. The next level up is the Archangels. These are beings so powerful and wise that humans cannot really conceive of it. However, on rare occasions, a human might encounter (or rather, be encountered by) an Archangel. It is actually mentioned only thrice: Once when the Archangel Gabriel is sent to help the prophet Daniel understand the vision of the end times (Daniel 8:16); again when Gabriel is sent to tell Zechariah of the birth of his son, John the Baptist (Luke 1:19); and finally when Gabriel appears to Mary to tell her about the birth of Jesus (Luke 1:26).

So humans, at our present level of development, do not encounter the angelic beings very often, and Archangels almost never. But the hierarchy goes on up from there: from Archangels to Principalities, Powers, Virtues, Dominions, Thrones—and you see we are completely beyond our element or any hope of understanding—but the lore continues up, to Cherubim and finally to Seraphim. That can hardly inspire or excite us, who cannot even remember the names of the seven Archangels who govern our solar system and all things that happen on earth (or so it was once believed). Their names are (according to whom

you ask): Raphael, Gabriel, Michael, Uriel, Simiel, Orifiel and
Zachariel (Zadkiel). All angel names end with "el" because they
are all servants of God (el = Lord, or God). Well, almost all. There
is one other story: Adam and Eve encounter a serpent creature.
A temptation is delivered, which finally results in what is called
"The Fall of Man." That was another encounter between humans
and an angel—an un-angel, or fallen angel. What rank? Oh my!
The story goes completely off our comprehension map. It was
Seraphim. Lucifer, the light-bearer, is said to have been the top-
ranking leader of the highest order of Celestial Beings—the
Seraphim. That will go over our heads! But for openers, it means
no mere Archangel could hope to stand against him for even
seconds. The plight of fallen humanity is grave indeed. What
kind and nature of creature could possibly help us against such
as Lucifer? But I stray, and get carried away . . .

Most interesting to humans, I suspect, is the theory of
"guardian angels." If we are going to get help from any of these
beings, that might get our attention. Even if the help is only a
warning, or maybe instructions for service—at least that is
something. But if some of these wondrous beings are actually
assigned to us—take a personal interest in us—then that is indeed
something else! As you well know, this was in fact the belief—
the assumed reality—for most of Christendom until very recent
times. Why did so many believe such a thing for so long? Did
they have experiences which supported such a notion? Were
they simply gullible? Was it just an easy symbolism for concepts
too complex to speak of in other ways? Whatever happened to
the angels?

Essentially, there are angels who are people, and there are
angels who are not people. Let us begin with the easy category.
"Angel" means "messenger of God." Anything or anyone that
carries God's word is automatically an angel. Most of us still say
and believe that God often speaks to us through other people.
When that happens, it is perfectly accurate to speak of that person
as an "angel." Indeed, in the passage from Hebrews that we read
this morning, if we continued we would discover that the author

is speaking of angels to include anyone who has carried the Word of God to people. It's confusing but interesting to find that even the name Gabriel means "man of God."

At least it is true that, in many Bible stories which speak of angels, it is difficult to tell whether it is a heavenly figure disguised as a man, or a man sent with a special message or task. In either case, the story is always focused on the message, not on the figure that carries it. So we seldom get to follow the "angel" back to wherever it came from—heaven above or earth below. What we can say with certainty is that some angels are humans. God uses people to carry a message, to perform a task, to intrude suddenly into a situation where this is needed—and afterward, they often fade back to another life or go on to another need after the crisis is over.

In any case, it caused me to stop and think of the number of people who have stepped into my life in special moments. Some of them are "regulars"—mothers, fathers, some relatives, certain friends are always shifting in and out of angel mode for us. Some of them rarely shift out of it. We come to expect it, to take it for granted. It is wonderful, but we no longer think of it as special. Well, it's important, but we don't think of it as unusual or different, because it becomes so familiar. You know what I mean. It is why we have Mother's Day, and birthdays, and most of our special days . . . to remind us to refresh our awareness of some of the most important blessings that perhaps lull us to sleepfulness by their very constancy. Anyone who tracks you through your growing-up years has got to be an angel. Nobody said anything about perfect. Perfect or not, none of us make it without some angels. For us, at least, they are God's messengers: "Welcome to Life. Learn and grow. Trust and receive. Someday learn to give as well." I am stretching nothing. Such people are legitimate angels.

Much more mysterious, though seldom quite as significant, are the people who suddenly show up at special times for us. Donald Spitler, when I was maybe eleven years old, came to speak at our church. It was one of those special-emphasis events that lasted for three days in a row. I'd never seen him before, though most everybody in our church circles knew of him. What he said was over my head, but somehow it moved me. He got wind of it and arranged to have my mother drive me all the way into Whittier, to his office, for a "chat." I was hugely impressed. I've never seen him since. Somehow, that man left a strong mark on me. Over the years, every time I think of it or hear his name, I feel grateful . . . though I'm not quite sure for what. I don't really mean to tell you about him—I'm trying to get you to remember your own angels.

Walter Pray was the speech teacher where I went to high school. He told me once, three years later, that he had seen a lot of scared kids in his time, but he never knew anybody who suffered the tortures of the damned like I did every time I had to give a speech. On top of that, I had a terrible lisp, a minor stutter, and a problem with what they used to call getting "tongue-tied." It wasn't really tied down, but sometimes when it moved, none of the right noises would come out. (I know . . . that still happens. But not in the way it did then.)

Hour after hour, month after month, Walter Pray worked with me after school. I'm sure he hoped that after the one required course, I would disappear. But I had to keep signing up for his courses. I had to learn to talk. To this day, I have no idea why he did it. No pay. No recognition. But he had studied to be a speech therapist—and if anybody ever needed one, there I was. But how did I get there? Whittier High School was only four miles away from my home. How did I end up in Fullerton, eight miles away, and stumble into maybe the only man in the state of California who could and would help me? I don't really mean to be telling you about Walter Pray—I'm trying to get you to remember your own angels.

I mean it. I preach this sermon hoping that every one of you will take a pencil and paper sometime soon and write down a list of the names of the special people who have stepped into your life when you needed them—especially the ones who just seemed to drop in "out of nowhere." It is an astounding thing to simply recall them on paper. And once you put down a few names, a whole string of others begins to come slowly back out of the memory banks. You have all been sent angel after angel—enough to shake the most ardent atheist to the roots. But for you, it will be gratitude and pleasure . . . and maybe the recall of some former life-themes that have grown dimmer than they should.

And finally, what about the angels that are not people? That could be anything from beyond the ranks of mortal earth, if there be any. What do you think? What can we say about such a thing? If there are messengers of God that are human (and we might have included animals and other earthly creatures), are there also angels from the spirit realms? In the King James translation, they are called "ghosts." But you know what is left of that word: Casper, and Halloween, and a few horror movies. What a fate for a word so high!

However, one of the main reasons I decided to go ahead with this sermon is the fact that I keep running into people who have encounters with spirit-beings in some fashion or another—and sometimes you shyly mention it to me . . . but you don't tell each other. That perpetuates the feeling that "I must be weird, and if I told anybody else, they would think I was crazy." Doubtless some would. But a lot more would say, "You know, that's really interesting and important to me. I've been wondering about an experience of my own, if you're willing to hear about it."

Some have encounters that seem to be with spirits of loved ones who have passed on. That's fine in the stories, but in "real" life it can be both entrancing and frightening.

Others encounter spirits that seem forbidding or friendly, evil or clothed in light. Some say that the Holy Spirit, who now deals with each one of us personally, has made the concept of guardian angels obsolete. But people with a very well-developed prayer life, and with long experience of the presence of the Holy Spirit, still have experiences with angels as well. C.S. Lewis called them "the Eldil." And have you read THE SCREWTAPE LETTERS? If there are angels, are there also devils dogging our steps? Oh my, I really hesitate to say such things out loud, in the open. It does sound so medieval, doesn't it? Or maybe it sounds a little earlier than that. Do you remember Jesus in Gethsemane? "Father, if thou art willing, remove this cup from me; nevertheless, not my will but thine be done." It is so impressive, we miss the next verse: "And there appeared to him an angel from heaven, strengthening him." (Luke 22:43) Did even Jesus need and have a guardian angel(s)?

My plea, however, is not for you to believe one particular way, or to disbelieve a particular way. My plea is that you talk to each other. You might even start today over coffee. Start asking each other: Have you ever had an encounter that made you wonder about angels?

Some people might think this is not a very practical sermon. But if there *are* angels and we are making it harder for them to get their messages through to us, that has practical implications! It might be a lot more important than some other topics we spend a lot of time on.

Please, make a list (with paper and pencil when you get home) of all the human angels you have encountered on your journey so far. And from time to time, when you get a chance, ask each other: Have you had any experiences that make you wonder if there are angels?

Wouldn't it be something, if you discovered that you really do have a guardian angel . . .

Matthew 5:11-12; John 16:21-22; Romans 5:1-5;
Philippians 4:4-7; I Peter 4:12-14; Revelation 19:4-7

Week Thirty-Nine

IS IT OKAY TO BE HAPPY?

Johnny Carson used to say, "You can tell it's going to be a bad day when your twin sister forgets your birthday." That does indeed have a novel twist to it, and tickles the funny bone. But I can think of a forgetting even more outlandish: a Christian forgetting to celebrate the dawn of Easter day. Of course, we celebrate it every Sunday. That is what the day is for, and why we set it aside. In a sense, we celebrate the resurrection every day that we wake up and remember God's love and Christ's presence with us. But Easter Sunday itself?! Who can stay in bed!? Who can fail to greet the dawn!? Is it possible to know anything of Jesus of Nazareth and not realize that this is the day of days!? No other independence day can touch it. No birthday can compete. Christmas itself is a pale harbinger, and indeed nothing, without Easter.

We are not always happy just because we are supposed to be. And sometimes, to our chagrin, we hit a mood when it is inappropriate to be happy, and we don't quite know what to do about it. But that is a minor inconvenience. Moods are always coming and going. This is still our day of joy, and no bad mood can last very long in its light.

Some of us were talking last week, and the subject came around to people we have known who just didn't seem to feel right unless they were suffering and sacrificing. At first we were feeling a little superior, being a little flippant about the whole thing. But soon we were in over our heads. We realized that we have the same problem ourselves.

What is it about the Christian Faith that seems so frequently to turn its advocates into people of concerned and somber visage?

It is true, isn't it, that prayer and Bible Study and pondering the Ways of God and the things we suspect God wants from us—well, it's serious business, and we get pretty serious about it. Having just come through Lent thinking about vows, and the meaning of Atonement, and the events surrounding the Cross—that does get us to thinking about hard realities. And the sheer effort of trying to understand things that shade from history into mystery is enough to furrow our brows.

Now suddenly we're supposed to be all happy, and light, and joyful. And why not? Our Lord is risen, and victory is ours because of His love for us! Why do we have to have answers to all the questions about the how and the when and the why of it?

Nevertheless, most of us have trouble with this business about being happy. We know it isn't because of our circumstances. We are well-clothed, well-fed, well-housed. We have each other. We have the love of God in Jesus Christ. We are engaged in an adventure called "Eternal Life." Nothing can separate us from the love of Christ. We are even out in the middle of the beautiful Puget Sound, on a magnificent day, on a fabulous boat provided by caring members of our own parish—who do it just to be nice to us! Can you imagine how many people in the world would call us lucky? I mean, if we aren't happy, can anybody ever hope to be happy?

There remains one problem, though, doesn't there? And it is a doozy! What if we don't have a right to be happy? What if it is making the gods or the fates of the future angry that we are so lucky now? Worst of all, what if it means we are crass and mean and uncaring to be happy—when so many other people are starving, hurt, hopeless and alone? Aye, there's the rub! Can we allow ourselves to be happy? Can we give ourselves permission to be happy—in the face of all that?

So you see, an Easter morning like this puts us in quite a bind. We start to rejoice. We want to celebrate and be grateful for what God has done. It all tugs at our hearts, and our minds, and our souls . . . and we start to feel the lifting, the joy rising.

But as it mounts, something else struggles within us to drag it back down. It's only a boat; I've seen the Sound before, lived here for years; the sun probably won't even shine; look at that kid over there—sure doesn't behave the way I would raise a kid to behave . . . etc.

That is only subterfuge, of course. That's just the technique. What really pushes the joy back down is the conviction that we have no right to it. We don't have permission to feel that good, or at least not to admit it on the outside. So, as Charlie Brown said, "We pray ourselves out of it." We should be thinking about the poor; planning more effective ways to bring peace; feeling compassion for the sick. Who has time for happiness here (in this world)? Never mind the fact that unhappy people breed unhappiness, are less effective, and create more problems than they solve, no matter how hard they work. Never mind the fact that happy people can care and work and feel compassion quite as well as—no, much better than—unhappy people.

It is a real issue, all the same. If we have friends who are grieving—friends who have suffered a loss, or who have encountered a serious failure—does it not seem somehow disloyal for us to be happy? And how often in my life have I known a time when none of my friends were in grief? I cannot think of a single time. Somebody I know or somebody I love and care about is always in some kind of serious grief or loss or peril. If that is not true for you, you do not know or love very many people. So where is there room for happiness? Can we never celebrate Easter, say "thank you" to Jesus, enjoy each other's company with unguilty and exuberant joy?

It was not recently, but the memory is still clear: A day when I had a funeral at 11 a.m., a wedding at 2 p.m., and another funeral at 5 p.m. It was in New England, where tradition is that people file by the open casket at funerals, and most of us hadn't learned yet to remember our Easter joy and confidence at such times. I remember walking into the wedding atmosphere after the first funeral, and feeling outraged at the merriment. Didn't these people know they were going to die? That indeed we had just buried a very special friend?! No, it was an entirely different crowd, and they had love and babies and high-hope thoughts on their minds. Of course they should, I realized just in time. Why should my mourning intrude into their wedding day? I tried to readjust my emotions. And I made it, too, by the time I left the reception . . . just in time to join the third group. I was all smiles and warmth and full of the energy of the wedding party (not what you're thinking), and suddenly it was clear that my mood was not fitting, and was in fact disturbing to the mourners around me.

What I'm trying to lead up to is the affirmation that knowing Easter gives us a mandate to be happy. Knowing Christ's resurrection is our permission to be happy, to carry joy with us all the time—regardless of whether it is wedding time or funeral time. Indeed, Easter outshines weddings and lifts funerals, and it is a joy and a happiness that should go with us into every occasion, with all people . . . and yes, whether they wish to share it, or understand it, or not.

We are the Easter People. Easter is our truth. And there is no problem or pain or turmoil or danger anywhere that can undercut or close down Easter. Therefore, nothing outranks or countermands our happiness. That is the change that is coming over us as we come more and more to believe.

Sometimes we remember the poor, the homeless, the hopeless . . . and it kills our happiness. Sometimes we also consider how far short of the mark we are in our own living, how much of our true potential is still unrealized. And that makes us feel unworthy to claim any happiness. First we should get ourselves together, get our disciplines rolling, get more accomplishments to our credit . . . and then maybe there will be time to think about being happy. That is what we say to ourselves.

Do unhappy people ever reach their true identity or approach their potential? Is happiness a reward for what we accomplish, or the awakening of gratitude for what God has done for us? How we do hold on to the LAW . . . to pride . . . to staying in control . . . to doing it for ourselves! Along that way, it is said, there lies no happiness. I've always sort of believed that, like, "because you're supposed to." And I could see that there was some real truth to it. The principles seemed sound and all. But down underneath, it still seemed—how do we tell it to ourselves?—it still seemed even more true that I would find happiness after I had worked hard enough, achieved enough, earned my way enough into security and acclaim. Then I could have what I wanted, do what I wanted, and be with the people I wanted. And that would be real happiness—not some sun coming up in the morning to remind me of the power and presence and love of Almighty God.

But I was wrong again. Happiness comes in trusting God. Happiness comes whenever I will allow it. If I don't beat it off with a stick because I don't deserve it, or because everything isn't perfect here, or because there is still a lot to do and there are people who are hurting . . . when I don't beat it off with a club, happiness just keeps winging in. It has nothing to do with outer circumstances. It has everything to do with the love and presence of God.

All my life I have said to people that happiness wasn't very important to me—that it wasn't something I expected, or went after, or even particularly wanted. Imagine my chagrin and embarrassment to discover that I am starting to become a happy person. I don't even know what to do with it! But I keep discovering, even in the midst of things that used to get me very upset, or frightened, or sad . . . I keep discovering that happiness is just sitting there—like the big collie dog I used to have—sitting there just waiting for that one word of permission to come bounding in. I don't have to find it, or manufacture it, or earn it, or deserve it. God in Christ has taken care of all that. The resurrection is collateral on the deal. I just have to be humble enough to receive it, despite all my reasons for being more comfortable with suffering and sacrifice.

Not all stories have a happy ending in the here and now. Happiness doesn't depend on that. But I was impressed by the story of Simon Pereins (as told by Guillermo Ochoa, a feature writer for a Mexico City daily newspaper). Pereins was arrested under the Inquisition back in the seventeenth century, and then thrown into a dungeon cell. To some small degree, at least, we can imagine what that would feel like—confined to a dark dungeon—especially if we knew that to be arrested was virtually the same as being found guilty.

That was pretty much the case with the Inquisition. No one was released. It was the end of your life to be arrested. The very best you could do was linger on in a cell that was dark, damp and full of bugs, hunger and disease. That would be your whole life until you died. What could you do?

What Simon Pereins did was mix paint. He took clay from the floor of the cell and took some of his food, and he made it into paint. Then he took fragments of cloth, strings and straw—from his clothes, the blanket and the floor—and made them into a paintbrush. He used his cell door as a canvas, and on the door he painted a picture of Mary and the Child Jesus. This was in the year 1667. The picture was so beautiful that his Inquisitors were convinced that he had seen a heavenly vision, and they set him free.

The picture still exists, and is called the *Altar Del Perdon (The Altar of Pardon)*.

I don't believe Simon Pereins painted thinking he would be released. Neither the painting nor his release did anything to free the other prisoners or to stop the horror of the Inquisition. But if you're a painter, it's best to paint. If you're a teacher, it's best to teach. If you're a farmer, or a banker, or a cook, or whatever—it is best to go on being who you are, doing what you do best. It is the difference between being happy and being sad.

Of course, Simon Pereins is dead now anyway. A long time has passed since 1667. So what difference does it make that they released him? Not much—in fact, none . . . except for Easter. This is only the beginning!

It is time for Jesus' people to accept happiness again. Try to remember that you don't have to wait for an Inquisition before you start painting. But whether the Inquisitions come or go, we know about Easter, and we are happy. We are the Easter People and we know . . . HE IS RISEN!

SECTION FOUR

AUTUMN

Ephesians 6:1-20

Week Forty

PRINCIPALITIES & POWERS

The sixth chapter of Ephesians is fascinating indeed, if you take it to be part of Holy Scripture. Many people take it to be some curious comments from an archaic time—meaning, it's interesting . . . if you like history. Imagine a time when people thought children should obey their parents, instead of vice versa. What must it have been like way back then? And how curious to advise slaves to be really good at what they do.

We could now come up with all sorts of opinions and observations about such matters. But if it is Scripture, that is a whole different matter. Then we are the children, and the parents, and the workers, and the bosses . . . and here are principles that are supposed to be operating in our lives, and affecting our behavior, and enlightening our understanding . . . and the more they do, the closer our lives will be to the pattern and purpose our Creator has for us.

Scripture is not inerrant, and not always obvious. Paul was not always right, nor did he pretend to be. I am not suggesting that we swallow Scripture whole, without chewing or digesting it. We are requested and required to "worship God with all of our minds." If it is Scripture, however, we approach with respect, with regard, with the expectation that we will find truth if we seek it.

None of you know any slaves, for instance. Is this passage then out-of-date and no longer worthy of our consideration? I know all kinds of people who still feel like slaves in various situations. Indeed, I have never met any person who was employed who has not found considerable help and light by contemplating this passage, once they have dipped beneath the surface and applied it to their own situation.

That is but one minor tidbit of the message of Ephesians. It is an altogether remarkable letter full of deep theological perspectives and practical advice. It is challenging and compelling. Christians have loved it and struggled with it generation after generation. We are at the tail end of the message today. That is, Paul is summing up, gathering all the loose strings together.

"Finally, be strong in the Lord and in the strength of his might. Put on the whole armor of God, that you may be able to stand against the wiles of the devil." Or as another translation puts it: "Finally then, find your strength in the Lord, in his mighty power . . . . "

Find your strength in the Lord. Paul is pretty certain about what will happen if we try to go on in our own strength. We can give it about the same chance if we try to depend on military strength, political strength, economic strength or academic strength. "Find your strength in the Lord, in his mighty power. Put on all the armor which God provides, so that you may be able to stand firm against the devices of the devil."

I would like to talk about that strength, and the armor which God provides. I would because I need it, and I need to have it clear, and I need so often to be reminded. So I'm going to do that in a couple of weeks or so. It seemed to me that I should give you fair warning. I can just imagine the communication hangups which are going to occur when we get into that. (Some intentional, and some innocent, no doubt.) In fact, we are already into it, aren't we?

Some of us are still trying to operate off of our own strength in this church, and predictably that is causing some mayhem. God is Creator—and without God's strength, this life does not run right. However, that is mild in comparison to trying to walk the Christian Path in one's own might. The life of the Christian is designed for conscious obedience to God—for willing submission to the guidance of the Holy Spirit. It will not and cannot begin to work under any other premise.

Once we claim faith in Jesus Christ—sign up as followers, so to speak—we get "put," "sent," "stuck" in situations where we are totally over our heads except for the support and help of Christ. *Find your strength in the Lord.* All other help is the proverbial clutching at straws. All other help is like the ironic spitwad in hell. Why do we keep getting surprised by that? How could we expect it to be otherwise?

We need to talk about putting on the whole armor of God, but that means we have figured out that we are in a fight. Some of us don't believe in Satan, so we end up blaming all the mayhem on other people. No wonder we get discouraged, and start thinking people are no damn good. Living in such a reality, pretty soon we have to start picking and choosing our acquaintances with greater and greater care—trying to find a way to associate with only those very few who are "different," "special," not like most of the others. With that view, the only people we can really trust are people we don't know very well.

All people are in a battle—a spiritual battle—whether they know it, or admit it, or not. All people struggle with a dual nature (at least). There is darkness and light within. There is good and evil within. There is a constant choice going on. There is help, support, backup for either choice! Is it possible that any of us have failed to notice? Can anybody have missed realizing, after having been alive this long, that sometimes our choices are cruel, that sometimes they are destructive, that sometimes the urge to negate is strong?

Yes, the urge to do good is immensely powerful, too. We wish to help others, to make a contribution, to strengthen someone else's efforts to accomplish.

It even gets mixed up a little. Sometimes we want to bring good, but it has to be our way. We feel we have to be in control of situations or people in order to do them all the good we want to do for them. Then we get good mixed with evil, and become all confused, and wonder if there is neither, or if all things are merely gray.

How can anybody have been alive for all this time and not know that they are in a spiritual battle? Have we not all tried to make it on our own strength enough to know what comes of that?

Supposedly none of us come to places like this—to churches, places dedicated to Jesus Christ and His WAY—supposedly nobody comes here very much until they have become thoroughly disillusioned with making it on their own. People don't choose the church—they don't turn their lives and their wills over to the guidance of the Holy Spirit—until they are desperate to find another, higher way to proceed with their lives. *Find your strength in the Lord.* If you have any other aces up your sleeve—any other good alternatives to turn to—you don't really belong here yet. That is not to say you are not welcome here. It just doesn't stick, this Christianity, until we are willing to go to any lengths— make any changes required—to have life in Christ Jesus.

So Paul continues: "Our fight is not against human foes, but against cosmic powers, against the authorities and potentates of this dark world, against the superhuman forces of evil in the heavens." That's it. That's verse 12 (REB). That's what I wanted to ask you about today. Is that Scripture for you? Or is that just some ancient person's illusionary mythology? "We are not contending against flesh and blood, but against the principalities, against the powers, against the world rulers of this present darkness, against the spiritual hosts of wickedness in the heavenly places." (verse 12, RSV)

Usually, it seems, when we think of the struggles we have in business, in trying to survive; or in marriage, in trying to develop lasting and loving relationships; or in politics; or in issues of peace, or ecology, or justice; or even in trying to improve and perfect ourselves—our normal assumption is that our fight, our struggle, is with human foes: human ignorance, or human recalcitrance, or human stubbornness, or human fear, or human anger. Yet Scripture says, "Our fight is not against human foes."

Isn't that something?! Have we really become so self-centered that we think we are the only force that matters, the only thing that makes a difference? Have we finally concluded that we are the only intelligent life-form there is—the only intelligence that truly exists in the universe?

Our experience sides with Paul, even if our vocabularies have become modern. Paul—and, incidentally, Jesus, Judaism, Hinduism, Zoroastrianism . . . all ancient peoples and religions and their adherents down to the present time—said, claimed and believed that we are not alone—that other intelligences exist, and not all of them are friendly.

Our fight is not against human foes. What a different perspective we suddenly get! The people we have trouble with— they are not the real foes. They are struggling with powers and influences that ensnare, twist, corrupt—even as we are ourselves. They do not need hating; they need rescuing. They are not the true adversary—even though at times it is easy to see it at that level. That is much of the secret of how Christians can love their enemies. They know that all people are children of God—that they are family, potential friends. They are *all* wonderful—if they can get loose from the dark powers that are holding them.

Two people get married. They have high hopes and great dreams, and it is clear that what they want for themselves and each other is probably quite close to what God wants for them, too. But then they get to thinking that it is just the two of them. And they discover some disagreements, some communication problems, some character imperfections. And they work to keep the vision they have of life together being beautiful and full of love—but it gets hard! After they work hard enough for long enough and it seems so much harder than it ought to be—and since it's just the two of them together—they start figuring somebody isn't trying like they ought to be. And each one knows it must be the other who is the real evil one, since each one of them is trying as hard as they know how.

When does it finally occur that there is another adversary, and that they aren't going to realize any dreams if they don't start getting help from beyond themselves? *Find your strength in the Lord. Put on the whole armor of God . . .* You put on the whole armor when you know you're in for a real fight—a fight where every inch of ground will be contended, and the fight is to the death. *Our fight is not against human foes.*

How can a husband and wife be in such conflict with each other? I mean, that's insane. They love each other, they need each other, they want to make life better for each other, to enrich each other. Life can't possibly be good for one if it's not good for the other when they live in the same house. It's insane. So why does it take so long for most of us to realize it is insane, and start looking for the real problem? *Our fight is not against human foes.* And marriage is only one tiny example. (Well, maybe not so tiny.)

On the other hand, almost every person experiences moments when they know they get "freed." At times, we get freed from forces that hold us down, or hold us back. Often we don't know exactly how. Usually we are quite amazed at how great the relief is, never having consciously realized how oppressed we were feeling. (Being convinced, of course, that we were alone all the time.)

Music, prayer, time alone, a walk in the mountains, a caring friend, the impact of a child, any of the many kinds of spiritual awakening—and our best expression is that we feel "freed." Something lifts; something that was heavy is taken off; some force loses its grip on us. And then how the energy and hope and love start flowing back in! Very often, in fact most often, the same people are in our picture, and all or most of the same circumstances remain. Yet we are freed. *Our fight is not against human foes.*

Am I trying to drag you back into a medieval world peopled with angels and demons, gods and devils? That is what some of you are thinking, isn't it?

Actually, I don't think of it as medieval—it's more ancient than that. I have my problem with the dark ages too, you know. I just don't understand how some of you can fail to see that we are living in one of the dark ages.

Anyway, it doesn't feel to me like going "back." It is more a matter of waking up. Our fight, as Christians, is with principalities and powers—the rulers of the realms of darkness. It is not with other humans who are brothers and sisters. They get caught and used and oppressed sometimes, just like we do. We all need to be freed—or some call it "saved."

Our tamed-down, civilized names for such powerful and ancient enemies are Anger, Dread, Fear, Despair, Boredom, Depression. But we lose round after round, and increasingly so, because we do not understand the power at work behind such phenomenons. We do not take them seriously! We half suspect we can still "climb out" of these little, inconvenient character traits whenever we really buckle down and make up our minds to do so. Seeing that they are killing so many of our friends, and even us, you would think we would get around to taking care of it sooner! The reality is, we have no chance against such foes in our own might. Being uncertain there is any help at hand against such formidable foes, we try to pretend for as long as we can that there is no fight. Or we simply succumb.

Few people in our day can swallow this kind of perspective in theory alone. I know that. I'm not trying to make things harder for you. But we all need the armor of God, and nobody takes the armor seriously if they don't know about the battle.

So I'm asking: Do you know we are in a great spiritual battle? Are you aware of it at work . . . at home . . . wherever you care . . . even within yourself?

Think of your own struggles with Anger, Fear, Meaninglessness (*ennui*—boredom). Test it out. If the Scripture passage is correct, three axioms will hold true:

1.) You will not make any real headway by your own efforts alone. (Even though it seems logical that you should and could.)

2.) The harder you try, the more enslaved you become. (If the trying is on your own power, that is.)

3.) As you "put on Christ"—turn your life and your will over to God in daily obedience—you begin to experience being freed. (How can you experience feeling freed if there has been no oppression?)

Test it out.

Ephesians 6:10-16

Week Forty-One

TO STAND FIRM

Self-reliance is out of the question. The "principalities and powers" of evil overmatch us, and may only be fought with the aid of the power of Jesus Christ.

Never mind what you think, or what I think, for just a moment. This is what the Apostle Paul is trying to tell us, is it not? This is in essential agreement with the major attitude and message of the New Testament, is it not? This is certainly the keynote of the sixth chapter of Ephesians. We can at least be clear that this is the truth, or part of the truth, as held by our tradition. Christianity does claim that there is Satan—that there are satanic powers, messengers, servants, agents. There are spiritual as well as physical realities. The spiritual dimensions contain powers of darkness as well as powers of light. And both have profound effect and impact on the physical realm, and on what is happening inside and all around us.

Part of the very core of our Gospel is the assertion that Jesus Christ has overcome the powers of Satan. "Death could not hold Him." The confrontation we see in the Crucifixion was not just— not merely—a matter of Jesus running afoul of the Jewish authorities, or of the way the Roman government executed Him. This was going on, to be sure. This was the way it was happening. It clarifies some ghastly, but nevertheless familiar, things about how structure and authority often operate in our world. But this was only at the very surface of what was happening. This was the physically "seeable" details of an incredible confrontation which had been—and was, and is still—going on between the powers of darkness and the powers of light. That is the backdrop and context and assertion of the New Testament. Jesus, on the Cross and in the Resurrection, was overcoming Sin, Death and the

Devil. "Conquered" is the best translation of the word they used. For the first time in earth history, it came clear that the powers of light and love were not as hopelessly overmatched as we had all secretly believed. For the first time in earth history, a light shined in the darkness, and the darkness could not overcome it. It even made us realize that some of the light we had seen before had not been as "overcome" as we had supposed.

Those who noticed . . . those who saw . . . those who believed what happened—were stunned, shocked, incredulous. It wasn't just the story they were seeing on the surface, powerful as that was. But it was also the implications—like endless peals of thunder after a great lightning bolt. They kept clearing their ears, and blinking and rubbing their eyes, and trying to clear their heads and hang on to their pulses and still manage, somehow, to keep breathing. "My God," they said. "This means the forces of light and truth have more power than we ever dared dream or hope! What else could it mean? Did we miss something? Is it just another ruse or trick of the Enemy? No. My God, it's true . . . and we can trust it and go for it." And with great shouts of joy, or deep resolves of a wonderful new anguish, they began throwing away all old life-patterns and all the heavy trappings that went with them. And they did whatever they had to do to spend their time and life with Jesus—or, more accurately, with the Holy Spirit.

However, the ancient enemy was not gone. Satan and all Satan's messengers, servants and traps were still everywhere in the world. Self-reliance was out of the question! No human was a match for such a subtle, powerful, intelligent, well-organized foe. The only difference was that now there was an Advocate . . . a Companion who could stand against the foe, who could and would show up at any time of the day or night to fight with and for us . . . a Spirit Being greater than Satan who could and would "stoop to our weakness" on a daily basis, at any time we had sense enough to cry for help.

That might not have been the way the great philosophers would have put it. But that is approximately the way the individual Christian thought about it, and felt about it. And it was not the

314 BRUCE VAN BLAIR

philosopher, it was that kind of everyday, humble Christian—
with that kind of trust and faith—who carried the light and shaped
the fellowship of believers which has carried the Gospel of Love
and Hope down to our present day.

Self-reliance is out of the question! Evil can only be fought
with the aid of the power of Jesus Christ. That is what Paul knows
and is trying to describe. It is not a few days after his conversion.
The first blush of naiveté has long ago worn off. The zeal and
enthusiasm of that first taste of the acceptance and love of God
in Christ Jesus has now been through at least twenty years of
tempering and testing. Paul has wrestled with the fevers of malaria,
and has been beaten and stoned and shipwrecked and left for
dead. He has made friends, and lost friends, and lived through
the pain of Church Councils at Antioch and Jerusalem that wrench
and divide believers from each other, and sidetrack the work of
the Gospel itself. I'm simply saying there isn't a whole lot that
hasn't happened to Paul to weaken his faith and make him
discouraged, downhearted and cynical. If we are looking for
reasons or excuses, it doesn't help to match hard knocks or
failures or bitter experiences with the apostles.

Satan misses no tricks, leaves no love-bond untested, allows
neither single child nor full army of light to pass by or accomplish
anything if he can help it. Paul is no longer a neophyte. His hope
of heaven is undiminished, and his joy in the companionship of
Christ is obviously very great. But he also knows he is in a fight.
Self-reliance is out of the question. Without Jesus by his side,
Paul knows how long he would last. Of course, for Paul it is worse
than for us. Satan has had a seven-level alarm out on Paul for
several years already. Paul can't make a move without every
ranking demon in the territory looking for some way to stop or
undo him. We know the pattern with those who serve too well:
Gandhi, Martin Luther King, Jr., William Tyndale, and on and on
(i.e., Chrysostom, Thomas Cranmer, Ignatius, Hugh Latimer,
Girolamo Savonarola, Thomas More, Thomas à Becket, Origen,
Polycarp, Raymond Lull . . .)

So here is Paul, chained to a Roman soldier (or at least with a constant guard), awaiting trial for the grave crime of allegiance to Jesus Christ. He is not upset, except that he hopes to speak boldly and fearlessly and tellingly for the cause of Christ. But he also knows and feels the drama that is going on around him and within him—the one that is deeper than the overt details make clear. And he knows that all his fellow Christians are also engaged in this greater, unseen battle in some way. Wanting to make that clear in a helpful way, and hoping to encourage his friends, he searches for an analogy. There beside him is a Roman soldier, and the images of warfare come to mind. Some of us might wish Paul had been in a more poetic mood. Or we suspect that the imagery of warfare is unfortunate because it is so easy to move with it back into feelings of anger and harm that undo the very points they are trying to make. .

Nevertheless, Paul muses . . . and the sixth chapter of Ephesians is what it is. I wouldn't be a bit surprised to learn that Paul was engaging in conversation the soldiers who guarded him (he usually did). And this letter about a different kind of warfare may have been one way he tried to reach them, before sending it along with Tychicus. But that is only my own musing.

The scenario of this analogy is not that of a lone, valiant, hero type. This passage is about a soldier "of the line" whose task—along with that of all the soldiers around him—is to hold the line. Paul's imagery is of a soldier doing his own part in the midst of an army, where, if everyone does their part, the battle will be won. There is no glory, no grandstanding, no fame or acclaim here. You do your own part at your own position, and hope the commanders know what they are doing.

When you really fight evil, nobody is likely to notice it in this realm. (Maybe afterward, looking back, a few will. But not at the time.) And the issue is to stand firm. Hold your place! Keep your position! God—the Holy Spirit—knows what he is doing and will take care of the strategy. Our part is to obey orders and stand firm.

Notice how much this is what Paul is picturing: "Put on all the armor which God provides, so that you may be able to stand

firm against the devices of the devil" (verse 11) . . . "then you
will be able to stand your ground when things are at their worst"
(verse 13) . . . "to complete every task and still to stand" (verse
13b). You can almost begin to hear Winston Churchill. (Yes, well,
Churchill got it from Paul.) "Stand firm, I say" (verse 14).

And why wear the shoes of the gospel of peace? "To give you
firm footing" (verse 15). "Keep watch and persevere" (verse 18).
So the mood and tone are clear. This is not a special or heroic
moment. This is the soldier's basic function, the thing for which
he is trained. Be ready, be watchful, be steady and consistent,
and when each onslaught comes . . . stand your ground, and
withstand the attack, no matter how fierce.

Self-reliance is out of the question. It will absolutely require
the armor that God provides. Nevertheless, once properly armed—
stand firm!

Paul now lists the necessary items in the order in which a
soldier would normally put on those items. FASTEN ON THE
BELT OF TRUTH. The first reaction, since this is such a powerful
passage, is to make this the biggest definition of truth we can
find. So we think things like, "Encircle yourself with all the
knowledge of God's nature and plan and purpose." That's a bit
grand, I suspect, for this image.

The girdle or belt is not really part of the armor. Pants had
not yet been invented. A person didn't want a lot of loose-flowing
cloth flapping around and getting in the way when they needed
to go into action. To run, to work, especially to fight, you "girded
up your loins," as the old language said. Pull all the loose stuff
in, flesh or cloth—get it firmly in place, and get ready to mean
business.

The belt of truth is not high knowledge of the eternal verities,
but the down-to-earth choice of honesty. In a fight with the powers
of evil, we need to have few illusions, few exaggerations, few
excuses, few fantasies about our prowess or our weakness. Put
on the belt of honesty (the capacity to be honest is a close relative
of humility), so you don't get entangled with false postures, or
pride, or unnecessary guilt or fear. Know yourself. Get the belt

cinched up and be who you are—no more and no less. Hard for Satan to play games with you if you have an inner honesty— have no need to color things up, no need to pretend. With God present, who you are will do just fine. Keep it clear and don't try to change it. The belt of truth: "Yes, I really did make that mistake. I am sorry." "No, I did not intend to hurt you, but if you wish to stay hurt that is your decision." "Yes, I would love to." "No, I have no interest in that."

PUT ON THE BREASTPLATE OF RIGHTEOUSNESS. Again it is easy to get the meaning too high. We will hit all the high meanings we need when we get to the shield and helmet. The breastplate, or coat of mail, covers the upper torso and especially protects the heart. I suspect that Paul was thinking not so much about the final righteousness of God at this moment, but rather about our own "love of the right." Remember that Paul is talking about our war with Satanic powers. If they can make us cynical about goodness, or persuade us that we do not really care about doing good, then such wounds will indeed cripple or kill us for any meaningful struggle against evil. We do love the right, love to see justice done, love to do deeds that genuinely help others. We have to protect this heart region. Put on the breastplate of righteousness so Satan can't take an easy shot, and convince us we don't really love the good or care about what happens to others. Goodness is armor against evil. This isn't self-reliance—it is still the armor that God provides, and God is the source of our goodness. But we still need to claim and protect our personal awareness of our own love of the good, our own personal hunger for righteousness.

LET THE SHOES ON YOUR FEET BE THE GOSPEL OF PEACE, TO GIVE YOU FIRM FOOTING. This is a bit strained to our ears. Isaiah 52:7 says: "How beautiful upon the mountains are the feet of him who brings good tidings, who publishes peace, who brings good tidings of good, who publishes salvation." Even that is not easily followed, though we remember it from music we love. It seems to suggest that people who carry good news do not mind the journey, however long or rugged. And what matter ragged or dirty feet, if they are in the service of carrying good news? Those who receive the good news are appreciative of those feet also. Something along those lines seems to be intended. Isaiah is talking about a great deliverance that God is bringing to Israel. And so the passage ends up connected with Jesus in the minds of the early Christians. Christians carry the message of the gospel of God's salvation to all people who will receive and believe it. All of that Paul knows and is alluding to.

Therefore, in the fight against the forces of darkness, if you remember your message—if you are ever ready to speak of Christ's deliverance to any person you find still in bondage—then your feet are on firm ground. Satan will not be able to unbalance you, will not be able to knock you off your feet. If we take our stand on any other message, or see our purpose in any other light, then Paul suspects Satan or his servants will be able to throw us pretty hard.

The gospel of peace (need I remind you?) is *not* peace in this world, or peace *with* this world! It does not mean we are going to be super-nice to everybody, or really polite and ingratiating to Satan or his servants. The gospel of peace is about peace between us humans and God. It is about the reconciliation between us and God that Jesus has made possible. Because of the death and resurrection—and because of the love of God for us that Jesus has revealed—we are no longer in a fight against God, or God's wrath, or God's judgment against us. We have changed sides, and the fight is now against Satan and his reign. That is what the gospel of peace is about—peace between us and God. No other peace is guaranteed, and peace with Satan (which some of us know all too well) is definitely repealed!

That's the shoes. The feet symbolize the foundation, the understanding. Keep a firm footing. Stand on the gospel of your peace with God. And if you're not afraid to mention the same good news to others, it may happen that some of Satan's warriors may switch sides and end up fighting along with you. In any case, that is what the fight is about: peace with God . . . reconciliation with God . . . friendship with God . . . loving God. That's what the fight is about, and what Satan is always trying to break up or undo in any way he can. Peace with God is the issue. Depend on it. Stand on it. Bet your life on it.

We didn't get to the whole armor yet. That leaves us in a precarious position, of course. But maybe at least we know we are in a fight, and maybe we even know which side we are on. It is not a fight against human foes. At least I hope it has come clear to us that self-reliance is out of the question. The fight is too big, too important, and too deadly for that. In this fight, without the power of the Holy Spirit, we don't have a prayer!

Ephesians 6:10-10

Week Forty-Two

THE SEVENTH PROTECTION

There is an old saying about losing the forest for the trees. It can go both ways, as we have all discovered. Sometimes we get so enamored of the vision, the larger picture, that we never get around to doing the details which would bring the vision to reality. There is a saying for that too. "They reject the road and not the goal. But lo, those who reject the road have rejected the goal already." That certainly has been the story of many Christian churches in America in the last fifty years. But that is not the subject of today's sermon.

It is particularly easy, with this passage in the sixth chapter of Ephesians, to get focused on the belt and the breastplate and the shoes . . . and actually forget what Paul is really talking about. Today we will want to add the shield and helmet and sword. Only, we need to keep such details in perspective. The imagery of warfare and armor, if we are not careful, can add to our tendency to get sidetracked. It is easy for us to get our aggressiveness triggered, and to consciously or unconsciously start thinking about this passage in terms of causes, crusades or problems we are having with various individuals, institutions or organizations at the moment. Some of us would love to have God "armor us" so we could march into some frays of our own choosing and be invincible, victorious and heroic—and become famous, and hopefully rich, in the process. Such thoughts, of course, have never crossed my mind. But you should be warned and wary. This is not what Paul is talking about.

Paul has specifically stated that our fight is not against human foes. It is against principalities and powers. Those of you attending the 9 a.m. Adult Class learned that these are technical terms for two of the nine choirs of fallen (or rebellious) angels. There is no

320

time for the details here, but that makes the passage doubly fascinating. Specifically, it makes it clear that this armor imagery is not intended for our pet peeves or causes, or for our battles with one another. In fact, the passage reminds us that our human foes are actually caught in Satan's bondage, even as we ourselves often are—and all of us need to be freed, not pitted against each other. It is indeed the work and purpose of Jesus Christ to free us from this very bondage.

Then let us be clear and keep clear: It is classic Christian wisdom that we live in a fallen—imperfect, rebellious—dimension. This world is not heaven! Things are not running here the way God designed and created them to run. All of us participate in this mayhem at all times, at least to some degree. We do not fully understand who we are, and what we are here for. We do not comprehend the true worth or value of each other. This is basic Christian theology—1A!!! We are separated—alienated—from our Creator to some degree. There is flak and mist and confusion in this, our primary relationship. We do not know God. We do not trust God freely and completely. We do not submit to or obey God with willing, childlike trust in all things and in all our affairs. And life will not, and cannot, work right or run right unless or until the creatures know, trust, love and obey their Creator.

We keep forgetting this primary condition, known formally in some circles as "The Fall." So sometimes we get shocked when we encounter trouble, or evil. Sometimes we are amazed when we make mistakes. Sometimes we experience injustice, or sorrow, or failure, or defeat—and we act surprised, as if we thought this wouldn't or couldn't or shouldn't happen. Where do we think we are?! Heaven?!!!

Strangely enough, we do keep forgetting. It is the mark of our origins. The soul or spirit within is created by God, and does not ever quite get used to this realm. Some spirit-memory seems to linger. (Or if we are newly created, the imprint of eternity is still stamped within us.) The evidence of our origin and destiny is quite strong within us, and it creates many problems for us here. We do innately think things "should" be perfect. Where does that come from? We do instinctively think *we* should be perfect. What incredible audacity! Yet we cannot shake it. We are ever discontent with less.

Mariana, some of you know, has had a tendency to be late to wherever she goes. One day it finally dawned on me what the missing link was. Her mind cannot fathom the idea of needing time to travel. Some residue of the spirit realm in her expects to transport from place to place instantaneously. Her mind does not want to remember, or face the fact on a daily basis, that the wings are gone. They aren't supposed to be gone! How enormously painful to have to realize that they are gone. All of us have some places in our lives where we simply cannot or will not admit that we are where we are—with the wings gone.

Is that also why so many of us fill our schedules too full? We keep forgetting, and keep expecting to accomplish a week's work in a single day. And sometimes we try to love too many people too well, or we go through times when we try to run away from all of it because it is so frustrating and painful and so hard to manage, with the wings gone.

In like manner, it is hard to remember that all of our loved ones will die here—that we ourselves will not be here long. We hear it, we know it is true, sort of, but our minds simply will not accept it on a daily basis. So we forget . . . and get devastated by the most obvious and certain fact in all the world. God has never ever promised, suggested or hinted that we would not all face death in many forms over and over and over in this world. But we keep acting shocked, angry, surprised by death—as if we were already in the eternal realms. Strange! And yet, is it not also one of the clearest hints of our true origin and destiny?

Well, we could and maybe should go on about this trouble we have remembering where we are. My point, however, is that whether we remember or not, this is Paul's perspective. It is classic Christian wisdom that we live in a realm that has trouble remembering, knowing and obeying its Creator. It is also certain, in Christian teachings, that this alienation is a reflection of warfare or conflict between the powers of darkness and the powers of light—between satanic legions and God's faithful. Only, we keep trying to make that seem big and wicked and ridiculous, so we won't have to understand it. Every time I want to do things my own way for my own reasons, I am satanic. It is as simple as that. Satan is just a cosmic prodigal son—a higher-dimensional spoiled brat.

Every time any of us wants to do things our own way instead of God's way, we serve Satan and strengthen his kingdom. It is as simple as that. No evil was intended, from our perspective. "Probably no evil is intended from that," we say, innocently.

It is not only Christian wisdom that Satan is largely in control in our realm (or world), but that most human beings are only dimly or partially aware of it. That is, we know the ways in which we are unhappy, lonely, angry, afraid, etc., but in spite of all that, we seem to be only dimly conscious of our bondage. It is the exception rather than the rule that we become aware of our slavery to satanic principles, individual power, control, autonomy, privilege. We even think that our real problem is that we haven't learned to be better and more effective at getting our own way.

So the whole human race tends to be in denial of its real disease and danger. At least that is the Christian perspective and belief. And Christianity goes on to talk about a Savior—a deliverer from this sin, this bondage.

The normal and expected reaction to the Christian message is: "You're crazy! I don't need a Savior. All I need, if indeed I will admit I need anything, is a little more money, a little more power, a little more authority. Then I would be happy. Then I wouldn't have any of these fears or angers or imperfections any longer. So if you want to do something for me—if you really care, really love me (like you Christians always talk about)—you'll give me some food, or money, or power, or something useful. But keep your Jesus. I don't need a Savior! I'm not under any bondage!"

Yes, Christians have been hearing that refrain from those clearly caught in this world's bondage for as long as they have been in business. Strangely enough, today you can hear it from inside the church almost as much as you do outside the church.

And no, that isn't terribly surprising either. Is not Satan a great strategist? First, a campaign to get people to disbelieve in his existence. The best technique for doing that is to get us to think we are too intelligent and too in control of our own lives to believe in him. Second, get us to believe that our real problems are because of other people, not because of our own bondage to Satan. Thirdly, confuse, divide and, if possible, silence the only crew that really knows what's going on. That would just about do it, don't you think? Then the whole world can go to hell with everybody working harder and harder to do more and more good against all the bad guys. And that way nobody ever will figure out what really went wrong. So we will keep revising the bylaws, and electing new leaders, and starting new groups and movements, and trying to punish those who don't help or cooperate. But no matter how well we do it, or how hard we try, it won't have any impact on our real problem: being out of touch with our Creator.

We are out of our rightful and worshipful relationship with God. That is all that is wrong. It is our only purpose and function to love and obey God. Nothing else is needed. There is animosity and alienation between us and God, and it needs healing, reconciling. Everything else will straighten if that straightens.

Paul sees it, and tries to help us see it. He wants us to wear the full armor of God so that Satan cannot take away our freedom and get us back under his bondage. That is the purpose of the armor Paul is talking about—to keep us protected against Satan's efforts to get us back under his control. Satan will try to do that by making us feel guilty and worthless, or by making us feel important and self-sufficient. Either way will work just fine. Satan will do that by making us feel discouraged, depressed and useless, or by making us feel strong, invulnerable and proud. Either way will work just fine. Satan will do that by making us feel terribly afraid, or by convincing us that there is nothing to fear. Either way will work just fine.

So Paul says we should put on the armor. And now the

function of the armor comes pretty clear. TAKE UP THE SHIELD OF FAITH against the flaming darts of the evil one—the accusations, the guilt, the fear, the discouragement. The shield of faith means, "God loves me because of the way God is, not because of my merit." That is made absolutely clear on the Cross. And indeed, no dart can stick or burn against that conviction. Jesus revealed what God is really like. It doesn't depend on us. Satan has no weapon against justification by faith. "Above all," says Paul, "take up the shield of faith" in Jesus Christ which allows you to know for sure that the distance between you and God is not God's idea, or desire, or judgment, or punishment. God wants you—loves you. The words are old. But the heart that finally hears them is released from Satan's grip, and protected from every dart Satan can hurl. *Above all take up the shield of faith.* Justification by faith, not by works—not by merit, success, bank account, good deeds, heredity, nationality, or correct political views—but by faith in God's undeserved, unearned love for God's own children.

And TAKE THE HELMET OF SALVATION to put over your head, so in case your heart is not connected to your mind, your head will start knowing that everything is going to turn out okay for you. I'm obviously not talking about this world, or normal human ways of evaluating who has "made it," or with what kinds of toys. God is not only love but POWER. And if God loves you, God will save you—meaning, your place in the eternal family is assured and guaranteed. If we don't know that, Satan will beat our heads in. That is exactly what Paul means! Without the helmet of salvation, Satan will beat our heads in with fear, anxiety, endless doubts, and images of horrid things happening. It is when we are frightened that we do our worst deeds, trying vainly to protect ourselves from things real or imagined—and if we are frightened enough, we don't care how. *Take the helmet of salvation.*

And TAKE THE SWORD OF THE SPIRIT, WHICH IS THE WORD OF GOD. You can think Paul means the Bible, if you want to. You know how much I keep after you to read and study the Bible—not that some of you pay any attention—so it is tempting

to use this passage for a little backup and extra incentive. But
that is not what Paul means. He is talking about how God will
give you the words you need to speak when it is your turn to bear
witness. That is, if you stay in contact with the Holy Spirit, the
Spirit will speak through you when you are called before courts,
councils, Satan's servants, whatever. Paul himself is about to face
the Roman emperor in the scariest and most important trial of his
life. That is clearly on his mind, and he is counting on this sword—
not his own eloquence, but the Spirit's inspiration.

It is sad that we have no report of this scene and speech—if
indeed the Roman court allowed Paul to speak. We don't because
all of the Roman Christians left Paul in the lurch—left him to
face the trial alone. Paul apparently lost this court battle and his
life. (Which does not mean that the Spirit didn't speak eloquently
through him; the Spirit persuades but does not coerce.) But we
can be pretty sure that Paul was not surprised, either at this
desertion by his fellow Christians, or at the decision of the Roman
court, because he remembered where he was—in a broken world.
And Paul would have died by now, in this world, no matter what
the Roman emperor decided. So the only thing that really mattered
to him was his staying faithful.

Oh, so much more I wanted to mention! Like how some of
you have such trouble with the notion of spiritual "dark" beings.
How strange. It is the only logical possibility to match the very
faith that you have. That is to say, you are very concerned with
and eager to believe in the premise that God does not condemn
anyone to hell or annihilation—yet you say that, for those who
do not fully or even partially awaken here, you expect God to go
on working with them in the higher realms until they *do* catch
on.

Well, what is God going to do with these beings he has
salvaged from the death of this world, while they continue to
exist and continue to live "out of God's will" in the next realms?
If God puts up with their remaining rebellion, disobedience and
willfulness, then they are by definition the "dark spiritual beings"
you suddenly don't want to believe exist. As Jesus said, souls in

this world or the next "who are not with me, are against me." And beings not in tune with God and working with God cause enormous damage—just like we keep discovering here. Only, they have more potential in the higher realms. You can't have it both ways. If you want God to be more "merciful" to sinners, it means greater suffering for the faithful. That's been the dilemma between mercy and justice since Genesis, chapter two. Where have you been?

As we move on from this sixth chapter of Ephesians, perhaps more regretfully for me than for some of you, I must draw your attention to one more thing. We have looked at six items that Paul calls "the whole armor of God." The belt, the breastplate, the shoes . . . the shield, the helmet, the sword. Six is a good number for protection with physical affairs, but seven is the holy number. Seven is the number of spiritual power. There are seven Archangels. There are seven days in the week, and the Sabbath, or seventh, is the holy day. There are seven moving lights, and seven candles represent them in all Biblical history. Seven is the number of spiritual power. Do you really think Paul is going to leave you with six? Paul is Pharisee through and through, by his own word, and he is rabbinically trained and spiritually very aware and trained and experienced and faithful. Do you really think Paul is going to leave you with six?

Paul designed his list with seven protections from the beginning, though many have missed it. In such a list, the seventh is always the last, the most important, and the most powerful item of all. I have told you a bit about the six. But you really should pay the most attention to the seventh protection. What is the seventh? Go get a Bible. Study the passage.

Genesis 39

Week Forty-Three

WHEN GOD DESERTS

Do you all long to grow in wisdom? It is an old assumption of mine that everybody would like to be wise, that each of us has as one of our goals an image of ourselves as one who, having lived on this earth through years of searching and striving, has come to the place of discernment. We would like to be among those who can see beneath the glitter and flash to the true values; who can look at the common and discern beneath the surface the caring of the Creator; who can experience the swirling, conflicting, confusing currents of all the busyness and activity and commotion going on, and still detect the steady flow of God's redeeming purpose underneath it all.

Wisdom is such an elusive virtue, however. Many wonder if it truly exists except as a word we use for those who agree with us. Unlike knowledge, wisdom is seldom among the practical and valued commodities of our world. It's nobody's fault. It's not that we wouldn't pay for wisdom if we could figure out where and when to get some. The trouble is, we are never sure where wisdom lies until it is too late. That is to say, wisdom is always recognized by our world in retrospect. Individuals may find it, or even themselves become wise. But the rest of us cannot tell for sure until after the story is over and we can look back on how things worked out.

In any case, wisdom is not knowledge. All the knowledge in the world cannot make a person wise, just as all the facts in the world do not add up to a single truth. Wisdom is never the foe of knowledge, but wisdom puts knowledge together in special ways that reveal patterns of meaning and purpose, direction and truth. Wisdom is to knowledge what faith is to reason. It takes that next step beyond. It discerns God, and with the awareness of God comes purpose and pattern, choices to be made, assignments given, and principles to be honored. The drama of Life begins, with all of its possibilities and terrors, if God really exists. Then we aren't just "here" by accident. All of it actually matters, including us and how we live every moment of every day. That is where we left off. The fear of the Lord (or the trust of the Lord) is the beginning of wisdom.

Getting into all that, it seems like it might be interesting to take a break—a kind of field trip—and go look for a while at a man of wisdom, and maybe get some further glimmer of what this is all about. Fortunately, we have records to provide us with such information, and all of us have copies of the record. So we don't have to start from scratch. I can reintroduce you to a man you already know very well, or we couldn't get anywhere in the time we have. Also, we do not have to wonder or argue about whether or not he was wise. The story is known and proved out, and has been for four thousand years. Joseph stands among the greatest sages and seers of all time. He was that, and he will go on being that, whether we like him, or agree with him, or learn from him . . . or not.

In his time, Joseph saved the Egyptian empire from mass starvation, chaos and ruin. In the process, he also saved the core of the Israelite nation. He therefore stands as one of the pivotal figures in "Western" history. Without him, God would doubtless have found another way. Nevertheless, we cannot imagine our history without him. Clearly the whole river (of history) changed its course by the influence and contribution of Joseph.

I know you know the story, but it's the sort of story we both know and never fully know. How well can we identify with Joseph? All humans are gifted in some ways. Joseph also was gifted. Looking back, we say he was gifted in very unusual ways. Perhaps. At least we can say with certainty that Joseph honored his gifts. He trained them, applied them, used them and claimed them constantly. To me, that is what first stands out most startlingly about Joseph. Throughout his life, wherever he found himself, regardless of the circumstances, we find him honoring his gifts in this fashion.

What are his gifts? I'm sure I don't know them all, but two stand out unmistakably. First, his primary gift is a special spiritual discernment. He doesn't just acquire "wisdom"—he is born with it. The outstanding mark is his ability to comprehend and interpret the meanings of dreams. But that is only the apex of his gift. The story makes it clear that Joseph senses, sees and perceives the pattern of life's events. He is a scholar and a thinker as well as a dreamer. He is a sage, a seer, a wise man, one of the magi.

Joseph's second gift is more mundane and practical: He is a terrific manager. He knows how to organize, how to keep records, how to take care of the details, how to keep everybody clear about what is going on and what they should be doing.

Notice what Joseph is not: He is not a king, not a warrior, not a leader type. At no time in his life is he ever number one. He is always backup, always number two, always the power behind the throne, the coordinator. He has no charisma, no personality for making friends, no vision or purpose of his own with which to inspire others. We might even say, if we didn't know the rest of the story, that Joseph was dealt a pretty weak hand. Despite that, he is sort of a super-clerk—a whiz at it—with a special interest in esoteric subjects.

So Joseph is a seer and an organizer. He is most often valued for his secondary, more useful, gift. But the first is higher and more dangerous, and that is the one that gets him into trouble. Either way, Joseph uses his gifts in the awareness that it is really God behind the forces and facts going on around him. So Joseph honors his gifts. He trains them and claims them all the time. But according to the story, he is also faithful. He tries to serve God. Whoever he seems to be working for, in his own mind he works for God. That is why he gets into so much trouble!

If you honor your gifts, you know you are important. If you honor your gifts—if you train and use and claim them—then you have to set yourself apart in some ways, if for no other reason, simply, than to make room in your schedule to honor the gift. What good is the greatest musician in the world without time to practice?

So Joseph's brothers learn to hate him. They do normal work while Joseph keeps the books and reads and studies. He wears the long-sleeved coat of a scholar (not a coat of many colors). Joseph also makes it clear that he has a special destiny. I suspect he was lonely and frightened by it, and hoped his father and his brothers might understand and help him to understand and live with it. But they thought he was being egotistical and superior, and couldn't stand him for it.

What a string of misfortunes seem to unfold for poor Joseph. His brothers are about to kill him when, "by accident" (of course), they get a chance to sell him into slavery for a profit instead.

How many years he was in Egypt before he rose (as a slave) to the position of chief manager for Potiphar, we do not know. His secondary gift of managerial skill was great, and he used it well. Then disaster again. Potiphar's wife. Once again, if Joseph hadn't been so aloof, so superior, maybe this second disaster would never have happened. So next we find him in prison. As an aside, it is a mystery that he was not killed. Why would Potiphar merely throw him into the guardhouse if indeed he believed that Joseph had accosted his wife? One suspects that Potiphar knew his wife better than she hoped, and appreciated Joseph more than he could afford to show.

The guardhouse is not as grim as a prison for hardened criminals. It is the guardhouse for political prisoners, those who have run afoul of Pharaoh or his household. It is the guardhouse Potiphar uses, as Pharaoh's Captain of the Guard. Nonetheless, it is quite a large establishment, we would imagine. How many years before Joseph rises to the position of chief manager of the prison? We are not sure, but it will be at least two years after that before Joseph is released.

What is Joseph thinking during all this time? Maybe: What was the meaning of those dreams I used to dream? What is the use of trying to be faithful, when all I ever get is scorn and abuse, hatred and ruin? Why should I keep praying and studying? Why bother to make myself useful? Prisoner and slave in a foreign

land . . . among strangers . . . with nobody to really care about
me . . . my own family hates me . . . what is the point or purpose
of any of it??!!

Perhaps this was exactly what Joseph said to himself as he
languished in prison. But there is no hint of it. Was Joseph morose
as he went about his prison duties—day in and day out, month
in and month out? Somehow I doubt it. Joseph seems to be the
sort of person who goes on doing his thing, honoring his gifts—
training them, applying them—running the prison better than it
had ever been managed before.

I suppose he *must* have wondered, "What am I doing here?
What good can come of this?" But some of us "languish" better
than others. Isn't that a wonderful word? *Languish.* How are you
at languishing? First I wanted to know, if you missed it: How are
you at honoring your gifts? But now also: How are you at
languishing? Everybody I know languishes part of the time. Part
of every lifetime seems to be spent in wrong places, on interim
tasks. Sometimes it seems like *all* of life is—as if we can never
quite find the right circumstances, the right combination. Then
we languish, wondering how long we will be in this place. Why
can't we get lucky, find the right niche, come forth into a situation
where we can make a real contribution and be who we really
are? So we languish. But some of us languish better than others.
How are you at languishing?

I think Joseph was great at it. Of course, he had a lot of
practice: despised brother, sold into slavery, household slave for
Potiphar, falsely accused of attempted rape, now prison. But
Joseph languished very well. Wherever he got put, soon he was
doing his own thing again: manager, organizer, seer, interpreter
of dreams. Usually there is some joy (praise and appreciation)
for the chance to be who we are, for the chance to serve—no
matter where we are. Usually, almost always, there is the *possibility*
of such joy, if we choose it. Joseph always seemed to choose it.

Everybody knows how Joseph interpreted the dreams of the
butler (cupbearer) and the baker in prison. And two years later,
the butler remembered Joseph when Pharaoh was troubled with

his dreams. So Joseph interpreted Pharaoh's dreams, and
eventually became the second-in-command of all Egypt. Then
he saved Egypt from famine, and eventually Israel, too. And how
poignant the meetings between Joseph and the brothers who had
sold him into slavery.

Many things here are too fascinating to touch on at the
moment, but one thing in particular I commend to you: It is hard
not to notice that, from the time of Joseph's boyhood, when he is
filled with zeal and faith and the visions of his own
destiny . . . from that time until he is thirty—for all those hard
and difficult years—it does look exactly like God has deserted
him. Almost nothing can go wrong that does not go wrong. And
Joseph is not making slow progress against difficult odds. He is
going backwards most of the time (from any fair, objective
perspective). His situation keeps deteriorating. Indeed, it does
look like God has deserted him. If, in fact, God ever did have a
special purpose for him, surely God has forgotten. Or maybe it
was all a boyish dream in the first place . . . the simple "delusions
of grandeur" that most of us have to outgrow from our youth.
(And if we indeed grow out of them, we are no longer of any use
to the Kingdom.)

What do you do when God deserts you . . . when none of the
plans materialize . . . when none of the opportunities come forth
or come true?

Can I get you to imagine this story for a moment from God's
point of view? Of course we can't really, but we can try—just
switch perspectives. Here is Joseph, your servant, with the special
gifts you have endowed him with. He is superbly suited for a
very special task, a very important task. The trick is to keep him
alive and to maneuver him into a place where he can use the
gifts at the crucial time. All of this must be done according to the
self-imposed limitations—that is, without directly violating
anybody's free will.

So you do what you can to alert Joseph, to awaken him to his
destiny. Naturally, you do that by means of the high gift you have
given him. Joseph has dreams, from early youth. You try to get

the information through to him. Something important is afoot. He has a very important role to play. Of course, he only gets vague bits and pieces of it, but he is game. He believes you and holds onto the plan—dim as it is for him.

Now, how do you get him to Egypt? Well, it's a little tricky, but it will probably work. First of all, you used up so much of Joseph's circuitry to build in the special wisdom and spiritual tune, that he is shorted in other areas like tact, relational skills, recreational interests. The objectivity and perfectionism that make him such a superb manager/organizer also make him uncomfortable to be around. He is always helping people by straightening them out, by telling them what they ought to be doing, by telling them what they don't want to hear. Fine, that gets him into Egypt. His brothers can't stand him.

But he lands in Potiphar's household. That's a true dead end. Potiphar isn't about to get rid of him. Potiphar has never had it so good. Joseph is a genius, and Potiphar's affairs are in fabulous shape, so Joseph is obviously there for life. Great. Potiphar's delighted. Joseph is comfortable and secure. But that's not what you designed him for. Now what?!!

"Even being God ain't no bed of roses." There isn't any way to get from Potiphar to Pharaoh—except through prison. Something has to jar Joseph out of his excellent position into the one where he really belongs. Joseph can't save Egypt or Israel from his position in Potiphar's household. Somehow God has to get him to Pharaoh. So Joseph goes to prison. It is the greatest promotion of his life—only it doesn't look that way for quite a while. What it looks like is that God has really deserted him—this time for good—this time for sure.

That is the real drama behind the story. If Joseph loses faith, despairs, turns away from God, lets his gifts atrophy, get rusty, get out of shape—then the whole thing is for nothing. Then Joseph will die believing that God has indeed deserted him. And God will have to figure out some alternative way to carry forth the plans and the true purpose. How close do you suppose it came? How close does it come with you?

God is a risk-taker, a gambler—always trying to match us to the tasks and situations we are designed for. But we have to honor our gifts and learn to languish faithfully. And we can now believe, by the power and love of Jesus Christ, that God never deserts us! Yet the risk is still very great—each time God has to promote us through some prison to where we really belong—that we will lose faith, quit, and let the gifts go to seed . . . because we think we have been deserted.

Jesus said, "You have been faithful over a little, I will set you over much." Do you hear that like a promise? Honor your gifts. It will help you to know what to do, and how to do it—and when, and where.

Honor your gifts. Learn to languish by running your prison well. And trust the promise.

II Timothy 2:1-3:17

Week Forty-Four

DAYS TO REMEMBER

Clint Ferrell tells me that in England in the 1600s and 1700s, it was sometimes difficult to keep the real estate records clear. Barons and Lords sometimes changed frequently, and there were no consistent land offices to keep track of the transactions. However, it was very important to keep such matters clear, since a dispute over who owned a major estate could easily lead to a war. So it became the practice to gather all the people of the village together at the time of a major land transaction. It would be announced clearly that such-and-such estate was being purchased by a new owner from the old owner for such-and-such a price. And when these facts were clear, they would beat all the children of the village. That way, for years to come, if anybody had a question about who owned the estate, all those who had been beaten could recall the day and verify the transaction. It had been a memorable day for them—a day to remember.

That seems a bit drastic and cruel to us. However, war is even more drastic and cruel. It got me to thinking about how important it is to remember some things—and what does it take to make us remember?

When the mind gets to toying with something like that, pretty soon it seems like life itself is one vast drama about remembering and forgetting. Our well-being, our very survival, depends upon our being able to remember certain important things. If we forget, we must start all over. And sometimes it costs many lives to re-learn that which has been forgotten. What will it cost if we forget Jesus Christ?

Pythagoras, 2,500 years ago, knew that the earth traveled around the sun, that the stars were suns, and that the earth was round. He taught that the universe was an immense place. He understood that just as there was a galaxy containing the sun, so there was a still larger grouping of galaxies that dwarfed our Milky Way system. Pythagoras knew, and taught, this information in the sixth century before Christ. But we forgot! From A.D. 1492 to 510 B.C. is over 2,000 years. That is a long time to be building systems on false premises—to be founding life on misinformation—simply because we forgot! On the other hand, if we are not ready for information, we cannot seem to hold on to it.

About 800 years before Pythagoras, Moses led the Israelite slaves out of Egypt. It was one of history's biggest miracles. The people swore never to forget it. It was a day to remember. It meant that God didn't like slavery. It meant that God *did* care about Israel, and had plans for this people. Our world never can seem to remember either one of these things. Anyway, the whole community gathered at the foot of Mount Sinai and received the tablets of the new Law. It was the Covenant between them and the God who had delivered them. It became crystal clear that day, and on many days to come, that the most important item in all of life was to keep that Covenant! The people heard it, the people accepted it, the people swore to keep it—to keep the Covenant—to teach it to their children, and to make sure that their children kept it. Yet they kept forgetting. It was imperative to remember, but they kept forgetting. That is the history of Western Civilization for 3,300 years now: trying to remember, and continually forgetting, our covenants.

Why do we gather here on Sunday? It is the Day of Resurrection. Knowing the Resurrection changes everything. It is a day to remember. It is imperative to remember. Because it is so important to remember, we are sworn to gather and remember it together at least once a week. Yet we keep forgetting. Even when we show up, sometimes we don't remember why. It is hard to remember. And when we cease to remember, everything reverts back to how it was before. Can you ever walk out of here sad, if you remember the Resurrection? Can you ever wonder whether or not to show up here, if you remember the Resurrection?

Paul says to Timothy, "Remember Jesus Christ." A strange

comment. How could Paul possibly think that a man like Timothy could ever forget Jesus Christ? But Paul knew that even he himself, at times, forgot. We all know that, at times, we forget. Yet, it is imperative that we remember.

Some days change the life of a whole people. In like manner, individuals have days to remember. People, for instance, remember the day they gave up smoking. Not all remember the date, but they do remember the day, and how long ago it was. It may seem like a silly little thing, in comparison to crossing the Rubicon or the Delaware, but it is a dramatic change in the life of an individual. So we remember.

The days we remember are days that change our lives. Before the special day, we thought and acted and perceived in one way. After the special day, we think and act and perceive in a different way. Thirty years ago, Doug Pursell was first-string center for the Stanford football team. He was standing outside the library one day, talking to some friends, when he looked up and saw Willene Van Loenen walking by. He had never seen her before, and did not even know her name. He said, "There goes the love of my life." He was to report later that he was never aware of such a thought forming in his brain, and that when the words came out of his mouth, he was even more surprised than were his friends. He had not been thinking about marriage, or long-term relationships, or family, or anything close to it. But he looked up, and there she was, and those words popped out of his mouth. He was so flabbergasted, she was almost out of sight before he realized that he had to find out who she was. Even I could have told him that she was Mariana's sister, but I wasn't around at the time. I *was* around to marry them in 1960, and she still is the love of his life.

I realize there are some days that change our lives and we don't notice anything special about them at the time. It doesn't make any difference if we remember them. The road forks, and we sometimes go one way quite casually, without realizing that a whole set of acquaintances and circumstances have been determined by it. Looking back, sometimes we wonder about fate. But these are not days to remember.

I am hoping, by now, that you are starting to think of the days in your life you most remember. I don't think I ever met a person who couldn't remember her wedding day. Doubtless there *are* some individuals who do not remember their wedding day, but I don't know them. Most of us remember the days that mark turning points in our lives. Marriage is usually one of them.

Can you remember graduating? Do you remember your first date? Most people remember their operations; their divorces; being fired from a job; getting a promotion or an award. I remember reading Tolkien's *THE LORD OF THE RINGS*. (Finally I began to understand what is going on here.)

Some days leave a mark upon us. Our lives are changed in some way. There is dramatic benefit, or dramatic loss, and life is never quite the same again. Sometimes benefit leads to loss, or loss leads to benefit, but we remember. These are the "passages," the pivot points of our lives. If we do not remember, it becomes for us as if these things never happened. We then go through experiences but gain nothing. We remain the same as we were. Or sometimes we begin to change, and then forget, and return to what we were before. Then we make the same mistakes over and over. We seem to get stuck on some important lesson, and life just keeps cycling around and around, over and over. We go back to smoking. We get remarried. We take a new job that ends up being just like the last job. Sometimes we seem to go for years without any new days to remember, as if we were stuck. Nothing is changing. Nothing is being learned. We just keep going around and around. Some people start getting *déjà vu*, and think it means they have had past lives. Sometimes it means they aren't doing very much in the present one—just going around and around.

Those of you who know me probably think I'm leading up to something. But I'm not. I just think it's a good meditation for our time together in God's presence. It is good to think about the days that are the most significant turning points in our lives. We were all born, and while we don't actually remember that, we celebrate it anyway. We remember it once each year. Things keep happening to us, or we take vows of one sort or another, and we get "days to remember." We lose something and/or we gain something, or we go through some trauma, and it becomes a day to remember. Life was one way for us before that day, and after that day it is different in some way. Everybody has some personal dates that, for them, are a move from B.C. to A.D. It is supposed to be that way. We are pilgrims. We are on a journey. We are not supposed to get too comfortable, or safe, or secure, or locked-in to where we are. God keeps trying to change us. That is part of the plan, part of the design. If nothing is changing in your life, you are keeping God very far away. If your world or your life is flat, you have forgotten Pythagoras on the outside, and Jesus Christ on the inside.

So I am hoping that, when you get home, you will make a list of your special days, your days to remember. I hope you will write them down, and bring them back to clarity and consciousness, lest you forget, and have to start going back over all the same old ground.

Most of all, of course, I hope you will spend time thinking about the spiritual and religious turning points in your life. On what day, especially, did you first decide to abandon your life to God? Such days are preceded by much preparation, and followed by many further decisions, and then re-decisions. Nevertheless, it is a memorable day when we finally decide to stop living for our own goals and desires, and start living to love and serve God.

Jesus said, "You must be born anew," and this new birth— this being born of the Spirit, this turning of our life and our will over to God—has always been the most dramatic turning point of any person's life. In early Christendom, it was celebrated by baptism, and sealed by the giving of a new name. Because such practices have been lost, it becomes more important than ever that we each find some way to celebrate and remember the day when we gave our life to God. You would think Christians would celebrate this day even more than they do their regular birthday. If we do not remember, it will all go back to the way it was before.

The way it was before, for all of us, is that we lived for our own sakes. We had our own goals, even if one of them was to win God's approval. We wanted to be in control. We made our own decisions. We were in charge of our lives. We maybe even tried to impress others with how good or godly or generous or kind we were. But we had not yet turned life over to new management, placed ourselves at God's disposal.

It is not always the happiest day, but it is the biggest turning point in our lives, when we decide to belong to God. When was that day for you? It is a day to remember.

Some people tell me that they have always been so in tune with God that when they turned their lives over in obedience, it made no ripple in their consciousness or in their behavior. The jolt was so mild when they decided to follow God's guidance in all things, that they have no memory of the changeover. I find that remarkable. Don't you think that's remarkable?

I had a friend once in AA who couldn't remember the day he had stopped drinking. None of the rest of us could tell either, seeing that we kept getting so much new evidence that he had not.

It is an easy dilemma to solve, however. All of us, today, in the quiet and prayer of the communion service, can turn or return our lives over to God's care. And we can swear once again to have no earthly goals except to serve and obey God. We can renew our vows to make no new decisions without seeking God's guidance, and to have no conscious motives except the desire to see God's Kingdom increase, and to want God's Will done on earth.

Saying and praying and meaning that with all of our hearts, and without any subterfuge in us whatsoever, some of us might even discover that this day itself has become a day to remember. We remember the conversion days that change our way of living forever after.

Deuteronomy 8:1-10; Hebrews 12:3-11;
II Corinthians 5:19

Week Forty-Five

FATHER OF FATHERS

Jesus once told a group of Sadducees (Luke 20:35-36) that in the resurrection, people would neither marry nor be married. Neither would we die, He said, but we would be equal to the angels. We would be children of God because we are children of the resurrection.

Now, that one incident introduces us to quite a few themes of great theological weight and merit. Way down from there—by comparison not hardly worth mentioning—there are some practical little details that have always fascinated me. Like what happens to me and Mariana? (Or to you and your mate?) Last week we celebrated our 31st wedding anniversary. Granted, that is a far cry from eternity. On the other hand, does that mean in heaven we lose each other, or are no longer special or close to each other?

Jesus didn't go into much detail, but I get very interested when He talks because I believe He really knows. Now, I get as frustrated as the next person, at times, by all the rules and traditions and restrictions. But from what I have seen so far, life without them is a good deal worse than life with them. So it bothers me to be told that in the resurrection, there isn't any marriage. I'm not sure what that means, but I suspect it means I had better get more serious about learning love and how to relate to another being because in heaven, it is going to take more than a house or kids or a piece of paper to keep somebody near me. Isn't that scary?

Again, I can't be sure, but Jesus does seem to be saying that there won't be any children in the resurrection. We will not die, so probably we will not be born either. And that always makes

me wonder why the Creator put such emphasis on children in
this realm we are in. Does that ever fascinate you like it does
me? I see the necessity for self-contained experience here—a
place of relative free will, and so forth. But is this our first
experience? Is this for openers? Or maybe this is like "solitary
confinement." And God says to the angels: "You keep on your
toes now, and keep in harmony with my ways, or I'll stick you in
a body and drop you down on earth for a refresher course in the
basics." In that case, we're all doing time here for some kind of
insubordination. That would explain a lot!

Maybe, on the other hand, this is a reward. What do *we* know?
If it is, and I ever find out about it, I'm definitely going to become
a Buddhist! Nevertheless, with insufficient information and our
kind of minds, we can come up with endless scenarios. What we
do know is that most of us who come to this realm—however we
get here—most of us experience a time when we are children
under parents, and a great many of us experience a time when
we are parents set over the growth and welfare of children. If you
believe in an intelligent, caring God . . . that has to be fascinating.
Why would God put such emphasis on this theme?

Apparently there is something so significant about children,
and parenting, that God wants most of us to experience it from at
least two angles. We can at least surmise that our experiences as
children and our experiences as parents are really a pre-planned,
carefully designed way to teach us the rudiments of what it
means—not only to be children under God, but a little of what it
is like from God's side of the relationship, too. A way to get true
understanding.

Back here in the daily round of life as we experience it, we
usually think of it as a normal sort of thing. You get married, you
have kids, and that leads into a whole series of big and little
decisions, crises, joys. Just because it happens with us and all
around us all the time, we get to thinking it is "natural" or
"common" or something like that. We forget that at every moment,
we are also into profound mystery that is trying to link us with the
vastness of God Almighty, and God's Eternal Plan. And it is

probably good that we forget sometimes, or it might make the burden even greater. But if we forget it for too long, or for too much of the time, we miss the very essence of what we are participating in.

One morning we'll talk about motherhood, but today I want to ask you: Is it possible to be a good father? It has been very important, to most of the men I have known over the years, to be a good father. And most of the men I know feel a lot of consternation and even guilt about how they have lived up to their visions of what kind of fathers they wanted to be. If attacked on the subject, they would tend to defend how hard they had tried. But sitting quietly and musing, it's an elusive thing to be a good father.

And sometimes it seems like the kids come out wonderful no matter what you do to them. And with other kids, the reverse seems equally true. Individuals come into this world with more agenda than we want to admit. They come "already made" in some very fundamental ways. Our parenthood may be profound, but heredity (as we think of it) is only the upper layers of personality.

That makes the question different. Is it *possible* to be a good father? With some kids, you almost couldn't miss. They start out wiser than their parents and keep one jump ahead all the way. And they're loving and appreciative to boot. With others, sometimes in the same family, well, there just doesn't seem to be any approach that will help. But the really terrifying thing is that none of us can ever be really sure when the whole picture will reverse. When do you decide? At what age do you take a photograph and say, "Now, this is an example of what a wonderful parent I have been. Look at my child—successful, popular, responsible, here in this picture at age thirty-three." What will the picture look like at forty-five? We may even think we know, but we never do. I have lived to see more than one despairing parent—and so have you—who was struggling, beyond all conscience or reasoning, with a perfect hellion at age seventeen. Then suddenly their child did a crazy turnaround—almost like they had found some vital missing piece—and they began to train and learn and grow with a voracious and creative passion. All at once, the poor parent is being thanked and congratulated, including by the kid, and they haven't the faintest clue what they ever did right any more than they could figure out what they were doing wrong before.

No, it isn't always mayhem. There are trustworthy principles that tend to work most of the time: Be consistent. Be fair. Provide. Don't spoil. Spend time. Be affectionate. Show you care. Believe in them. And there are lots of hints about such things in any bookstore. But mostly, mothers read such books, and that's because people who think like mothers write most of them. But let's not get into that.

So the roles are changing, and the rules with them. And that's no secret to anybody. It's been going on for quite a while now. But change has a tendency to cut only so deep, and then revert to pattern, if there really is one. What are some of the images you have of "father"? It will depend on your experience, of course, so this is not a true-or-false quiz. But let me remind you of a few majors.

PROVIDER—PROTECTOR. I don't know if that is a classic image of "father" in the minds of most women, but I can guarantee you that it *is* in the minds of most men. Women and counselors and many children talk a lot about how they would prefer love and affection, time and attention, feelings and caring in the place of some of the "providing and protecting" they have received from their fathers. Men hang their heads in shame, and sometimes even try to change. But it won't fly! Ten billion years of genes aren't going to change their vote, for a little current logic or a few tears. If you're the father, you provide and protect. If there's time left over for other things, that's dandy. But the greatest fear of the father is that he will not be able to provide or protect.

Lots of people think it is John Wayne who makes men think this way—the macho image. But it isn't. It's Billy Bigelow who haunts our dreams. And behind that, a father knows that his primary function is not to be liked or approved of, but to provide and protect. In many instances, that is no longer working out in our society. But a father knows it anyway.

DISCIPLINARIAN—STANDARD SETTER—PRIEST. That is, carrier of the family ritual, tradition, heritage, ceremony, religion. This image of father is indeed much faded. The "oughts" and "shoulds" and "musts" are very unwelcome in our society. Many fathers no longer attempt to keep this role. But I often suspect that it has only gone underground. The other side of this coin is the father as teacher, trainer, mentor. To grow up in a home often meant, for all practical purposes, to be an apprentice to one's father. You remember *The Karate Kid?* Mr. Miage was often asked where he had learned this or that skill. His invariable reply was, "Father teach." Why did that resonate so? Why did that strike a chord so deep for so many? Maybe some folk are beginning to miss it. How many of you ever saw the movie *Bambi?* It's really crazy to show that movie to young boys in our society. It's going to do a lot more damage than carloads of sex and violence. There is the Great Stag. You don't often see him, except occasionally from afar. He is tireless, usually alone, always vigilant, always living only for the protection and care of the herd. There is, however, one time you will see him: When you need him the most. And then he is there for you, and no sacrifice is too great. Bambi has lots of cute adventures, but what Bambi really wants more than anything else in life is to grow up to be just like that Great Stag, his father. And every little boy who watches it is feeling archetypal music coming alive and singing to him from the depths within.

A lot of fathers have faded out or quit. We have grown uncomfortable with the Biblical passages that speak of discipline, that remind us of the old roles, that use the analogy of God as Father. In real life, the perfect patterns are often missing and we have to do the best we can. More and more of us are trying to learn to get along without fathers—without discipline, without the traditions and rules and goals that they represented . . . and without the tyranny that sometimes comes with it, too. And the pendulum may be reversing once again. We are discovering that men who are afraid of women and children do not make good fathers either. Men who take on more and more the role of mother sometimes make good mothers. But it's no substitute for fathers.

What goes wrong is not that fathers act like fathers and so we have to wipe away that role. It is when the fathers forget the fathers—and the Father of fathers—that we get mayhem and disaster.

The experience of raising children is one of the great revealers of what it is like between us and God. We see in our children all the themes of rebellion and adoration, of fear and enthusiasm, and of trust and betrayal that are continually being played out between us and God. And we get to "see it," sort of, from God's side. You punish your child, and know for the first time how God must feel with us. And when your child forgives you and gives you a big hug, you start to learn why God values repentance. And when your child excels and your heart swells, you start to learn why God takes His hand away and makes us learn to do it ourselves. The parallels are endless.

So it seems that God wants most of us to experience childhood and parenthood in some fashion—that we may become aware of some of the greatest themes in life. And I, at least, have concluded that it is not possible to be a "good" father. God alone is the Good Father. Two things seem absolutely imperative, nevertheless, if we are not to become disastrous fathers: We must remember what it is like to be a child. And we must stay child to the Father of fathers. Each time we deal with our children, we must cling to the image of how God deals with us. And each time our children respond to us, we must keep realizing how it reflects the way we respond to God. And even when we feel like throwing away the rules, or quitting, or putting aside all the principles we believe in—just to get out from under the pressure of it—then we must also remember how it would be for us if God walked out on us.

So we need to remember the Father of fathers, and we need to remember that we are still children. Sometimes the second is even harder than the first. So I want to close with an essay written by Robert Fulghum. My friend, Donel McClellan, read it at the Conference Annual Meeting in Olympia, and I have been waiting to share it with you. It is called, "All I Ever Really Needed To Know I Learned In Kindergarten." [Editor's note: Five years after the first publication of this book, Mr. Fulghum's essay and other writings were released in a wonderful book by the same name, published by Ballantine Publishing Group.]

"Most of what I really needed to know about how to live, and what to do, and how to be, I learned in kindergarten. Wisdom was not at the top of the graduate school mountain, but there in the sandbox at nursery school.

"These are the things I learned: Share everything. Play fair. Don't hit people. Put things back where you found them. Clean up your own mess. Don't take things that aren't yours. Say you're sorry when you hurt somebody. Wash your hands before you eat. Flush. Warm cookies and cold milk are good for you. Live a balanced life. Learn some and think some and draw and paint and sing and dance and play and work some every day.

"Take a nap every afternoon. When you go out into the world, watch for traffic, hold hands, and stick together. Be aware of wonder. Remember the little seed in the plastic cup. The roots go down and the plant goes up and nobody really knows how or why, but we are all like that.

"Goldfish and hamsters and white mice and even the little seed in the plastic cup—they all die. So do we.

"And then remember the book about Dick and Jane and the first word you learned, the biggest word of all: LOOK. Everything you need to know is in there somewhere. The Golden Rule and love and basic sanitation. Ecology and politics and sane living.

"Think of what a better world it would be if we all—the whole world—had cookies and milk about three o'clock every afternoon and then lay down with our blankets for a nap. Or if we had a basic policy in our nation and other nations to always put things back where we found them and cleaned up our own messes. And it is still true, no matter how old you are, that when you go out into the world, it is best to hold hands and stick together."

II Samuel 18:24-19:8

Week Forty-Six

THE ONE AND THE MANY

Sometimes we have trouble with Christianity because Jesus was only one person. Even if He does end up the eternal Holy Spirit who called the worlds into being, we say to ourselves that, on earth, He was still only one man. How can it be true that all of us can relate to only one man? It doesn't make any sense that we could all identify with the Cross and awaken to our salvation by knowing ourselves forgiven there. Jesus was only one man. His ministry was in only one country. He came out of one culture and tradition and religion. It all happened at one time in history, and that was a long time ago. These things we sometimes say, or think within ourselves. And then it seems to us that we have thought or said something important, or even profound. We tell ourselves that maybe these really are authentic objections. Sometimes that throws people off the path for a long time. (Not that God is unable to build our wanderings back into a path that leads us home.)

Let us skip all the backdrop and buildup, and come straight to the culminating scenario of our day. It is the Last Judgment, the Day of Reckoning, only from a humanistic point of view. It is The Great Courtroom Scene, only it is Humanity that is irate. Humans may be in the dock, from God's point of view. We did not keep the covenant. We were not obedient. We did not love God or each other with passion or consistency or devotion. That caused a lot of trouble.

But God is also in the dock, from Humanity's point of view. In this scene, the voice of The People will also be heard. The People are angry about the experience on earth that God has designed and put them all through. God is, after all, accountable for God's actions too! The Creator is responsible for what is set in motion and left running. The Creator should keep a closer watch, or turn it off—not just let things get so out of hand.

So Humanity's spokesperson steps forward to bring evidence before the Court. In this courtroom, there are no technical difficulties. As Counsel for Humanity speaks, there flashes into every mind the clear and authentic scenes of what he is saying. As he talks, countless people begin to appear and recede in an incredible procession: wounded and dying victims of war . . . mothers trying, without success, to gather food for their starving children. Scene after scene comes before the Court: disease, heartache, broken dreams, broken homes . . . people enslaved, betrayed, tortured, lonely, imprisoned, cast away. By the time Counsel for Mankind has finished, all in the courtroom are weeping uncontrollably—including God and all of God's Angels.

After a necessary recess and all are again composed, the Archangel Michael steps forward as Counsel for God. Michael's words also translate instantly into thoughts and visions within the minds of all present. And everybody is present. Michael begins slowly, speaking of God's hopes and intentions, and how it was necessary—imperative—that human souls should experience freedom in a self-contained environment before being given access to the eternal and endless dimensions. Michael then shifts to the design of creation—how most of the suffering was unnecessary, and how all creation was designed to lead humans into awareness of their dependency on God and on each other. The scenes begin to flow more rapidly, showing what the earth could have been like if people had honored Nature; had honored the commandments even they themselves believed in; had sought to live in harmony and love and cooperation. Every mind filled with pictures of life on earth showing beautiful scenes of cities and farms and villages, where people planned and studied and worked for themselves, but also for the common good. Diseases were healed; poverty was only a starting over; wars were talked-out long before they turned into organized violence. All people felt a desire as well as a responsibility to obey God as the very first priority. Even people who were dying were far from miserable, for they were in the midst of loving friends, and they had all realized that they would meet again.

Then when the Archangel Gabriel steps forward to speak, the entire assembly knows that this is no mere speech. This is the design. This really could have been true . . . should have been true. Then Gabriel's voice changes, and he begins to show what God has done to lead Humanity into this better Way. New images form—of Moses, Buddha, Socrates, Jeremiah—and countless stories of light and enlightenment come before the Court. Finally, the scenarios come to a halt, and there is a brief pause. Then there appears a man carrying a cross up a hill. Again, the entire assembly is in tears, including God and all of God's Angels.

Except . . .

Except for Counsel for Humanity, who steps forward now and waits. After a long time, and the assembly is settled and attentive again, this spokesperson begins to speak. Pictures again flash clear in the minds of every being present. The scenes are flashing back and forth, back and forth—between the man with His cross, and the suffering scenes of all the sons and daughters of earth down through the ages. For a long time, the pictures flash—Golgotha against all the rest of the world's suffering. Finally, Counsel for Humanity raises his arm, and his fist is clenched. And he lifts his voice and cries until it rings throughout all the halls and corridors of that great courtroom: "One Son is not enough! One of Yours for all of ours is not enough!!"

To Christian ears, there could hardly be a greater blasphemy. Jesus was not enough?!? The Eternal Spirit . . . descended in human flesh . . . come in mercy instead of in wrath . . . trying to teach and reveal . . . preferring to suffer and die rather than harm us . . . and it is not enough??!!

Mostly we are appalled at what happened to Jesus. We can barely believe that God would send the Son. In no way was that ever fair or right. The feeling of utter unworthiness—and the shock of our importance to God in Christ—has literally undone and redone and converted us generation after generation. Our own ingratitude, and the ingratitude of the world, is already an enormous paradox, and our greatest crime. To suggest that one Son is not enough—it is unthinkable . . . and it should be unspeakable.

How many sons, then, would it take? If we will not listen to one, who is crazed enough to believe we would listen to the many? It doesn't take long to figure out who is playing Counsel for Humanity. What an age we live in: so greedy and ungrateful; so self-centered, and yet so lonely; so crass, yet so hungry for meaning; so eager for some purpose, yet so empty for God. Is it any wonder that the blasphemies mount? Strange and offensive as they sound to our ears, we must learn to listen, to hear, to feel the pain beneath the utterance, and to respond. It is our world. We are Christ's witnesses now. What do you say to the friend or neighbor who wrestles with such thoughts, or who speaks them boldly?

It brings us back to a principle that is ancient, not modern. It affects our perspective on many things. The track of its wisdom is found in some form in every major spiritual path around the globe throughout history. You recall it in teachings like: "Inasmuch as ye have done it unto one of the least of these my brethren, ye have done it unto me." (Matthew 25:40) The point of the Good Samaritan story, in its context, is that we must stop trying to be perfect for everyone, and start trying to help one neighbor at a time. We do not find truth in the many. We find it in the one.

When we are young, we think that "more" means more important. Tigers can do more damage than leopards, so tigers are more important. To be important, a thing must be big. The many are more important than the few. Even when we are young, something in us knows better. But as we learn to count and pay attention to the outer world, for a while we forget the unseen realms, and lose the truth.

An airline crash that kills two hundred people is more

important than a crash that kills only five people? A rock concert that draws three thousand people is more important than a prayer meeting that only four people attend? Do you not still catch yourself thinking this way from time to time?

Is a symphony more beautiful because seven hundred people listen to it, than it would be if only two people hear it? It takes more than two to play a symphony. That is a different principle, also very important. There must be a musician for every part. We have run into that truth before, and we will again. But do seven hundred listeners make the symphony more beautiful than two listeners? The thunder of applause will be greatly different. But the symphony can be heard by the one. The many cannot hear beyond the reaches of the one.

How is a big war different from a small feud? More people experience it, but what they experience is, in every case, experienced and perceived one person at a time.

What makes me care about humanity? How do I know that humanity is important, if I have never had a single friend? You already know what I am trying to say. I am only trying to get you to remember. When I was a young boy, in third grade, I had a dog named Brownie. Not much of a name, but a lot of dog. Every creature on our small ranch loved Brownie. The goats let her help lick the kids dry when they were born. The cat sometimes curled up next to her to sleep. Even the chickens never ran from her. She loved and protected everything, and everything loved her back.

I watched a car kill Brownie. We were both off on a wide shoulder of the road, where we were supposed to be. Brownie was up ahead. The car swerved clear out of its lane to hit her. It never slowed down. One blink and my reality was changed forever. I had seen pure evil. It called forth within me evil to match!

When I reached Brownie, she was still alive. I don't know how much it hurt her when I gathered her in my arms. She tried to lick my face, but she was too weary. It was about three-quarters of a mile to my house through the orange groves. I tried to be careful, I never put her down, but she was dead by the time I got home. I learned many things that day that I will never learn any clearer. If every dog in the universe had been killed that day, could it have made me any sadder? If you had killed every person on the face of the earth that day, you could not have increased my grief. It doesn't mean others weren't important to me. But whatever capacity I have for sorrow, it was already full that day. That has happened to me on some other days since, as it has for you. It is never a matter of the many. We care one at a time. Even when we do grieve for the many, it is because we remember the one, and project it outward.

To seek the truth, we do not seek the many. We seek the one. Through the one, we begin to comprehend the significance of all. One Son is enough . . . if you know Him.

How many sons did David have? How many faithful friends had fallen in battle to save David from Absalom's rebellion? Even David could not stand the sight of Absalom for years because Absalom had killed his own brother, Amnon. Yet David's grief is complete as he mourns for Absalom. Everything else recedes from his consciousness. He does not mourn for Absalom his son who was a spoiled brat, a murderer, a treasonous leader of a rebellion whose purpose was to kill all of David's most loyal friends, and then also David, and then take over the kingdom. David is not mourning for his son Absalom who wanted to kill his own father and king. He is just mourning for his son, Absalom. Even Joab, who makes all of Hollywood's hit-men look like pantywaists by comparison—even Joab is barely able to pry David out of his grief in time to save the kingdom.

The loss of one is a total loss. Grief is not the only illustration. It does not take a cast of thousands to discover love. It takes one other. We know nothing at all about love until we learn to care for one—one at a time. You think monogamy wasn't God's idea? I can tell you it wasn't man's idea!

Some things cannot be added unto. Quantity does not alter, does not qualify, does not change grief, or love, or truth. As long as there is one person anywhere who is not in the church . . . who is not within the beloved community . . . who is not known and loved and forgiven and cared about—the Kingdom is incomplete. Do you still think that only a few will be saved? If so, you don't know or understand very much about Jesus yet! Only, we are supposed to be helping. Truth is not found in the many. It is found in the one. Who teaches us about leaving the ninety-nine and going after the one who is lost?

Everything we learn that has any true significance, we learn personally, and in a specific instance or experience. We do not find the truth in the many, or from the many. We find it in the One. If we know Him . . . and believe Him . . . and follow Him— all things will be revealed. Even in the midst of chaos and confusion as incredible as our world now produces, we find salvation in and from the One. One Son is enough.

In that Courtroom Scene, however it actually happens, He will be the true Counsel for Humanity—one at a time. He will be our Advocate. If He cannot clear us of all charges—nothing can! No one else is even going to try.

Psalm 139:1-18

Week Forty-Seven

PLAYING GOD

I was in a conversation recently with a person who said to me, "You always sound so certain of your faith. I have a lot of doubts that you don't seem to have. It must be wonderful to feel sure that God exists, and cares—that God wants us to live in special ways and do certain things like tithe, and study the Bible, and pray, and love our neighbors, and all the rest. It must be wonderful to do all those things if you really believe. Only, I have a lot of trouble believing it in the first place. So for me, a lot of it doesn't make much sense."

It could only have been three or four days earlier that I heard approximately the same comment from another person. It got me to thinking. It has been a long time since I addressed issues from so early on the Path. After seeing God at work in my life and in the lives of so many other people, all the brave ways in which I had doubted God's existence slowly lost their luster. Every time any of us walked the Way, or even took a new step on it, we were blessed in some way. I still remember how to doubt the Way. But mostly, those doubts just sit off in a corner somewhere, collecting dust. New doubts are more interesting. I do not doubt God, I doubt the church. It still seems to me that we are a faint image of what we are intended to be. God seems very real to me. God is Great and doing great! But I wonder about myself. Sometimes I don't seem very real.

Some of *you* seem pretty real to me. I watch you becoming real persons. It is the most astounding and important and wonderful thing in the world. I can feel Jesus just jumping with glee every time you take a new step and get more real. Sometimes even *I* take a new step, and I can feel His joy then, too. So it's true that my doubts have changed. I think Jesus is the only true person who ever lived on earth. The rest of us are Pinocchios trying to figure out how to be real, and maybe learning slowly that the Way is to follow Jesus.

Now these two conversations have reminded me of the other kind of doubts. I used to be more plagued by doubts. There is no way to come onto the Path except by going through them. And I wonder . . . am I still able to be at all helpful to someone who is wrestling with such doubts? I don't know. But I would like to try. I certainly think a person with such doubts should feel very welcome in a place like this. Anybody toying with the Path or anywhere on it should feel at home here. So I want to go way back up the road this morning, and say just a few things about dealing with the early doubts.

First, I suppose, I better dust off my own doubts, so you will know I have them. They never go away, you know. Categorically, faith is never a matter of proof. Faith is always a choice, a risk, a leap. We weigh the evidence, but all the facts are never in—not in this world. Faith decides to bet life one way instead of another. So intellectually, the doubts are never banished once and for all. After enough experience, they recede into the corner and get neglected. But I can still go find them if I have to.

I'm a little rusty at this, so bear with me. Start imagining big cities. Millions upon teeming millions of people. Don't just stay in Seattle. Think of Calcutta, Hong Kong, Mexico City, London . . . and hundreds of lesser cities all over the globe. How many single individuals are at this very moment eking out a living, each one with hope and despair and aspirations? And does each individual think, "My own life is important"? Do you really think some god cares about all these mites, any more than we care about all the ants that crawl on the banks of the parking lot?

How could all the tragedies keep happening to all these people—in prisons, in hospitals, in mental institutions, in slums (and in some cities, those are the lucky ones—at least they can get off the street)—how could all these tragedies keep happening if some almighty god cares?

Sometimes you can look up into the sky at night, and it doesn't feel warm and beautiful. It just seems cold, and endless, and far away. What does any of it matter? The stars go nova, and if there are any worlds nearby, they are totally destroyed in seconds. Is our corner of space any different?

Even on our own planet, we notice what a tiny portion of its billions of years here have had anything to do with humankind. And if we evolved from primitive animals only a few million years ago, why do we suddenly conclude that it was some god's design from the beginning, or that we have some special destiny beyond this accidental moment?

And now that we have developed world-killing weapons, and our history shows that we always end up using our weapons, how much longer can it be before we blow our world to extinction before its time? Is it not inevitable that some of our species will do that, no matter how hard or fervently some of the rest of us work and pray to prevent it? And do you think some god will step forth to prevent it?

What is all this self-centered, wishful thinking about God, or love, or meaning, or some life beyond this one? Should we not grow up, put away our childish fantasies, see life as it really is, make the best of it while we can, and stop deluding ourselves with complex, irrational religions? Just because we are lonely and afraid are no reasons to invent gods or to build churches.

Well, I can't do it real justice in so short a time, especially being out of practice as I am. But you can probably tell that, under the dust, such thoughts have crossed my mind. There are lots more, there in the corner. I tried not to add any new ones to your pile. I might be able to. I was a good doubter when I was young. It is doubting, after all, that drives us to seminary. Doubts plague us until we have to drop our lives and go seek answers. Then if we keep meeting God along the way, pretty soon we forget why we came and find ourselves busy with other things.

I want to tell you three things about doubting that I hope will be helpful. The first is: Never be afraid of your doubts. If you worship God, and your God is real, then obviously God is not going to be afraid of your questions. If God designed your mind to be so questioning, then God doesn't fear your doubts, and neither should you. I am trying to say that much damage is added to doubting by those who feel guilty for having the doubts in the first place. Failure to doubt is no mark of saintliness. It signifies either a lack of intelligence, or a fear-frozen mind. Check the lives of any of the saints. The greater the saint, the more doubts they have wrestled with.

On top of this, we must add that most breakthroughs to new understanding come through doubting. The Holy Spirit loves our doubts, if those get us back into dialogue; get us thinking again; get us uncomfortable enough and stretching enough so that we can get some new insight. In His time, Jesus was the only Jew in Israel who dared to doubt that Moses was the final word, or whether the traditions were truly honoring what Moses had intended. Jesus doubted absolutely everything (with respect). Otherwise, He could never have grown open enough to let God do so many absolutely new things with Him.

Never fear your doubts. They are leading you to new insight. Just remember that you are body, mind, emotion, and spirit. Doubts are only one portion of the intellect part of your mind. Keep a little perspective. Pay attention, but don't take it too seriously. You can only doubt up to the capacity of your own mind. That's impressive to you and to me. But it isn't exactly absolute intelligence either! There is a lot we cannot comprehend, even when we do wake up and pay attention. God isn't counting on our intelligence alone. That's no insult. It's just comforting.

The second thing is this: Be fair. Eat the whole meal. Most of the time when we doubt, we cheat. We take a tiny piece of a doubt, take it out of context, and then we cherish that doubt, turning it over and over in our minds and "enjoying" it without noticing or dealing with all the implications.

.If you begin to believe in Jesus as the Christ, you end up
with a whole constellation of beliefs: God, the Holy Spirit, the
Church, Eternal Life, and the whole vast array of values and
teachings and principles that Jesus represents—until, as we say,
you have a whole new way of thinking and feeling . . . until a
whole new way of life is involved. You can't just believe in Jesus
as the Son of God, for instance, then turn around and claim that
there is no God. You see, one thing is connected to another, and
all of them hang together and affect everything you do or think
about.

Well, doubts are the same way. They come in constellations.
Only, we cheat. We try to pick one good-sounding doubt out of
the pile, without noticing all the others that are connected and
come with it. For instance, I may have suffered a cruel blow, lost
a friend or a relative, or a job. If I am new in the faith, and the
hurt is too great, one release is to get angry toward God. We don't
reason it out at such a time. It is more emotional pain than it is
rational doubt. And often it can be healthy and healing to blame
God, if we go to God with our pain and anger. But sometimes,
after the grief subsides, we still keep the doubt. A person ends
up saying God doesn't exist, or God is no damn good, because
God didn't save the loved one.

Only, we cheat. We keep the rest of our convictions about life
just as they were before. We forget that all of them are based on a
belief in God. And then we pretend that all we threw out was our
belief in God's existence. But if there is no God, there is no meaning
either. It is an accidental universe. There is no plan. What we do
doesn't matter. There are no morals because there is no authority.
Groups or civilizations may get together and make up rules, but no
rule is better or worse than any other. There is no standard to measure
by unless there is an authority. And all concepts of authority trace
back to God. If there is no God, it is just a matter of who can collect
the most opinions. The opinions have no validity except for a
temporary condition of "might makes right."

When you doubt, don't cheat! Eat the whole meal. If you
want to stay with your doubts, then change your life to match.

There is no love, there is only self-interest. There is no nobility, no future to hope in, nothing to live or strive for beyond keeping comfortable and amused while you wait out the accidental time you have stumbled into.

It isn't fair to entertain just one tiny doubt while you sit in the comfort of all the rest of the benefits of faith. If your doubts start to trouble you, then get serious. Eat the whole meal. Compare the full program of doubt with the full program of faith. Otherwise we cheat. The trouble with cheating in this game is that we end up in limbo—halfway in between, where nothing ever comes clear.

People talk about hypocrisy in the church! And they're right, of course. We don't live up to what we claim to believe. But the hypocrisy outside the church makes *us* look like amateurs. I've never met an atheist or an agnostic yet who didn't still talk about and live for either truth or excellence or love or beauty—and usually some combination of all of them. That's just flat-out dishonest. Where do they think those things come from? The very concepts and possibilities are grounded on and presume the existence of God.

Don't cheat! Eat the whole meal. It will help you a lot when you struggle with your doubts.

Thirdly, and finally, I want to urge you to play God. You never thought you'd hear me say this, but I don't mean it the way you think. Sometimes we use the phrase "playing God" when we are talking about power games, and pride, and people who try to be in control of their own lives and of everybody else's. That's not what I'm suggesting.

This third suggestion, though, is my favorite. If it helps you as much as it does me, I'll be pleased that I preached this sermon, and I hope God will be, too.

Playing God is a mental exercise wherein you pretend you are in God's shoes, and you redesign this place the way you think it ought to be. It's a lot of work, but a lot of fun, too. Frequently, it is more entertaining than even the best television program.

This wonderful game is really best played with paper and pen, so you can't forget what a wonderful "creator" you would have made. You put down on paper the things you would have done, the ways you would change things, if you were God.

Then, after you list the changes, you have to meditate for a while on all the repercussions that would come from those changes. You have all done it at times. I am urging you to do it a lot, and seriously. Do you remember some of the simple ones? Most of us said, when we were children, "If I were God, there wouldn't be any pain." And then we slowly began to realize how horrible that would be: People dying needlessly everywhere because they had no warning of the damage. It would be like a kind of perpetual and absolute leprosy. Of course, we never could have evolved or survived under such circumstances. So our first brilliant improvement as creators was not so good.

Next, we usually wiped out death. You think we have a population problem now? Then wipe out birth. Terrific, that just eliminated all of us. And so it goes. And that's only for openers.

See if you can follow this one: God has designed us so we only have to endure so much pain. Beyond that level, we black out. You can't increase the pain beyond that level. A human will go unconscious. Now, what if God's design reduced that threshold even slightly? We would die easier. You see that? It would take less to put us out of commission. Things we survive and recover from now would be fatal if God reduced our suffering one iota. And what if God made us hardier, able to endure and survive greater damage than we can now? Then our suffering would increase dramatically. We would be much harder to kill, but the price would be horrendous pain! Do you really think you can improve the ratio? Do you really think you are more merciful, more rational, more practical than God? You will suspect so and assume it, until you learn to "play God" seriously, and well.

Playing God is a wonderful game to play with your doubts. Try and try and try to come up with one single improvement you could make. Well, you say, that's only because we are used to things the way they are. We have never known a different reality, so naturally we will conclude that things must be this way.

Hey—that didn't stop you from complaining an hour ago! Why think of that now, when I'm giving you this terrific game to play that can really help you?

Try not to wipe us all out. Don't cancel our free will, so we have no more capacity to love. But "play God" long, and hard, and well. You'll find out why bad things happen to good people a lot clearer than the book told it. You'll even find out why good things happen to bad people, and maybe even why Jesus said, "No one is good but God alone."

The Psalmist tells us that we are fearfully and wonderfully made—that God has designed it all with intricate caring down to the smallest detail, and all of it is intertwining in patterns and purposes far beyond our comprehension. Do you believe that? Faith trusts that it is so. In any case:

Do not fear your doubts.

Don't cheat. Eat the whole meal.

Play God.

If you're having trouble believing, get good at doubting. God is happy to pick you up at either end. Just don't hang out in the middle.

Philippians 2:1-18; Matthew 25:14-23, 29

Week Forty-Eight

YOU ARE ON A PATH

Imagine that you are out in the wilderness. It is your desire to survive. What are the ten essentials, and would you remember to bring them with you? (You know: knife, compass, matches—things like that.) I know some people who would consider it downright uncultured not to be familiar with such things.

I was listening to a television program a few days ago that was speaking of survival tactics after retirement. They were talking about the five necessary components for a good life: health, a place to live, money to live on, friends who care, and something to do. In this program's view, that covered the essentials.

Whether in the wilderness, after retirement, in high school, or any other time . . . we might claim that there is another essential more important than any of the ones yet mentioned. In our language, it is usually called "faith." Some of us have come to the conviction that faith is one of the most important dimensions of life—that, in fact, a person really isn't well-off without it.

So what are the ten essentials of faith? Or what are the five necessary components for a healthy faith? We could make such lists. We each really should. What an excellent project for a Sunday afternoon. Make a list of five things you have to "take with you" if you are going to have a sound and healthy faith. And after you have your list, take care of it!

It may or may not appear on your list, but one of the things we have discovered down through the ages, and in every culture around the globe, is that one of the essential ingredients for faith is a group with which and in which to live it. Because faith is so intensely personal and affects us in such private and inward ways, we often claim it to be an individual affair. But history shows otherwise. Faith is always lived and expressed in the context of some community. Even at its most dramatic moments of breakthrough, or departure from old ways, faith still operates out of a tradition, and in some conscious effort to be accountable to what God has revealed to the community in the past. From such a stance, faith looks to see what God seems to be asking in the present, and for the future. Faith is a very personal thing. But it operates and grows in community.

Faith does not grow in a vacuum. People misunderstand why the church keeps urging its members to participate, to show up for drill, to come to meetings. It is nothing new. The church has been talking this way from the beginning. Maybe sometimes in our day it has been done for crass or materialistic reasons. But normally, that is not the case. The plain truth is that people who drift away from the fellowship atrophy. The church doesn't just tell you to come because it worries about its attendance record. It tells you to come because it knows your faith will shrivel up if you don't. How many great football players do you know who never play on any team? That's how many Christians there are who are not part of any church. How many spiritual people can you name—from any time or place in history—who operated outside of a tradition and a community?

To be sure, there are many and various training programs, approaches and life-patterns recommended for acquiring and becoming proficient in faith. There are, on this island alone (Mercer Island, Washington)—if we count only those with formal staff and land and buildings—there are twelve faith organizations in which you can live and train and grow. People say to me, "Wow, your island is really over-churched, isn't it?" But I think, "Not until each of the twelve has twenty-five hundred members." We don't have to close down yet.

Have you followed me so far? Faith is one of the essential ingredients of life. Some of us have realized it is even the most essential ingredient of all. It turns out that faith, while intensely personal, grows and thrives only in community—stays healthy only when attached to a tradition. Therefore, those of us who seek faith and wish to be people of faith must find and attach ourselves to the best training school, parish, congregation, church or "whatever you want to call it" . . . that we can find. If there is a better tradition or approach than the one we follow here, then we ought to become part of it. If we can find or receive new or different or additional ways to enhance our growth and experience in faith, then of course we will want to adopt them. But we don't just fool around. Faith is too important!

Everyone is on a Path. Their life can be seen as an unfolding story. I believe the Holy Spirit tracks each and every one of us. But we don't see ourselves as being on a Spiritual Path until we notice that—until we awaken to that Presence and that reality, and start to see the coincidences in terms of patterns, and start to recognize themes and directions and common denominators. That is when we start to get excited about our lives, and excited about the lives of those around us.

So if you are here, I rather expect you to recognize by now that you are on a Spiritual Path . . . that those around you are also . . . and that everybody is, but everybody doesn't know it yet. And if, knowing that, you have chosen this congregation to be your faith home, your faith community—then glory a little in the Path we're on, in the WAY we try to follow. Claim the disciplines with joy . . . try the training programs with enthusiasm . . . walk the WAY eager to experience the ways of faith that our tradition claims to be the most authentic.

For instance, there is a reason why our tradition stresses your individual freedom and your responsibility to hammer out your own commitments. There is a reason why I am granted freedom of the pulpit. There is a reason why you are not required or expected to believe or agree with what I say. I am not granted freedom of the pulpit just because our Conference is too lazy to set regulations! There are anguish and revelation and generations of scholarship and study and prayer behind our tradition not to take the Bible literally, not to approach the Bible as the infallible words of God. We have no firm creed, not because creeds don't take shape and form among us, but because we insist on dismantling them whenever they do.

The reason our denomination and our tradition do these things is because we place so much emphasis on the Holy Spirit. We really believe, within the United Church of Christ, that you are each on a Spiritual Path, and that the Holy Spirit is in touch and in contact with each one of you who will allow it and cooperate with it. Therefore, we keep clearing the decks and trying to make room, so the Holy Spirit can have more space and more elbow-room in whatever work the Holy Spirit wants to do with you. You need to know this—and need to be able to explain it to others. We don't hand you a creed in this tradition because we expect you, in company with the Holy Spirit, to be building your own! If you are too lazy or too unmotivated or too shy to be doing that—then you would be far better off in a creedal fellowship. Do you see that? Any of the great, historic creeds of the Christian Faith are far superior to *no* creed! The vast majority of Christians do live in creedal fellowships.

Our tradition and church were formed by and designed for people who cannot fully embrace or totally commit themselves to a creed somebody else has handed to them. More importantly, our tradition holds that we cannot fully turn our lives and our wills over to the care and direction of God until we stop swearing total allegiance to other human beings, or to human organizations, or to pieces of paper. (No matter how lovely the words on them may be.)

Well, I don't mean to get you back into Confirmation Class, or to start a series on the traditions and beliefs of Congregationalism. You are on a Path. I hope you know that. And you have chosen to link your Path to this church—to this congregation and tradition. So know it, claim it, let it help you . . . or find one you will let help you. Walk this WAY eager to experience the ways of faith, and to understand them better all the time, and to build them into your life with each passing day and week.

Does it make any difference what church you go to; what sermons you pay attention to; what kind of training you get; what group of people you have for your church—your faith family?

We always answer "no" to such questions—"No, these things don't make any difference." We don't want to offend anybody, or start any fights, or act superior. And that's all understandable. But do you notice? This is the only area of life where we would give such an answer! Do you tell your kids it doesn't make any difference which friends they hang around with? Do you tell each other, when your child is ill, that it doesn't make any difference which doctor you go to? There are lots of good coaches, lots of good schools. There are lots of good people, and lots of good tools. But in every other area of life, we still say it makes a difference. Only when it comes to faith and to the church and to the things of God do we sometimes try to say that it doesn't make any difference. Any God will do; any religion will do; any church is as good as another. That can only make sense to people who don't intend to spend much time in any of them! And they say to me, "We're all headed for the same place, you know—heh, heh." I wonder where they come up with such a startling piece of information. It only takes ten minutes in any airport to figure out that just isn't true.

If you come to church every possible Sunday, and get involved with the people here, and get serious about the disciplines that WE RECALL each Sunday, and follow them where they lead you—will you have a stronger and more effective and more skillful faith by the end of the year than you would have if you did none of these things? I can promise you: Absolutely, YES! It is clearer and more certain to me than the sunrise. I have watched the principle in action, and watched the evidence mount over many years, with quite a diverse cross-section of people. I have seen people grow strong in faith. I also know that happens to people when life gets tough and faith is thin. But that is *my* experience. Do you know it too?

If it was known to you that, by going to the Covenant Church or the Presbyterian Church, you would end up with a stronger faith by the end of the year, would you continue to come here? You would be crazy to make such a choice. Make your best choice, but then give it all you have.

When Jesus said, "You must become as little children," He was thinking of "Disneyland enthusiasm." A kid walking into Disneyland for the first time wants to see it all—take every ride, explore every corner. I actually know people who come to church with the exact opposite approach. They come to be convinced of as little as possible; to believe the very minimum that they can; to try as few faith disciplines as they think they can get away with and not be kicked out; to let it change them and their way of life as little and as marginally as possible. Even the Holy Spirit just sits back and waits with people like that. Maybe in some other season of life, they will arrive with a more genuine interest.

I just wanted to "straighten the furniture" a little bit. Now I want to tell all of you: You are on a Path. Early Christians called it THE WAY. God has plans for your life. You know some of them, perhaps, but not all of them. Parts are clear and parts are dim or misty, if you are like the rest of us. But you are on a Path. Probably by now you know it.

If you are on a Path, what does that actually mean? What is it like to walk this Path? Let me remind you of the ABCs of faith, of walking with the Holy Spirit.

1.) The hard step, and the first one, is mental. You must assume that God personally and specifically is conscious of and cares about and is paying attention to every last detail in your life. Please pay attention to how we phrase this. I did *not* say you had to "believe" it. Humans love to get hung up on beliefs (by which they mean philosophies or theologies, or theoretical arguments with themselves and each other). You can waste years on theoretical beliefs, and nothing will come of it. Never mind believing it. Authentic belief comes after years of experience. We are talking about walking the Path—the action side of faith. We take a chance . . . go do it . . . see what happens—and we can talk about what we "believe" afterward.

So you assume that God knows and cares about every detail in your life, down to the smallest item. You treat it as a working axiom. Whether you believe it or not in any absolute way, you act as if it were true—to the best of your ability.

2.) The second step is the same as the first. I'm just trying to break it gently. You also assume that everything you encounter, everything that happens in your life—down to the last detail—is part of God's design, part of God's plan for you. Each day is especially   designed,   created,   furnished,   choreo-graphed . . . precisely for you, containing the very things you need to deal with in order to learn and grow and become that which God wants you to become.

In terms of the Path we are walking, then, we refuse to get into philosophical head-trips about accidents, exceptions to the rule, God's plans for everybody else that cannot possibly coincide with God's plans for us. We simply say to our minds, if they want to argue: "Good point! Fine logic! I'm sure all those points are excellent. But I have no interest in your theories right now. Right now I am following a Path. And the WAY requires that I assume that the days God brings me are the days God wants me to have—down to the smallest detail—each and every day. If I don't assume that, I cannot respond correctly. I will miss the signals. I will not be able to stay on the Path." (So, dear mind, "Sit down and shut up for Jesus." In reality, of course, we are not talking to our higher mind, but to our skeptical inner self.)

3.) Having got this straight, we start looking for God—for God's   instructions   and   guidance—in   our   everyday experiences . . . and only in everyday events . . . but always and every day! We stop looking for the "big stuff." (Big stuff is only a collection of little stuff anyway.) To be faithful in the common, little things becomes our highest aim—how to respond to each new event, in each conversation, in each encounter. We consider all of it part of the Path—the WAY—because we assume God has put it in our way on purpose.

It is imperative, of course, to keep a sense of humor, to keep lighthearted, to be full of gratitude and expectation and a steady conviction that God actually has our best interests at heart (and in mind) in the final analysis. If we started to get grandiose or anxious or heavy-hearted with such a perspective, it would undo us rather quickly. Sometimes a day unfolds into interruptions or challenges or things going wrong, until our minds are sure that either we are dealing with the absurd, or we have stumbled into the core of evil. But if we are on the Path, it doesn't matter. Well, it matters, but it doesn't change anything. We just keep trying to respond to each detail as it comes, as if it were a very intentional and carefully designed part of God's plan for us for that day. We try to respond as obediently as we can—asking for forgiveness when we know we blew it. And we just keep on doing that because the hours and events keep on unfolding.

That's it. That's what it feels like—how we take it from our side—when we know we are on the Path, trying to walk the WAY. Of course, we remember that nothing is ever what it seems. What is going on here in the physical dimension does not look the same or have the same significance as it does when seen from the spiritual dimension. We also keep letting our souls practice to see the difference between these very different perceptions. But that is just for fun. That isn't what makes the difference.

What matters is the absolute assumption that everything down to the tiniest detail is part of the plan. And that it is our task— our only real task—to respond to each detail as it comes as closely as we can to what we think God is directing us to do. When we have it close enough, God will move us on to new experiences. As we learn to be faithful over a little, God will set us over more.

Now, you have always known this, right? This is what it means to be on the Path, to walk the Christian WAY—trusting in Jesus, or the Holy Spirit, or whatever your words for it are. But just in case, I've lined it out for you once again. If, by chance, this does sound strange or new and you are interested in the Path, you might want to come talk to me or somebody about it quite soon. Beginners can have more trouble with it than you might think. Some of us spend quite a few years trying to do everything our own way before we are willing to try this new WAY. Shifting from "our way" to this WAY can be quite a shock. That's why they call it "conversion."

Luke 10:25-28

Week Forty-Nine

WITH ALL YOUR MIND

A lawyer stepped forward to put a question to Jesus. "What shall I do to inherit eternal life?"

It is a good question. We all ask it. How can I make it? How can I succeed? What is the right course to take? What is the true requirement of life? What is the survival kit?

It is also a trick question. Is it really a matter of what we humans do as individuals? Does it not, rather, depend upon how the whole society behaves? Or beyond that, maybe it is all up to God. But even if it does depend upon individual human choice, does anybody really know the answer?

Apparently Jesus did not find it a trick question at all. He turned the man to the core of Jewish tradition and teaching. "What is written in the Torah?" And the man knew, of course. Everybody knew the words: "You shall love the Lord your God with all your heart, and with all your soul, and with all your strength, and with all your mind; and your neighbor as yourself." And Jesus said, "You have answered correctly. Do this and you shall live."

So it was not a trick question. It was a trick answer. How many of you have figured out how to worship the Lord your God with all your heart, soul, strength and mind—and your neighbor as yourself? Yes, it is the right answer. But who knows how to use it, how to put it into full effect? It is one of the "endless answers." That is to say, no matter how far we track it, it keeps opening out before us. No matter how much we live by it, it keeps suggesting and requiring more. Only after much experience and pain and frustration do we begin to realize that all the "right" answers, all the true answers, are like that. How could it be an appropriate reply to the question of eternal life if it did not have this "endless" dimension to it? You can keep applying this answer for a hundred lifetimes, and more, and it won't wear out on you, it won't leave you with nothing else to do.

There are five categories to this answer. Each one is imperative, and worth a study all its own. Yet all five must be in balance together. You would think this would form the core of all our educational systems. What could we possibly want our children to know and practice and study and work at more than this right answer to the meaning and purpose of life? But to teach the children, we have to know it ourselves. And as we have said, to know it ourselves takes endless lifetimes. To some, this might sound discouraging. All it means is that we have to keep working at it, earnestly but patiently, a little bit at a time—every day.

So let's talk about censorship. It isn't everybody's favorite subject, but we have to start somewhere. We aren't really sure when censorship started, but it has been a major item from earliest times. Some people think it was around the time of Moses, when Israel decided it was wrong to marry outside Judaism, and wrong to be friendly with people who worshipped other gods. But most folk say it actually started in the Garden, when God told Adam and Eve that they had to stay away from the fruit of one of the trees. From that day to this, we have had a lot of trouble with censorship.

How do we worship the Lord our God with all our minds? Does that mean we study and consider everything, but always bring it back to allegiance under God? Or does it mean we think and look at only those things that are "godly"—approved by God? And if so, who decides ahead of time what is approved and what is "ungodly," seeing that God has created all things?

In any case, despite the problems, censorship has always been a necessary part of every serious spiritual path. We don't always think of it in just that way. In the early church, some of the regional bishops began to make lists of the writings they had found most beneficial to their own prayer and study. Just as you tell your friends about a book you particularly like, so they were telling their friends about the books they found most helpful. The practice caught on, and turned into a process that eventually decided which writings would be included in the New Testament and which would not. To choose anything eventually turns into a rejection or exclusion of that which is not chosen. And this is the principle of all censorship.

When the church puts some books on a recommended list and others on a banned list, and leaves the rest without special comment either way, we tend to get scornful. We say things about "freedom" and "oppression" and being "open-minded" or "narrow-minded." We don't very often comment about the church trying to be helpful.

I remember some of my own scathing comments, when I was young, about fundamentalist churches that tried to forbid their members to dance, or see movies, or read some of the books I thought were terrific. It was years before I realized that they were only trying to be helpful. Most of their church members were not experiencing oppression. They were encouraging their church leaders to give them guidelines, to help steer them through the maze of possibilities.

The greatest censorship of all is TIME. We do not have time to experience everything, watch everything, read everything. How I sometimes *wish* we had a more trustworthy censorship program in the UCC! If I could read, watch, participate in only the top-quality books, plays, television programs, movies, events, etc., and avoid all the trash—what a boon that would be! Of course, with my training, I wouldn't believe it if it were offered. Neither would most of you.

It's time I was getting to my point, if I'm ever going to. And my point is this: Nobody else will do it for you, in our tradition. You have to develop your own censorship program, or you are creamed! The purpose of this sermon is to persuade you to go home and develop a proper diet for your mind. And the reason is: "You shall worship the Lord your God with all of your mind." It is one of the five primary obligations—one of the five primary secrets—for moving out of death into Life.

The mind is the key (not the source, but the key) to our attitudes, our expectations, our way of processing information and making decisions. That is no surprise to any of us. It is nonetheless beyond appropriate emphasis that the way we feed, discipline and use our minds is critical. It affects everything!

1.) What input does your mind get each week to nourish it on its spiritual path and in its spiritual disciplines? The mind must have nourishment to grow and stay healthy. We all know it. Twenty minutes to an hour (depending on your attention span) once a week is not going to keep the mind focused on God. "You shall worship the Lord your God with all of your mind." If not, then you will not inherit eternal life. Translated, that means the quality of your life will not be very good—not what you need, not what you hoped for, not what you were designed for.

2.) What is your mind's function as worshiper? That is: How does the mind worship? Do you worship with your mind by excluding all things that do not seem godly? Or do you worship with your mind by studying all things until you discover how they are godly? In either case, how do you adjust and correct for the fact that your own time is so limited, and your own mind is inadequate to deal with all things?

After all, it is the mind that questions the existence of God, just as it is the mind that sometimes concludes, "Abba, father, all things are possible unto Thee . . . nevertheless, not my will but thine be done." (Mark 14:36)

We come from the wing of Christendom that is not afraid to doubt. We do not censor things because we are *afraid* of them—at least that is not supposed to be the reason—we censor things because they have proved to be unhelpful, a waste of time. As a result, many of us go through periods of dark doubts. And we trust God to be patient and even approving of our journeys into darkness and despair. And that is because when we come out, our faith is no longer mere theory. Nor is it a product of group pressure or approval.

Maybe some of the results of that are deeper wounds than we should have, and more individualism than is good for us. But it is our Way. The question remains, after we get through such nights of doubt: How do we then turn to worship God with all of our minds? What portion of any given week do we dedicate to Adoration, Gratitude, Contemplation, Intercession, Obedience, Dialogue?

Since we have no censorship in our wing of Christendom, it means we must each become our own censors. Surely we cannot conclude that we have no need of discrimination and discipline. Some people just let their minds do anything at all—think about anything they want to, for as long as they want to; go flitting from subject to subject; get stuck on some pointless object for weeks, or months, or even years. We know the results. There is no way we would want such a fate for ourselves, or for anyone we care about. "You shall worship the Lord your God with all of your mind." So the purpose of this sermon is to persuade you to go home and rework your diet for your mind. Nobody else will do it for you, in our tradition. In our tradition, we are each responsible for our own spiritual disciplines, for our own spiritual path. The price of freedom is always heavier responsibility.

What do you eat with your mind? What do you let it nibble on? Do you also train it constantly for its primary task: to worship the Lord your God?

Consider specific things. How much television, and what programs; how many books, and what kind. The principle of censorship is not just a forbidding. It is an effort to improve the fare. According to your time and your identity, your fare cannot be the same as another person's—even if you are both totally faithful. But it is true that if you spend an hour a day reading a newspaper, it is robbing you of a book a week, and vice versa. And also remember (because few do today) that sometimes the mind needs time to think and digest what it is taking in. Speed is not the answer to our limitations. For some people, speed-reading only means their minds are inundated with more and more trash. Even if you speed-read Plato, Kierkegaard or Brunner, or most of the Bible—and even with high comprehension—you still need at least twice as much time to think about it as you took to read it, or it might as well have been trash.

Along this same line: How much time do you take each week to sit and think? "You shall worship the Lord your God with all of your mind." That can't mean just input—just what we read, watch, see, hear from others. The mind needs time to produce its own thoughts, to contemplate the information and the experiences coming through. There is supposed to be a difference between a computer and a human mind. A computer holds only what has been entered into its memory. Nothing comes out except that which went in. It always comes out the same as it went in. You are supposed to have thoughts of your own, and creative ideas, and new ways of perceiving things. That takes time: time to sit and think; time to contemplate; time to go over things and draw conclusions and ponder possibilities . . . scary as that is.

Finally, do not forget about unofficial time. In some ways, that may be the most important of all—in terms of character formation. I'm talking about all the odd moments through every day when we go off and leave our minds running, without really noticing it. Driving time, walking time, shaving time . . . time in the shower, and doing dishes, and gardening . . . time when we are alone, doing anything habitual. The mind is always busy at such times. It daydreams, or goes over recent conversations, adding in all the comments it might have made. It thinks about victories that eluded us, or sexual encounters we might have had, or money we wish we had, or people we wanted to admire us.

At such times, our own minds seem only half aware of what they are picturing. But we are also getting set up for our real attitudes, and expectations, and choices. That is not time off. We are still supposed to be worshipping the Lord our God with all of our minds.

I remember, with chagrin, going through one of those "phases" a couple of years back. It lasted, it seemed, like forever, but at least six months. My mind kept imagining scenes of great wealth. In my right mind, I know I am already wealthy, but this was daydreams of millions of dollars. Every time my mind was not occupied with a task, if I did not interrupt it with strong demands, it would return to endless scenarios of how it would be to have lots of money. Some of it was instructive, some was pleasant and imaginative, some was very entertaining. But clearly, I was way off track.

For a month or two, I didn't give it much notice. Some of us are asleep enough to suppose that our private thoughts are nobody's business—including our own.

Then I heard myself say some things that were foreign, and realized I meant them. So the alarm finally went off. This is not who I am, how I want to live, what I care about, or what I have dedicated my life to. So I started struggling with my mind, and found I had let things go far too long.

So I started tracking where all this trash was coming from. It wasn't evil, it seemed. I wanted to help some people. That's what got it started. And I pictured what I could do if I had lots of money. And then I saw it. I wanted to help people with money instead of with faith. They needed bucks, not God. After years of knowing better, it had been so long since I went through the ABCs that my inner self forgot. In the end, it did not escape me who I was imagining would get the credit for all this "help." So it was evil after all—right at the core of where real evil really comes from: wanting to play God.

Understanding all of that still didn't break the grip of my greed. The thoughts kept recurring at every careless moment, until the simplest, fundamental principle came back into focus. I was shifting from trusting God to trusting money for my security! That broke it. My heart started laughing, and all the scenarios looked as dull and pointless as they really were. And so they finally faded away, and left me in enough peace to go back to life. Do you ever go through stuff like this? The greed thing isn't bothering me at all, lately. But I wonder what my mind is working on now that will turn out to be a dumb sidetrack a few months hence. After all, the mind is like a spoiled child. If we do not train it constantly, it gets into all kinds of mischief.

We cannot control all the subjects and scenes that cross our minds. The mind is made to process information, and to be curious, and to be imaginative. The mind will consider anything. Sometimes that embarrasses or worries us.

We cannot control all the subjects and scenes that cross our minds. But we *can* decide what we will dwell on . . . what we will hold in focus . . . what we will mentally nourish, and hold onto, and keep, and give our minds permission to work on. If the mind does not dwell on God, it dwells on something else.

This sermon hopes to persuade you to consider and then set up a serious and well-balanced diet for your mind. In our culture, and in our wing of Christendom, nobody else will do that for you. You have to do that for yourself, or be overrun with trash. If we wish to LIVE—to inherit eternal life, to be disciples of Jesus— we seek always and in all ways to remember: "You shall worship the Lord your God with all of your mind."

Romans 6:8-23

Week Fifty

SIN

Lent is here again—forty days to get ready for Holy Week, and prepare ourselves for resurrection. It is not likely that we will believe in the magnitude of the Easter Resurrection unless we have a medium-size resurrection at least once a year, and a smaller resurrection experience at least once a week. It is just another way of saying that we need to stay awake to the realization that we are already living our eternal life. This isn't all of it, but this is part of it. We are expectant and eager for what lies ahead, but we are already into it.

Lent comes every year to remind us that we aren't really here to wait for heaven. Lent is a time of special focus, and new disciplines. Traditionally, Lent is a time when the saints give up something. Corrupted as that has often become, it is still clear that Lent is a time of earnest endeavor. Ninety percent of the Christian Faith is about what God does for us. God's love is a gift, a mercy, a grace . . . an undeserved and unexpected BLESSING of power and beauty that we can neither earn nor repay; that we cannot turn on or turn off; that we cannot manipulate or control. We can only receive or reject. The other ten percent of the Christian Faith is about how we respond to God's love. And that ten percent is always more than we can keep up with.

So Lent begins with our sins, our struggles, our disciplines, our efforts—mostly our efforts to please God, to get closer, to bring our lives in line with God's Will and Purpose. Then Lent moves on to far vaster themes, and to that which the Christ does which we cannot do for ourselves. But Lent starts with the assessment of where we are. Lent reminds us that the spiritual life is also a steady discipline and training on our part. Our efforts will never make it, never be enough. But they are nonetheless important. It is part of our gratitude and part of our response. We don't just kill time waiting for Jesus to do everything for us. Even though that will end up being the case, we still try to cooperate. It is often quite true that our efforts at self-improvement are disastrous. Often they get in the Lord's way. Many times, the "improvement" is worse than when we started. Nevertheless, it is still necessary!

I remember as a young boy trying to help my father with various projects. My "help" always cost him more time than if he had done it himself. My "help" always introduced flaws and accidents and even disasters into the project that wouldn't have been there if he had done it himself. Often, after I was gone, he would have to fix the work we had done together. It was the same way when my son was young and tried to help me. It is always that way between us and God. But there is no other way for us to learn. God's love is the power that saves us, but we try to help . . . and we mess it up . . . and we learn a lot in the process. Eventually, God's grace saves us in spite of all our "help." Only, my father didn't like it if I stopped trying to help. Even though it was making his task harder, he didn't like it at all if I stopped trying to help. And I didn't like it if my son stopped trying. We can be pretty certain that God doesn't like it either. Sloth is still one of the Seven Deadly Sins, especially spiritual sloth. Or, as Henry David Thoreau said, "As if we could kill time without injuring eternity!"

Lent begins with an inventory of our condition. That results in ashes on our heads. Ash Wednesday is an old, traditional and beautiful way of saying, "We aren't perfect yet, and we know it. We aren't finished yet. We have lots left to learn and know and grow into. And we still do a lot of things wrong, and leave a lot of right things undone." Lent begins with the reminder that time is short, that we are mortal here, that there is much we need to be doing—and some things we need to stop doing or be done with.

In short, Lent begins with the reminder of sin—with our seeing afresh the condition of our sin and the seriousness of that sin. Lent begins with a renewed awareness of ourselves as sinners.

Somebody in the Confirmation Class asked me what the position of the United Church of Christ was on penance. I assured the class that if they walked among you at coffee time asking about "penance," at least half of you would say you had never heard of it, or would claim only a vague and fuzzy notion of its meaning. I further supposed that the response would be even less rewarding in most other UCC congregations they might visit. In short, the UCC doesn't think much about penance because it mostly doesn't believe in sin. At least it doesn't like to talk about it. People think it is negative. It doesn't leave people with an upbeat feeling. (So the UCC likes to talk about nuclear war, urban planning, refugees, world hunger, how to choose only "good guy" companies to invest in, and other upbeat subjects like that.)

It seems pretty clear that we cannot engage in Lent unless we can face and talk about sin. And we cannot really participate in Holy Week or Easter either, if we are afraid to look at sin. It's like looking at an answer without a question, or a solution without a problem. According to the Christian Faith, sin is the basic condition of all life on this planet. If we do not understand and identify that basic presupposition, then everything else about the Christian Faith will be hopelessly distorted. Sin is the basic condition of all life on this planet. We should know that, expect it, get used to it. (Imagine the change in perspective—no more perfectionism!) From the Christian perspective, all that God does here is done with that in mind, and done with that as the context and circumstance of everything. The problem today is further complicated by the fact that we no longer know what the concept of "sin" means. Or we know, but keep reverting to the popular usage. I have reminded us of the real definition of perhaps no other word more often in the last three years than this one. Still, it is easy to revert back to the more familiar meaning. When that happens, the miscommunication is terrible. We simply must come to the place where we can call ourselves and each other "sinners" and know there is no personal insult intended. If we are not sinners, what are we doing here? Being a sinner is the only true requirement for membership in the Christian Church.

I suppose the reason "sin" is such a volatile word is because judgment, condemnation and hell seem to follow so close behind. If we are guilty of sin, then it is hard not to assume that we are about to be judged, then condemned, and certainly sent to hell. Supposedly, we know better. The whole story and message of the Christ who came to us stands for precisely the opposite. It all happened to reassure us that this is not what God in Christ does about sin, or to sinners. But we have a hard time believing that, no matter how brave we talk. And we have a hard time trusting each other to really believe it.

A woman who was called to jury duty told the presiding judge that she was not qualified to serve because she did not believe in capital punishment. The judge said, "You don't understand, ma'am. This is a civil case involving a man who spent five thousand dollars of his wife's money on gambling and other women." To which the woman replied eagerly, "I'd be happy to serve, your honor, and I've changed my mind about capital punishment."

A college sophomore who had spent most of the school year in one kind of trouble or another received the following card from his parents, who were vacationing in Greece: "Dear Son, we are now standing high on a cliff from which the ancient Spartan women once hurled their defective children to the rocks below. Wish you were here."

Somewhere deep inside, we have that uneasy feeling that maybe—just about the time we buy the Christian Message and admit that we are sinners—maybe the lady will change her mind about capital punishment . . . maybe the Great Parent in the sky will decide to throw us over the cliff after all. So we decide not to think about the whole thing very much—maybe take a stab at giving up some minor habit during Lent, fully expecting to regain it after Easter, and that's that.

There are three words most often used in the Old Testament for our word "sin"—*chata, awon* and *pesha.* The first characterizes sin as failure to meet a standard or arrive at a goal. To sin is to miss the mark, as when you shoot an arrow and miss the target.

The second word sees sin primarily as an action that is irregular, "crooked," a deviation from the normal behavior patterns. C.S. Lewis loved this one, and often used the words "bent" and "warped." The third word sees sin as an infringement upon a psychic totality. We say, "being out of tune with nature, or God."

The common denominator of all three of these is still separation, alienation. In the first case, the missile is separated from its intended target, the person from the intended goal. In the second case, it is action separated from the true or normal pattern of action. In the third case, it is separation from an awareness of the life principles themselves, or from the Creator of those principles.

To ponder sin in this light is amazingly revealing. Suddenly all sorts of teachings and concepts and principles in Scripture start to make sense, and become helpful, and get downright exciting. Jesus saves us from sin by "making us get rid of all our bad habits"? Heavens no! That isn't even talking about the same subject. Jesus saves us from our separated state by reconciling us to God—that is, putting us back in communication, in relationship, with God.

The next thing that happens most often, I find, is that people say (to themselves sometimes), "That is really helpful, and it makes so much sense," yet they cannot make themselves believe that Paul and Luke and Jesus were smart enough to know this better definition. How can I persuade you? The early Christians would never have turned the world upside down if they had thought sin meant what you think it means. They were not getting thrown to the lions and burned at the stake and crucified along the highways of Rome because they were enthralled with giving up smoking, or cutting down their TV time, or losing some weight, or even quitting their adultery. That kind of thing has its importance in its proper context. But the Christian Faith enthralled and converted a pagan world over issues larger than that! Because of Jesus Christ and all that had happened, people realized they were caught in an entire way of life that was literally built and running on principles of separation, alienation, loneliness, aloneness—and that's what *they* meant by SIN. They were sinners, and everybody was caught in this web of life, running on the energy that divides—us from God, us from each other, us from nature. Everywhere you turn, everything you experience, all of it always ends up in separation.

You get married because you fall in love and want to be close and share and care—and what happens? Professor Hans Jurgens asked five thousand German husbands and wives how often they talked to each other. After two years of marriage, most of them managed two or three minutes of chat over breakfast, more than twenty minutes over the evening meal, and a few more minutes in bed. By the sixth year, that was down to ten minutes a day. A state of "almost total speechlessness" was reached by the eighth year of marriage. (Daily Mirror, London)

You have children because it's a miracle of life, and you want to raise them perfect and fill them full of love and the idea of "family"—people working and living together in joy and harmony through thick and thin. It's so beautiful we can't even think about it very long without hurting inside for longing. But then we try it and what happens? Sometimes we taste it for a while, just enough to remind us it's possible. Sometimes people in a crisis find each other; sometimes in war, people find each other; sometimes a cause, or a significant enough project, or something of great beauty or potential draws us together for a little while. But then the crisis passes, the war ends, the cause gets organized, the thing of beauty becomes familiar . . . and what happens? Everywhere you turn, everything you experience, all of it always ends up in separation. We live in a realm running on the principles of sin, and we are caught in it as sinners, and there is no escape.

At least there *was* no escape. Then Jesus came and said: "You can't fix it! No matter how well you keep the rules, it won't get any better. You have to leave the entire system. You have to die to it all. You have to be born anew to a different WAY. And even after that, the only hope is that the power and love of God will indwell you, invade you, come into you and replace the entire system and way of separation—replace your wanting to be alone, to do it yourself, to be in control, to do everything your own way. Let me in—I'll bring you a new way, a togetherness way, a way of Love. You're also free to stay in the old way. But it is a way of aloneness and separation. You may think you can fix it. You can try. But it is separation, and it will stay the way of separation."

"The wages of sin is death." (Do please start translating this, and other passages on the subject, as "The result of separation is death.") If you follow the principles of being alone and apart for long enough, you will die totally. If you follow the alienation way for just today, you will be more apart and alone by tonight than you were this morning. It's inevitable. Resentments, fears, hatreds . . . getting even . . . suspicion, competition, pride— where else can they go, except to separation that gets wider, and colder, until life cannot exist. Of course, along the way there is behavior that reveals the condition we are in—the condition of our souls. But those are symptoms. Jesus Christ was never trying to put Band-Aids on symptoms! He was certainly not trying to sweep any of it under any rugs. He was trying to heal the *condition*—SIN—the state of alienation, and doing all things by the principles that maintain alienation.

We are sinners. And we will stay sinners until the grace and love of God can change every part of us—from thought-wave to the least deed we do. We can't do that for ourselves—it requires a Savior. But we can cooperate. Only, cooperation begins with our recognition of our condition: Sin. We are SINNERS.

Forty years ago, malaria killed at least half the people who died each year. How was malaria conquered? Not by killing mosquitoes! By developing quinine and similar medicines that counteract malaria from within the life-stream itself, from within the hemoglobin. So with sin. It isn't conquered by going around slapping mosquitoes—individual sins. It has to be healed at the source and core of things—our closeness to God. Christianity isn't about sins, though we keep getting sidetracked on such things. Christianity is about SIN—the Great Divide—the Great Separation between us and our Maker. And that is what Jesus came to heal. That is what Jesus is about: reconciling us to God.

Colossians 1:11-20; II John

Week Fifty-One

SWEET & SOUR

The only organization I know of that takes inspiration from the second letter of John is the Order of the Eastern Star. The church secretary in my first parish was the highest, most-exalted, glorious potentate—I could never remember the exact title, but something like that—of the Eastern Star for the entire state of Massachusetts. I don't know anything about the order, but I used to tease her that she didn't know much about it either. A lot of the meaning and symbolism apparently focused around some of the famous women of the Bible. One of them was Electa. So I would ask Ethel, "Who was Electa? What did she do?" And Ethel would say to me, "I don't know, but she was very important."

I was only about twenty-five and didn't know, yet, how careful you have to be not to offend your secretary. So I would ask, "Ethel, are you sure Electa is somebody mentioned in the Bible?" And she would say, "Oh yes, sure." And I would ask, "Where?" And she would say, "I don't know exactly, but she's in there."

So then I would ask, "Ethel, why is it called the Eastern Star?" And she would say, "Because of the Christian star. You know, at Christmas—the one the wise men followed. You're supposed to know these things." And I would say, "Ethel, I do know these things, and there's nothing in the Bible about any wise men following an eastern star." Now she did know where *that* passage was, so she would get out the Bible and show me Matthew 2:2. "We have seen his star in the east, and have come to worship him." And she explained to me how traveling east had been symbolic of seeking truth and spiritual enlightenment ever since.

Then gleefully I would get out my map and ask her to show me where the wise men had come from, that they could travel east and end up in Bethlehem. So we had many delightful discussions about camels with waterwings, and how rumors get started with careless reading of information. And I would say things like, "How can you be the highest, most-exalted, glorious potentate of the Eastern Star and not know that the star was in the west or who Electa was, when these are foundation principles of your whole order?" And then she would say . . . things I won't repeat here.

In John's second letter, "Electa"—the elect lady—refers to the church. The letter assumes that the church is made up of special people—the lucky ones, the chosen, the elect. John knows we aren't saved by any special merit, brains or behavior of our own. Yet the church is the elect lady—the lucky ones who are called out of aimlessness and sin into the special grace and purpose and love of God in Christ.

The other day I was talking to an AA friend, and I suddenly got a fresh demonstration of how this kind of thinking developed in the early church. My friend was saying how he considered those of us in AA to be the lucky ones. Out of the thousands of us destroying and being destroyed by the disease, only a few of us get the incredible blessing of finding ourselves in the program, and then we find the program so helpful that we often catch ourselves feeling sorry for "normal" people. There was no pride whatsoever in my friend's comments. He was simply feeling grateful.

It suddenly dawned on me that this was precisely what happened in the early church. People were released from their guilt and fear, from feeling worthless and hopeless about life. And they realized that through no merit or fault of their own, they had found themselves in the incredible fellowship of the church, and being filled by the grace and power of the Gospel Message. They felt grateful, and wished everybody could get a taste of what they had found. Generations later, their comments—now canon Scripture—were perceived as a doctrine of exclusion and judgment, rather than as simple comments of wonder and gratitude.

Today, the selectivity and exclusiveness make us uneasy, and rightly so. We don't want to be ungrateful for all God has done for us, or unmindful of all that Jesus went through and endured to reveal greater truth and to reconcile us to God. On the other hand, we know atheists, humanists, Buddhists, Muslims, etc., who are pretty nice people. Whatever any of them believe, it is my belief that God loves them as much as God loves us.

When John wrote, the church was still quite small, and Judaism was widespread, well-established and very influential. Frequently, that influence cost Christians their property, jobs and lives. The animosity between brothers is always hottest because neither can believe that the other will not come around. John's writings in the New Testament reveal his anger and pain. And those writings in turn have inspired countless generations to maintain the tragic separation. Christians in various ways and times have "repaid" the Jews a thousand times over, and more, and many of us are ashamed and deeply regretful of that part of our history. Yet it is still our history.

If the Pope wants to make pronouncements that are helpful and important, he should drop the subject of birth control (a subject that seems beyond his grasp) and instead say, "We [the church] are sorry for the way we have spoken and acted and treated God's Jewish children and all the other children who have disagreed with us over the centuries. We do not repeal our faith or the truth by which we believe we are being saved. But we would affirm our fundamental Christian truth that God loves all the people outside the church at least as much as God loves those inside the church. And while we naturally claim that inside the church is a wonderful path and the best way of life on earth, we wish courage and endurance to all spiritual pilgrims, and hope we can be as warm and helpful a friend to all of them in the future as we have been a scourge and enemy to them in the past."

I'm not really trying to put words into the Pope's mouth, although I would if there were any way in the world I thought I could. But back to reality. I am using this example to illustrate how a lot of us feel today, and how troubled we feel about the flavor of exclusiveness and the "we alone will be saved" kind of attitude that seems to permeate so much Christian tradition and concept. It is a "sweet and sour" experience to explore and struggle with many of our basic Christian assumptions and beliefs.

It is sweet to contemplate Jesus' incredible devotion and love and obedience. It is sweet to begin to discern that this opens for us the possibility of daily and constant experience in the presence of His Holy Spirit. It is sweet to begin to feel and realize that this changes us from within—grants us peace and confidence and a deep inner joy, and a hope for the future that is beyond all human language.

It is sour indeed to add to this any hint or indication that anyone without the same experience or the same awareness and conviction is somehow outside of God's care, or consigned to some kind of special punishment or displeasure from the God of Love.

It is sweet to hear in II John that we are the elect—the ones God has especially set aside and chosen. It is sweet to be reminded that love is the primary principle of our fellowship—that we are called and chosen not only to receive love, but to learn to love one another. It is sour to have this same letter, without break or explanation, flow smoothly on from words and concepts of love into a diatribe against anybody who does not acknowledge Jesus Christ in the flesh. Suddenly we are calling them deceivers, linking them with the Antichrist. And so, the loving letter to the elect lady ends with the demand that we are to utterly reject, condemn and refuse to associate with anybody who does not see or understand things exactly the way we do.

It is sweet to think of the church as a fellowship of believers, of people seeking together, and growing and sharing and learning together—supporting each other, in ways large and small, through the turmoil and sorrow and joy and potential of this life's experience. But it is sour if the church is self-righteous or smug or thinks it has all the answers, or admits only those who think according to prescribed ways. It is sour if the church talks or feels like a group of superior citizens, instead of like a family of sinners who help each other unreservedly, knowing everybody needs all the help they can get.

It is difficult to rejoice completely, or to enjoy spontaneously, when we keep getting a mixture of sweet and sour. It's hard, also, to invite others freely, when we are half-delighted and half-ashamed of who we are and what we represent.

As if that weren't enough, the sweet and sour analogy flips around the other way too. It may be sweet to see more and more people in our time who want to be inclusive; who see and long for a greater unity between all peoples, lands and religions; who want to heal the ancient rifts at last, and build bridges between all the alienated brothers and sisters and traditions.

But it is sour, bitter indeed, that these same people so often have little or no comprehension or experience of the Gospel. Flitting around the edges or over the surface of Christianity, they seem to have missed the core of the atonement. Jesus is not really the Christ to them. The Cross and the Resurrection seem only stories to them, akin to George Washington's cherry tree or Aesop's fox that decided the grapes were sour because he couldn't reach them.

It's easy to talk about giving up Christianity's exclusive claims—giving up the core and tradition and faith of the church, and becoming universal and all-inclusive—if you have never tasted the real grace of Jesus Christ to begin with. What seems logical, intelligent and civilized to some, remains unthinkable for some of the rest of us. And we forget that some don't realize the incomparable loss if Jesus Christ gets homogenized into a figment of modern Western imagination. No need for prayer, for revelation, for guidance from the Holy Spirit if the truth is in you because you are really God, or part of God, or your own salvation, or your own savior.

Sour indeed! The word is suddenly quite inadequate. I sometimes have trouble keeping kind thoughts for fundamentalists, but I would turn Pentecostal long before I would swallow pabulum like that! (Not that they would have me . . .)

Despite the sweet and sour, the church is still mostly sweet for me. I think the institutional church is a silly, inadequate, contradictory, irritating, feeble shadow of what it ought to be. Its people fuss and fizzle, fight and fume, get bored and forget all their vows and disciplines, get lost in details, and all the rest. But the institutional church, despite all of this, is still the best institution this world has seen so far! And, far more impressive to me, it can still connect with that invisible church which truly *is* the body of Christ.

So I know it is sweet and sour. And I'm glad we can share that together, and not try to sweep it under any prayer rugs. We are the church in our day, and we have the privilege and responsibility of shaping it according to the measure of our own faith and prayer and experience.

Hebrews 7:1-19

Week Fifty-Two

THE SERMON ON THE AMOUNT

Today is going to be fun because we get to talk about money. Somebody asked me last year, "How come on Covenant Sunday you talk about money when there are so many other dimensions to the covenants?" I said that was easy: Money is the labor of our hands. It is the practical core of dedication in this life. Therefore, we start there, and move up from there. If a person hasn't learned to tithe, what chance would he have to learn prayer, or service, or any of the more difficult disciplines of spiritual devotion?

Money is a subject that not everybody, but almost everybody, is interested in. People who are not interested in money are leeches. They are living off of somebody else. Somebody else is taking care of them and making all the practical decisions for them. Do not confuse that with sainthood, which is trusting in God, not in other human beings. Even saints are supposed to be good stewards, and most of them are therefore also interested in money.

Today is going to be fun because we get to talk about money, and we are all interested in money. Money is a resource. It can be put to use in almost any direction. It can help with an amazing array of goals and interests and objectives. If we find companions with the same goals, we can pool some of our money and accomplish amazing things. As Benjamin Franklin said, "The use of money is all the advantage there is in having money." It sounds so obvious when he says it. But I keep forgetting. Our whole culture keeps forgetting.

The thought of lots of money is fun to contemplate. The thought of losing money is fearful to most of us. Is that not logical, reasonable and understandable? No great mystery here—except when we try to pretend it isn't or shouldn't be so.

It is, therefore, logical that all the pragmatic issues of life should cluster around whatever monetary system any civilization sets up. If we have any goals, any dreams, any fears, any desires, any concern for helping others—then we also have an interest in money. Status and reputation may enter in. How much will we sacrifice or risk to get more money? Already we have crossed the border into spiritual affairs. For many people down through the ages, money has been of interest because it can be used for religious aims or purposes. But where is the line between greed and devotion? Between responsibility and pride? Between stewardship and stinginess? Humankind has stumbled, and sometimes been broken, over such issues from the dawn of time. Socrates proclaimed, "If a rich man is proud of his wealth, he should not be praised until it is known how he employs it." That was back in 400 B.C. Not how much, but how do we use it? That is the issue. How we use money tells what we care about, what our values are, what we really believe is important. No matter how much we have—or how little—our use of it still tells the true story.

This is going to be the sermon on the amount. I get to cut away all the confusion and tell you what the Christian solution is. I get to announce to you once again what the Christian Life is like when it comes to money. Christianity assumes that the way we deal with our money is part of our spiritual path. You get to hear the message again and decide whether or not you will live by it. Isn't that clear and simple? It should also be a delight. "We make a living by what we get, but we make a life by what we give." Or so said Winston Churchill.

I happen to know that only a few of you have ever experienced—have ever actually tried—the Christian pattern when it comes to money. That means you have something wonderful in store for you! The Christian Life is not discovered in thinking about it, or in imagining it. The blessings and peace and joy of the Christian Pilgrimage come in living it, in experiencing it. If those in a community/congregation/faith family finally come to the point of dedicating themselves—of living the spiritual disciplines of the Christian Way together—then the joy of sharing and caring and believing together increases manyfold. Church is no longer something external. It is our life, our being—who we are and what we are about. Among other things, conversion is a move from the theoretical into the realm of the actual.

To cut any possible confusion, this is the sermon on the amount. The amount you owe to the Kingdom each year is one-tenth of what you earn. How long has this principle been in effect? At least four thousand years now. Has this amount ever been enforced? It is required in Judaism. Christianity considers it a spiritual privilege, and does not enforce it. In Christendom, it is considered that everything we have belongs to God and we are merely stewards, trying to manage and use all our resources as God would want them managed and used. But it is also Christendom's teaching that at least the tithe—the first ten percent—of our income must go to the church.

I hope you agree that I have preached more inspiring sermons on this subject in the past. I mean, you have heard some of the world's best sermons on stewardship, and I hope you're grateful. Today I am more interested in clarity than in inspiration. I am not responsible for what you do about tithing—thank God! I *am* responsible for what you are *taught* about tithing. When you get to the Pearly Gates, will St. Peter say, "I don't understand it. You have been a faithful church member for years. You should have a tremendous account with us by now, but this record shows you never even gave the minimum. What happened? Is there some mistake?"

If at that point it turns out that your minister never told you straight, never made it clear, never lifted up the Biblical principle because he didn't want to disturb or bother you . . . then guess who is going to be in trouble?! But if it turns out that your minister told you straight, called you to obedience, and you just decided you knew better than the Bible, better than your minister did, better than four thousand years of faithful followers did . . . then I don't know if you'll be in trouble, but at least I won't be. Not on that score. Now, I'm not terrified of every kind of trouble. But there are some kinds of trouble I want no part of. "Fear of the Lord is the beginning of wisdom."

I'm not asking you to tithe to please me. I don't think hardly anybody could make themselves tithe just to feel like a big shot, or to feel super-generous. A few people might tithe because the church is important and needs money. That moves me, but not enough to make me tithe.

However, a lot of people tithe because they know God asks it, and they wish to be obedient to God. Christianity is about turning from our own aims and goals—our own little kingdoms— to living in and for God's Kingdom. We talk a lot about turning our lives and our wills over to God. Well, one of the first and most obvious parts of that decision, if we mean it, is that we turn our money over too. One of the first steps or marks of the authentic spiritual path is that our money gets dedicated along with our hearts. So we tithe as part of our spiritual pilgrimage.

I read to you what may have sounded like an obscure passage for this sermon. Abraham is called "The Father of Faith." He is the first patriarch of our tradition. He himself came out of some pre-Zoroastrian Persian religion. But it is shrouded in the dimness of ancient time. Abraham's conversion is the beginning of Judaism. It is as far back as we go, with any historic comprehension. And Abraham is already giving a spiritual tithe to Melchizedek, priest of God most high.

Let us keep clear. The Bible speaks of bringing to the Lord both tithes and offerings. The tithe is owed. The tithe is minimum for citizens of God's Kingdom. The tithe is like a spiritual tax. After the tithe is paid, many who can afford it bring offerings: gifts of love or devotion, gifts for a special cause or a further purpose. Ten percent of your income is obligatory; after that, you can bring offerings if you choose to.

Our daughter, Willene, was in China for a couple of months this summer. That is a whole saga in itself. But she made an intriguing vow upon her return. I am interested to see if she will be able to keep it. She said, "I will never complain about paying income taxes ever again." She explained that, upon her return, when she drove her car for the first time and came to an intersection, there was a signal light there. It enabled some of the traffic to stop and some of the traffic to proceed, and everybody didn't jam into the intersection until nobody could go anywhere. She sat in new amazement and awareness until the cars behind her had to honk to signal that the light had changed. And she yelled out, "What a great idea, America! You're wonderful!" She saw that everywhere there were attempts to improve things for everyone. They weren't perfect. She had known that before. But they were attempts. Streets got repaired, and even cleaned. There were fire departments, and communities hired their own police, and on and on. She saw it with new eyes, and made her crazy vow: "I will never complain about paying incomes taxes ever again."

Do you know what a tithe is? Has it been too long—so long that the origins are lost? If I say to you the word "tribute," will you know what I mean? From the dawn of time, people have paid tribute. All people always pay tribute to something or someone. They pay it in gratitude, or out of fear. They pay it in allegiance, or in anger. But tribute must be paid. Sometimes we pay tribute for protection, or for increased services, or even because we honor and believe in the leaders to whom we pay it. But tribute must always be paid, one way or another, to one leader or another. Always people pay tribute to the king. If there is no tribute, there is no king!

Are we getting simple enough? Why do we pray each day, "Thy kingdom come"?

If we live in, serve in, believe in God's Kingdom, we also pay tribute. We pay taxes to an earthly kingdom. But those of us in this place also belong to a Kingdom not of this world. Our hope, we say, is in this other Kingdom. So we tithe—we pay tribute. We support and back our King. We want the church—the place on earth that represents our King—to be a place that continually draws more people into the Way of the King. If there is no tribute, there is no King! If we do not pay our tribute, we serve notice that we do not really believe in or serve this King. About one-fifth of our members pay no tribute at all. I don't understand that. If you make ten dollars all year and give one to the King, it is not a small gift. It is all that is asked. But to give nothing at all? I don't understand that. Of course, I don't understand not wanting to give the tithe, or being willing to give less than a tithe.

Sometimes, in my imagination, I think of life without the church—life without any place to learn about Jesus, and to know, to follow, to share the Christian Way. I come away from such times swearing I will never complain about tithing again. And I almost never do. It is a pleasure, a joy, a privilege to pay tribute to our King! It is part of the Good News of the Gospel that we finally know a King who is worth giving to—that we have found in Him a purpose and a vision that make it at last satisfying to give, to dedicate ourselves, even to sacrifice. If we give our tribute rightly, it will bring increase to the Kingdom and turn into great blessings, not only for us, but far beyond our present borders.

I know some people who seem to resent the fact that the church spends money. To hear them talk, you would think that it should be the church's first priority to cost as little as possible. Anything not absolutely essential to bare survival is suspect, if not treasonous, in their eyes. What a strange attitude to have toward one's King.

A church member was complaining about how the church spent money on music, playgrounds, parking lots, office equipment and salaries. "And it's always asking for more money," the person concluded, with both whine and disgust in his voice.

Another member, listening to this familiar line for the thousandth time, finally replied, "We had a child. She cost us quite a lot of money, even as a baby. Then it was school, and she always seemed to need more clothes, and she wanted to go to summer camp. Pretty soon, she wanted music lessons, and instruments cost a bundle. Then it was college. Do you know how much it costs to go to college? But she died partway through college. And you know, since then, she hasn't cost us a cent." And he turned on his heel and strode away. There is a way for the church to cost far less, or even nothing at all. Will I ever complain about tithing again?

Do we really resent paying tribute to our King? Some of the world really would prefer Him dead, cut off, silent. That we know. That has always been part of the story. If He is not to be shut off, we will pay tribute, and gladly. You cannot just live an ethical life and keep Christ's Kingdom alive. You cannot just run your own business or your own affairs in "a Christian manner" (though that is terribly important) and keep Christ's Kingdom growing in this world. You cannot just give to all the many fine charities and humanitarian organizations, however noble you or they are, and keep Christ's Kingdom available in this world. When people seek the information or the experience or the fellowship of the Christian Life, they cannot go to the Red Cross, or to the Boy Scouts, or to John Hancock, or to any other company or organization—no matter how inspired or helpful they might be. When people want to know or be a part of Jesus and His Kingdom, they go to church and become the church. And if they don't find anything there, they quit, or seek a different kingdom. Where people do not pay tribute, there is no King! (At least not for them; though the King exists, He is incognito.)

Here is a parable: Watching the ball is to tennis what tithing is to the spiritual life. Tithing is a constant reminder of our purpose, our allegiance, our tribute. Paying tribute keeps us remembering what our purpose is, what we are living for, whom we live to serve. If you do not tithe, your Christian game is about as good as the tennis game of a player who does not watch the ball. He may try very hard, and use great energy, but things never come into focus.

Every Sunday, in WE RECALL, we read: "We move earnestly toward tithing to 'our' church." *Our* is always in quotation marks. It is our church because this is the church we are part of, but it also belongs to Jesus Christ, so *our* cannot be possessive. Some of you have been "moving toward tithing" for a long time without making any progress. It is important to realize that spiritual growth does and will get stopped if we do not accept the disciplines of the spiritual life. And that it opens up into unending vistas and experiences if we truly turn our lives over, and live for the King and the Kingdom. If God isn't good enough or important enough to receive our tribute, then by definition we haven't started to worship yet.

I realize that if all of you, or even most of you, started to tithe, it would have a dramatic impact on our church's budget. We could pay off debts, take on new projects, accomplish many things we cannot even consider now. It will cross your mind that I would like you to tithe so this could happen. Let me tell you something: I would love to see that happen! There probably isn't anything in this world that seems more exciting to me than to be able to live in a church which really decided to live its faith.

Maybe you aren't going to believe this, but it's true: That is still not why I have preached this sermon. First and foremost, I care about your spiritual health and growth. I know the interior difference—the difference in a person's personal relationship to the Lord—when they do not carry their commitment and devotion to the level of tithing. And I know how much that begins to change when they do. That is what I truly care about.

If you do not pay tribute, you have not yet claimed this king as your King. For Christians and Jews, the minimum tribute is ten percent of your income. This is the sermon on the amount. The amount is ten percent of your income.

So you can do as you like—meaning, as you believe—about tithing. It is the Congregational way. But don't tell them at the Pearly Gates that you didn't know any better. Because they're going to look it up to see what church you came from, and who was teaching there.

THE STEPS
THROUGH LENT,
AND BEYOND

Together, each week, WE RECALL:

It is necessary for us as Christians to pray every day, to study some portion of the Scriptures each day, seeking in grace and praise to discover God's will for our own lives on a daily basis. As part of our discipleship, we also work to increase our love for one another. We move earnestly toward tithing to "our" Church, that the Kingdom may increase its resources. For the same reason we try to tithe our time and our conversation. Finally, we hope that our faith and love and discipline will increase until it flows beyond our fellowship and becomes a blessing to others.

I John 1:5-2:2; Luke 18:10-14

Ash Wednesday

THE EIGHTH STEP

*Made a list of all persons we had harmed,
and became willing to make amends to them all.*

All human beings feel guilt. The polite word is "remorse." The dictionary definition of remorse is "the keen or hopeless anguish *caused by* a sense of guilt." All human beings feel guilt. *For all have sinned and fall short of the glory of God*—the state of perfection or total wholeness we long for yet have never experienced. (Romans 3:23) Some people seem to "make us feel guilty"; some people think the church produces guilt; some people play off our guilt more than others; some people try to use our guilt to get us to react or perform as they want us to. But they do not produce the guilt—it is already there and they merely use it. Neither does the church produce guilt—it is already there. The church focuses either on helping to heal the guilt or on using it to control its people.

The question is not, "Should we feel guilty or not feel guilty?"—though it is often put that way. Many statements imply we have such a choice. But our choice is whether to deny it or deal with it—whether to pretend it is not there, or to go through the process of cleaning it up, of healing. The fact that guilt is such a huge reality in human existence suggests that the Creator designed us with this potential for guilt—and that its purpose is to guide us toward important corrections and necessary changes. In this sense, guilt is good—if it warns us about wrong directions and helps us turn in new directions. But we all know that guilt unprocessed is a killer. Guilt is spiritual acid. Mixed with other things—like sorrow, confession, repentance, penance, the receiving of forgiveness—it is wonderful. But guilt unmixed—

guilt just sitting there by itself—guilt, like acid, eats through and destroys everything we try to become or accomplish.

This Lent, we are talking about steps to take—things we must actually do—if we want to make spiritual progress. We are not talking about being saved—that is God's part. We are not talking about *making* God love us, or persuading God to love us, or earning salvation, or forcing our way into grace. But it should be no secret that after any person is truly converted, they change: their life changes; they start *being* different and doing things differently and for different reasons. If not, the conversion was a fake—a misfire. It is no surprise that our world is full of false starts, and no surprise that much which passes for religion is counterfeit—intended or unintended. Nevertheless, some steps characterize the spiritual path. People who are serious about their religion take steps, they do something about it. Always the majority of members in any well-established religion seem *not* to take steps: nothing much happens for them; eventually they quit, or they settle for just going through meaningless motions. Every established religion is covered with the dust of inertia and the debris of people who no longer take it seriously. Always we must get beneath the surface, back to where the power and beauty and excitement are.

There are many ways of listing the steps of the spiritual path. All of them share some similarities. The wars between the various ways to line out the spiritual path are mostly futile—a problem of semantics, a quarrel over turf. Most any step we take in sincere devotion to God will lead us on, give us growth—even if we do not do it perfectly, and even if the step itself is flawed or faulty. The only thing that does not lead us on—gives us no growth, or even sets us back—is doing nothing, taking no steps, not bothering to try to incorporate our faith into our practice. So the Twelve Steps of Alcoholics Anonymous—the Twelve-Step Program, as it is often called today—is only our jumping-off place, and a very good one. Just a reminder: We are not studying AA or taking an objective look at a Twelve-Step Program. Our purpose for being here is to walk a spiritual path—to not just talk about spiritual growth, but to take steps toward spiritual growth.

Ash Wednesday begins Lent. Every year for hundreds of years, Ash Wednesday has begun Lent. It is interesting that Ash Wednesday, and even Lent itself, is neglected or nearly neglected by more and more Christians. Look around you. It doesn't look much like Christmas or Easter, does it? Not very many people think it's important to take the step represented by Ash Wednesday. Every celebration and ritual of Christianity represents a spiritual step the saints of the past have found most useful, even crucial, to their spiritual growth. What often looks to us like dull ritual or mere habit was once the dynamism of faith in action—faith being practiced. Sometimes we have to dig, almost excavate, some of the rites and rituals of our religion to find what the valuable step was all about. Sometimes it is just sitting there waiting for us, and all we have to do is see past the veil of our familiarity.

Ash Wednesday is about remorse (guilt), feeling sorry for all that is wrong, and especially about our own personal contribution to what is wrong or evil in life. Some of the anguish of Ash Wednesday is the sheer awareness of the wrongness of this realm—all the alienation from God, and all the cruelty, stupidity and pain that come out of that. But eventually it comes down to us, and to specifics: our own mistakes, our own stubbornness against God, our own blunders and alienation.

It is interesting that in our culture, remorse—being sorry or feeling apologetic—has become a step so out of style. We are a culture that considers it a weakness to apologize. We are a nation that thinks it is negative to admit faults or make amends or even to admit the dark side of life. Lent has a hard time in our culture, and Ash Wednesday has a hard time even in Lent. We begin Lent by facing our guilt and sin. We don't get consoled. We don't get forgiven. We don't get told it wasn't our fault or it doesn't matter or that everybody does it. We just begin by facing our guilt and sin (alienation). So not many people come to Ash Wednesday.

But *we* are here. That is, we have come to Ash Wednesday on purpose. And so it is our purpose to take this step of remorse—

to be sorry for our sins and to end up penitent and willing to make amends. It is a *step to take*—actually something we are intending to do. It may not sound like a very earthshaking or momentous undertaking—to make a list of what we are sorry about, and to get willing to make amends. Its repercussions, however, are sometimes enormous.

In the Twelve-Step Program, spiritual steps are usually distilled into even more specific and focused procedures. What is lost in breadth is made up for in clarity. The hard part is in getting started, not in trying to understand all the applications and innuendoes of all the theories. So the step says, "Made a list of all persons we have harmed." That's the first thing. You need to do that. Start it in your head right now. Just enough to taste it. Just enough to know you will continue it after this service, or early tomorrow morning. *Made a list of all persons we have harmed.* That's a specific assignment for remorse—for sorrow—for admitting our sins.

"Well," you say, "I have done a lot of harm that was not directly related to specific people I could name." But you can get to that some other time. "Well, a lot of other people have done some harm to me." And maybe someday you should take paper and pencil and deal with that too, but for right now, how about a list of people you have harmed? "Well, I have harmed myself." To be sure—and you can each put yourself on your list if you want to. You are a person you have harmed, without a doubt, but that is actually a more advanced step. Keep it simple: make a list of all people you have harmed. A seemingly clear, simple and direct assignment, but how hard we often make it—and how seldom we actually get to it. "Well, define *harm*. Well, how recently are we talking about? Well, some of these things I can't do anything about, or I don't even know where the people are anymore, so why bother with them?"

Who said anything about *doing* anything about it? All we said for this step was "make a list." Is that so hard? You bet it's hard! Hard to sit and look at the harm we have done. Hard to connect that with real people, no matter what we may think of some of them. Hard to realize, since we insist on jumping the gun, that much of the harm we have done is irreparable. And hard to realize that if we start taking steps, probably one will come along telling us to do something about this list. But we can never get anywhere taking all the steps at once. How many places can your feet be at one time? So we take it slow—one at a time. *Made a list.* Forget everything else. Make the list.

Are you thinking yet about some of the people you have harmed? It isn't fair to ask, I know. Just wanted you to taste a little of all the dodges we try to make, so they won't surprise you when you do sit down to make your list later this evening, or early tomorrow morning. If you start to go to sleep tomorrow night and have not yet made your list, then you know you are dealing with some heavy shields and denial. I told you about only a few, just enough to warn you. Do you know where I came up with them? They are all ways I have tried to avoid, duck and dodge taking the Eighth Step.

Ashes are what we get when something has been destroyed, when something has gone up in smoke. In ancient times, people poured ashes on their heads to show their sorrow at having destroyed something, lost something, ruined something—at having experienced the loss of something dear. So ashes are what we use, symbolically, to show our sorrow and remorse. But how empty a ritual if we use the ashes but they stand for nothing—if we claim the sorrow but it is not real.

Willingness to change—to be changed, to let God in, to give God some say in our affairs—willingness comes most often out of pain, remorse, sorrow. Waking up to the fact that we don't like things the way they are is usually the prerequisite for us to make any significant change. So the second part of this step is to become willing to make amends. Not to make them—just to become willing. Many people skip lightly over this part because, again, it doesn't seem very significant on the outside. But everything hinges on our willingness, and our willingness is never as automatic or complete as we assume at first glance. We have reasons to keep our sins, or they would be gone already. Every single one of them is attached to views we hold, resentments we cherish, excuses we have set up, and even to certain opinions we have constructed about how life can't get any better than it is or we can't be any different than we are. To become willing to make amends invites all kinds of things to be readjusted, or perhaps to come tumbling down. Even if joyful in the end, the return of a hope is a most disconcerting and messy affair, causing terrible restructuring of our way of living.

I was looking for an illustration to cut through the theory, and thought I would tell you about peanut brittle or some of the other stories I have been told. But for this one, I better tell you what I know. A little over ten years ago, I came out of the alcoholic treatment center in Cabrini Hospital. I thought my marriage was probably over. I assumed my career was over, as soon as we could make some arrangements. Of course, the biggest change was that the whole system of denial and rationalization that had grown up over the years was crumbling. No system can handle it all at once, but I was starting to see the wreckage—what I had been doing with my life and relationships—only without all the excuses.

It was too much. I either had to start drinking again or I had to get through it, but I couldn't stand it like it was. So I started running every day. And I started saying a mantra as I ran. It came out of the tradition somewhere, just started repeating in my mind, over and over, to the cadence of my feet: *Jesus Christ forgives your sins, relieves your present suffering, restores you to wholeness and strength.* Mile after mile, day after day, month after month I ran. Often I couldn't see the path for the tears streaming down my face. I ran, and I repeated that mantra.

I didn't believe it, of course. That is to say, I believed in all the truth of it and behind it—in the power of Christ, etc. But I didn't believe I was forgiven, or ever could be. I didn't know if the pain would ever lessen, or if I would ever get back any of the power I had once known. But I said the mantra, and I wept, and I ran. It was mostly desperation—the only way I could make it through the days.

But because I was working the step—not even realizing what I was doing—Christ was able to work also. Months later, I began to realize that the forgiveness had started to come. I do not know how else to say it. Forgiveness was out of my hands. It was beyond me. But I could feel it when it came. And I was no longer interested in being coy or holding it off or theorizing about it. I simply took it, like a thirsty man in a desert takes water that is offered.

Jesus Christ forgives your sins, relieves your present suffering, restores you to wholeness and strength. Slowly it sank in—and got real. I believe it today, incredible though it seems to me. But I don't think the Christ could ever have reached me with this offered forgiveness if I hadn't stumbled my way into the step of remorse— of Ash Wednesday.

It is Ash Wednesday. In worship together, and more thoroughly when alone, we take the step of remorse—sorrow over the sin (alienation) of the world and, more specifically, sorrow for the ways we ourselves are caught in it and contribute to it. Very specifically, we make a list of the people we have harmed, and we seek the Spirit's guidance and help in becoming willing to make amends. We do not make amends yet. The sorrow has to do its work. The willingness has to sink in and get very real and authentic. We do not wish to procrastinate on our pilgrimage, but neither are we in a hurry so that we take the steps carelessly or go so swiftly that the steps have no time to do their work within us.

Make a list—get willing. That is sufficient for the time being. Do it. Do it well. Don't just know about it. Don't just understand it. Take the step. Do it. Do it well.

So now we commemorate this step by putting ashes on our foreheads—the mark of our sorrow, the mark of our remorse. Even our sorrow and despair we show in the sign of the Cross that stands for our eventual healing, our salvation and our hope. But none of it is activated unless the remorse is real.

Matthew 5:1-16

First Sunday in Lent

POWERLESS

Step One
We admitted we were powerless over alcohol [sin]—
that our lives had become unmanageable.

Most of you are not in AA. I am aware that it may annoy
you if I seem to be "pushing" a program that is not your own.
I also take a chance of irritating those of you who *are* in AA,
since you know more about the steps than I do. Almost
everybody in AA knows more about the steps than anybody
else. Yet I have wanted to show the mix of the vast richness
and heritage of the Christian Faith with the simple "do
something about it" approach of the Twelve-Step Program.
Because it has the possibility of being both interesting and
helpful to many, I have chosen to try this series.

Step One in AA is Step One on any spiritual path I know
about: *Blessed are the poor in Spirit, for theirs is the kingdom of
heaven.* "We admitted we were powerless over alcohol [sin]—
that our lives had become unmanageable."

Jesus' Sermon on the Mount begins with the Beatitudes. The
Beatitudes and the Lord's Prayer itself are early Christian "Step
Programs." The Beatitudes are, besides being beautiful poetry
and powerful teaching, the Nine-Step Program of the early
church. The Nine Steps of the Beatitudes actually have greater
breadth than the Twelve-Step Program of AA. The AA Program,
of necessity, is focused for people who are already debilitated,
defeated and not thinking straight. The steps must be short, clear
and simple. It starts out with a mandate to forget everything and
everyone else ("go to any lengths"), if necessary, until you get

your own life in order. *First take the beam out of your own eye.*
(Matthew 7:5)

When dealing with the Nine Steps of the Beatitudes, it is well
to remember that the rest of the Sermon on the Mount (Matthew
5, 6 and 7) is commentary, explanation and illustration of the
Nine Steps already set forth. Jesus is talking about a Way of Life,
a Program for Living for those who want to follow Him into a new
Kingdom—just as the AA person is telling himself and his fellow
drunks: "If you want to get sober, if you want out of your present
life, these are the steps you must take."

Correlation between the Beatitudes (Matthew 5) and the
Twelve-Step Program is not exact, yet often we can feel the Twelve-
Step Program zeroing in on the specific and personal application
of a Beatitude principle. It takes no imagination to realize that
the similarities are dramatic:

First Beatitude .... **First Step**
Poor in spirit; humble   The old "humility" and the present
(Matthew 5:3)   "powerlessness" are a close parallel

Second Beatitude .... **Fourth & Fifth Steps**
Mourn   Take inventory, confess
(Matthew 5:4)

Third Beatitude .... **Third Step**
Meek; obedient to God   Turn will and life over is a nearly
(Matthew 5:5)   absolute corollary

Fourth Beatitude .... **Sixth & Seventh Steps**
Hunger for righteousness   Ready for and asking God to make us right
(Matthew 5:6)   is personal application, but on target

Fifth Beatitude .... **Eighth & Ninth Steps**
Merciful   This is a reversal: made a list of all who had
(Matthew 5:7)   harmed us, and became willing to forgive
                                   them all—and then forgave them

Sixth Beatitude .... No corresponding Step
Pure in heart
(Matthew 5:8)

Seventh Beatitude .... **Tenth Step**
Peacemakers   Admitting wrongs is our side of
(Matthew 5:9)   peacemaking

Eighth Beatitude .... **Eleventh Step**
Persecuted for righteousness   Knowledge of His will for us,
like the prophets   spokesmen for God, people of prayer
(Matthew 5:10-12)

Ninth Beatitude .... **Twelfth Step**
Salt; light   Salt practices these principles in all
(Matthew 5:13-16)   affairs; light carries the message

In the Big Book of *ALCOHOLICS ANONYMOUS,* at the end of the Ninth-Step discussion (pages 83-84), twelve promises are mentioned—the rewards of working the steps. Jesus names the promise of each Beatitude as an integral part of that Beatitude. Jesus' promises are a little higher and more astounding and far-reaching. The promises of AA are more mundane, but still head in the same direction. I shall leave these comparisons to those who are interested enough to pursue them.

I have learned that I am never really sure what you are hearing. What I think I have established is not only the interesting parallels between the Twelve-Step Program and the Sermon on the Mount, but also the necessity—for all of us who are religious and hope to grow spiritually—the *necessity* for us to take steps, to work a program. Again and again I am appalled at how many church members, how many people who call themselves "Christians," are working no program, walking no path, taking no steps to get anywhere at all. Please do not misunderstand me: I am not sitting in judgment of them because I am unhappy with

them. They are unhappy with themselves, and with their lives. I
happen to run into them, and we get to talking. It is in trying to
discover why they are discouraged and hurt that I discover they
are not walking any path, are not taking any steps, are not working
any program, and often do not seem to know that one even exists.
No one ever bothered to mention to them that Christianity is a
pilgrimage—a Path to walk—a WAY of Life. That is what is
appalling. Many people read the Beatitudes but do not realize
they are about a way to live. They say the Lord's Prayer as mere
words, and do not realize it is the distilled essence of how Jesus
goes about His life—and how He intends all of His disciples to
go about their lives.

The biggest change in my religion since I graduated from the
Drinking Class (you never graduate from being an alcoholic) is
the realization that the grace and mercy of God is grace for the
Path, grace for walking the WAY. Grace is free for the taking, but
it is nothing at all for those who do not take it and then walk with
it. There is nothing more pathetic than a "Christian" who sits in
the same spot and keeps sucking in forgiveness just to keep
sitting in the same spot. I am not saying any of this "at" anyone
here. I'm just trying to establish premises. All of us have active
guilt patterns. If I joggled yours, that was not the purpose. But I
know that if I were sitting there and you were talking about this,
it would joggle mine.

Blessed are the poor in spirit. "We admitted we were powerless
over sin—that our lives had become unmanageable." Twin
statements about how to begin walking a new Path—into a new
Life. Not an indictment, but a step to take—an awakening, an
awareness to live from, and to live out of. To take a step, we have
to look for the verb: *admitted.* I must *admit* my powerlessness,
my inability to manage my life well on my own—by my own
wisdom, strength, purposes or desires.

This First Step seems so obvious and simple, how can it be a
stumbling block to so many? Can I make the world the way I
think it ought to be? Can I prevent all the disease, stop all the
hunger, right all the injustices I see going on around me—and I

mean every single day? If I had any power at all, I would certainly make a dent in some of this immediately. I sit in meetings—both with alcoholics and with nonalcoholics—and hear people anguishing over this step, over whether they can admit to being powerless. But if they have power, why don't they *do* something?! Take a walk through downtown Seattle—there are many people there who need somebody with "power" to help them. Take a stroll through Harborview Hospital—there are many people there who could use somebody with "power" to help them. We have crises of major magnitude going on all over the globe. If you have power, go fix them!

"Well," you say, "that's not fair. I have only *a little* power." And that's true, you do. But two things get me into this First Step with ease: One is trying to fix some of the things that are wrong. The other is tracking the word "little." Just how "little" is your power? Don't cheat now. We aren't talking about the power of God carrying you. Some of you have been doing more than normal humans should be able to—and have been doing so for years—because you are not afraid or ashamed to let the power of God carry and sustain you. That doesn't count. "I, by myself, am powerless." That is what each one of us must admit in order to enter the Program—Christian or AA.

I am powerless against sin—the principle of alienation that operates everywhere in this world. Not only am I powerless to stop the mayhem in the Middle East or in downtown Seattle or sometimes even in this church, I am even powerless to prevent myself from contributing to it. I wake up in the morning and devote myself to being a child of The Light. And sometimes by 9:30 a.m. I am embroiled in a situation where there seem to be only choices between varying shades of darkness—and sometimes one of them is me. Do I manage my life well? In comparison to what? In comparison to the way some of *you* would manage my life, maybe I do it quite well, and vice versa. But that isn't fair either, because many of us already know that "it is necessary for us as Christians to pray every day, to study some portion of the Scriptures each day, seeking in grace and praise to discover

God's will for our own lives on a daily basis." We wouldn't make this statement, and couldn't take it seriously, if we hadn't worked the First Step.

Nevertheless, from time to time, I forget. Something goes wrong—for me or for one of you or for somebody else I care about—and "off I go" to fix it. Spencer is dead and his church is too deeply in debt, and I am going to heal it or fix it? I never know for sure when God will give me the authority to do something way beyond my own power, or when God will empower me to assist some person to whom God has assigned a redemptive task. But that is at the other end of the Program, clear up at Step Eleven. As a matter of fact, that cannot happen at all—truly— unless I have taken many steps in between.

So first I have to take the First Step. (Strange logic, isn't it— taking the first step first?) First I have to admit to the level of my own personal power in the context of the evil and sin within and around me. I am unable to save myself, unable to save those around me, and unable to save the world. By myself I am powerless, and the more I govern my life by my own light and for my own purposes, the more unmanageable it becomes. I can always tell when I am taking the reins back into my own hands because the fear level shoots up. Some of you call it anxiety or worry, but I call it fear. Always when fear rises, anger is not far behind (though often, people who cannot admit anger get depressed). When I admit I am powerless and realize it truly, the fear drops almost instantly back to normal.

Of course, I already believe there is a God. Though I am powerless, God is not. Remembering who is truly in charge drops my fear level. That also is cheating. I already know the Second Step. So do most of you. But I have great compassion for those walking this Path for the first time. For them, admitting they are powerless feels like being held out over the bottomless void and, the moment they admit they are powerless, they will drop. It is one of the great Catch-22 places in life. If you do not know or trust God, Step One is the way in, but Step One feels like the admission of utter destruction: I am the only power I know or trust, and I am powerless. That is how Step One feels to most people, at one time or another in their lives. So when I say Step One is simple and obvious, it *is* for you who are spiritually awake and aware. We need to keep taking the step to counter our pride, and to put our perspective back straight, but it is much easier after you have already "come to believe," which is Step Two.

In our religious tradition and heritage, power (like love) has always belonged to God. All power comes from God. Obvious, I know, but just thought I should mention that this step is as old as the hills: *Once God has spoken; twice have I heard this: that power belongs to God* [it is not mine; I am powerless] (Psalm 62:11); *Do not say to yourself, "My power and the might of my own hand have gotten me this wealth"* (Deuteronomy 8:17); *Then Jesus, filled with the power of the Spirit* [not His own power] (Luke 4:14); *Stay here in the city until you have been clothed with power from on high* (Luke 24:49); *You shall receive power when the Holy Spirit has come upon you* (Acts 1:8); *But we have this treasure in clay jars, so that it may be made clear that this extraordinary power belongs to God and does not come from us* (II Corinthians 4:7); *My grace is sufficient for you, for my power is made perfect in weakness* (II Corinthians 12:9); *That I may know him and the power of his resurrection* (Philippians 3:10); and I Corinthians 1:27; II Chronicles 14:11; Ezekiel 34:4; Psalm 35:10; Romans 5:6; II Corinthians 13:4; II Corinthians 2:7-10; II Chronicles 20:12; I Corinthians 1:18 & 15:43; Ephesians 3:20; Psalm 78:22; Ecclesiastes 8:8; Isaiah 40:29; Zechariah 4:6; Luke 5:17.

Faithful people have been working Step One for at least four thousand years—the "First Step" has always been an integral part of our WAY. How it came to be lost or neglected, I'm not sure. If it takes AA to remind us, so be it. But whatever it takes, we *must* be reminded, because there is no way to get into or go on with the Christian Life unless, in some manner—deeply and earnestly—we have taken and keep taking this First Step. So if you are not an alcoholic, have you taken the First Beatitude? *Blessed are the poor in spirit*—the humble, those who know their need of God, those who know that power does not belong to or come from them. A "Christian" who has not taken the First Beatitude, the First Step—what are they like? Either they sit in the seat of the spectator or, in the words of the First Psalm, they sit in the seat of the scornful.

TWO THINGS—TOO QUICKLY:

1.) There is a whole movement rising (again) in disdain of this approach. And there are many different groups and approaches within this movement. We simply need to be aware of it. Many of our best friends are already in it. Some of it is actually angry toward AA and the portions of Christianity that still know and practice the Christian WAY. Its emphasis is on claiming our own power, realizing our inner potential, making our own destiny. Often the power of the mind is a place of central focus and teaching. Annoyance, and often outright anger, toward Jesus (especially Jesus as more than a man) usually accompanies this perspective. It is logical that a savior would not appeal to those who believe they have the power to save themselves. Jesus the man may be slightly interesting, but Jesus the Christ is anathema. I suspect that this movement will grow with astonishing speed in the near future. It has much to recommend itself to the longings and opinions of American culture and to the frustrations of our time.

2.) One of the places of greatest stress for us "normal" Christians of this era—that is, stress in light of the First Step—is the feeling of vertigo when it comes to thinking of moral and social responsibility. If we are powerless, why do we feel so guilty when confronted with all the causes so many people are trying to get us to be part of? Most of these appeals recite the refrain: "You can make a difference." Some people worry that taking the First Step will make them "care less" about the plight of others. Those in leadership positions worry that the Twelve-Step Program will become a handy excuse for thousands of people to stop participating in the important "help efforts" they are trying to promote. This is not a baseless charge. Both AA and the Christian

Church can become very narcissistic through some of the phases of growth, and many people do get stuck (sometimes for years) in one phase or another along the way. Some people get stuck in the phase of social action, so why wouldn't some people get stuck in the phase of personal healing and nurture?

But enough. It is Lent. We need to keep taking steps if we are going to make progress. As my father used to say, "If you're coasting, you know you're going downhill." So start. Whether for the first time or, more likely, in review, start with the First Step: *Blessed are the poor in spirit.* "We admitted we were powerless over sin—that our lives had become unmanageable." Or perhaps you would like it to be even more familiar, like in a prayer you are supposed to pray every day.. Can you truly pray the Lord's Prayer without taking a First Step? *Thine is the kingdom and the power and the glory, for ever. Amen.*

Thine is the power, not mine. I, by myself, am powerless. And without Your help, my life is unmanageable. Is that not our prayer?

Matthew 16:13-26; Mark 10:23-31

Second Sunday in Lent

CAME TO BELIEVE

Step Two
Came to believe that a Power greater than ourselves
could restore us to sanity.

If we have admitted we are powerless (Step One), a Second
Step and a second question come forth with great urgency: Is
there any power and, if so, where is it, or who has it? Many different
answers are given to this question, and in a sense, every human
answers this question in some fashion.

The atheist says there is no power—all is random and chaos.
The agnostic says they're not sure if there is power, or where it is,
but they're looking for it. The humanist says that power is in the
collective human spirit or in the potential of the human mind or
in alliances of human cooperation. Judaism says power belongs
to Yahweh. Christianity says power is in Yahweh but that we
humans know its nature in Jesus Christ, and experience it in the
Holy Spirit of Jesus Christ.

There was a time when dozens of religions were all claiming
power for their own particular god and for their own particular
way of worshipping their god. In that regard, times haven't
changed very much. We still have various world religions vying
for human allegiance. Under them comes the inevitable pantheon
of lesser gods—the gods nobody claims to worship but that many
truly worship: money is power; sexuality is power; property is
power; the ability to get votes is power; there is power in numbers;
power in justice; power in information; brainpower; might makes
right; evil is invincible; health; youth; and so on. We live in a
world where various people and groups are worshipping at all of
these different shrines—sometimes staying loyal to one for years,

or for a lifetime; sometimes going from one to another in a frantic search for "where it's at."

I have now made it sound like an intellectual game, a philosophical question. For most people, most of the time, the issue is not that genteel or polite or clear or sterile. Caught in the midst of busy days and constant emergencies—living in the midst of endless noise and confusion, finding life laced with fear and joy, doubt and delight, guilt and grace—most humans are not even thinking about which gods they are serving or believing in, at least not on a conscious level, not most of the time. We are just making it through the days.

Working the steps of a spiritual path requires intention and decision and focus. Nevertheless, it does not feel like a philosophical exercise. Taking a step is always visceral as well as mental. It is not so much about certainty as it is about seeking. Taking a step is not like writing a term paper (or a sermon). Taking a step puts your life on the line. There may or may not be much danger, but taking a step necessarily moves you to a new position. Finding out if we like the trail is a matter of experience. Taking steps changes stance, and always feels like a risk. It is a matter of theory when we are being intellectual; it is a matter of testing it out—finding out—when we *take* steps. There is always a difference between Abraham walking out of Ur toward a new land, or Jesus walking out of the wilderness to take up His ministry, and someone devising a vast system of interconnected theories that look good on paper. With the vast system on paper, we often become certain, make grand claims and feel sure we know the outcome. Actually *taking* the steps is real life, and we don't know for sure what each new step will carry us into, or where that will lead, or how we will manage. Taking the steps is real, and wherever they lead, only then is it a real journey—part groping, part elation, and always risk and adventure.

Came to believe that a Power greater than ourselves could restore us to sanity. The AA wording of this Second Step sounds particularly inane and muted—to the ears of Christians. There is no quarrel with the step, no objection to it being the Second

Step. It's just that the wording is so generic and pale. Nothing of the love of God in Christ Jesus our Lord; no hint at the vast tradition and heritage that might give a person hope and confidence in taking this step; no tinge of comfort or confidence from the Cross or the Resurrection.

Came to believe that a Power greater than ourselves . . . How flat. That could be my wife, your boss, our police force. Having admitted our powerlessness, it could be almost anything. On second thought, that is a bit hasty—my wife, your boss, our police force are unlikely to restore me to sanity. The obvious point is that it is a Power greater than myself, and the true point is that I don't have time or cause or reason to define it. Step Two is one of the mystery places of life. Having just admitted our powerlessness, if we are sincere about it, then there is suddenly a great vacuum—a great empty place is created within. Almost inevitably, we feel another Power at work in our lives, one we had not noticed and could not notice while we thought the power was ours.

It is true that many times a person in the wake of Step One will put faith in another person, a mentor or a program—for a while. If it sticks there for too long, it can become a problem. But normally, in a short time, the person realizes that the real Power is working *through* the mentor or the program. But for a while, it doesn't matter. It is a crucial step, but it is a transition step. Having trusted in our own power for as long as we could get away with it—having finally come to the end of that road, hit a dead end—we have to seek and come to believe in a Power greater than ourselves. There is hardly any transition greater than this, in terms of the shake-up of our personal lives—to start relying on something outside of and beyond ourselves. That is Step Two. Small chance we will get it right or know it clearly or define it correctly—at first. It is a forced out: if we are powerless, we have to find a Power outside of ourselves—or surrender to meaninglessness and chaos. It is also the beginning of our exploration into realities like obedience, humility, gratitude. Such concepts are not possible, and in fact are gibberish, as long as we imagine we have power and are in charge of our own lives.

I do not mean to minimize the barrenness of this language for the Christian. AA is trying to save people who are dying from alcoholism. Many of them have prejudices and animosities toward the church, or they have turned adamantly away from the "god talk" employed by various Christians they have encountered. Many of them come from places and traditions outside the church. In any case, AA does not and will not speak a specific religious language lest this causes it to lose some of the people it might otherwise save. After they stop drinking, they can go find a church if they want to.

From my perspective, this is a sad reality, but it is reality. It is of great sadness to me that AA cannot name the NAME of the Power that saves us; cannot mention or claim some of the reasons why we trust this Power; cannot say anything much about where it is leading, or what the purpose is, or how wide the mercy; cannot direct its gratitude or move into a higher allegiance. AA presses the line pretty hard, and even crosses over in small ways on a regular basis (like closing each AA meeting with the Lord's Prayer), but what is sad to me is that Christendom has so represented itself that this is necessary. In general, our creeds have become so literalistic, so judgmental and so full of fear and hell that the grace and love of Christ—and the Pilgrimage He calls us into—are now so obscured that we have to pull all the true names out of the picture for a while in order to allow the true Power to begin to work again in many people's lives.

On the other hand, even for those of us who know and honor the names, there is benefit in the simple language of the Second Step. Even if we know that the power belongs to God—and is made known to us in Jesus Christ—even then, it is good to admit we do not have the power of definition over such names. Walking the Path, it is absolutely true we do not know what the day will bring, or how God's power will direct or save us. Taking it back down to simply "a Power greater than ourselves" can open us to the honest reality of the step. We follow like little children this Power that we trust. And our trust is a hope due to unverifiable, interior awareness that some Presence has been caring about us and trying to help us far longer than we have realized. It often starts from the awareness that we have survived better than we could have expected or deserved; that we have new chances we did not coordinate or plan; that we have inner awareness and longings we did not design or manufacture. Taking it from there, we try to follow. Incredible as it is, it is not really a good reason for terribly precise definitions.

Step Two is a step of hope. "Came to believe" is the action end (the verb clause), but the step keeps moving, right past the believing—even past the Power we are going to trust. What the step really wants, really longs for, is to be restored to sanity. We get tired of being crazy. We would like to be restored to sanity.

A brief aside, since we do get tangled up in language. We are not talking here about a strict definition of sanity according to the latest definitions in clinical psychology. This step is not speaking in a court of law, where we are determining sentence according to whether or not the accused is to be considered insane. We are talking about down-home, rule-of-thumb sanity. From an alcoholic's perspective, it isn't sane to go on drinking when the cost is so high and mounting. Jobs are impaired, threatened, then lost. Relationships are hurt, threatened, lost. Joy and hope turn to depression and guilt, or to anger and guilt (nice choice). Health is impaired, threatened, lost. Life is hurt, threatened, lost. Looking back, it doesn't seem sane that we kept on drinking. Nothing fancy, just down-home, rule-of-thumb crazy.

For instance, I know a man who didn't like that his wife was giving him advice all the time—telling him what to wear, how to speak, where to go, who to like, how to spend his time. Each time she started to do this, he either got angry or clammed up and left the room. He reasoned that, in time, she would change her behavior. If, every time she gave him such instructions, he got angry or left the room, pretty soon she would stop doing it. But instead she gave him more and more advice about how he shouldn't get angry, what he could do to cure his anger, how he shouldn't just stop talking and leave the room, and how he should seek professional help to teach him how to relate better so he wouldn't just clam up and leave the room. But he continued to get angry, or clam up and leave the room. He knew it had to work, sooner or later. But the fact was that it only made it harder and harder for them to love each other. So year after year, he went on getting angry or leaving the room, and she went on giving her advice—ten years, twenty years, thirty years. That's *insane*—doing the same thing over and over and expecting different results. At least that is AA's definition of insanity: doing the same thing over and over and expecting different results. Last time I drank, I got drunk; this time I'll drink, but it will turn out differently. Last time I got angry and it made the relationship worse; this time I will get angry and it will heal and cure things between us. That's insanity.

Speaking in this vein, it isn't sane that the world keeps sinning. It isn't sane that we keep reproducing at a rate destined to destroy all quality of life on this planet. It isn't sane that, as a people, we keep trusting in lies and cleverness instead of walking a path of honesty and integrity with each other. And once started, the list mushrooms. We do not live in a sane world. We spend half our lives trying to fit in, trying to adjust, trying to find our niche or make a place for ourselves—only to discover that we do not live in a sane world. And if we have found our niche or made a place for ourselves or become adjusted so we feel comfortable here, then *we* are crazy, flowing along in happy synchronization with an alienated, corrupt and crazy world. If you take your bearings from this world, you are crazy! This world does not know what it is doing, does not live in The Light, is not fostering peaceful, holy or just life-patterns for its people.

We discover ourselves powerless over sin—powerless to change our dwelling place as long as we are on this crazy planet. I have often looked forward to dying, in sheer eagerness and anticipation and curiosity about the next realm, but I have never been suicidal. Brief moments, maybe two or three times in my life, but never a serious contemplation—because I know this place is crazy. If I thought that it was sane, that this was all there was to look forward to—people starving and killing each other and the massacre of nature—I'd be out of here yesterday. But since the world is insane, and I am too, then I need to stay and learn—need to find a Higher Power who can restore me to sanity—until I can learn to live and be sane, even in the midst of a crazy world. Then I will be ready to try the next realm.

But how about this Second Step in full light of the Christian Faith? Is it really a different WAY, these Twelve Steps? Suppose you have already "come to believe," as many of you have? While that may have been a fascinating experience, back when it was fresh and new and happening for the first time, does that mean this Second Step is of no relevance to you, or that you will never have cause to take it again?

Most of us here have come to believe that God in Christ will restore us to sanity. In Christendom, we always believe that "creation" is well-made, that people are of incredible value, that the foundational reality is wonderful. The Doctrine of Original Sin, for instance, is quite the reverse of what many people today try to make it sound like. The Adam and Eve story is about alienation—a relationship lost. It is popularly called "The Fall"—that is, it is about a good thing going wrong; a beautiful creation going out of focus, getting lost, turning from its purpose and potential, toward evil and destruction. If Christianity were negative about creation or people, it wouldn't be called The Fall—there wouldn't be any place to fall from.

Christendom talks of sin as bondage, as enslavement. Jesus forever talks about restoring us. If we lose our life—turn away from the lost life, the one under bondage—we will find true Life. Old man . . . new man. Old birth . . . new birth, or rebirth. If you die to self . . . you will discover or be given your true self. Always it is a message of restoration—to a life fitting what the Creator created and intended. Salvation frees us from a bondage that corrupted and distorted our true nature until we lost hope. But Jesus saves . . . restores . . . restores us to sanity—to true hope and true purpose. Jesus saves—a Power greater than ourselves restores. Same step, except the words have been changed to protect the innocent, or deflect the prejudice.

Step Two is a step of hope. "Came to believe that a Power greater than ourselves could restore us to sanity." *God was in Christ, reconciling the world to himself* (II Corinthians 5:19); *I came that they might have life, and have it abundantly* (John 10:10). If you lose the old life which is under the bondage of fear and guilt and alienation, you will find your true life.

In the midst of the world we live in, the schedules we try to keep, and all the insanity of the ways we try to work our plans and our relationships, it is hard to "believe" that anything can restore us to sanity. This is especially so when, everywhere we turn, we run into more insanity and discover more of our own insane ways. But the Second Step is a claim and a promise: We are going to go on believing in the Power greater than ourselves, and therefore trusting we will be restored to sanity—to the being God created us to be. No known timeline, no fixed date for when this will be accomplished. It is being accomplished all the time— as we walk the steps.

But the Second Step is our declaration of hope and, therefore, of our independence from discouragement and despair. And within Christendom, we make it even plainer: *Jesus Christ forgives your sins, relieves your present suffering, restores you to wholeness and strength.*

God, You have the power. Thy Kingdom come on earth. Restore us to sanity. Thank You for giving us back our hope.

John 3:1-8; Romans 6:3-11

Third Sunday in Lent

MADE A DECISION

Step Three
*Made a decision to turn our will and our lives over
to the care of God <u>as we understood Him.</u>*

It is always fun to argue over which spiritual steps are the most important, or to discuss which steps are our favorites. Of course it is silly, as if the destination were not the reason for the journey—as if the journey itself were not a process wherein each step or phase is part of a larger whole. If you take out steps 4, 18, 32, 75 and 94, what happens to the person trying to run the mile? It isn't just difficult, it's absurd. Without all the steps, the journey isn't possible. I don't mean it goes wrong; I mean it doesn't exist. The thought of canceling out some phases of a journey because we don't like them is ludicrous. And it is ludicrous that we humans are frequently guilty of claiming we want to reach certain destinations without having any intention of taking some of the steps that will get us there.

It is true that some of the steps on any journey are more mundane than others. The step just before you come to a beautiful view is seldom as famous as the one with the view. It is just as necessary, but it calls forth less appreciation. Step Eight, for instance: "Made a list of all persons we had harmed, and became willing to make amends to them all." Few of us jump and cheer when we come to that step. Many of us put it off, and even try to make the journey work without it. It takes some of us a long time to figure out that we cannot get to the beautiful view without it.

Step Three, on the other hand, is a great favorite with many people. In Christendom, we normally refer to it as "conversion."

Actually, people hate this step the most before they take it, and love it the most afterward. Of all people, I do not want to detract from its importance in any way. But we need to keep remembering that marvelous as it is, it is only one step along the WAY. This becomes particularly intriguing when we stop to remember that some people, and even whole organizations, sometimes talk and act like this Third Step is the whole journey, the whole point, the whole purpose—and that, having taken the Third Step, we have reached the destination. That is, some people talk like conversion is IT: You are converted or you are not. If you are converted, you are "saved," you're "in," you made it and it's over. The whole drama of life, for them, is seen in terms of the Third Step only. After you are converted, your only remaining function is to help convert others. You are into or out of heaven, or into or out of hell. Being converted is the difference, the whole difference and nothing but the difference. Pretty soon all of life is shrunk down to the Third Step. The journey has disappeared and there is nothing worth living for, or being alive for. No more journey—just hold on to your ticket and try to get others to get a ticket so they can hold on to theirs, day after day, year after year. Never mind anything else, just get your ticket.

I'm certain God is going to take all these people into heaven. But when they get there, they are going to find themselves standing in line, tickets in hand, waiting to go through some gate. Only, nobody is ever going to come take their tickets. They will just have to wait in line until they get tired enough or bored enough to TAKE STEPS to get themselves where life is flowing. So we might as well be taking those steps right here, and now.

All disclaimers aside, if we do not try to make the Third Step the only step in the journey, it is indeed a marvelous step. In fact, it is one of the steps that brings us to a marvelous view. "Made a decision to turn our will and our lives over to the care of God <u>as we understood Him</u>."

It sounds a little mechanical, but there are four key phrases in this step:

MADE A DECISION
TURN OUR WILL AND OUR LIVES OVER
TO THE CARE OF GOD
AS WE UNDERSTOOD HIM

These four segments do have to hold together to make a step, but they each carry an important dimension of the step.

I.) MADE A DECISION

It is a most unnerving thing (we humans never get used to it) that there are consequences to our actions. Our intentions have great influence on our actions, but the consequences respond to the actions, not to the intentions. Most unnerving. It was my intention to hit the brake, but I hit the accelerator instead. Will the consequences arise from my intention, or from my action? Sometimes it just doesn't seem fair.

If I meditate on it for very long, it can be almost paralyzing. Every single thing we do has consequences or repercussions. We stay oblivious to it much of the time, just to keep calm. But every word we say and absolutely every thing we do is weaving the pattern of where our lives are going, what they will be like, and what we will be like. Sometimes we take a big action out of sequence and notice that it does indeed have vast repercussions. For example, getting married clearly has dramatic impact on all that follows, but thousands of lesser choices and deeds were part of that "getting married." Had we done the little ones differently, the big one would not have happened.

What we do and what we decide are always and forever putting us into new positions. We can make choices, but we cannot choose the consequences. As my mother used to say, "You get to decide whether or not to jump, but you do not get to decide whether you will go up or down." (And she had an endless array of applications.) Choices have consequences. We get to make the choices; we do not get to control the consequences. Sometimes we can find and receive a forgiveness that stops the ongoing wave of consequences, but the consequences up to that moment remain. Receiving forgiveness is a new action that sets a new wave of consequences in motion—and interferes with the prior wave of consequences.

Whenever we are taking consistent steps in any direction, the wave of consequences begins to mount. You cannot become a Hitler or a Charles Manson in an afternoon. It takes years of making decisions and taking actions to get so far down a path. Neither can we become a St. Francis or a Teresa of Avila in one afternoon. It takes years of decisions and actions, each one building and counting on the last.

Just so, if we are dealing with the Third Step—it cannot be out of the context of the other steps. It is a decision. We are faced with a choice, and this choice is the direct result of having taken Steps One and Two. Many people try to take Step Three as if it were a loner step—or a first step. They make a decision to turn their will and their life over to God, but they have not admitted powerlessness or come to believe that a Power greater than themselves can restore them to sanity. If they think they still have power enough to run their lives well and do not recognize any need to be restored to sanity, can they take the Third Step? They can indeed make a decision to turn their will and their life over to God, but it will not be the same Third Step we are talking about. It will be, for them, a first step, and it will be on a *very different* path. They come to God in pride rather than in humility, and they sign up because they have so much to offer, not because they have needs or problems of their own. You can argue that it is a more noble and admirable stance, a superior way to come to God, and I would have to agree—by definition. But it is imperative to see that it is not the same path.

Having been through the admission of powerlessness and then having come to believe in a Power greater than ourselves— and only in that context—we find ourselves facing this Third Step. Should we go back to where we were? Clearly that is

increasingly untenable. Should we go on looking for other
options—maybe a new job, a different location, a better friend,
or some power we have not yet discovered? Always an option,
but time is running out and the First Step leaves us somewhat
desperate. Nevertheless, the Third Step is not automatic. We still
have to *make the decision*—a conscious decision, in cold blood
(so to speak). Should we go with this Power we have come to
believe in, or not? Indeed, the Third Step is not automatic. Many
people make it through Steps One and Two and flat-out balk at
Step Three. Alcohol is the number-one killer in the United States.
Many people come to Step Three and commit suicide rather than
decide to turn their lives over to God. Thousands, facing Step
Three, go back to drinking, which is merely a slower form of
suicide. Thousands come to Step Three from other defeats and
patterns and cannot or will not make the decision to turn their
wills and their lives over to God. Every one of them gets some
kind of death, some form or level of suicide. No indeed, it is *not*
an automatic choice.

I am simply saying that it does no good to slough over the
first phrase. Step Three is decision time. And on some levels, we
hate decisions, especially when they sound like commitments.
Step Three is nearly a total commitment, at least as far as we
have any understanding about it. This Step-Three decision is by
its nature one of those "no turning back" places. That becomes
more and more clear as we look at the rest of the step.

II.) TURN OUR WILL AND OUR LIVES OVER

No need to belabor this phrase for very long. It makes it very
clear what this decision is about. Nobody turns will or life over—
to anything or anyone—if they still have any shred of hope left
that they can handle things themselves. The images are clear:
selling out, surrendering, letting go, giving up, turning it over.
We hate every one of them. The more we hate them, the more we
understand what is going on and why, and the clearer the choice
becomes.

If you turn your will over to some new Power, what is left to reverse the decision at a future time if you don't like how things are going? It is no wonder so many turn away, even though they are looking into the face of death. God is always our very last choice, the lover we settle for when all other options are gone. Sometimes we tease and kid about it: "When all else fails, pray." But it's no joke. It is our reality. To be sure, some of us pray for years—with ourselves still in charge. We even think we are religious. But that isn't really prayer, it's superstition. God is our mascot—maybe he will bring us luck. If we are still in charge, it has nothing to do with the real God or with being truly religious.

When all else fails, we begin to pray—really and truly—and not before. "I was *driven* to my knees, in the sheer realization that there was nowhere else to go." (Abraham Lincoln) Why is this statement so powerful? I agree with the truth of it. I believe in prayer. I have enormous regard for Lincoln. So why does it make me want to weep? Because I feel in that phrase the anguish and the turning point for all the people I have ever admired, down through all the ages. I can feel Jacob and Joseph, Moses and Jeremiah, Jesus and Paul and Peter, and the thousands who have carried our faith and become part of our tradition. And I remember my own turning points, the big ones that mattered and stuck—the ones that shaped the only part of life that still matters to me.

To turn our wills and our lives over—in the sheer realization that there is nowhere else to go—that's conversion. If it isn't on that level, it isn't conversion, and it isn't the Third Step. *They left everything and followed him.* (Luke 5:11) When you hear that rooster crow, there is no more time for debate or discussion. You are faced with a decision. You either go hang yourself like Judas, or you turn your will and your life over like Peter. Nothing else makes any sense. There are no other options.

III.) TO THE CARE OF GOD

It is not true of everybody, but many folk do comprehend at an early age the significance and flow of the First and Second Steps. It is a big, scary world, and some people seem to understand from a very early age their vulnerability and weakness. They know they need help and protection. Almost from the beginning, they look for some Power bigger than themselves that they can count on. For some of these people, Steps One and Two have been a way of life for as far back as they can remember. They are forever taking the Third Step, except they keep rewriting the second half. They turn their will and their life over—to mother, to spouse, to church, to a political party, to each new lover, to each new job, or to each new cause that strikes their hunger to do something noble and wonderful.

On the one hand, we have this enormous human reticence to turn our wills and our lives over to God. On the other hand, we have this incredible propensity for turning ourselves over to everything *except* God—sex, friends, golf, computers, what have you. (Or, what has you?) The Third Step is a decision to turn our wills and our lives over to *God*—not to a religion, not to another human being, not to anything less or other than God. *The fear of the Lord is the beginning of wisdom.* (Psalm 111:10; Proverbs 9:10)

I will not comment fully, but the phrase says "to the care of God." This is not the macho step where we are going to do God's will in the world, fight evil and injustice, play Joan of Arc or St. George or any other great role. That comes in Step Eleven, a long way from here. Underline "care." Many people miss that little word in this step. We are early in the journey (at least in the description of it). In Step Three, we aren't doing anything for God—God is going to care for us. We aren't in any condition or position to be servants yet. That's hard and dangerous stuff. We are still broken, probably mangled. It doesn't matter that some of it is our own fault. God has to heal us, feed us, clothe us, soothe the terror, dismantle the guilt, restore our identity, bring us back to calmness and peace. Some of the other steps are about how God does this. The point is, we are turning our wills and our lives over to THE CARE OF GOD. We will probably be asked to do some difficult and unusual things (from our perspective) just as soon as we turn the reins over, but those things are about our healing and being nurtured.

We don't love ourselves or take care of ourselves, even when we use those very phrases and try to. Many times we say it: "I need to learn to take care of myself . . . I have to watch out for number one . . . I'm going to take better care of myself . . . " But then watch what we go and do. Turning our wills and our lives over to God is the first time we are ever truly loved and cared about and taken care of. And it is *never* the way we would have done it.

Step Three is not about taking on new assignments or "onward Christian soldiers" or let's go build the Kingdom or feed the hungry. Step Three is turning your will and your life over to God's caring for you. You may smell an assignment coming. You may even be told about it because that is often part of the healing of your identity. But that is not Step Three. Step Three is turning your will and your life over to *God's caring for you.*

IV.) AS WE UNDERSTOOD HIM

It is patently obvious that we do not understand God. This Third Step does not mean to imply that we *do* understand God. It does mean to state as forcefully as possible that we cannot allow anybody else's understanding of God to stand in for us. Specifically, we cannot allow a pastor, a church, a creed, an ecclesiastical hierarchy, a relative, a peer group or anything or anyone else to interpret God to us or for us. Nothing can be allowed to stand between us and our own relationship with God. We must be responsive to our own prayers and meditations—or we are not walking this Third Step. So we will be wrong about God, and we will make some mistakes about what God wants of us. But that doesn't matter because God can correct and redirect us—as long as something doesn't keep getting between us and God.

This is not about being proud of how well we understand God, as if we thought we had God figured out or we had the right views or the correct theology. It is the very humble realization that we have to start from where we are—and that it *must* be from where *we* are—and that this new Path and WAY depend upon our keeping it one-on-one between us and God.

You must be born anew. (John 3:7) *Take up your cross and follow me.* (Matthew 16:24; Mark 8:34; Luke 9:23) *Have you forgotten that when we were baptized into union with Christ Jesus we were baptized into his death? By that baptism into his death we were buried with him, in order that, as Christ was raised from the dead by the glorious power of the Father, so also we might set out on a new life.* (Romans 6:3-4)

In endless phrases and imagery, the New Testament talks about Step Three. What it talks, let us walk.

Luke 4:1-13; Luke 6:37-45;
I Corinthians 11:23-32

Fourth Sunday in Lent

A SEARCHING AND FEARLESS INVENTORY

Step Four
Made a searching and fearless moral inventory of ourselves.

This is one of those steps that everybody realizes would be very good for everybody else to take. It is also one of those steps few people take with any thoroughness unless life starts to fall apart on them. In our society, we normally put it off until we have to pay somebody $125 an hour to make us do it. Sometimes even then we fight the process and act like it is the psychologist's job to do it for us.

The AA version of this spiritual step is somewhat limited. That is, AA is concerned specifically with alcoholics and is focused primarily on that part of the spiritual step most necessary for reconstructing a life torn apart by drinking. So AA doesn't focus, in the beginning, on a full inventory. It wants a moral inventory. Around AA tables, people don't spend much time talking about accomplishments, achievements, honors won, distinctions earned, how to carry on the dream of perfecting society. They are busy with the wreckage. The focus is on a moral inventory, and the focus of that is on what they have done wrong. A true inventory, of course, is not just moral, it's spiritual, relational, personal, social, practical—the whole scope. And it would include the full spectrum of life, not just the negative side.

There is also that little ending phrase, "of ourselves." Inventory of ourselves. Obvious, you say? From the evidence all around us, one of the hardest lessons of life is to learn to stop taking the inventories of others—and to start taking inventory *of ourselves.* Jesus underlined it clearly in the story of the speck and the plank. (Matthew 7:3-4)

Legend says the inscription "Know thyself" was written by the gods on the Temple of Apollo at Delphi, the true center of the world, maybe five hundred years before the birth of Jesus. The Fourth Step is not new to the spiritual path.

Let's try to get clear from the beginning: The Fourth Step calls each one of us to take a searching and fearless inventory. But perhaps you don't like the language of an accountant. Then this step calls us to take a thorough and honest look at our lives— not ducking anything we find; not skipping over anything embarrassing; not minimizing the good or the bad, and not exaggerating it either. Inventory, assessment, evaluation. Calm, honest, unblinking.

We can talk and muse about this step forever—which is what we are doing right now (at least it will seem that way to some of you). But *taking* the step is the only thing that will bring benefit. It doesn't matter how good or boring or interesting this sermon might be. What matters is: Will you actually go home and *work* this step? Do it. Take it.

Last week we talked about turning our wills and our lives over to the care of God. The Fourth Step is the beginning of the practical side of that caring. God knows us. God cares for us (loves us) through, around, under and beyond all that God knows of us. The problem is, we do not know ourselves. As Paul says: *For now we see in a mirror dimly, but then face to face. Now I know in part; then I shall understand fully, even as I have been fully understood.* (I Corinthians 13:12) Now that we have turned will and life over to the care of God, the first practical task is to take inventory—to get some clear concept (to the best of our ability) of what it is God has to work with and care for. We try to get all this information and perspective about ourselves into our heads—into our conscious minds—so God can have a better chance to talk with us, to communicate, to put ideas into our heads. That is why it is so important to be fearless and honest and thorough. Any way in which we warp the picture, doctor it up, smooth over the rough places, leave out the painful stuff or the motives that scare us or make us ashamed—any way in which we "touch up" or obscure or leave out things in this inventory of ourselves will dramatically affect the level on which God will be able to care for us, heal us, work with us. What we "touch up" or delete, God can't fix because we have erased it from the agenda. This makes it extremely difficult for God to get on that subject with us.

Our inventory will turn out to be the agenda of God's caring for us. The good we acknowledge from the inventory, God will lift up and re-create, empower and build into our futures. The wrong and the painful, God will correct and forgive and redeem and heal. We will leave things out, but not if we can help it—not because we are careless or afraid or secretive or proud. Some things are buried so deep we simply cannot find them anymore. And God will help us to get to them also, in due time. Some of our memories are partial and confused, so the inventory will not be perfect. But it will be the clearest and most honest look at ourselves and our lives that we can manage—no-holds-barred. That is the step. It is all that is asked in the Fourth Step, and is the next thing that's required if we are to proceed on the spiritual path. *Made a searching and fearless moral inventory of ourselves.* And if you are not coming out of a particularly painful and traumatic time, then make it the full-scope inventory, not just moral, and not just what you've done wrong.

Let's tie back into the spiritual path as we think of it and understand it, in light of the Christian tradition. Last week we talked about conversion (Third Step). It is my understanding that "inventory" always comes after conversion. That is, each time a person goes through a genuine conversion, inevitably there follows the step of assessment. It is mixed with humility and often with feelings of deep inadequacy that God must first heal before bringing reassurance. Nevertheless, the Fourth Step is the next step after every classic conversion I have ever known about.

Moses is saying, "I cannot speak well enough; I do not have sufficient reputation; I already blew it back in Egypt; nobody will listen to me; why should they?" and so on. Right after the burning bush, Moses is taking inventory. And God is dealing with him according to that inventory. Isaiah is a man of unclean lips who doesn't feel that his parental and cultural background has given him sufficient maturity or self-esteem with which to speak to or for the Almighty in his troubled, complex and indeed convoluted time. And he would probably still be talking like that if the angel hadn't purified his unclean lips with the burning coal. The inventory followed on the heels of his conversion, and it is necessary before he can accept the commission—the call to get on with his life.

The entire concept of Lent itself is understood in the context and tradition of taking a Fourth Step. Lent is a time for taking inventory. Traditionally and formally, Christians have considered it necessary to do a serious Fourth Step at least once a year. Lent, in turn, comes out of Jesus' own Fourth Step (which is patterned after Elijah's Fourth Step, which is patterned after Moses' Fourth Step, and it is clear to me that Jacob and Joseph knew the Fourth Step). After Jesus' own conversion (baptism), He went into the wilderness for forty days and nights—to be with Satan and with angels, to deal with the negative and the positive, darkness and light—for a searching and fearless inventory the likes of which the world had never seen before, and has never seen since. And we are followers, so we get baptized like He did (turn our wills and our lives over) and we also take inventory like He did. At least that is what the Lenten season hopes for on our behalf.

In a letter to the church at Corinth, Paul says: *If we examined ourselves, we should not fall under judgment.* (I Corinthians 11:31) If I were a fundamentalist, I could surely wale on that one: "You want to stay out of hell? Take a Fourth Step now!" That is not my language, but the point is just as good. Don't wait until God has to do it for you. A Fourth Step is a necessary part of the spiritual journey, and it needs to be very clear among us that this Fourth Step has always been a major step on our Path, one of the pillars of the Christian WAY. Why does it seem that there are numerous

Christians in our time who do not know this . . . who do not think it is important . . . who have never taken a serious or earnest Fourth Step? Certainly every person thinks about themselves and their lives from time to time—this or that desire or problem or choice, as it comes up, as it is happening. That's the Brylcreem theory of Christianity—"a little dab'll do ya." But a true Fourth Step, like any true inventory, is not very useful unless we get the whole picture laid out and clear before us. And that takes work. It isn't just a casual musing here or there, missing the real issues forever.

What are some of the reasons people do not take a Fourth Step? The first and clearest reason is *time*. It takes a lot of time to sit down and go over your life in a thorough and fearless manner. The information and learning patterns were different in Jesus' day, and memory was on an entirely different plane. Most modern people need to write in order to get a clear inventory. A good Fourth Step is not unlike writing an autobiography, except it is shorter because you write it for yourself to understand. This requires a lot less polish and explanation, and it includes things you wouldn't publish. Many people think they don't have time for such a task, or that it is self-centered to spend so much time thinking about themselves. Interesting that there is a strange correlation between having no time to ponder about ourselves, and being people who do great damage to ourselves and others. As John Dryden commented: "Look around the habitable world: how few know their own good, or knowing it, pursue." (JUVENAL, X) Or Geoffrey Chaucer: "Ful wys is he that can himselven knowe!" (THE MONK'S TALE, line 251) People who do not do Fourth-Step work do not know themselves. They do not know who they are. They do not know why they are here. They do not even know what makes them happy or sad or angry, or what makes them behave the way they do.

It is not just a time problem. Behind our busyness, we suspect there is a fear—an avoidance, a denial. It would be no fun, we assume, to find out that much about ourselves. It would be no fun to be reminded of all our mistakes, to see the remains of dreams and ambitions we once held dear, to face the waste of time and talent—to look into the eyes of God (so to speak) and say, "This is what I have done with the life you gave me." We think it would be no fun at all. And nobody ever did a sincere and earnest Fourth Step without a lot of tears. But there are huge surprises in the Fourth Step as well. Though you feel the ravages of Satan in the past, you will feel the closeness of God in the present. Though you feel the draw of Satan's plans for your future, you will know the power of God's caring—and know you can have a different future. But at the very center of the Fourth-Step experience, you will encounter a new clarity about your own life and the path you have been walking. It will feel good and clean, no matter what the wreckage or the accolades, to have things so open again between you and yourself—and between yourself and God.

Therefore the Fourth Step is worth your time, and worth overcoming your reticence or fear. St. Augustine, in his *CONFESSIONS* (which came out of his own Fourth Step), made it clear that the search to know the self and the search to know God, though quite different in motive, are absolutely necessary to each other. The path to knowing the self and the path to knowing God are the same path, the same journey. I guess that's because God made us. In any case, both require contemplation, reflection, time to think and ponder, time alone, time to listen and pay attention to threads and themes deep within—all the things our society dislikes and most people are sure they have no time for.

There are many ways to approach a Fourth Step. Word processors are a big help because you can insert things as your memory clears. I will suggest one approach for those of you who need a technique to get started. Divide your life into increments of five years. It may take a little time to figure out which grade you were in and where you lived, etc., for each five-year increment. After you have the five-year segments mapped out, put the names and events you remember in each of the five-year sections. Some people, of course, will appear over many segments;

others will appear in only one. Put them all in anyway. Then go back and start writing everything you remember about those names and those events and what was going on with you, for each five-year period.

You may discover, for instance, that "Mother" was not the same person in all the five-year segments—or that you were not. You will discover many things, some beautiful, some ugly. And as you write, memories will come back that you had no idea were still in your head at all. If you are new to the Fourth Step, and if you give it a reasonably high priority (that is, all or most of your spare time), it will take you three or four months to complete. Just so you know approximately what we are talking about.

Before I close, I should mention that the Fourth Step is virtually impossible if we have not already walked through Steps One, Two and Three. Of course, anyone can take an inventory of sorts, if they set their mind to it. But apart from the presence and reassurance of God's caring, the human psyche cannot face the inner self. Human beings are afraid, on some deep inner plane, that at the core they are evil and dark and satanically selfish. We cover it up and try to make sure we don't *act* that way. But deep within, we are always afraid that somehow the veneer will be torn away and we will be exposed for what we are, and then nobody will have anything to do with us ever again. Only in God's presence and reassurance do we dare to believe that at the core we are children of Light, and that the darkness is the veneer—coming from all the hurt and betrayal and pain and abandonment that happen to us in this broken world.

Having taken Step Three, Step Four reveals the darkness— brings it out where we can face it for what it is. And Step Four also reveals that we are more than our mistakes and our evil. The Light begins to glow and shine again—from within. And not from any game or trick or willpower of our own.

I am reminded of a poem I love by William Blake. I do not often chance a poem with you, but here it goes:

The Lamb

Little Lamb, who made thee?
Dost thou know who made thee?
Gave thee life, and bid thee feed
By the stream and o'er the mead;
Gave thee clothing of delight,
Softest clothing, woolly, bright;
Gave thee such a tender voice,
Making all the vales rejoice?
    Little Lamb, who made thee?
    Dost thou know who made thee?
    Little Lamb, I'll tell thee,
    Little Lamb, I'll tell thee,
He is called by thy name,
For He calls Himself a Lamb,
He is meek, and He is mild;
He became a little child.
I a child, and thou a lamb,
We are called by His name.
    Little Lamb, God bless Thee!
    Little Lamb, God bless Thee!

Just to reiterate, I hope this sermon has made it clear to you what the Fourth Step is about, and how it fits into our tradition and is a basic part of any serious spiritual path. However, talking about the step is not the same as taking it. Knowing about it brings none of the benefits of working the step. Do it. Take it. Let us pray . . .

Isaiah 6:1-8; Acts 22:2-5; 26:9-12; James 5:16

Fifth Sunday in Lent

CONFESSION

Step Five
*Admitted to God, to ourselves, and to another human being
the exact nature of our wrongs.*

One of the remarkable things about the Biblical record is its openness. Yes, there are endless unanswered questions. If you are like me, you wish somebody had taken the trouble to go interview all the people Jesus encountered—say, five years later—to find out what their lives were like because of that encounter. The synoptic Gospels feel too short, as if writing were hard work, or the writers were busy with important ministries and eager to get back to them. Nevertheless, one of the remarkable things about the Biblical record is its openness.

Though not always so among us in this church, in our society in general it is still fashionable to be secretive, to be closed off, to keep the bad mistakes and wounds and problems to ourselves. Though that tendency may be changing in our time, the Christian Church—once an open, sharing, working community of friends—has become a museum piece, a place to get dressed up for and put on airs. "Church" has become one of the last places in our society where people can be open or honest. Everybody needs to look good, act holy and impress each other with godliness, or at least cleanliness, and a mask of calm and competence. A person can visit many a sanctuary in our land for months, even years, and never guess that anybody there is having any serious struggles or defeats or doubts.

This scenario is not at all the impression we have of the early church, or of the Biblical record as a whole. The Bible was interested in real life. It still is, until we try to make it too perfect or holy. It is remarkable and worthy of notice that the Biblical heroes are not whitewashed. Whatever struggles there have been with editing and collecting, mostly the stories are not "cleaned up." From Genesis to Revelation, the people are in trouble and the people are in transition. The real hero is God, who keeps forgiving, restoring, inspiring, healing, guiding and leading any who are willing to confess their need and turn to God.

No time for a complete list, but just to make the point: Noah is a drunk; Jacob is a liar and a thief (inspired to be so by his mother, Rebecca); Moses is a murderer; King David is a murderer and an adulterer; Solomon is an idolater; Isaiah has a dirty mouth; Peter denies; Paul persecutes followers of the WAY, and most would say is also a murderer; Mark is a coward; John is a racist. It's hard to find perfect people, except among the pretenders. So God deals with the likes of you and me. The stories aren't about how perfect these people are, but about what happens to them when they repent, confess, turn to God.

What I am leading up to, of course, is the fact that confession has always been a major and necessary part of our tradition. *If we confess our sins, he is faithful and just to forgive us our sins and to cleanse us from all unrighteousness.* (I John 1:9) What if we do not confess our sins? What if we have no sins? There are no provisions for such a contingency. Such a state could not exist as "church," so the church has no category for it.

It isn't an enemy who tells us of Peter's denial. It isn't a smear campaign that defames the Apostle Paul. The Book of Acts reveals that it is Paul himself who keeps telling his story. He doesn't want anybody to think he or they are qualified for Christianity because of good behavior, excellent spiritual credentials, or superior record or performance. Just as important, he doesn't want anybody feeling they are dis-qualified because of bad behavior, terrible spiritual credentials, or inferior abilities or performance. In the Christian Way of Life, the hero is never us— not ultimately. The hero is God in Christ, who takes us as we are and heals, transforms, sanctifies, makes new.

"Admitted to God, to ourselves, and to another human being

the exact nature of our wrongs." *If we confess our sins, he is faithful and just to forgive us our sins and to cleanse us from all unrighteousness.*

Step Five very frequently comes after Step Four. That is what you would expect, is it not? You might think this is sarcasm, or right on the verge of it. But unfortunately it is all too common for Step Five to be skipped or neglected, even after Step Four has been taken. It is equally unfortunate that Step Five is sometimes attempted before Step Four has been accomplished. No need to dwell on it for long, but people who confess without taking a thorough and fearless inventory do very often confess the wrong things; or confess in such a way that no healing comes; or confess as a technique for gaining sympathy or for setting things up so they will not be expected or required to change. Just because it is a spiritual step—recommended by AA and at the core of the Christian tradition for thousands of years—does not mean that it works automatically no matter how we approach it, or what our motives. Most of us know people who very frequently *say* they are sorry but rarely show any evidence to support such a claim. They say they are sorry, but there is no behavioral change. How long does it take you to stop believing them?

One of the earliest stories in the Bible is the story of Cain. He murders his brother Abel, but there is never any hint that he is truly sorry. He never repents. He never confesses. The result is that the sin dogs his steps for the rest of his life, and even drags its ugliness into succeeding generations. The story makes it clear that God is willing to work with Cain, that God is eager to stop the evil from spreading and ruining life beyond the ruination already wrought. But Cain will not have it. Cain is too proud to repent or confess. So Cain lives with it, is stuck with it, and carries it forever.

Having turned our wills and our lives over to the care of God (in Step Three), we become engaged—or embroiled—in a process that is truly the business end of God's caring. Steps Four through Ten are the steps *we* take—our side of the process, our *cooperation* with God's caring: God's healing, restoring and nurturing us back to health and strength. However, Steps Four through Ten are far from the full story of what is going on. God is always more active than we are in this process and in the caring. But if we do not work Steps Four through Ten, then we are balking, holding back, hanging on to old ways and all they stand for. Can you picture in your mind a mule, all four feet planted, with someone in front gently tugging on the reins? God does not coerce. If we have turned life and will over to God's caring, we walk the steps. If not, the journey is still theory without practice—nothing happens, nothing changes.

We can only work one step at a time, but it is still no secret what God is about. We come powerless, and seeking a Power greater than ourselves. We turn our wills and our lives over to the care of some Higher Power—our best understanding of it. We turn it over to God. What is the situation? The situation is that, according to our own definitions, we were defeated—or we would never have made it through the First Step, never mind the first three. The truth is that we carry such weight of fear, guilt, remorse, dashed hopes, broken dreams, old resentments, rejection, betrayal, abandonment and injustice—the truth is that we carry this *enormous* weight—until it becomes so heavy we are no longer able to carry it. We can shuffle along for a few steps sometimes, or crawl through the days, but we cannot run or skip or dance anymore. And the weight doesn't always show up in any direct, tangible way. It may crop up in disease, depression, anger and/ or doubt. But for the most part, we are only semiconscious of all the weight we are actually carrying. We think that putting it out of our minds—putting it behind us—means it will no longer weigh us down.

That is not how it works. An unconfessed sin is a dead weight on the back of our souls. Unless we feel true sorrow, repent, confess it, ask for forgiveness, make amends and receive the forgiveness of God, then we carry this weight forever. Most of us spend years trying to believe life doesn't work this way—that maybe it works for others, but not for us. We spend years trying to beat the dealer, trying to find some other approach or philosophy or system that will not require us to work Steps Four through Ten—remorse, repentance, confession, absolution, penance. (Does it sound like AA is pure Catholicism? Well, maybe Catholicism made pure.) In the tradition of the church, no Christian is supposed to take communion unless they have gone to confession. It has been terribly stylized and ritualized, but it reminds us of the truth—once vibrant and vital—that if we don't keep clearing off the weight of alienation and sin, we will soon be too heavy to move.

So Lent has always been a time for prayer and fasting, a time for inventory, a time for confession. It is a time to lose weight and get back into shape—spiritual weight and spiritual shape. Step Five is not the full package, just the confession part of it. One step at a time, remember? "Admitted to God, to ourselves, and to another human being the exact nature of our wrongs." Have you ever done that? After taking a thorough and fearless inventory, have you ever sat down with another human being and gone over the exact nature of your wrongs? If so, you walk light. If so, you will go on doing this step from time to time because you have experienced the lifting of the weight and will never again be content to live under the crushing load. It's too hard, too heavy, and makes it impossible to get anywhere or make any real progress.

Inventory without confession is dead—a waste of time. How many of us stumble for years over this simple principle? We think that if we take the inventory—clear our minds, get the facts and the information straightened out and clear before us—that is what matters. Why burden anybody else with it? Why embarrass ourselves further? Just make note of it and move on, let it go, be done with it. How has that worked for you? Has it taken the weight off, cleared your guilt, restored you to joy and peace, put the spring back into your step? Inventory without confession is dead—a waste of time. *Therefore confess your sins to one another, and pray for one another, that you may be healed.* (James 5:16) Healed of what? Healed of our guilt. If we do not move on from Step Four to Step Five, we will know what our sins are but they will not be healed. The weight will not be lifted. In accountant language, we may have all the right numbers in the columns and everything figured correctly, but without confession (Step Five) we will never get out of the red.

Staying with the discipline of Step Five, the confession comes in three parts. Thousands of Twelve-Steppers claim to have taken a Fifth Step when they have only done the last third of the step—the least important part of it. This is a vast improvement over no Fifth Step at all, but I am always surprised when people will not take the step as it is stated. They jump to the conclusion that the first two parts are automatic, or unimportant, and rush off to do their Step Five with another human being. They think this is the real power of this step, but it is not. I strongly recommend that you listen to the step and do what the step tells you, in the order it tells you: first to God, then to yourself, and finally, to another human being.

ADMITTED **TO GOD** THE EXACT NATURE OF OUR WRONGS

God knows everything. God was present when we did the inventory. So that takes care of that, right? Wrong! Even though we know God knows, it is a very difficult, revealing and necessary process to walk into the presence of God on purpose and, in a calm and unhurried fashion, go over the list of our wrongs and the memories that are attached to them, giving God ample time to reflect on each item with us. "Dear God, this is the situation you put me in—this is what I made of it. This is the life you gave me—this is what I did with it." One at a time—no hurry, no avoidance, no ducking. Not with God in the background somewhere, but with God right there looking at you and invited to comment, to interact, to work it through with you.

It is an incredible experience. It is the deepest of the three confessions, and the one from which we learn the most. It is the one in which we discover the most tender understanding, and the one in which we discover threads and themes within ourselves that we did not understand or know before. It is the confession that will not gloss over or make light of what we have done, yet brings us to far greater appreciation of all of life—including our own. It is also true, in many ways, that unless we do this confession in God's presence first, we will not have received the assurance or confidence or forgiveness necessary to approach the other two levels as we should.

ADMITTED **TO OURSELVES** THE EXACT NATURE OF OUR WRONGS

Again we assume that, having written the Fourth Step, we automatically "told ourselves" or admitted to ourselves the exact nature of our wrongs. Again I suggest a second look. There are many layers of the self within. While the Fourth Step is often an incredible inner awakening and inner confrontation, the Fifth Step still calls for this admission to ourselves. Some of our Fourth Step is done with the analytical self, the objective information-seeking part of our brain. Unavoidably, the process is spread out over many weeks. Having gone to God with the results of the inventory, and especially with the exact nature of our wrongs—having discovered that the true Author and authority of the universes cares about us despite what we have done and failed to do—we still have unfinished business with our own inner being, especially with our "higher self," or soul.

Something inside us has been very hurt by our failures, mistakes, wrong turns, evil choices and wrong motives. Necessarily we have avoided these very subjects, even inside ourselves—hiding behind rationalizations and excuses and busyness and noise—until we have become strangers to our own inner beings. Now we need to repair the channels and get reacquainted, and it cannot happen without a Fifth Step. We discover we have hurt and disappointed our own inner being more than anyone else—except for God. And this confession is absolutely necessary if we are ever to become friends with ourselves again.

As with God, we must take unhurried time to go over the Fifth Step with our higher self, our inner being. It feels strange at first to go over the material again, when maybe only a few days before we went over it all with God. But the dialogue and the experience will quickly show itself to be very different. And the result will heal a different place within us.

ADMITTED **TO ANOTHER HUMAN BEING** THE EXACT NATURE OF OUR WRONGS

The credentials of the person are not mentioned. It does not have to be a professional counselor or a priest or somebody superior to us. Clearly AA believes in "the priesthood of all believers." In one sense, it hardly matters which human being listens to your Fifth Step with you. This person represents all human beings. What we do and who we are impact the others who live here, so we confess to another human being, who symbolizes them all. And having admitted to that person the exact nature of our wrongs and finding ourselves still alive—perhaps even still able to talk, still be cared about, still allowed to be part of the human family—there comes this incredible new awareness that spreads all through us.

God knows, our truest inner self knows, another human being knows—knows what we have been afraid to know, or admit, or own up to, or confess . . . often for years. But afterward we are still alive, still cared about, still accepted—and without all the secrets, subterfuge, pretending, masks and postures. Can you believe that? Not until you take a full Fifth Step you can't.

I do not understand how anybody who does not know about the Cross could ever bring themselves to do the first and deepest part of a Fifth Step. Perhaps that is why so many Twelve-Steppers jump quickly to the third phase of this step. The authority and acceptance of another imperfect human being is a much smaller chasm to attempt. But I hope you will not settle for it. The healing is too small and partial and short-lived for those who would live in the Kingdom. Besides, you *do* know about the Cross, and the mercy that has no borders and no limits. Aim for that, my friends.

Mark 11:1-11, 15-18, 27-33

Palm Sunday

COURAGE TO CHANGE THE THINGS I CAN

We have momentarily left the Twelve Steps of AA and their deep roots in the Christian tradition. We shall return to them sometime after Easter. Meanwhile, we turn our attention to the events of what is called Holy Week, or Passion Week—the culmination of Jesus' earthly life and ministry.

However incredible the ministry of Jesus—the teachings, the healing, the miracles—however much we might be impressed by the baptism, the wilderness trials, the gathering of the disciple band, the power of the relationships being formed—without the events of this final week (Palm Sunday through Easter Sunday), it is extremely unlikely that we would ever have heard of Jesus.

As for Holy Week itself, we can focus on what Jesus is saying and discover from that a perspective on what is happening. He gives many instructions; He does much teaching and arguing with His opponents; He talks with the disciples at the Last Supper; He speaks a few words during the arrest and trial, and from the Cross. We get one perspective and dimension by listening to what Jesus *says*.

We get a different perspective and dimension by paying attention to what Jesus *does* in this last week. There are times and ways in which actions speak louder than words. Focusing on what Jesus does, we could very nearly conclude that it doesn't matter what He says. The story is carried in the actions alone:

- Jesus enters Jerusalem in prophetic, Messianic style.
- He scatters the money-changers.
- He assumes the right to command—to teach and lead on the Temple premises—all week.
- Jesus enacts the New Passover. Instead of warding off the Angel of Death and being freed from slavery, this *New* Passover

(Last Supper) enlists all who partake of it as servant/slaves of
God, ready to die for God. Do you want freedom and life—or
slavery and death? Actually, the two Passovers do not stand in
contradiction, for one is grounded in the physical dimension and
the other is grounded in the spiritual dimension. Yet the symbol
message of the Last Supper is a nearly total reversal of the First
Passover.

•   Jesus waits in the Garden when He could have (should
have) run.

•   The Crucifixion and the Resurrection are deeds about
which we speak endless words, and we need to keep talking and
sharing and trying to comprehend the full magnitude of such
events. But in a sense, they require no words. They speak forever
just by the force and power of the actions themselves.

If we have approached Holy Week from these two directions
(what Jesus says and what Jesus does) and spent time with each
dimension and perspective, then perhaps we can take a third
look and see Holy Week as the climax or pivot point of all earth
history. All that comes before leads up to it; all that comes
afterward springs from it, and takes power and direction from it.

In any case, we have come to Palm Sunday again. Much of
the world around us is not walking with Jesus through Passion
Week. Some think they have gone beyond it. Many are more
engaged with worries and concerns of their own. Most are mostly
unaware.

But we who are sworn to be followers want to follow Him still.
It is not that we do not have our worries. We are aware of living in
a scary and threatening world, and in very troubled times. Only,
instead of drawing us away from Passion Week, as if that were
long ago and we have no time for it, we are drawn to it more than
ever—seeing all things illumined by its light, defined by its
themes, given purpose and hope by its outcome.

How, then, do we come to Palm Sunday? With things sacred
and familiar, we must always find some way to break through the
veneer of past worship and sheer familiarity—the veil that tells
us we already know all about it. It doesn't take much, if we are

willing—just enough to get us started, to get us engaged again, to get us thinking and feeling again.

Courage to change the things I can. That simple phrase is my way back into Palm Sunday this year. It doesn't have to be yours. It doesn't matter what gets us back into it, as long as we come fresh and real and willing again. But I am using that phrase this year, and some of you may want to also. It comes from Reinhold Niebuhr, one of Union Theological School's most famous teachers. He was never my favorite theologian (Emil Brunner was, closely followed by Anders Nygren). But I've read everything he ever wrote because he was Frank Weiskel's favorite teacher, and I worked with Frank Weiskel, so it was survival for me to know Niebuhr. Long after everybody has forgotten Niebuhr and all the books he wrote, great and small, the world will still remember a prayer he gave us—one of the shortest prayers in history: *God, grant me the serenity to accept the things I cannot change, courage to change the things I can, and the wisdom to know the difference.* This "Serenity Prayer" is said thousands of times every day by people trying to get their bearings, who want to remember the principles by which they live, and who are seeking the presence and help of God. Interesting (not that it matters) that it comes out of the Evangelical and Reform side of the United Church of Christ.

Now forget all of that. The benefit comes if we pray the prayer, not just look for its origin and pedigree. But I was realizing, as many of you might also, that mostly when I use this prayer I am contemplating the first phrase: *serenity to accept the things I cannot change.* There are endless applications, and control issues are so numerous and so insidious that some of us find ourselves praying the prayer all through the day some days.

The second phrase is of equal importance, even if some of us get to it less frequently: *courage to change the things I can.* To me, this is the epitome—the distilled essence—of Palm Sunday. Palm Sunday is the strongest action Jesus ever took in this world, humanly speaking. You may be more impressed by the calming of the storm, the feeding of the five thousand, the Sabbath healings, the raising of Lazarus, or whatever. But Jesus could have calmed every storm that ever hit the Galilee, and they never would have crucified Him for it. He could have healed every person in the nation—and on the Sabbath—and some would have fretted and grumbled, but they never would have crucified Him for it.

It is the political action Jesus took on Palm Sunday—and the way He followed it up throughout the week—that got Him crucified. Palm Sunday is the strongest action Jesus ever took, pragmatically and politically. It was the threat and challenge to political power and influence—to who was in charge, to who had the right to govern. That's what got Him crucified. Claiming to be the Son of God wouldn't get Him killed until He started using it as a reason for claiming authority in the real world. That puts everything in a different light. Jesus wasn't kidding—He was serious about changing things. *Courage to change the things I can.*

Moses can preach about freedom and justice until he is blue in the face and old and gray, and it doesn't really matter and nobody will mind very much. Not until he walks into Pharaoh and says, "We all have to go three days' journey into the wilderness to worship our God." *That's* different! Who has true authority? Who is in control of what will actually happen? Clearly that forces a confrontation.

To be sure, priests and Pharisees and even King Herod have been wondering about Jesus because He makes noises that sound more authoritative than what they are used to. He's been getting their attention, from time to time, as His movement grows and spreads—and they wonder what He is leading up to. But when Jesus takes over the Temple the week preceding Passover, confrontation is no longer avoidable. Remember: There is no separation of church and state. This is not just a church—not even a really big church. This is the Temple—the center of the nation's life.

Courage to change the things I can. What did Jesus think He could change? That is what blew me back into Palm Sunday this year. What did Jesus think He could change? How does that compare to what I think *I* can change? Or to what you think *you* can change?

I read and re-read the story and contemplate it this way and that. I try to comprehend and understand it from this perspective and that. But no matter what I do to it, *He* is trying to change the world. *Courage to change the things I can.* Jesus is intentionally doing things, taking steps, making plans, organizing and training disciples, strategizing—and none of it makes any sense until we see it heading straight for Palm Sunday . . . Passion Week . . . the confrontation . . . the bid for taking over the country in a peaceful, spiritual coup. To be sure, it is a backup plan. Nevertheless, Jesus is serious about changing things—about changing the whole world.

What am I serious about changing? What are you serious about changing? How are we followers of the One who set out to change the world if we are not trying to change anything ourselves? I'm not talking about changing our bank accounts, or changing from overweight to trim, or from too busy to more relaxed, or from steady work to retirement. What is it that you pray for when you pray for *courage to change the things I can?* Dangerous thinking. In the light of this story, that very nearly goes without saying.

We do not dare lose sight of the fact that Jesus goes at it from the foundations. To change anything, at least in the Christian tradition, we begin by changing ourselves. More accurately, we begin by letting God make changes in our own lives, in us personally. Jesus gets baptized. The dove descends. He finds a new identity—at least a new awareness. Jesus goes into the wilderness. Everything about His own life and purpose changes. We'd never heard of Him before this. After this, He is different, His schedule is different, the way He spends His time and life is different. All authentic change begins with ourselves.

Jesus gathers a support community—a disciple band, a church *(ecclesia)*. That is the second phase of the change. He begins introducing others into the change that He Himself has experienced. They live it together, act upon it, act it out. So the disciples' lives also change. They find new identity also. After this, they are different, their schedules are different, the way they spend their time and life is different. So the change starts with the One, and spreads to the many. Yet each of the many has to change at the point of the One. That is, each has to decide. Each receives the change first as an individual. Each must experience conversion, even as Jesus did. Jesus is always willing to wait for this. It cannot be faked—no mass conversion, no substitutes. Each must walk the Path in his or her own right. Those merely riding the coattails of others weaken and endanger the whole mission. (Was that Judas' problem? I don't know, but it's ours.)

Jesus moves into Palm Sunday with His own change and the change of His followers already in place. Further changes will come, yet no one attempts this larger change until their own change—individually and as a body—is authentic.

Have you ever known people who try to change the world without any personal change, and without any personal change in those they enlist for the cause? "If I can get everybody else to shape up, do things right, then maybe my own life will be okay."

Jesus' life is okay already—even as He rides the donkey toward Jerusalem. No matter what happens or how the people react, Jesus' life is already authentic, centered, dedicated, devoted. There is nothing anyone can do to change that. Is that where some of His courage comes from? Can you fathom a Palm Sunday apart from courage?

Jesus, of course, is not on a level to challenge the whole world to change. On Palm Sunday, He challenges the authority of some of the political/spiritual leaders in the capital city of a tiny nation that is no longer truly a nation. It is a vassal province— a "waystation" of the Roman Empire. And He cannot even "hold" the Temple in this pseudo-capital city, even for one full week! Is this "courage to change the things I can"?

Do I try to measure that phrase according to what I think I can actually, sensibly, successfully change? If I can actually change it, then I should take courage and do so. Otherwise, if it isn't pretty clear I will be able to do it—be successful in the attempt—then I am off the hook. That is how I think. Is that how you think too?

Palm Sunday shatters that illusion for me. I am convinced Jesus fully intended to change the world. From my perspective, it is very clear Jesus did change it, and goes on changing it. But from a worldly perspective, Palm Sunday is as far as He got. Yet all of the change He truly wrought came after Palm Sunday. It came *through* Palm Sunday, and because He dared to do it.

"Courage to change the things I can" is not about successful outcomes, not by anything I can know or measure. Jesus—the One we follow—was living *toward* the change, out of His own personal change, with everyone who claimed this change with Him. They lived for it, lived toward it, and believed in it with all they had and were. That was *their* notion of "courage to change the things I can."

This is very disturbing . . . and very comforting. First of all, it means I have to rethink all my notions and convictions about what I am trying to change—and on what basis. Secondly, it means I can go back to living for some changes I had given up on. It doesn't have to be grand. I don't have to be in some high position or in some moment in time where my own mind can believe I might be successful and accomplish change in some good and final way. No, I get to live for it, live toward it, and believe in it with whatever I have and am. Where it comes out is not in my hands, any more than Palm Sunday and Passion Week were in Jesus' hands.

If I make the change in my own life, then I can look for others who believe in the same change—and we together can live for it, and nothing in this world can prevent it. So I'm singing *Hosanna!* again, and I hope you are too.

Mark 14:22-50

Maundy Thursday

ALTARS AND TABLES

We are here primarily to take communion. It is the highest sacrament of the Christian Faith. We have taken communion many times before. In all likelihood, we will take it many times after tonight. Sometimes it has been mere ritual for us. Other times we have felt the sacrament lift us into its truth—the unity and power and presence of the Christ who loves us, who comes for us, who does so at any price, whatever it takes.

Remember me. That is about all it takes, from our side. Because of who He is and what He does, remembrance is about all it takes to get us back into the possibility of communion—of life together, walking and sharing and doing things together. *Communion*—with union, in harmony with each other.

Perhaps we start out, this night, being grateful that Jesus still wants communion with us. I am, at least. That always seems like miracle to me. Through my life, over the years, there have been times when other humans didn't seem to want very much to do with me. There was Dorothy Cooper, back in the first grade. Sometimes she was friendly; sometimes she preferred Bill Gaines. I really didn't understand why—one way *or* the other. But it's painful. If somebody likes you, will it last? If not, why not? What did you do? Usually it's unclear. So what's changed since first grade? Same song, second verse. It was merely previews of coming attractions.

Life has bumps. It just does. The road isn't smooth. Most people don't make it over very many bumps with us. Maybe one. Maybe two or three. But the bumps keep coming. After a while, they blame us, or they think other people will be smoother, or maybe they just need a change of scenery. It looks to them like a better opportunity somewhere else. Anyway, they are gone again—

physically or mentally or religiously or relationally. Once in a while we find a friend—somebody who for some unknown reason stays, or at least keeps coming back. That's one of the miracles of life.

Rejection, betrayal, turning away, walking off or away or apart—that isn't strange. That happens all the time, all over the world, on endless levels and in endless dimensions. Wanting to be with us—wanting communion, wanting to stay in it together—*that's* the miracle!

When we hit a few big bumps, I expect people to scatter. It's the way of the world. So I appreciate it when some don't scatter. It isn't the same for everybody, I'm sure. But for me, the folk who don't scatter easily are the people of Christ. That has been my experience. I can only presume that it's because they know Somebody who doesn't scatter on them.

Each time I come to communion, I am grateful that He still wants communion. It is a mystery to me. Others, more or less my equals, do not always want very much to do with me, or they get tired of me or find better things to do. But this One, the Son of God—far greater, far busier, with friends in places so high I cannot even fathom it—this One *always* wants communion with me, and is always eager to share time and life and to go on together. That makes life worth living. Never mind that it is always startling, always miraculous—it makes me grateful, grateful that I get to go on with Him.

Beyond the gratitude, or because of it, I am also reminded this night that wherever there is communion, there is, so to speak, an altar and a table—a sacrifice and a shared meal. Jesus cannot come here tonight—cannot be here, cannot participate with us—without some kind of sacrifice. It comes clearest, no doubt, in the context of the first time—the Last Supper with the disciples. It was sacrifice for Him to show up on earth at all. Incarnation is a terrible reduction, from heaven's side. Coming into the physical realm at all—the limitation, the strife, the bickering, hurt, anger, disease and alienation—it was a great sacrifice just to come here. We aren't so impressed by this, since we are here too. But even *we* can feel the sacrifice in "this is my body, broken for you . . . this is my blood, poured out for you." Staying with the disciples on His terms, showing them His kind of life and truth and love—and revealing it and making it possible for them as well—that is what it was costing, what it was coming to. Jesus *could* turn away, close it back down again. But to keep it open, to keep it available for them as well, that was the price: body broken, blood poured out. Altar and table are mingled—sacrifice and shared meal are intertwined beyond all hope of being able to separate them, ever again.

This is the night when that all comes together—and it is more than we can fathom, more than we can absorb, more than we can endure: Judas leaving early, feet getting washed, all the last instructions about serving each other and loving each other as He has loved us. This is the night we go to sleep on Him—the night He prays to be released from it all. This is the night of final testing. *Nevertheless, not my will but Thine be done.* This is the night of the arrest, the night of the kiss, of a cock crowing, of best friends running away, and nobody left to ride the bumps with Him.

Oh well, it's a hard life, and He brought it on Himself, right? Right?! We inhabit a world where such a thing is done, to such a One?!! Ever since He made it clear, we realize that it goes on all over the place, all the time: This world is not under the reign of God, and there is no hope for us. That is what we had not known, and could not make ourselves see. This world is not under the reign of God, and there is no hope for us . . . unless . . . unless there is some way whereby and wherein we can return—convert, repent, be transformed—be allowed back into the reign of God.

Beyond the gratitude, or because of it, I am reminded this night that wherever there is a communion meal, there is, so to speak, an altar and a table—a sacrifice and a shared meal. *We* cannot come here tonight either—cannot be here or participate—without some kind of sacrifice: our pride; our belief in our wisdom or right to be in control; our individualism, and the fear and loneliness that go with it.

You see, it is a New Passover. The first was deliverance from bondage to Pharaoh in Egypt. This second one is a release from slavery to sin (alienation = being apart)—release from bondage to Satan, and all the guilt and shame and fear and sorrow which come from that.

There will be other kinds of sacrifices too, perhaps—things that get dropped from our lives as a result of our being in His presence. But they are questionable sacrifices, being let go more from lack of continued need, desire or interest than placed on God's altar as something precious.

This is the night our communion meal begins. It locks us into the transition between the earthly ministry of Jesus of Nazareth, and the continuing ministry of the Holy Spirit of Jesus Christ. Jesus is said to have given many hints and even clear teachings to let us know that this was happening. But we are so startled by death and cruelty that it blurs on us. So this communion meal continually reminds us: He is with us. Insofar as we will allow it, He walks with us still. Nothing we or our world can do to Him will or can change His offer—this meal, our bond—not anymore. We can refuse it, or wander off, or forget. But He is here, and waiting. And this meal is the reminder.

So we come again, this night—as disciples of today, yet feeling great kinship with the disciples of old. Jesus has told us parables and taught in graphic imagery throughout all the years that we have journeyed with Him. Now He comes to this Last Supper—His last chance to talk with us human to human; His last chance to be helpful, to instruct, to encourage and express feelings (love). What will He say? Sic 'em? Rah rah? Hey guys, it's been fun?

He says *Remember me.* Even more, He says *Do this in remembrance of me.* Do this breaking of bread and drinking from the cup in remembrance of body broken, blood poured out—the clearest and most graphic proof we know of God's mercy . . . of God's total forgiveness . . . of God's true and passionate love . . . of God's intention to be with us, and for us. Gathering all that we know of Him—His way of teaching, His love of parable and imagery, His own compassion and unusual powers, His confrontation and courage, His startling prayer life, the movement He has been leading with a disciple band at its core, the prayer He taught us, the true identity we finally concluded was the truth about Him: Messiah, Christos—we bring it all into this moment, this night, this meal. And we hear Him say to us: *Remember me . . . Do this in remembrance of me.*

Could I ever say such a thing? Could you ever say such a thing? If we do not feel the magnitude, and the contrast, how can we understand? What have I ever been or done that the world should remember? Why would I want it to? Please, I am not feeling lonely. Especially not here, especially not on this night. I know I have friends. I remember some of my friends who have died, and some of my friends and loved ones would remember me, for a while. That's fine. But that's different.

That is not the same as this *Remember me*. That is not a beacon in the night to show the way. That is not a lifeline for no matter what happens, or what storms come, or what disasters hit. That is not a promise of deliverance, of help, of shelter, of sanity, of Light and Love. If we are friends, we remember each other—and I am not knocking it, it's wonderful. But this *Remember me* is all of those things—and more. This *Remember me* is the shadow of a great rock in a weary land. This *Remember me* is a beacon in the night, and a lifeline in the storm, and a promise of deliverance and sanity and Light and Love. To remember Jesus is to remember everything: God, love, future, eternal life, how to live, what to care about, hope and faith, and what is really going on here.

In this meal, Jesus says to us: "We are on a journey. Sometimes it gets hard. But I show the WAY. Keep together. Keep with me. *Do this in remembrance of me.* Because every time you *Remember me,* it will allow me to communicate with you again. It will tune your mind to my channel, and you will sense and feel and hear me with you—wanting to have conscious contact, just like always. But it requires occasional attention from you— hopefully, sometimes, undivided attention."

Do this in remembrance of me.

Mark 15:43-16:20; I Corinthians 15:3-9;
Acts 22:6-11

Easter I

I'M IMPRESSED

Easter is the most impressive event that has ever happened in human history. But things do not impress all of us in the same way, nor are we impressed by the same things. There are even some among us who would automatically refuse to be impressed by anything that seemed to impress so many others. Strange is human nature.

Maybe the first thing we should do each Easter Morning is hold a great contest to decide who believes in the Resurrection the most: the liberals or the fundamentalists; the Catholics or the Mormons; the businessmen or the professors. Eventually we could get to us and decide which individuals among us really believe in the Resurrection the most. Wouldn't that be a good idea? Sounds pretty "Christian" doesn't it? Have a big contest, rate everybody's faith, kick out all the unfaithful, and shame everybody who doesn't believe correctly. Hey, it builds bigger churches than this one!

But that's not our problem. It's Easter, and so I will make a proclamation: I do proclaim to you, in the name of Jesus the Christ, that you are loved by the God of all Creation. And that the Christ, who put His life on the line for you, has shown you how much and how deep is that love. Especially I proclaim to you, in the name of Jesus the Christ, that if you do not yet believe in Him, yet He believes in you. If you do not yet know God, yet God knows and loves you. If you come here with whatever level or dimension of doubt, still you are welcome here. And though you may not believe it yet, God wants you in eternal life, and it is the power and love of God that will keep offering it to you—no matter what you think, and no matter how much or how little you deserve it.

I know that you have and will run into many teachers and preachers who tell you differently, who put all kinds of threats and restrictions on this Gospel. And yes, they tell me that I am going to hell too, because they say I don't believe it properly either. But it's okay, I don't believe them. I believe in Jesus, who came to those who did not believe it properly, and made a way for us also. So don't trust anyone who tries to lock the Message back up into their tiny frames of who God loves, and on which conditions of behavior or belief. What we believe *does* free us to participate and cooperate more consciously. But what we believe does *not* change the heart of God. Jesus' coming here—His teaching and healing and life here—proclaims God's love for us. The Cross and the Resurrection are about *how much* God loves us. That does not go away because of anything we do or don't do, believe or don't believe.

Believe in gratitude and joy, as much and as fast as you authentically can. But do not be threatened by haste or hell. God wants us to believe and to know Him truly. Yet such things cannot be coerced and still remain true. "Truth, like love and sleep, resents approaches that are too intense." God will give you all the time you need—in this world, or the next. No fires are waiting to burn you more than those which already have. The fires of remorse and sorrow and loneliness and fear that have burned us in the past will also burn us in the future, until we find our God. But that isn't some religious creed, it is just our reality for as long as we are alienated—estranged from God, from ourselves, from each other.

So we try to trust God's love. If we get confused or perplexed by the words or the systems or even by the way somebody uses the Bible, we keep remembering that Jesus came and how He died, and that witnesses for two thousand years claim they know His living presence. If words get confusing, we watch the actions of God—especially with Jesus—and we include what we ourselves experience in our own lives.

So let's talk about Easter. The first thing we need to do is take away certainty about the details. I know that sounds strange at first. So many people are trying to know everything down to the last detail. But Easter is not a scientific convention. No videotapes were running. Easter is a faith affair, not a scientific experiment. It is important to know and admit that we do not know the details with any certainty. Easter is mystery—*mysterium.* If you can explain it all, you flunk! (This is not to suggest that you go to hell; it's just me saying that if you come here with no doubts, you don't understand the situation.)

As soon as we get technical, we get into trouble. On the other hand, we are physical beings, so we are always getting technical. Whether we agree with each other, or whether or not we even discuss it, each one of us has a technical image in our head when we think about the Resurrection of Jesus. Is it a physical resurrection, a spiritual resurrection, or some kind of combination? Once on that level, we start arguing, and often we intersperse the arguments with phrases like, "Well then, you just don't really believe . . . "

I do not believe in the physical resurrection of Jesus. But the moment I make such a statement, we are instantly into word games. We got technical. The word "physical" to me (and to the dictionary, for that matter) refers to the body—to the body as I experience and know it, as all of us have always known it. The physical is imperfect: it wears out, it gets sick, it gets old, it dies. If you say to me "physical," that's what I think. That's what that word *means* to me. Everything I have ever known that was physical was in decline—wearing down, wearing out—from mountain peak to my big toe. I do not believe in the physical resurrection of Jesus. Obviously for me that would be horrible—pathetic, trivial, ridiculous. Easter has got to be bigger than "physical" or I would have no interest in it. I would conclude we were talking about resuscitation instead of resurrection.

I understand a little about the mind-set of Apocalypticism in the century before Jesus, and I know there have been threads of our tradition which perceived and expected everything to be physically based. New Jerusalem would be the actual city of Jerusalem made perfect, right here on earth. Resurrected bodies would be our physical bodies, only made perfect, and dwelling here on a perfected earth. That is at least some improvement. Then we have more than a physical resurrection—at least our physical nature is transformed so we are super-physical. We could at least say, "I believe in the super-physical resurrection of Jesus." But I don't believe that picture either. It is much too small and limited. The implications (no sun or moon) are that God will "freeze" the earth in some perfect state, and those who make it—who "earn" the transformation—will spend eternity on this earth, only without pain, decay, aging, etc. Does that get you all excited? I am not impressed. I am not even interested.

According to this tradition, those who die stay in their graves until the day of resurrection, then everybody comes out at the same time. Of course. There isn't room here for both shows to go on at the same time, so the dead have to wait for the living, for the present mess to run its course, and then when this phase is all finished, we can change the stage setting a little, and bring on the eternity phase. Act V, Scene Two Billion. Boring! I am not impressed with the merely physical. Haven't been since about sixth grade. I realize that some people who speak of the physical resurrection of Jesus mean it as a compliment, as something more real or grand in their eyes. Not for me. That makes it small, petty, foolish—for me, it is not worth the effort.

Some people, however, are impressed with the physical. If it isn't physical, they think it isn't real. People whose minds work like that do believe in the physical resurrection of Jesus. Usually they don't mean what I mean by physical. That is, they think of a body not limited by time and space or disease and aging. They don't think the resurrected body of Jesus will die. So they think it is some kind of spiritually transformed physical body, which is actually pretty close to what I mean when I say I do not believe in the physical resurrection because it is too limited. (So sometimes we mean the same thing, at least sort of, but argue like we despise each other because we do not use identical words.)

Do you believe in the resurrection only of the spirit? For me, it depends on what you mean by "spirit." Lots of my new-age and "liberal" friends mean a sort of gaseous vapor, like Casper the Friendly Ghost or the cohort of Mrs. Muir. I'm even less impressed with that than I am with a reworked physical body. Even now I hate it when things slip through my fingers. If you're going to saddle me through all eternity with a form that can never get a grasp on things, I'm not going to be very grateful. I think God personally invented hugs, and I don't think heaven can run right without them. Besides, heaven is more, not less.

Paul's phrase is "spiritual body." What is a spiritual body (besides being a contradiction in terms)? What is a spiritual body capable of? I have no notion. I've never touched one, certainly never used one. I expect to get to do that some day. Suddenly the technicalities are absurd, and science is silent simply because no one with a spiritual body has ever turned it over for scientific investigation. A spiritual body, for sheer lack of definition, is whatever we imagine it to be. Maybe it has substance, if it wishes, but not substance as we know it. Jesus appears and vanishes. *Later he appeared in a different form.* (Mark 16:12) Sometimes people don't recognize Him, except in the breaking of bread— that is, in the communion meal. (Luke 24:31, 35) Even Mary of Magdala doesn't recognize Him at first, and if anybody in the world would, she would. (John 20:14) When Jesus appears to the disciples, they think He is a ghost, a spirit. (Luke 24:37) It is not a "body," at least not like anything we know or think of as a body.

Okay, so Easter is *mysterium.* Technicalities don't help us. In fact, they only confuse the issue. What we do know is that some people had experiences with the Living Christ which convinced them that He was alive. Nobody—NOBODY— EVER BELIEVED BECAUSE SOMEBODY *ELSE* SAW HIM. Track it with me:

• Mary Magdalene was the first to see Jesus. She told the disciples, but *they would not believe it.* (Mark 16:9-11)

• Two disciples encountered Jesus on a country road. They went back and told the others, *but again, no one believed them.* (Mark 16:12-13)

- The women from Galilee returned from the tomb and told the eleven disciples, *but these words seemed to them an idle tale, and they did not believe them.* (Luke 24:1-12)

- The whole Gospel of John is about people not believing, including the story of Thomas, whom we have nicknamed Doubting Thomas. The other disciples tell him, "We have seen the Lord." But Thomas refuses to believe until he sees and touches for himself. (John 20:24-28)

It isn't just Thomas, you see. They were all like that. They had walked and worked with Jesus, and Jesus had told them what to expect—told them that He would rise from the dead, told them to be ready for it. And still they would not believe each other when it happened. NOBODY BELIEVED BECAUSE SOMEBODY *ELSE* SAW HIM.

But *you* are supposed to believe because somebody else saw Him? His own disciples would not believe until they themselves saw Him—would not even believe each other—but you are supposed to believe because I, or they, or somebody else tells you? *That* is His plan? That is what Jesus was counting on? He would appear physically to a few folks for a few weeks, and they would tell everybody else, and it would work? All over the world, all through the ages? Until now, when *your* faith is supposed to depend on somebody telling somebody down through the generations for two thousand years?! You believe on the basis of an eyewitness two thousand years in the past??!! No wonder we have a society in which hundreds of thousands can believe in the Resurrection but it doesn't make any difference to them. We are just as depressed, afraid and self-centered as before. We can believe in the Resurrection but it doesn't cut our greed or interfere with our adultery or idolatry? It doesn't bring the joy that transforms, or put us into living churches that demonstrate the Way of Life which knows Christ's Kingdom is real?

You understand, I presume, why fundamentalists are so adamant about the Bible being inerrant. Since their faith depends on the absolute accuracy of the record which tells about Jesus' appearances, any hint that the record might have flaws of any kind is terribly threatening. Easter is *because* the Bible says it is, *and the way* the Bible says it is. Therefore, they try to make it sound like it had precision, that the technicalities are all in place, and that no "good" person can doubt that it happened just as it is portrayed.

Except that Matthew is sure the disciples see the Risen Lord for the first time in Galilee, while Luke thinks it happened in Jerusalem. They can't even tell the difference between one end of the nation and the other, but I am forbidden to wonder if they got all the other details right, like *what happened to the body?*

That's the wrong Easter! Easter is about a LIVING LORD! And you don't have to be petrified from fear that some ancient record isn't perfect, not if you believe in a *Living* Lord. If Luke got confused, so what? For all we know, he had never been to Israel, and didn't know the difference between Galilee and Judah. Or, in this case, it is more likely that Matthew failed to read Mark's Gospel carefully. Do you think that might actually matter if our Risen Lord is really RISEN?! If Jesus is alive, the Bible is precious for whatever information we can get from it, but Easter doesn't stand or fall because somebody saw Him two thousand years ago. The truth is, we believe just like they did. That is to say, we believe when we *encounter* the Risen Christ *ourselves.* Just like them, we do not believe it until after *we* encounter the Risen Christ. We may long to. We may be very eager as we hear the witnesses, and feel the soul stirring within us. But it takes true encounter before we truly believe—the kind of belief that changes our lives: our values, our goals and how we try to reach them, why we are alive, what we live for, what we care about, and where our hope lies.

Paul lists the appearances of Jesus (I Corinthians 15:3-8). Paul doesn't know anything about an empty tomb. What he does know is that he has personally encountered the Risen Christ on the Damascus Road. And Paul knows that every other apostle (messenger) has had some kind of encounter with the Risen Christ as well (verse 7).

Now I'm impressed! Now we are talking about a Risen Christ who is really here with us—who is at work among us, and who keeps on coming to us, encountering us, changing us, sending us. The Resurrection is about our encountering Him, too . . . and about our living life with Him also.

Have you ever wondered why Jesus did not appear to Pilate? What about to the Chief Priest, or to the Sanhedrin? That would have been appropriate, don't you think? "Hey fellas, remember me?" I would have liked that scene. That's just about my style— which is one of the big differences between me and Jesus. But don't sidetrack me. What about Jesus appearing to Caesar? Why not settle it once and for all, if that really is the purpose—if we are going to do this resurrection thing in some overt way that nobody can ever doubt, ever again. Why doesn't Jesus just walk in on Caesar and make it *really* clear—to the whole world? "Hey bud, move over, I'm back." (Jesus as Rambo.) This also would have saved the lives of a lot of His very dear friends.

But that's not like Jesus, is it? It's not like our God to do it that way. That's how we keep wanting them to be, how we keep wanting to make it sound, but that's not how they operate. They offer, make it possible, invite, encourage, come to share and influence—just as much as we are comfortable with, just as much as we will allow it. But no shoving, no coercion, no breaking the Prime Directive (the decision of God never to do anything that would destroy our free will). A Book with no errors would be like the Resurrected Jesus walking in on Caesar: it closes the options, takes away the learning and growing on our part, turns from faith to fact . . . and in the process, cuts out love and life and meaning. That's how to get automatons, not living, growing souls. Why do we try so hard to make the Resurrection fact and certainty, when God and Jesus work so hard to keep it faith and prayer?

If we want Easter, we can only find it like the early disciples did—in our own personal encounter with the Living Christ. Oh no, you say, don't tell me we have to go back to "life as usual." If by "life as usual" you mean prayer, turning it over, walking day by day, trading in our control and our purposes for Christ's unseen

Kingdom—doing it in faith (uncertainty), making mistakes, getting forgiven, feeling the mercy and grace and guidance and presence of the Risen Christ ourselves—in our own lives—then *yes!* Then *Yes!* Then . . . YES! He is risen! (He is risen, indeed!) And He didn't go back up to heaven in some way that leaves us waiting for Him. He is risen and here! And Easter IS the Second Coming. So He is *really* risen! And we have life with Him here, and now . . . and forever. Amen!

Mark 10:17-22; Matthew 19:27-30; Galatians 5:22-6:2

Easter II

THE PROMISES

From the Big Book of *ALCOHOLICS ANONYMOUS:*

We are going to know a new freedom and a new happiness. We will not regret the past nor wish to shut the door on it. We will comprehend the serenity and we will know peace. No matter how far down the scale we have gone, we will see how our experiences can benefit others. That feeling of uselessness and self-pity will disappear. We will lose interest in selfish things and gain interest in our fellows. Self-seeking will slip away. Our whole attitude and outlook upon life will change. Fear of people and of economic insecurity will leave us. We will intuitively know how to handle situations which used to baffle us. We will suddenly realize that God is doing for us what we could not do for ourselves. (pages 83-84)

We left off on the Fifth Step, heading for the Sixth, and I thought it would be fun to compare the Twelve Promises of AA with the benefits you expect as a Christian, right here in this present life. But what I really want to do today is talk more about an even bigger promise—God's Promise in Easter—so I am making just a few comments first about what might have been a sermon on the Twelve Promises of AA, confident you will fill in the blanks if you want to.

The AA Program assumes that if a person works the Twelve Steps faithfully, earnestly, patiently and consistently, the Twelve Promises will come true for them in this life. Of course, this same wisdom has also been the understanding of the Christian WAY. If we become followers of the WAY—work the spiritual disciplines of the Christian life—then the gifts of the Spirit will be ours.

The Twelve Promises of AA may seem impossible—or at least

far into the future—to a person just coming into the Program. But they are definitely intended for this present life. What about the immediacy of Jesus' promises? Mark 10:30 says that anyone who gives up home, etc., for the Gospel "will receive *in this age* a hundred times as much . . . and in the age to come eternal life." Matthew is already cutting that back, and he seems to suggest that maybe the only rewards are later, in heaven. But I wanted to ask you: What kind of promises or benefits do you expect from walking the Christian Path or WAY—here, in this life, now?

Instead of taking steps and waiting for the promises to be given to them as a gift, some people try to work the promises and wait for the steps to be given to them as a gift. Though a total reversal, I do not think it is always an intentional apostasy. It is a trap we easily fall into. Some people try, for instance, to work on being more loving (or more patient or less angry or more caring), thinking that, in making this effort, their lives will become more and more Christian, more Christ-like. This—instead of working the steps, taking up the disciplines, and then waiting for the gifts to grow in their own time and way. That is, instead of following the WAY—praying every day, studying the Scriptures each day, tithing for allegiance, carrying the Message, choosing a spiritual mentor, doing deeds of kindness in secret, finding and following a vocatio, confessing and repenting and claiming forgiveness— instead, some people go out after the gifts themselves, trying to *act* grateful or peaceful or loving or patient or kind, trying to grab such things directly.

So, some people try to work the promises and wait for the steps to be given to them as a gift. As a matter of practical interest, we should remind ourselves that we are not in charge of the promises. It's none of our business how loving or wise or kind or good we think we are. Our side of it is working the steps, walking the Path, doing the disciplines of the Life we have chosen. The work is work, even though sometimes it is very good work and even fun. The promises are gifts, and they come as gifts. And they don't come at all if we try to fake them, pretend them, manufacture them or work on them directly.

"Truth, like love and sleep, resents approaches that are too intense." The steps we can take; the rest we wait for in patience and in confidence.

*   *   *

Happy Sunday after Easter! (Or Happy Easter, if you are Eastern Orthodox.) I hope the power and glow of Easter Truth is not receding from your conscious minds. We are the Easter People. We switched our worship day from Saturday to Sunday so we might be reminded at least once a week that our lives are to be centered and powered by Easter. And also to declare that we trust Jesus enough to bet our lives on His grace, even though Torah says we should worship on the Sabbath. *Remember the sabbath day, to keep it holy.* (Exodus 20:8)

While we may be interested in the promise of eternal life, that is not the biggest deal about Easter. All humans in all religions in all ages and cultures have always believed in eternal life. Down through the ages, only a tiny handful of wounded optimists, and an even tinier handful of elitist philosophers, have disbelieved in life after death. Easter is not startling because it declares a life after death—the world has always believed in that. Easter is startling because it declares that Jesus Christ is with us—will stay with us—and will go on loving and guiding and strengthening us—in this world and the next. *I will be with you always.* (Matthew 28:20) That is the Good News! Longevity may be interesting, but *that* we have always presumed, sometimes in expectation, sometimes in trepidation. But quality of relationship, bonds of love—never to be alone or forsaken or abandoned or despised (not ever again, at least not by God), never to be punished except as correction, always to be cherished and forgiven and picked back up and welcomed back home—*that* was the incredible message the Cross and the Resurrection flung out across the world.

The bondage of the dark power—the bondage of Satan: the belief or suspicion that we are no good, hopelessly flawed, endlessly doomed to our diseases and despair and fear and guilt, bound to all our past mistakes and bad memories and hard experiences—that is what Easter challenges and defies. We are always inventing new words for our sin—our condition of alienation from God. But you can track the message through whatever vocabulary is current in your mind: dysfunctional, co-dependent, low self-esteem, victim, abused, self-centered, self on throne. The words change, but the reality does not.

Easter's claim is that this alienation and lostness are over because of the great "I am with you." The Eternal One—the Word made flesh, the Christos of God now transformed from time-locked and space-locked man of Nazareth to totally available Holy Spirit of Jesus the Christ—*is now with us!* All of us are always lonely, but the deep, tear-us-apart loneliness is gone forever. All of us know fear, but the horrible dread that cripples the soul and shrivels our delight in life is gone forever. Of course Easter transforms our expectations of life after death, but only because the Christos will be with us there too. We are relational creatures. We are not transformed by longevity—we are transformed by love. *Easter is not about how long you live, it is about who is with you!*

So I tried to proclaim to you last week what I believe the Scriptures have always proclaimed: That Easter is far bigger and greater than a physical body, as we know it. Heaven knows I tried to speak to you as clearly as I possibly could. Heaven knows you tried to hear me as clearly as you could. Heaven also knows you did not all hear me saying the same thing last Sunday. What a fascinating thing to hear my Easter sermon coming back to me in so many different guises. Some of you told me you got into discussions within a day or two of hearing the sermon and still found yourselves arguing about what I had said and, even more, what I had meant. Hold that scenario in the back of your mind for a bit, if you will.

In case you have wondered, I do not at all doubt Jesus' ability, capacity or power to appear before us—right here, right now—in some "substance" that we would mistake for a physical body. It would not truly be a physical body, as we define and understand that term—first of all because it "appeared." I have a physical body. It does not appear here or there. I have to cart it around with me. It is a constant hassle to get it where I want it to be. After I get it there, it's a hassle to get it to behave the way I want it to. You don't make a hole-in-one every time you tee off, do you? The body is an incredible thing, a bloody miracle (if you'll pardon the pun). But it is also endlessly limited, and endless trouble. It is always hurting and wearing down and wearing out. Or it's hungry or cold or hot or misbehaving. If Jesus appeared in recognizable substance, which I am sure He could, it would not be in a physical body as we know or understand it.

I do notice, however, that Jesus is not appearing here in some substantive form—not right at this moment. Not only that, Jesus has failed to appear here in any substantive form for a great many years now. On top of that, He has failed to appear in any of His other churches, of whatever denomination or persuasion, all across the world, for a great many years now. (Wouldn't that be a wonderful way to clear up our confusion—if Jesus would appear physically in only the churches that believe His message correctly and do His will best?) I do believe, and it seems to me that the evidence is too overwhelming to doubt, that the Christ has been present in all of these churches—present, alive and powerful . . . transforming lives . . . guiding, correcting and inspiring all who would allow it. And often we have known it most in "the breaking of the bread."

Nevertheless, I have asked you what you think Jesus' real plan is for making His Resurrection known to the world. If it is to be the "physical appearance" approach—so that the world would have to accept it as absolute certainty—why didn't He just appear to Caesar and go through some tests and demonstrations and establish it solidly for everyone's benefit? For that matter, Jesus could still do that today and clear up all the problems. He could walk into MIT or any major hospital and suggest a battery of tests, with the news media present, and say to us: "I'm getting sick of all this confusion and doubt. Do whatever you must to be persuaded—document and publish the findings—and then start following me like you are supposed to." Wouldn't that be a compassionate and loving thing to do? This is what some say He did for Thomas.

Jesus does not do it that way for us. He has not done it that way for almost two thousand years. So why do the records say He did it that way for the early disciples? Do I think the Gospel writers are liars? How do I dare to doubt the Gospel stories?

The earliest witness to the Resurrection of Jesus is the Apostle Paul. That is to say, the earliest account we have comes from Paul. Paul tells us Christ "appeared" to many believers, and he names some of them (I Corinthians 15:3-8). He also says Christ appeared to him—to Paul. Paul makes no distinction between the appearances to the others and his own appearance experience. It is in fact the reason for his claim to apostleship—a claim he holds equal to anybody else's claim, despite his record as an enemy and persecutor of the church. We would classify the Damascus Road conversion as a spiritual experience, and we do not question its validity, reality, impact or efficacy as a result of the fact that no "physical body" appeared to Paul. Nor can we even vaguely imagine that the impact on Paul (or on all the other people Paul subsequently influenced) could have been any more real or effective or dramatic if the Lord had appeared to him in a "physical body" rather than speaking straight to his mind, as the story indicates.

I take it, then, that those who insist we must have a "physical resurrection" to make Easter real are mistaken. In fact, I *insist* that they are in error. If we are to measure by any standards we can understand, if we are to compare the results of resurrection method, we would have to conclude that the physical-appearance approach with the eleven disciples was not nearly as effective as the spiritual-appearance approach was with Paul. In short, no one can claim that the physical appearances were necessary or more effective or more inspiring or more "real" than the spiritual appearance that converted Paul.

Why are people still so enamored with the physical? Your

dog hears better than you do. Your cat smells better than you do (please do not misunderstand). Any hawk sees better than you do. The physical spectrum of our awareness is known to be terribly limited. The Northwest Audio Society has met in our church each month for years, and *they* have to have instruments to tell them if the sound is as good as they think it is. What you perceive in your soul about the physical stimuli you pick up is always far beyond anything provable. Yet every one of you lives for what the soul within you apprehends. And God always speaks to you more powerfully from within than by what you taste or touch or see. As Paul says, in the very same chapter: *I tell you this, brethren: flesh and blood cannot inherit the kingdom of God, nor does the perishable inherit the imperishable. . . . For this perishable nature must put on the imperishable, and this mortal nature must put on immortality.* (I Corinthians 15:50-53) Do you think Paul believes in the physical resurrection that so many people are pushing today? Guess again!

At least fifteen years after Paul's letter to the Corinthians, we have Mark's Gospel telling of an empty tomb—and evidence to suggest that somebody else tacked onto Mark the stories of Jesus appearing physically to the disciples. And five to ten years later than Mark, we have the full-blown appearance stories. Who is most likely to reflect the original understanding of the nature of Jesus' appearances—Paul, or the Gospel of John?

The summer before I was in the sixth grade, I rode my horse to one of my favorite hide-outs in the hills above where I lived. I sat under a beautiful pepper tree, with my dog beside me and my horse grazing peacefully next to the tree. Suddenly I found myself in an entirely different place. A Being of Light was beside me, and we stood on a kind of hill, gazing out across a valley. It was clear I could not go there, though I cannot explain how I knew, and across the valley was a community of people going about their business. They lived in such peace and joy and productivity and love that it took my breath away with the longing to be among them.

The Guide beside me said no words in English that I recall. Yet when I was returned to the pepper tree, several things were very clear to me. One was that someday I would be in that incredible place. A second was that I should become a minister, and in my case that meant I had to start doing my school work. The third, and by far the most overwhelming awareness, was that this place I had "seen" was reality—and the place where I live, here on this earth, is shadow, partial, incomplete. Real people were *there. Here,* we are only pretending, getting started, trying life on, trying to be real. Sometimes it makes me want to go around the world telling people: *TIME* magazine is fiction; if you want the facts, read *PINOCCHIO.* We are wooden puppets trying to become real people.

Do I believe that my vision was the Christ appearing to me? I already told you it was no "vision"—it was the closest to reality I have ever been. Not one day of my life has been the same since. It doesn't make me special or right about anything, but it changed my sense of reality forever. If Jesus had stood before me in a body I could touch, would it have impacted my life more? That would be tame by comparison. Would I have believed it more? That isn't possible.

So I try to tell you how real that experience was, but there are no adequate words. I should know better than to say anything at all, for such things cannot be communicated. Yet from time to time I get in situations where keeping quiet doesn't seem right either. Suppose you believe this happened to me, even though it is not your own experience. And one day you are trying to explain my behavior to somebody else, so you tell them the story—trying to make it clear to them that what I saw was more real to me than reality itself. What words would you use? "He actually saw this Being of Light. He actually saw this valley." And that's absolutely true! I can see it, clear as crystal, still today, so indelibly is the memory impressed on my mind. But did I see it physically before me?

Nobody is lying. Nobody is trying to mislead. That is not the problem. The problem is that if you think reality is limited to the physical, your world is too small. Our language has always been too small for the truth—and for the mystery and the presence of God. Why do you think Jesus spoke in parables?

In any case, I tried to tell you two things this Easter. First, Easter is not a message about life after death. We already had that message. Easter is about Jesus being with us—now, as Holy Spirit. Secondly, don't try to believe the Easter Message because somebody else may have seen Jesus two thousand years ago. Watch and wait for your own experience—expect the Risen Christ to "appear" *to you* in a spiritual experience that will change your life and perspective, just as it has been happening for all His followers down through the ages.

ENTIRELY READY FOR RECONSTRUCTION

Step Six

*Were entirely ready to have God remove
all these defects of character.*

Jesus frequently tells parables of gardening—planting, sowing, pruning. Among them is this story about a fig tree that is not producing any fruit. This fig tree had been planted in a man's vineyard. Not unusual. The fig tree was cherished for its shade as well as for its fruit and, like the grape, symbolized prosperity and peace. The grape, the fig and the olive are all used, sometimes vaguely, to symbolize Israel. When Jesus—not in a parable but in real life—cursed the fig tree outside Jerusalem for not bearing any fruit (Matthew 21:18), it is often assumed to be a metaphor of His disgust for the Temple not bearing spiritual fruit.

As everyone knows today, the fig tree is fertilized by a tiny wasp that bores its way to the center of the fruit. Without this wasp, or a gardener who hand-pollinates every fruit, the fig tree bears no fruit. We do not know if Jesus, or the gardeners of His time, knew about this wasp or its function. Perhaps this vineyard keeper had conscientiously destroyed all the wasp nests in his vicinity. Or maybe we extend the story's meaning to be a parable of the Holy Spirit—that is, if the Spirit does not penetrate to the core of us, it means we cannot bear fruit for the Kingdom.

In any case, this is a parable about a fig tree that is bearing no fruit. It is taking up space, using the nourishment of the soil, but it bears no fruit. It takes, but it does not give. It receives, but is unable to bear. Yet it is the function and nature of a fig tree to produce figs. If this tree had heart and voice, surely it would be very sad, perplexed and confused. Why is it unable to produce fruit? There are three great sorrows in life: the awareness of evil, the loss of loved ones, and the inability to bear fruit (to produce, to accomplish).

The owner of this vineyard is understandably disappointed. Grapes could be growing where this fruitless fig tree stands. Or another tree could be planted that would bear fruit. In any case, the owner is about to give orders for a replacement. But the gardener intercedes. "Let me give it some extra loving care and attention," he says. "Give me one more year. Let me cultivate the soil and give it special plant food. If it doesn't respond after that, then you can give the word and we'll take it out of here."

To what do we identify in this parable? God is the vineyard owner. Jesus is the gardener. If we are not God or Jesus, that leaves the fig tree. The fig tree is Israel, or the church, or you— or all three. The fig tree is a precious and well-loved symbol. It is no insult to be represented by a fig tree. It is, in fact, a high compliment. But this fig tree has a problem: It bears no fruit (using agricultural language, as Jesus does). It is somehow alienated from its true nature and purpose (sin, if you use church language). It has flaws (character defects, if you use recovery or Twelve-Step language). It is in trouble, externally and internally (no matter what your language).

Right here, in the middle of the Twelve Steps—fresh from Easter and full of grace and promise—I thought it might be good for us to stop and do a little theologizing. There are some strong parallels between the Christian Pilgrimage and the Twelve-Step Program. Different people would explain and describe both in different ways, but I can tell you what I notice on my own path, and see if that resonates with anything you are experiencing on your journey.

We live in a time, and in a land, that does not like the concept of sin. Many people would like to find a religion, or start a religion, that is based on creation as good and without any "Fall"—that is, without any separation from or animosity toward God. They would like a spirituality that is fueled by joy and built on the positive characteristics of human life and all life. They would like all motivation to spring from innate goodness, moving from there toward perfection. In short, they want to represent themselves and see others as untainted with sin. Either that, or they think the solution to sin is to ignore it, focus on the positive, and simply outgrow whatever negative or evil tendencies (mere circumstance or coincidence) still cling to them.

It is—let me simply call it interesting—it is interesting to see alcoholism as a parable, or parallel, of the classic understanding of sin and salvation. The alcoholic—and I better get real and say "at least this alcoholic"—the alcoholic in earlier drinking days often thinks he is living the grand and good life. He feels joyful, adventurous, alive and free.

I am talking about human perception, or at least mine. I worked hard, played hard, drank hard, had lots of friends, got invited everywhere. I was justification—and not by faith—for what other people wanted to do. Of course, not everybody approved, but that was simple: they were hypocrites. That is still the word I hear constantly at AA tables to describe those who go to church. More and more, a drinker learns to mistrust non-drinkers, whom they see as hypocrites—as judgmental, boring, rigid people. And alcoholics within the church "love" concepts of grace, unconditional love, endless forgiveness—anything that supports their pattern of continued drinking. (Whenever someone "loves" the concept of unconditional love, it's time to wonder what life-pattern they are trying to protect.)

The key, at this phase, is that the alcoholic *thinks* he has a wonderful life and *thinks* he lives it very well, does a lot of good, loves people greatly. It does not occur to him—yet—that everything is centered around drinking and serving the desire to keep drinking. It does not occur—yet—that there is also damage going on in other areas of life that cannot be attributed to self-righteous hypocrites. It does not occur—yet—that alcohol is in charge, that the person lives to drink and is becoming a slave to drink. He thinks alcohol is a friend—that it frees and empowers and energizes, that it is the spice and the uninhibitor which really make life fun and worth living. This entire perception problem we summarize today in the word "denial."

The alcoholic does not believe he has a drinking problem. He has more and more problems, but they are all external. More and more people become hypocrites, more and more politicians become corrupt, more spouses become impossible, more bosses become unreasonable and unappreciative, more children become aloof and disrespectful—the longer a person drinks.

My point, of course, is that sin works in the exact same manner. The sinner thinks he has a wonderful life. He does what he wants when he wants to. He has to make a living, of course— work and pay bills and deal with various structures of society. But inside this frame, the sinner is a free agent. He can buy anything he can afford, go to whatever places and events please him, associate with whomever he wishes, turn away from whomever he wishes. He is a free agent—in charge of his own life. To be sure, if the sinner breaks too many laws or hurts people in certain proscribed ways and gets caught, then society will step in and he will no longer be as free an agent. But even so, the sinner is in charge of his own life—whatever the outer circumstances. That is, he is alienated from God—unaware of any relationship with a Creator; unconvinced about any communication between humans and God; unimpressed with the possibility of responsibilities, obligations, duties, assignments or corrections from any God to whom ultimate allegiance is owed—and at the same time, equally unaware of any affection, concern, caring or love that may be coming from this same God.

The word is still "denial." The sinner thinks he lives the good life and thinks of himself as happy and positive. The idea of giving up his sin—his independence (alienation from God = independence)—is abhorrent to him, like giving up drinking is abhorrent to the alcoholic. He sees no damage in his disconnectedness. He also blames troubles on externals—outer places, people and things. Most of all, he cannot see that his optimism is based on things transient and passing away, or that the kinds of love and relatedness he seeks are shallow and temporary. Like the alcoholic, he consigns all such considerations to a future he insists is distant and irrelevant. Like the alcoholic, he says, in words and/or deeds: "I am happy. I don't need a savior. Everybody should be tolerant of all people and all opinions and all lifestyles. I don't need to be changed or converted. I don't need to admit defeat or surrender or turn my will and my life over to any god. I don't need to get sober. I am fine the way I am. In fact, I'm a terrific person, and only self-righteous hypocrites fail to realize this."

As an aside, you realize that what most people in our society call "sinners" is not what we are talking about. Our society thinks a sinner is a law-breaker because the law is our society's only standard of measurement. In Christian language, a sinner is one who does not have a personal relationship with Jesus Christ. That is, he still runs his own life, makes his own decisions, feels primarily responsible to self, and feels free to please the self— even if that includes (as it often does) doing very nice things for other people.

In terms of alcohol, when a person reaches third-stage alcoholism, life stops working as well as it once did. Blackouts increase; the ability to hold liquor becomes erratic; relationships get strained to the breaking point; paranoia and isolation keep increasing; the growing damage becomes more and more clear to friends and relatives. In short, the person has many opportunities to break through the denial and seek recovery, because life is not working and things are getting worse.

In third-stage sin, life also stops working as well as it once did. Do more people turn toward religion in their twenties, or in their fifties? Life based on false principles gets harder as it goes. I wonder if it was designed that way on purpose—like a gentle hint. Character flaws don't go away with age, they get worse— unless something changes us.

In third-stage sin, depression increases; the ability to laugh off fears of death, or meaninglessness, decreases; things that once seemed like endless excitement and hope are no longer able to inspire; loneliness, even in the midst of familiar relationships, keeps increasing. People begin to wonder why the world looks so bleak, why their energy seems to leak away, why their creativity and enthusiasm aren't what they used to be. Threads of criticism and negativity in their outlook and conversations, even though they try to control them, keep increasing. In short, the person has a growing opportunity to break through the denial and seek the God who made them, who knows them, and who loves them.

There is no recovery without the admission of powerlessness. Until a person knows that alcohol is an enemy, there is no chance for sobriety. Extremely obvious, isn't it? Well, there is no conversion without the admission of powerlessness. Until a person knows that their independence from God (sin = alienation) is the enemy, there is no chance for peace or, in the formal language, for salvation or reconciliation. We turn to Jesus for reconciliation with God.

And now we come to it, I think. The alcoholic eventually comes to the place where a decision must be made. Either he goes on drinking unto death—or he seeks recovery. But recovery does not end with the admission of need, or the desire to get sober. Awakening opens the *possibility,* but it still requires *walking* a WAY, taking steps. In other words, an alcoholic who wants to recover must make severe, wide-ranging changes in his way of life. There is no alternative within the borders of recovery. If I say to the alcoholic, "Hey, believe anything you want, think anything you want, do anything you want, but just keep claiming a desire—keep wanting to be sober," how far do you think he would get? Well, he might do just fine, if he truly wanted to get sober, because he would know I was an idiot and wouldn't pay any attention to me. He would trot himself off to a place where people really meant business and worked a program and really stopped drinking.

But the liberal church keeps talking just this way: "Hey, believe anything you want, think anything you want, do anything you want, but just keep claiming you believe in God's love no matter how you live or think or behave." You don't have to make any changes. You don't have to take any steps. You don't have to live for God in any way that seems inconvenient or demanding. Our denomination is in the Christian camp called "liberal." For many reasons, we are happy about that and consider it the best choice available. Nevertheless, we need to be aware of our flaws. The liberal church has a tendency to downplay sin and play up "unconditional love," to speak as if the Cross and conversion and total allegiance to Jesus as Savior and Lord were somehow optional—that it's okay, if you like that sort of thing, but there are really dozens and dozens of ways, and who are we to say one is better than another? There *are* dozens of ways, and we can have great regard and respect for those who represent them. But that is no mandate for you to be ashamed or mealy-mouthed or vague when it comes to an appropriate time for you to represent the way *you* believe—the WAY *you* walk and live.

Every species, every form of life, has to have a certain environment to thrive—or even to survive. One of the things we learn from watching life on planet earth—whether in the model of alcoholism or the model of sin—is that humans do not thrive in an atmosphere of unconditional love. We would all very much like to think that we would: give us everything we want, never scold or condemn us, and we will all turn out beautiful, loving and wise—because we are so inherently good to start with. But the facts do not support this proposition. When we have everything our own way, get everything we want, and nobody corrects or punishes us, we do not get beautiful—we get spoiled, arrogant, self-indulgent, domineering and ever more demanding. Strangely, our stamina diminishes, our health suffers, our compassion shrinks, and our courage disappears.

I came across this little saying, though do not know the source: "The cultivation of humility: When we think that we can do anything we want, we become arrogant. This arrogance causes sickness: spiritually, mentally, emotionally, and physically." We are designed to serve a God and a purpose higher than ourselves. When this higher loyalty and allegiance calls us into discipline and focus and service and sacrifice, then we begin to thrive, to find an inner peace and a true joy. Until then, all our efforts to run our own ship merely lead us into more self-indulgence, depression, irritability and confusion.

So eventually we become entirely ready to have God remove all these defects of character—all our separateness from our Savior—all our alienation and rebelliousness and sin. This step doesn't end those things, but it does put us on a WAY, a Path, a Pilgrimage that changes who we are, what we are about, why we are here, and how we go about it.

Luke 11:14-26

HUMBLY ASKED

Step Seven
Humbly asked Him to remove our shortcomings.

Steps Six and Seven certainly run in tandem. In fact, some people new to the Twelve Steps think they are the same step, that somebody just worded it twice so it would come out to twelve. What is the difference between being entirely ready to have God remove all our defects of character, and humbly asking God to remove our shortcomings? Certainly not very much difference in the wording, or in the conceptual side of it. But in the walking— in the doing—there is a gentle but profound difference.

People new on the Program are encouraged to move through these steps quickly. If you are still toxic from substance abuse, or just coming out of a major crisis, that is the best approach to Steps Six and Seven. You have done a moral inventory in Step Four. You confessed to God, to yourself and to another human being in Step Five. The Big Book of *ALCOHOLICS ANONYMOUS* covers Steps Six *and* Seven in two short paragraphs at the top of page 76. We ask ourselves a few questions and then ask God to help us be willing (Step Six). Then in Step Seven we say a brief prayer: *My Creator, I am now willing that you should have all of me, good and bad. I pray that you now remove from me every single defect of character which stands in the way of my usefulness to you and my fellows. Grant me strength, as I go out from here, to do your bidding. Amen.* And that's Step Seven.

Do it sincerely but swiftly. Glean whatever good you can, as you whisk on through, and get to the steps that can lift the weight of guilt and shame. It's no good sitting around contemplating Tao when we need to be repairing damage and getting our lives moving in a positive direction. It's no good sitting around contemplating the nature of evil when we are in the heat of the battle and about to go under. So page 76 takes all of the books on all of the shelves of all of the self-help sections of all of the bookstores, and adds in most of the wisdom of psychotherapy and all the hours and hours of counseling, and then throws in most of the theological doctrines of sin and salvation (from whatever religion or perspective you like), puts them all together in two short paragraphs and says: "Okay folks, we are now stopping off here at Steps Six and Seven. Take your time. You have ten minutes. Let's *move* it!" That is exactly what needs to happen the first time around. Take the stance. Make the best move you can toward it. Get whatever good you can grab as you go. Then get on with cleaning up part of the wreckage so there will be some space to move and breathe in.

But what about five or ten or twenty years later? What about when the glaring errors and sin and insanity are long since past, and life has returned to the spectrum we call "normal"? Then we discover that life still isn't right: all things are partial; friends and family everywhere struggle with issues that threaten to undo them; people are in trouble the world over, and the planet itself seems to be in trouble. Having rid ourselves of many consciousness-deadening habits and attitudes, we keep seeing it and feeling it with ever greater clarity and power—both inside and around us. Only now we believe ourselves forbidden to deaden the awareness. Getting sober, on whatever level and from whatever form of avoidance, is a great blessing. It is nevertheless a mixed blessing.

What happens eventually is that we can no longer go flying merrily through Steps Six and Seven with a lick and a promise. We start contemplating Tao, and wondering about the nature of evil. In other words, we begin to wonder about the quality of our inner beings, and to see that this is connected with the way the world runs. Like the vast majority of the people we know, we are not raping, burning, killing or stealing. Yet the world is still in trouble. And on "normal" levels, so are we: Relationships are not what we thought or intended. Success has almost nothing to do with what we expected, or longed for. Anger and loneliness still dog our steps, and occasionally erupt in ways that surprise and dismay us. Fear is forever calling our shots, when we wanted and promised ourselves that love would, or that prayer would. And we begin to see that it is thousands upon thousands of pretty good, pretty wonderful, pretty caring (most of the time) people who make up our society, and make it what it is. It isn't the criminal fringe that is ruining everything; if everything else were okay, we could handle that element fairly well.

No, something else in this life resists our desire to be what we most want to be like. Is it something dreadful and powerful? Is it mere inertia, or carelessness? Is it just the fact that there are so many of us, and we are all trying to learn how to share and get our own way at the same time?

Hey, lighten up! It's Mother's Day!

Daughter Jerrie, age twelve, wanted ballet lessons in the worst way. Her mother drove her five days a week for four years. Mom longed for the day when Jerrie would get her driver's license. The day Jerrie passed the driving test, she also quit ballet. Stunned, her mother asked why. Said Jerrie, "I don't want to do all that driving."

Sharon Miller of Vicksburg, Mississippi, says that when she married her present husband, her daughters accepted the new relationship. After a new son was born, her daughter Elizabeth was saying grace at the dinner table. She prayed: "Bless this food and bless all my brothers and sisters, steps and halfs."

Nancy Fuller of Bethel Park, Pennsylvania—age six—had a bit of a temper. One day, after stomping up to her room, she called out, "How do you spell 'hate'?" Her mother called back the answer. Two minutes later, Nancy called down, "How do you spell 'love'?" Again mother answered. A few minutes later the note fluttered down the stairwell: "I hate you. Love, Nancy."

Michele, three years old, told this story: "They played in the snow and had hot chocolate with marshmallows and drived and drived and crashed and lived happily ever after."

A rude, disagreeable preteenager of eleven had driven her

mother to distraction. One day in exasperation, her mother asked
her how it was that she always seemed welcome in so many of her
friends' homes. "Well," said Lisa indignantly, "you don't think I
act like this at other people's houses, do you?"

Michael was not quite three years old, but he loved his first
day of preschool. When his mother came to pick him up, he
screamed, "I'll call 1-800-CHILD-ABUSE if you take me away
from here!" (Motherhood is getting harder and harder, isn't it?)

Cathie Fife of Lincoln, Nebraska, tells it this way: I came
home from delivering my fifth baby. The first morning, baby
screaming, stitches hurting, Jenny, my seven-year-old, said,
"Today is the mothers' tea at school." I said I couldn't possibly
be there. Jenny put her hands on her hips and admonished, "If
you can't be there for ME, why are you having more children?"

Maybe I tried, but I didn't really change the subject, did I?
Broken homes, self-centered people, love mixed with hate, people
twisting good advice to serve their own aims, people acting bratty
while knowing better, people taking other people for granted, life
mixed up with death. How do we get willing to have God change
us? When do we realize we do not have the power or the skill to
make ourselves over into what we want to be?

Sooner or later, we return to page 76 (literally or figuratively)
and realize there were mountains of material packed into those
two brief paragraphs. "Are we now ready to let God remove from
us all the things which we have admitted are objectionable?"
Last time I tried to answer that question in earnest and get clarity
on it, it took most of my meditation time for nine months. It does
little good to pray the prayer of asking, if I am not yet ready to
receive what God wants to bring.

What does it mean to truly pray, *My Creator, I am now willing
that you should have all of me, good and bad?* All of me? Most
people, through most of their lives, give God only their good
side. They think it is *their* responsibility to clean up or eradicate
the bad stuff. After they get it cleaned up, then they can bring to
God whatever is left. God cannot do very much for us if we bring
the good without the bad. God cannot do very much for us if we

bring the bad without the good, either, though a few people try to do it that way. They bring only the guilt and shame. They never let God encourage or rejoice with them or take pride in anything they have done or tried to do. (Pride, remember, is not a sin for the Creator—only for the creature.)

In Step Six, we get ready. That is, we look to all the motives behind our character defects: we look to see why they have served us, and why we cling to such attitudes and approaches; we get honest about how anger has helped us to survive, about how pouting has brought us what we want, about how our disapproval has been used to manipulate and get our way. And yes, we look to the backlash: how this anger has stayed with us; how the pouting has marked our personality; how the disapproval has backfired into negativity we end up living with well after whatever incident that sparked it is long gone. But all of it is a carefully wrought, intricate and interconnected pattern we have developed over all the years of our lives. Are we really willing to let God mess around with this pattern—this pattern that is our carefully constructed survival kit?

We cannot pray effectively against our own will. God ignores the prayers we do not really mean—they do not register as prayers. There is a popular saying: "Be careful what you pray for, you may get it." But in reality, that statement moves past its intended irony. Sometimes deep within us, we actually mean more than we realize. Often we send prayers we have not identified as prayers, but that register as prayers anyway.

In taking Step Seven, we "humbly ask Him to remove our shortcomings." We are not in charge of the reconstruction. We give God all of us, the good and the bad. We acknowledge, deeply and happily, that we have neither the skill nor the power to overhaul ourselves. We turn all our self-help projects back over to the Creator—knowing that in our hands we get the timing wrong; we get the order of procedure wrong; we frequently tear out the good with the bad, or even mistake the two for each other. *We cannot correct the flaws!* Most people do not know this when they are young. Without God, we are good but powerless . . . or powerful but evil. Young or old, we sometimes forget that.

BRUCE VAN BLAIR

Is it our Jewish heritage or our Yankee ingenuity that keeps convincing us—which *assumes*—that if we are not perfect, it is because we are not trying hard enough, or we don't care enough, or we must be truly evil? All evil comes from good motives which have been twisted and bent, sometimes almost beyond recognition. All evil comes from good motives, but with us playing God instead of serving God. If we take on the task of remodeling ourselves, we fall into Satan's traps forever. Doing it that way, we will forever be pulling up by the roots things which were carefully planted by God.

To overhaul the self is futile. We always do the guilt thing—scold, shame, mutilate—thinking if we get uncomfortable enough, it will force the change. Or we do the spiritual "bask in the sun" routine: I will sit here and image and image until the natural power of my own inner goodness wells up and takes me over.

Humbly asked God to remove . . . in God's own way . . . in God's own time. Which includes, of course, the fact that we stand ready, at any moment, to receive our marching orders—what we will do or stop doing or do differently—one day at a time. It doesn't matter to us what we do or don't do, get or don't get, accomplish or don't accomplish. Not anymore. It is interesting to watch and fun to see, but it doesn't really matter. It is God's life, after all. God made it. If God wants to ruin it, that's God's problem. If God wants to bless it, that is God's privilege. What has it got to do with us? We are only obedient servants. Our gratitude for the Presence is just as strong either way, no matter what happens. Whoever heard of servants, anywhere, being loved as much as we are?!

Jesus once told a story about Steps Six and Seven. There was this guy who had a demon. You can dub-in anything you want, but I'll say he had a drinking problem. This fellow had a really miserable life because this demon—his drinking—ruined everything. No matter how much good he did or how much effort he put in, everything kept getting undone by the demon. He could live a sterling and faultless life for two or three or twelve or even thirty days at a time, but eventually the demon would come and mess up everything, ruin it as if he had never even tried. So finally, life got truly miserable, and it was obvious there was no hope unless he got rid of the demon.

So this guy decided to throw the demon out. And he did. Humans have a lot of power, in a way, when they put their whole minds (wills) to something. So this guy threw the demon out—no more drinking. After a while, his mind started to clear. He realized he was really better off without this demon. He started feeling good about it. So he began to get everything in order: cleaned up the house, shaved, went out and found a decent job, straightened out his affairs, started paying his bills and climbing out of debt. He was very pleased everything was looking so clean, and his friends and relatives were amazed at what he had done.

But inside there were still lots of things out of balance, unattached and out of adjustment. They didn't show up at first. Nobody suspected that the demon had many friends or that they might still be hanging around and paying attention. Well, the demons loved what they saw: this clean and lovely house, just waiting for their occupancy and attention.

So the man didn't drink anymore, but after a while it was clear he was getting more and more irritable and overweight, his moods were wild, and often he went through deep periods of depression. He went from woman to woman or into periods of being a recluse, and he hated his work. To hear him talk, you would think most of the people in the world were crooks or idiots. At some point, despite his initial joy at getting rid of the first demon, he turned into a cynical, self-centered, unloving, negative, unhappy being.

Jesus leaves His parable right there. He doesn't go on to say: "You can't do this job yourself. You can't leave your life empty and hope to escape the demons. You have to fill your life with God and God's Kingdom or you might as well keep drinking—it'll be faster, and easier."

This is the parable of the dry drunk. Dry drunks don't work the steps, they just kick the demon out. They do not replace the demon with God.

Matthew 5:13-26; Luke 19:2-10;
Romans 5:6-11; Colossians 1:13-22

MADE DIRECT AMENDS

Step Nine
*Made direct amends to such people wherever possible,
except when to do so would injure them or others.*

The song of the true Ecologist:

> *All things dull and ugly,*
> *All creatures short and squat,*
> *All things rude and nasty,*
> *The Lord God made the lot.*
> *Each little snake that poisons,*
> *Each little wasp that stings,*
> *He made their brutish venom,*
> *He made their horrid wings.*
> *All things sick and cancerous,*
> *All evil great and small,*
> *All things foul and dangerous,*
> *The Lord God made them all.*
> *Each nasty little hornet,*
> *Each beastly little squid—*
> *Who made the spiky urchin?*
> *Who made the sharks? He did!*
> *All things scabbed and ulcerous,*
> *All pox both great and small,*
> *Putrid, foul and gangrenous,*
> *The Lord God made them all.*
> *Amen.*

That is from *MONTY PYTHON'S CONTRACTUAL OBLIGATION ALBUM*. Monty Python, I understand, has this song sung beautifully, and movingly, by an English boys' choir. I don't have the record or I probably would have played it for you. To recuperate from that, here is something from Carl Jung's commentary found in *THE SECRET OF THE GOLDEN FLOWER (A CHINESE BOOK OF LIFE)*. It is one of the best descriptions of grace and conversion available in non-religious language:

> *The greatest and most important problems of life are all in a certain sense insoluble. They must be so because they express the necessary polarity inherent in every self-regulating system. . . . They can never be solved, but only outgrown. This "outgrowing," on further experience, was seen to consist in a new level of consciousness. Some higher or wider interest arose on the person's horizon, and through this widening of his (or her) view, the insoluble problem lost its urgency.*
>
> *It was not solved logically in its own terms, but faded out when confronted with a new and stronger life-tendency. It was not repressed and made unconscious, but merely appeared in a different light, and so, did indeed become different. What, on a lower level, had led to the wildest conflicts and to panicky outbursts of emotion, viewed from the higher level of the personality, now seemed like a storm in the valley seen from a high mountain top. This does not mean that the thunderstorm is robbed of its reality, but instead of being in it, one is now above it.*

We come today to Step Nine of the Pilgrimage, according to the Twelve-Step Program of Alcoholics Anonymous: "Made direct amends to such people wherever possible, except when to do so would injure them or others."

What happened to Step Eight? We need it for context: "Made a list of all persons we had harmed, and became willing to make amends to them all." Actually, this series started with Step Eight, back on Ash Wednesday. Suddenly we have several irons in the fire. A list of all people we have harmed? Who has time to keep up with the present moment, the demands and interests and responsibilities that come pounding in each day, never mind trying to pick up the pieces of the past? And it is a convoluted affair, this business of people we have harmed. We didn't mean to harm most of them—or did we? Some of them harmed *us* a lot more than we harmed them. Some people seem sure we harmed them a lot more than we think we did. What is harm? What is an amend? How can we make up for water that has long since flowed under the bridge? We don't even know where some of the people are now. Some of them may even have passed on. It is a convoluted affair, this business of making amends.

A great many people jump track when it comes to Steps Eight and Nine—whether in the Christian Program or the Twelve-Step Program. *If you are presenting your gift at the altar and suddenly remember that your brother has a grievance against you, leave your gift where it is before the altar. First go and make your peace with your brother; then come back and offer your gift.* (Matthew 5:23-24) Did Jesus belong to AA? People of integrity and justice have known in all times and cultures that they must right at least their own wrongs or the world will keep getting worse. If we do damage and do nothing to counterbalance that damage, not only will the world keep getting worse, but we ourselves will keep getting worse. It does seem, sometimes, that our culture and generation have lost sight of this truth. Perhaps in reality we are no worse than the generations before us. Perhaps the sheer weight of numbers and the way the media operates today serve to obscure how many honorable people still walk the earth. Nevertheless, the amount of resistance we encounter when dealing with Steps Eight and Nine—inside or watching those around us—is enough to make us wonder what has happened to the love of justice, and the sense of honor.

On the one hand, the love of justice seems to have gone public. That is to say, there seems to be great concern about the larger issues of justice. We read constantly about the flaws, or possible flaws, of public figures. We hear of major efforts to right vast wrongs: wrongs against nature, against the poor, against gays, against the homeless, against education, against the home, against women, against racial minorities. Perhaps part of the problem is that we are so used to being confronted with a vast and general injustice that the subject no longer registers with very much power. As a friend of mine said in a recent letter: "We used to have to go to church to be made to feel guilty. Today I can get my guilt almost anywhere. Read any newspaper, watch public television, go to a Rotary Club luncheon, open my bulk mail, talk to a friend at work. Everybody knows something I should be doing that I'm not—and it's amazing how many of the world's problems I am responsible for."

Christianity is no refuge from life. Neither is the Twelve-Step Program. On the other hand, both of them really are. A religion that offers no different way to live is not a religion. Anything that offers a different reason for living and a different way to live *is* a religion. Nobody is interested in religion as long as the life going on around them (in general) seems fairly pleasant and satisfying— or at least that these are possible. Religious people all have one thing in common (and it is not the way they worship or understand God): they try to live in a way that is different from the normal life going on all around them.

Somewhere the mayhem, confusion, aimlessness, greed, self-centeredness and inner anarchy have to stop. We go onto a path that has focus, that draws us. Immediately, and inescapably, that means limitation. The focus and direction bring expansion—new levels and experiences. But it also limits, by definition. Some things are now forbidden. Some things we have no more time for. That is always the cost of focus and aim. That is why Jesus calls the WAY straight and narrow. Some people forever mix and mess everything up with judgment and damnation. It is simply the nature of a path, of any focused way, that it narrows the options in order to make progress in a desired direction. *Straight is the way, and narrow the gate, and few there be who find it.* (Matthew 7:14)

What happens to all the other people? The ones who don't choose a path? Nothing happens to them—if you mean do they get thrown somewhere, like into a lake of fire. They just go on living normal lives. They stay on the same plane, wander about doing all the things that normal people do: They work. They eat. They go to movies and games. They make love and have children and do things with friends. They pay bills and take trips and get sick, and are sometimes sad, sometimes happy. They do some good and do some harm, and surely God loves them as much as he does you or me. But they do not consciously choose a Christian WAY, devote their lives to Christ's Kingdom, give themselves to the disciplines of prayer, study, tithing, obedience, evangelism, reconciliation, sanctification. Nor do they walk the Twelve Steps, which, some of you are catching on, have a lot more in common with Christianity than most people realize.

Some people actually come onto the Christian Path or into the Twelve-Step Program with a conscious awareness that they are giving up their great passion for justice on one level. A strange reversal, many say. They are not giving up all passion for justice, just reducing it way down. On a serious spiritual path, we give up our efforts to right all the wrongs of the world. Instead, we get serious about righting our own wrongs. Steps Eight and Nine are an amazing awakening. Focused on the vast and general wrongs, we had somehow overlooked many of our own. Thinking about how other people, companies, groups, organizations, bodies and/ or countries should be more just, we somehow missed seeing all the injustices we have ourselves let go without recourse, apology or amends.

Take the beam out of your own eye, says Jesus (Matthew 7:5), and then you will perhaps see more clearly how to help the teeming millions solve all the earth's problems and injustices (to paraphrase a bit).

But the truth is that, once started, Step Nine is a marvelous adventure. The truth is that, costly as it is and nervous as it makes us, properly executed Ninth Steps make an enormous difference to us. Regardless of the reaction and response of those we make amends to, a Ninth Step well done changes our lives. It lifts great weight off of us—weight we often did not know we were carrying. It changes our self-esteem dramatically. The inner impact surpasses all normal logic. There is simply something very clean and healthy and uplifting about trying to apologize for and then undo, or compensate for, the damage one has done. Life is not about the bright and beautiful only; some of it is dull and ugly. It is no good to just ignore it—to leave it as it lies.

People in a Twelve-Step Program tell endless stories of their experiences doing Ninth Steps. It is far better to be in a fellowship of people working a similar program, if we mean to take these steps. The thing about further injury is serious business. Making amends is no task for people who are unclear about their own motives, who are careless in their approaches, or who are in some kind of hurry to get through their list. An amend worth making is worth making prayerfully, and after thinking through the possibilities and implications. Often an amend is made for the harm we have done, though the true situation is far larger than that. It can be perilous to be sincere in our amends for the harm we have done—without getting drawn into the harm others have done or the injury we ourselves have sustained. The task calls us to clean our side of the street and leave others to decide when or if they will make amends for the damage *they* have done.

It is an excellent thing to have a sponsor or a spiritual mentor with whom to check over an amend before it is made. We are endlessly capable of unbalanced thinking in situations where we are directly involved. Again and again, a friend can see where we are about to be too hard on ourselves or too easy on ourselves, or where we have missed a dynamic that would make our amend offensive or harmful, even after we have sincerely tried to design it appropriately and well. A poorly done amend is frequently worse than none. Of course, many situations allow us to invite the injured party to help us decide on the proper amend. When this is appropriate, it is an excellent way to proceed. But we should come with at least some offers and suggestions. On the other hand, some people are vindictive or have an exaggerated view of the damage we have done. If you allow them to suggest the amend, you will soon be back into a whole new incident.

"All things dull and ugly, all creatures short and squat . . . " We do tend to thank God for very limited parts of life, for that which we have judged and found worthy or pleasant, at least from our own perspective, at this moment in time. In Step Nine, we include our failures, our wrongs, our evil, our blunders and our mistakes, and put them right in the middle of our spiritual walk. God can be wondrously healing and loving in the middle of our wrongness—when we get honest and repentant.

The true mystery of the Ninth Step is that while we are busy making amends for past damage we have done, God is busy too, without our realizing it. God is busy lifting us to a new level of life and awareness, where problems that have long stymied and stopped us—problems having nothing to do with our amends, that we know of—are suddenly manageable. The Ninth Step has nothing to do with it—we think. Yet doing the Ninth Step seems to change us in some subtle way that allows this to happen.

As Jung was saying: Sometimes the answers to life's most baffling and painful problems are not found in any logical confrontation with the problems themselves, but are suddenly answered almost effortlessly when we move to a different level of life ourselves. Such is the grace and mystery of God's mercy.

Or as Paul puts it: *For if, when we were God's enemies, we were reconciled to him through the death of his Son, how much more, now that we have been reconciled, shall we be saved by his life! But that is not all: we also exult in God through our Lord Jesus, through whom we have now been granted reconciliation.* (Romans 5:10-11)

And: *He rescued us from the domain of darkness and brought us into the kingdom of his dear Son, through whom our release is secured and our sins are forgiven. . . . For in him God in all his fullness chose to dwell, and through him to reconcile all things to himself, making peace through the shedding of his blood on the cross—all things, whether on earth or in heaven.* (Colossians 1:13-14, 19-20)

For any of us who wish to lighten our load . . . get new clarity . . . make progress on the Pilgrimage . . . experience new dimensions of the grace and mercy of God—we can make a list of all the persons we have harmed and get willing to make amends to each one of them. Then we can make direct amends to each in turn, whenever possible (or as God makes it possible), except when to do so would injure them or others.

WHEN WE ARE WRONG

Step Ten
*Continued to take personal inventory and
when we were wrong promptly admitted it.*

What a life! Not like the one out there, is it?

If we get a little distance and look at the spiritual pilgrimage through the Twelve-Step Program from an objective stance, Steps One through Three are about conversion—about the purpose and direction of our lives being radically changed. Steps Four through Nine describe the actions we take to realign our lives with the new awareness and the new direction. Steps Ten through Twelve are about how we maintain and continue growing in this new life in the ongoing present moment.

Steps Four through Nine deal with the past—with what we did, what we were like, what we must do to repair damage and make a clean break from the way we were. If we do not take Steps Four through Nine with sincerity and thoroughness, the past will inexorably draw us back into our former patterns. In the spiritual realms, we cannot cheat. We can pretend to have peace or love or patience, but pretending does us no good. Only the genuine article changes us.

Likewise, finding the new awareness and relationship with God described in Steps One through Three is marvelous—a new lease on life—and sometimes the only link left with life. But it will not and cannot last unless we claim it and make it real by building it into all our past and present patterns and realities.

Eventually, necessarily, we move past this reorientation period and come back into the present moment—albeit now a *new* present—wherein we attempt to live each day with the God we have discovered . . . with the God who has saved us . . . with a patient and steady eagerness to be helpful and to be part of the new life (Kingdom/Program/Purpose/Truth) we have found. I think this is not some sudden or complete change we make from one phase to another, like coming around some corner that separates us forever from the work of past steps. Bits and pieces of the past keep catching up with us, or coming out of the shrouded memories which are no longer so frightening that we have to keep them locked away. So we do not throw away Steps Four through Nine after we have worked them as thoroughly as we can for the moment. They are good friends and we will visit them often. But it does come time, eventually, to shift most of our focus to Steps Ten through Twelve, where we continually struggle—or have the adventure, depending on the mood we are in—of living our new life in the present.

Many or perhaps all of us skip lightly through, or even leap-frog over, Steps Four through Nine early in our spiritual journey. We are longing and eager to be helpful, to participate in the Kingdom, to be grateful to God and the community that has helped and loved us, so we rush to Steps Eleven and Twelve and start working there as hard as we can. Often we do some real good and pick up some excellent experience. But one way or another, we also get undone—run out of steam—go dry and empty. Sooner or later we must go back and work the earlier steps thoroughly. The later steps require a strong and solid foundation.

Steps Ten through Twelve are the Song of the Servant—the disciple/apostle, the converts who are happy to live for the God who has found and rescued them. Steps Ten through Twelve are not the Song of the Smug—not for those who have "arrived," or who have no more problems, or who have learned to maneuver so well that they never get into hard or harsh situations anymore. We must keep remembering: There is trouble that we cause because we are wrong, or don't do things right. And there is trouble that comes from being faithful. One of our motives for leaving our old ways is to escape the trouble—the anguish of our old lives—whether it's loneliness, fear, guilt, idolatry or whatever.

It is, therefore, a shock for most of us to discover that the new life also leads us into trouble, confrontation, anger, sorrow, etc. The new trouble is indeed different—with a very different impact on the inside. But such subtleties escape us early on. We are not signing up for peace on the outside—for wealth or fame or worldly success. We sign up to have God guiding our lives and to be servants of the Kingdom. A very different deal. We dare not forget it. Neither are we signing up to be perfect, to make no more mistakes, to have no more anger or confrontation or evil in our lives. We dare not forget that either.

So here we are at Step Ten—having come through so much; having admitted powerlessness and turned our lives over to God; having confessed our sins and gotten honest about those whom we have harmed; having made all the amends we could understand and design (at least so far). So here we are, ready to step boldly into the light—and that's right. Even so, this next step is asking us to be instantly and eagerly ready to admit and confess all the mistakes it knows we are about to make, and will go on making. How is that for confidence? How is that for self-esteem? Actually, it is wonderful—if we have discovered that humility instead of pride is our friend. It is reassuring to know we are not expected to be flawless just because our lives are under new management. It will be a different layer and level of mistakes, but we haven't graduated from this alienated realm, and we have not been invited to sit out our remaining time here. So get ready to make mistakes—and lots of them. Only, catch them fast—see them for what they are—and keep it clear and in the open. That is the message of Step Ten. If we let mistakes slip past Step Ten in the present, they will soon be building themselves into our pattern of life and our system of rationalizations, convictions and defenses. Then they will become entrenched and start causing trouble from deep within. As time goes on, they will become more baggage from the past, and we will have to do Steps Four through Nine to be rid of them—six steps instead of one to be rid of them. That is costly in time, energy, guilt, joy, love and all the rest. There are better things to do with our lives, if we can learn to keep doing it the simple, easy way: keep working Step Ten in the present. *Continued to take personal inventory and when we were wrong promptly admitted it.* We will either keep working Step Ten in the present, or forever work Steps Four through Nine about the past. The only other alternative is to go off the Program altogether ("lose our faith," in the Christian language). But we have been there, and don't enjoy hell all that much.

How do you feel about the Apostle Barnabas? He is one of the men I am exceedingly eager to meet, when I get to the other side. "Son of Encouragement," his name means. Not many are called apostles, but Barnabas is (Acts 14:14). An incredible man—*a good man, full of the Holy Spirit and faith,* the Scripture says. So I want to ask him: "Which one of you was wrong and unwilling to admit it?" Of course, by now he knows. Was it Paul or Barnabas who missed an important Tenth Step?

Barnabas is the fellow who sold an estate and gave the money to support the poorer members of the church at Jerusalem (Acts 4:36). Barnabas is the fellow who, when nobody else would have anything to do with the converted Paul, befriended him and introduced him to the apostles at Jerusalem. Barnabas is the fellow who was sent by the Jerusalem church to look into the reports that Gentiles were being accepted into the church at Antioch. When Barnabas arrived, he was thrilled by what he saw happening, and not only did he encourage it, he took a journey to Tarsus to see if he could find Paul. Paul, meanwhile, had spent eight or nine years getting his Fourth through Ninth Steps taken care of. The two of them came back to Antioch and worked together for a year in what quickly became the most dynamic center of Christian growth and ferment in the world of that time. After a trip to Jerusalem with an offering for the church there, Paul and Barnabas, and a cousin of Barnabas' named John Mark, were soon ordained (set apart) by the church at Antioch to carry the Christian Message into Turkey (Asia Minor)—on what we call the First Missionary Journey.

Paul and Barnabas were a great team. Clearly Barnabas (a Levite from Cyprus) was a man of generous spirit. He was largely responsible for Paul's acceptance into the Christian community, and the earthly reason Paul was drawn into the missionary movement. They had great respect and love for one another. They went through hell and high water together. It is one of the great sadnesses of the early record that this incredible bond of Christian love was broken. *The dispute was so sharp that they parted company.* (Acts 15:39) They never worked together again, in this lifetime. As far as we know, they never met or spoke with each other again. Neither one broke with Jesus; both went on serving the Kingdom. But this great separation, rift, alienation (sin) dwelt between them. Never mind the Ten Commandments—where was the Tenth Step?

This is not how we think it should be. Doubtless it was not how they thought it should be either. How judgmental some of us might have been, had we been there to watch. Can you hear us? "And you call yourselves Christians? I certainly want nothing more to do with you or your faith, if this is how you act." We say such things to each other, sometimes. Would we say such things to apostles like Paul and Barnabas? Daily they risked everything in their love and devotion for Jesus, yet they came to this dispute with each other that they could not resolve. So they parted company, yet each went on working and living and dying for the Christian WAY.

These weren't neophytes. It is not an easy world. Always there have been arguments. This one is all the more poignant because it was not between enemies, but between two of Christendom's best friends. Most of us carry in our heads an idealized picture of how Christians ought to act—how "real" Christians should act— and for many people there is an unexamined belief or expectation that, back when the faith was young and the early church was pure, people lived above the petty quarrels and immature behaviors that so disturb us and maybe even disqualify us from calling ourselves "true Christians."

Well, no such age of harmony and faithful enlightenment has ever existed on the face of the earth. I don't think that means it shouldn't. I don't think that means we want harmony and love between us any less, or that we are any more content with our imperfect behavior, poor communication skills, or impatience with each other's differences. But it *does* mean we are not disqualified for our imperfections. It *does* mean we face the same challenges and foibles as all the other servants of God—even the best we have ever known. And that is what tells us how much we need this Tenth Step—and how constantly we need to work it—or things will get a lot worse than they already are.

Peter and Paul argued (and Barnabas sided with Peter, in Galatians 2:13) and, stunningly, Peter did a Tenth Step to save the day that time. James (the brother of Jesus) and Paul were great adversaries. It is clear there were various schools or factions of Christianity from the very beginning. Some were for Apollos, and there were Chloe's people, and some followed Paul, and there was a Johannine cult, and then things started to proliferate. When we stop to think about it, it was inevitable that the church would grow and develop in various cities and regions. And when these different "pockets" of faith ran into each other, they would enrich each other—when it was positive. But sometimes they would quarrel about who was doing it right or better, about who was understanding it more correctly or more helpfully or more faithfully.

There has never, ever been a time when the church was not in argument. Do you expect it to be a mark of your sainthood that you will never, ever be in another argument? Step Ten is not an emergency measure. It is a daily necessity for those who intend to walk the WAY in the present moment.

Well, what about Jesus? He was the man of love, and some even say He was "sinless." Nevertheless, there is one way in which Jesus was a lousy role model. When did He ever say He was sorry? (The Syro-Phoenician woman?) When did He ever apologize, or make amends to anybody? Some say He made amends *for* everybody—but when did He make amends *to* anybody?

Jesus quarreled with almost everybody, from King Herod to the rich young ruler, from Samaritan harlot to Nicodemus, who sat on the Sanhedrin. He quarreled with His mother and brothers. He quarreled with Pharisees and priests. He quarreled with Peter *(Get thee behind me Satan, you are a hindrance to me)*, with Martha, with Judas and, indeed, with all of His disciples *(O ye of little faith; will you also go away?)*. He quarreled with John the Baptist and with Pilate and with Moses *(It was said by the men of old . . . but I say unto you . . .)*. He quarreled with Satan and the demons. He quarreled with disease and poverty and even with death itself. Many times, we suspect, but one time we are sure: in a garden, He quarreled with God—and took His only known Tenth Step. *Nevertheless, not my will but thine be done.*

Was Jesus sinless? We have a problem with terms, don't we? Sin is a condition of alienation, not a specific deed. Jesus was caught in the middle of an alienated world far more than any of us are—because His awareness of the Kingdom was far clearer than ours is. And so His life was a constant quarrel with all the compromises and half-truths and capitulations and surrenders that seem "normal" to us, but that grated on His awareness of God's Kingdom—of authentic love and reconciliation. No pretend peace or harmony soothed or comforted Him. Death was better than cooperating with the way things are run here.

Jesus, it seems, seldom if ever apologized—never demonstrated the Tenth Step on a human level. An amazing number of His followers follow Him in this one way with unerring and consistent dependability—seldom thinking themselves wrong, they never admit when they are. The church itself sets this example, ensconcing itself in creeds and statements which it then defends as if the worth of Jesus' life or ministry were somehow dependent upon these statements being right, down to the last letter.

Sometimes there are faint signs of hope. Galileo was recently exonerated after only 359 years of condemnation. Four centuries ago, he was forced to kneel before a great assembly, with his hand on the Gospel, and renounce as heresy the truths he had maintained (essentially, he championed the Copernican theory, which suggested, among other things, that the earth moved around the sun). Galileo was then sentenced to the dungeons of the Inquisition for an indefinite time, and every week for three years he was required to repeat the seven penitential psalms of David. Galileo deserved it, of course, having declared that the literal understanding of Scripture with regard to physical phenomena led to absurdities. I suppose they felt that with Galileo in prison, recanting, the earth and the sun would be forced to behave themselves. Despite the recent Tenth Step of the Catholic Church regarding Galileo, I still sometimes hear of issues based on discrepancies between Scripture and evolution, and wonder if we will have to go through it all over again.

In any case, the church has not yet officially admitted that it has been wrong about the Virgin Birth or the Second Coming of Christ, about birth control, about the nature and purpose of hell, or about what is required to receive the mercy and love of God. Consequently, it continues to mute and garble its primary message about God's love, about the presence of the Holy Spirit, about the power of grace, about the true function and purpose of the church itself—which is a support community for pilgrims, not a political movement, a morals SWAT team or a museum of ancient history.

Every one of us, I suppose, who takes any spiritual path or way seriously, finds some step or requirement or discipline more odious or difficult than the rest. So I have hated the Tenth Step, finding myself among those who say: "Seldom am I wrong . . . never shall I admit it . . . and *promptly* isn't even relevant."

On the other hand, it beckons with both peace and promise toward a better and calmer life, one wherein we expect ourselves to make mistakes and to find forgiveness, and so we are able to learn from all that we experience. The Tenth is also a step that promises we can keep clearing our relationships from the debris of resentment and anger that constantly threatens to bury them.

I find it clearest in contrast. When we are wrong, do we: Go hide in shame? Feel really guilty and worthless? Resign? Try to blame others? Run away? Not at all! It is really very simple:

Promptly admitted it. That's it? If we catch it fast, before the damage sinks in and takes root, it's that simple? That's incredible! Yes it is. The spiritual Pilgrimage *is* incredible.

Continued to take personal inventory and when we were wrong promptly admitted it.

John 14:15-29

Pentecost

THROUGH PRAYER AND MEDITATION

Step Eleven
*Sought through prayer and meditation to improve our
conscious contact with God as we understood Him,
praying only for knowledge of His will for us
and the power to carry that out.*

Suddenly the Twelve-Step Program opens out into a full-blown religion. That is ironic, since many people in AA hate that word and even brag about how AA is a spiritual program but not a religion, or even religious. Sorry, but religion is when we intend to *do* something about our spiritual awareness. Religion is when we move from theory to practice; from feeling to commitment; from vision to establishment in the real world. Such a move, in our kind of world, will be endlessly mixed with errors, frustrations, misunderstandings and challenges. We *never* keep our commitments as pure and powerful and steady as we intend to— as we still long to and want to. Frequently these commitments are tied in with alliances, with covenant bonds with others. How these alliances are working can have a major impact on the commitments. We are committed to the church of Jesus Christ, and this is primarily between us and Jesus. I mean, it was His idea; He is the one who designed it; He is the one who calls us into it. Nevertheless, sometimes the way things are going among ourselves has considerable impact on that primary commitment to Christ. In theory, we know this shouldn't be so, but experience does not always match theory.

Falling in love is a lot like a spiritual awakening. That is, the emotional impact is powerful and beautiful. We sense ourselves coming alive and awake in ways we had not been before. Life looks different and we feel different, and all things seem full of a new wonder. To our dismay—sometimes to our anger and frustration—the awakening does not last on this level. One way or another, no matter how we try to design or understand it, we either make a strong commitment (often called "total commitment") to this relationship, or somehow it begins to wither, to shrink, to dribble through our fingers. We cannot stay "in love" on a feeling level. We have to do something about it—build it into the pragmatic patterns of our days, our schedules, our plans, our goals. In other words, one way or another, we have to get married—we have to get "religious"—or lose it. Religion is to spirituality what marriage is to love.

No matter what we call it, if we introduce this Eleventh Step, it has turned into a religion. You intend to find and do the will of God. To the best of your ability, of course. Allowing for elements of confusion and uncertainty, of course. With a certain amount of fear and trembling, of course. Nevertheless . . . sought through prayer and meditation to improve our conscious *contact with God* as we understood Him, praying only for *knowledge of His will for us and the power to carry that out.*

Clearly this step is much too big for one little sermon. I do have a perspective to highlight—a reminder, a gathering of threads that we might all enjoy. But let me first mention some of the things we will not have time to talk about, at least not in any depth. I don't want anyone walking out of here thinking we have "covered" Step Eleven.

1.) There are many ways to seek conscious contact with God—many ways to increase our awareness of God. Step Eleven only mentions the ways of prayer and meditation.

• Some of you tell me that you feel "close to God" in **nature,** especially on ski slopes and golf courses, but also in boats and planes and while gardening, hiking, fishing, hunting. I know people who have been profoundly moved in each of these settings. I have been so moved myself. For instance, I've had profound spiritual experiences hunting deer near Pasamagammit

Lake in northern Maine. Times away in the wilderness, alone,
may even lead to a religious experience. Even if we didn't know
that, our tradition makes it clear in the stories of Jacob, Moses,
Elijah, Jesus, Paul and many others.

• Sometimes people are deeply moved and spiritually
awakened by **art**—dance, music, painting, poetry, etc. Though
often scorned today, architecture and the church have had a
love affair going for centuries. Art has a way of reaching past
normal defenses and framing things in new and unexpected ways
that carry us into new awareness—and sometimes to new
awareness of God. Recently I finished reading *THE HERALDS OF
VALDEMAR* by Mercedes Lackey. The majority of people I know
would call this neither art nor literature. I have profound pity for
them, because I found in that book a deep and very moving
experience of the reality of the church and the Christian
pilgrimage—a new level and a different expression of John
Bunyan's *PILGRIM'S PROGRESS*. It helped to clarify and encourage
me in my own religious walk.

• Everyone knows, and I think most are willing to admit,
that **being in relationship** with other people is one of the ways
that can improve our awareness and contact with God. People
sometimes inspire us with their faith or wisdom or devotion.
People sometimes "carry" the love, or a message, or the caring
or forgiveness or encouragement of God to us. We not only
appreciate those people themselves, but we sometimes actually
feel the very presence of God with us because of them.

• **Exploring our heritage** through history, archaeology,
going on pilgrimage—seeing where it happened, contemplating
what happened, putting ourselves back into the tradition and
drama of how it developed—is one of the classic ways of drawing
closer to God and improving our conscious contact.

• One of the most famous and specialized ways of inviting
more conscious contact with God is to **read and study the Bible**—
inviting God to communicate with us as we ponder and reflect on
those whom God influenced most powerfully in the past.

• Some people seek conscious contact with God by

exploring God's creation—giving themselves to scientific study in honor of the Creator. Others study creation and, with no intention of paying any attention to the Creator, find that their studies draw them into profound spiritual awareness. Any genuine search for truth—any attempt to expand the realms of human knowing—can increase our conscious contact with God.

• **Work and service**—deeds of compassion or caring, efforts to make life better for others—have sometimes turned into profound spiritual awakenings. Sometimes people look back and realize that they didn't design it at all—that they have been instruments of God.

In no way have I exhausted the list, but it is long enough to make the point. Step Eleven in no way implies that prayer and meditation are the only ways to seek conscious contact with God. Step Eleven is profound and startling because, among the many ways there are to draw closer to God, it singles out prayer and meditation. Among all the ways to draw near and come close, this step says we will pray and meditate. All those other approaches remain open to us. They are not forbidden. But neither are they Step Eleven. We will pray and meditate. *It is necessary for us as Christians to pray every day.* We will allow additions, but we will allow no substitutions. If we do not pray and meditate, we are not working the Program. And if we do not pray and meditate, we are not walking the Christian WAY.

As an aside, the Twelve Steps were developed in the 1930s, not in the '60s. The influence was from the Oxford Group Movement, not from Eastern religions. In this context, "meditate" does not mean yoga exercises. It means to ponder something deeply. Especially, it means to *listen* for God's guidance.

2.) There are lots of ways to seek conscious contact with God, but the Eleventh Step is interested in prayer and meditation. Likewise, there are lots of things to pray about, but the Eleventh Step has a very narrow focus. Just for contrast, let us name some things most all of us would agree are fit and proper subjects for prayer.

• **Thanksgiving** is often taught as the first and most important ingredient of any prayer or worship. Indeed, any increase in our level of thanksgiving improves the quality of our spiritual life across the board. Many have made gratitude the key and cornerstone of the Christian WAY. Nevertheless, the Eleventh Step is not about thankfulness.

• **Praise and adoration** are the favorite prayer categories of many of the saints. Awareness of God's glory, and delight in the sheer perfection and majesty of God, seemed more important to them than always reducing it down to *their* needs or problems. Our current culture has become too self-centered to understand such a perspective, but at least we can identify with notions of **appreciation.** Surely some of our prayers could include sheer appreciation for who God is and what God is like. But having mentioned it, we shall leave it for today, since it has nothing to do with the Eleventh Step.

• Many people pray for **discernment,** or for wisdom. It seems legitimate to ask God for some of the virtues necessary for Christian living: patience, love, peace, joy, compassion and constancy. Requesting such gifts may be among the higher requests we can and should make, but we shall say no more about it today, since it has nothing to do with the Eleventh Step.

• Many of us pray at times for other people—the whole dimension of prayer called **intercession.** Sometimes we pray for other people because they are sick or in trouble, or we sense they are at a crossroads or at a standstill. Sometimes we want special blessing for them. Sometimes we simply love them and bring that into God's presence because it feels good to talk with the God of Love about the people we love. Surely praying for other people is a fascinating and important dimension of prayer, but we shall say no more about it today because it has nothing to do with the Eleventh Step.

• Lots of times we bring concerns to God—everything from world peace to the injustice we feel we are suffering in some specific area of our own life at the moment. Truly we need to bring both **our concerns and our heartaches** to God, on any level and at all levels that are troubling us. But we shall say no more about that today because it has nothing to do with the Eleventh Step.

None of these prayers are forbidden to us. None of them are mocked or in any way denigrated. They simply are not the prayers of the Eleventh Step. All of the other steps can be done prayerfully. For instance, prayers for forgiveness may accompany the Fourth and Fifth Steps. The Third Step is truly a step of prayer—on a very different level from the Eleventh Step, and for a very different purpose. All of which brings us back to the clear realization that Step Eleven is a step of great focus and purpose. It cuts to the core and the quick of where we are heading and how. To get to this focus, it intentionally and ruthlessly cuts away all generalities and all other purposes—no matter how noble, sentimental, commendable, true or right. Step Eleven says "only." Praying *only* for knowledge of His will for us and the power to carry that out. Nothing about praying for God's will for others, or for the country, or for the company, or for the world. We are down to it! Now "I." There is no religion until we get to "I"—the self that loses self to find the self in God. "*I am your servant.* What do *You* want *me* to do—in the here and now? I fully intend (with Your help) to do it."

That doesn't cut through the religious—that cuts through all the subterfuge to get to *true* religion. We aren't doing the cleanup from the past anymore. This isn't about our hangups or our character defects anymore—though we surely have some left. This isn't about our drinking or our smoking or our weight problems or our relationship problems. This isn't about our success or failure in the society around us. This isn't about our resentments or our appreciation for whatever situations the world has handed us, or about how we feel we have been treated.

At Step Eleven, we pray and meditate for one reason, for one purpose only: "Okay Lord, what do You want from me? Anything You want, You've got it—only help me to hear clearly, and give me the strength to do whatever You ask." Of course, our prayers about the "power to carry that out" will get far more specific each time we know what each new task is.

Truly the Eleventh Step is the Pentecost of the Twelve-Step Program. Just as truly, many will spend more energy trying to misunderstand it than they will trying to work the step. We have to be careful and constant, or we will be among them. At Pentecost, the Holy Spirit descends upon the followers. It is the birth of the Church. That means no more sitting around mourning the Crucifixion or cheering about the Resurrection. The Holy Spirit descends—the Holy Spirit comes personally to each believer. And that means it is time to get to work, time for the followers to carry on—each in his or her own way and setting—what Jesus started and taught and showed. At Pentecost, we move beyond the spiritual and get religious—we start to build it into reality, live for it, really mean it, bet our very lives on it.

On the other hand, we can debate what is meant by "tongues of fire," or argue about speaking in tongues, or stick our tongues out at each other, or wonder who was there, or try to make up some new creed about what we all have to believe—until by chance, or subconscious design, we have lost the whole point. But Pentecost and actually working the Eleventh Step are synonymous: each one of us guided by the Holy Spirit, each one of us doing what the Spirit is asking of *us*—not of anybody else, not of everybody else, and *not* on the condition that anybody or everybody else does what they are supposed to. *Praying only for knowledge of His will for us and the power to carry that out.*

We read from the 14th chapter of John's Gospel. John pictures a conversation between Jesus and His disciples on the last night of Jesus' earthly ministry. Jesus is trying to tell them He has to go away in order to send the Paraclete—the Holy Spirit. In other words, Jesus is trying to talk to them about the coming Pentecost—the time, very soon now, when He will be with each one of them personally as Holy Spirit. And He will then guide and direct each one of them, if they will cooperate. *I will not leave you bereft; I am coming back to you.* (John 14:18)

Jesus, in turn, is fulfilling the prophecy of Jeremiah, who had predicted Pentecost six hundred years earlier: *The days are coming, says the Lord, when I shall establish a new covenant with the people of Israel and Judah. It will not be like the covenant I made with their forefathers when I took them by the hand to lead them out of Egypt. . . . For this is the covenant I shall establish with the Israelites after those days, says the Lord: I shall set my law within them, writing it on their hearts; I shall be their God, and they will be my people. No longer need they teach one another, neighbor or brother, to know the Lord; all of them, high and low alike, will know me, says the Lord, for I shall forgive their wrongdoing, and their sin I shall call to mind no more.* (Jeremiah 31:31-34) What can we possibly imagine fulfilling this vision, except Pentecost—the coming of the Holy Spirit to be with each one of us, as close as our own minds, guiding and directing each one of us through each and every day?

Jeremiah . . . Pentecost . . . Eleventh Step . . . John's Gospel—all are giving us exactly the same picture: the New Testament, the New Covenant. *If you love me you will obey my commands.* What commands? Over and over, we go back to the *old* commands. Or we try to get new ones out of the Sermon on the Mount. Or we jump down to the new commandment to "love one another." Phooey! Jesus is talking about the New Covenant— the new time of the Holy Spirit He is promising. *If you love me you will obey my commands.* What commands? The guidance of the Holy Spirit, of course! The commands you get when you are in prayer—when you are working the Eleventh Step. The commands that come to you personally, as you wait upon the Holy Spirit of Jesus Christ—in prayer—on a daily basis. Not the commands of the Old Covenant. Not the commands you get from me or your parents or even from reading the Bible. This is a *New* Covenant—written on the heart—the Holy Spirit present and with you—alive and real on a daily basis. Those are the commands we obey if we love Him, because this is the new WAY and Life Jesus lived and died to bring us, to introduce upon the earth. Try to hear it:

If you love me you will obey my commands; and I will ask the Father, and he will give you another to be your advocate, who will be with you for ever—the Spirit of Truth [the Holy Spirit of the resurrected Jesus]. *Peace is my parting gift to you, my own peace, such as the world cannot give. Set your troubled hearts at rest, and banish your fears. You heard me say, "I am going away, and I am coming back to you." If you loved me you would be glad that I am going to the Father; for the Father is greater than I am. I have told you now, before it happens, so that when it does happen, you may be part of it.*

We don't have to understand all of this. It's just fun to see how the Eleventh Step and Pentecost and the promises of Jesus and the power of the New Covenant are all linked together, and are part and parcel of the same Message and Purpose of God. We don't have to understand it—we just need to keep working the Eleventh Step, and the rest will take care of itself.

TRIED TO CARRY THIS MESSAGE

Step Twelve A

*Having had a spiritual awakening as the result of these steps,
we tried to carry this message to alcoholics [sinners],
and to practice these principles in all our affairs.*

It is not a rule, but many step meetings find it helpful to treat the Twelfth Step in two meetings rather than one. The stories and experiences we need to share about "tried to carry the message" are more than enough material to occupy one evening. Likewise, sharing about "practice these principles in all our affairs" is adequate agenda for a whole meeting. I have chosen to follow that split agenda in these sermons.

We can start to feel the fullness, now. It seems a perfectly logical thing that people who have discovered a way out—a release and a healing from something that was ruining them, destroying their lives, literally killing them—it seems a perfectly logical thing that having found a way of recovery, they would tell others caught in the same maelstrom.

Of course, nothing is as easy as it looks from the outside. People who are overweight should just stop eating too much. Why this national falderal? Why always make a big deal out of everything? Just decide to stop eating too much and get back to a normal weight.

Why make a big deal about greed? Everybody should just stop wanting more than their share, and the world would be a lovely place. What's so complicated? Just decide to stop being greedy, and get back to a normal level of selfish desire.

Or why all the fuss about critical, judgmental people who make life so miserable for others? Why don't they just stop being judgmental and learn to love their neighbors? Just decide—make a decision and be done with it.

Can you imagine Mark Antony actually losing an empire for Cleopatra, or King David going through such torments for Bathsheba? How could any sane human jeopardize reputation or peace or the security of children for a few minutes of pleasurable twitching? Why don't all humans simply decide never to be that stupid?

Nothing is as easy as it looks from the outside looking in. Beneath the surface of our "simple" problems, there are oceans of fear and anger and pride and loneliness. Making human resolutions against the tides of such oceans is truly like the proverbial spitwad in hell—the resulting ash never even reaches the first flame. Sometimes, of course, we do make important decisions and stay committed to them. But when we are really proud of ourselves, it is when we are comparing our puddles to someone else's ocean.

Nothing is as easy as it looks from the outside. It takes a spiritual transformation to break us out of any of our deadly patterns. We can switch from one deadly pattern to another relatively easily—from sex to greed, from alcohol to drugs, from smoking to overeating, from fear to anger. The celebrations are wonderful and the congratulations heartwarming, but it only takes a few months to discover that the frying pan is little improvement over the fire.

It takes a transformation to free us because staying natural (of nature), and trusting ourselves, merely switches us from one prison to another. It requires a Higher Power. From our side, it requires a conversion, followed by a new Way of Life. For that very reason, carrying a message of such magnitude is terribly important. For that very reason, carrying a message of such magnitude will encounter endless opposition—especially from the very people it is trying to reach.

It sounds perfectly logical that those who have found a way of release would tell others about it. The official word in Christendom is "evangelism." An *angel* is a messenger (of God).

An *evangelist* is one who carries a message (from God). Every recovering alcoholic knows and believes he or she is supposed to be finding ways to work the Twelfth Step—is supposed to be carrying the message to other alcoholics who still suffer. But it is highly amusing to me that so many recovering alcoholics have such scorn for the word "evangelism" and for the church's attempts at evangelism, when they themselves are evangelists and take their own Twelfth-Step principle straight from the Christian Church. If you do not carry the message, you lose the message yourself. If, having found grace for yourself, you do not carry word of it to others, that grace will soon shrivel in your own life. Bill W. himself could not stay sober until he started carrying the message to others. Desperate to stay sober, and desperate for a drink, he stumbled into the principle of evangelism—and it literally saved his life, and started AA. I'm not talking about the fringes, about a "Sunset Step"—a nice touch after the drama is over. Evangelism is the heart and core of the Program—AA or church. It works with all kinds of sin, and it is the only thing that works with most of them. Carry the message until it sinks in. Teach it if you want to learn it.

I do not find it amusing that so many modern-day Christians have deleted evangelism from their understanding of discipleship. I do not find it amusing that half the members of this church have never made a conscientious effort to bring one single human being into the Pilgrimage and fellowship of this church. You may think this sounds like a scold. If so, you must suppose I have no understanding of the things I have just said.

It is a sorrow to me that, even in a church as intentional and faithful as this one tries to be, so many have still experienced such faint grace in their own lives—have had such small experience of release—that they have no message to carry with confidence and enthusiasm. It does not happen very often that a person experiences the grace and love of God—the freedom of the new Life—and then keeps quiet about it. The problem of evangelism is not that we have the message and refuse to carry it. The problem is that we do not have the message. We cannot carry what we do not have.

So it is not a scold or a complaint at you. Some among us do carry the message with joy and delight, simply because God has done so very much in our lives. It is still a sorrow to me that anyone could participate here for very long—be part of the worship and fellowship and study and prayer—and not find enough of the transforming power of the Holy Spirit to turn them into enthusiastic messengers. Some of you still have no Twelfth Step in your Christian Program. That can only mean you have not had a spiritual awakening as a result of living the Life we claim to live around here. Is this because you pay only lip service to the principles we claim here? Is it because the principles we claim do not work like we have said they would? Is it because you come for different reasons, and get what you want, but do not want the spiritual transformation? I do not know the answers to these or all the other related questions. I am simply saying that for me it is a great sadness.

This church—marvelous as it is, and more satisfying as a spiritual fellowship than any other I have ever served—is still a mere shadow of what a fully inspired and thankful Christian community would be like. Most of us still do not pray every day, not in a way that turns our lives over to the guidance of the Holy Spirit. Most of us do not study the Scriptures each day with a similar intention. Most of us do not tithe. Most of us do not put our identity as followers of Jesus among the top ten priorities in our lives (tithing time or conversation). Most of us do not work to increase our love for more and more members of this fellowship. I guess it stands to reason that as a body, we work a very weak Twelfth Step. Few of us take that last phrase of WE RECALL to heart, the part about "spread beyond our fellowship to become a blessing to others." We are conscientious people and we try to be nice, but we are still a long way from home. There is evangelism going on in and from this church, but to say it is at half-mast would be a compliment beyond our deserving.

I love you. I think you are wonderful. I know something of the problems and challenges many of you face. I see constant evidence of your caring for one another, and even for me. It's close, so close, to breaking loose some days I can almost taste and smell it. But there is also the rebellion and resistance: I have a right to my own life; I don't need to get sober; I do enough already (you probably do *too* much and that's the problem); let somebody else carry it for a while; I can't afford any new changes in my lifestyle right now.

If we don't let God in, we are going to lose it. And this is only half the sorrow. There are people out there who have no spiritual family, who do not know that one like this exists, who do not realize that sin (alienation) is a disease of denial which infects the whole world. If you have any release and recovery from it yourself, can you possibly stand by and carry no message to those who still suffer? Don't you know that lonely hurts? And money can't fix it? Don't you remember how fear paralyzes things on the inside that don't show for a while on the outside? Don't you realize it is a terrible thing to have no guiding purpose for your life—nothing to live for beyond yourself or the people you know? Don't you know that Satan loves to charm and hypnotize us with trinkets and baubles—so that we spend our whole lives on outward trivia? Trivial Pursuit is not just a game. For many in our time, it is a way of life.

There are thousands of ways to carry the message. There is no need for us to get into one of those conversations about how we don't like the way some other people have tried to evangelize. As Scripture says, *Who are you to judge somebody else's servant?* (Romans 14:4) There are thousands of ways to carry the message. You can sit in Twelve-Step meetings and just shake your head in amazement at the endless array of avenues and coincidences and approaches by which the Spirit spreads the message through those who are serious about carrying it. If you are bold enough to follow the impulse when it comes, the Spirit will use and abuse you too. No doubt about it.

So the step reads: *Tried to carry this message.* Often the word "tried" is seen today as a big excuse, a secret decision to fail before we get started. In this case, it is a humble reminder of spiritual reality. The message is alive and has a life of its own. The message belongs to God, and carrying it doesn't give us any rights or privileges—only joy. We *try* to carry the message, yet never know when it will take. Often when we carry it best, speak it most eloquently, put it better than it has ever been put before— nothing! Nothing happens. And other times, when we are tired and discouraged and half our attention is on other problems, we awkwardly stumble into some feeble attempt to speak of the light by which we try to live—and, like magic, the message gets through. The message is alive and has a life of its own. It belongs to Another, and its power comes from Another. That doesn't just put us in our place, it ought to free us from our terribly human concerns of perfectionism and wanting to look good and do everything right. There is no right way. We are only messengers. When the message wants to reach a person, or when a person is ready to hear it, it will get through. It has nothing to do with us. Our part is simply to carry it. The Twelfth Step says nothing about what will happen as a result. The results are not in our hands.

Tried to carry this message. Some of you cannot or will not hear the step. You insist on rewriting it. Your eyes make it read: carry this message *well* . . . or carry this message *successfully* . . . or carry this message *poetically*, or in *deathless prose* . . . or carry this message *in a way that made me famous* . . . or carry this message *in a way that made everybody love me.* And on and on. If we just leave it like it is, it will be fine. *Tried to carry this message.* Let the Author of the message stay in charge of the results.

There are some things, in my opinion of course, that the church knows far more about than AA. That's only logical—the church has been around longer. It knows more about prayer. It has incredible resources of tradition and Scripture by which to frame and comprehend the principles that AA has gleaned from it. It has the story of Jesus and the Holy Spirit, and it names and thanks the Power that makes it all work. It has the experience of trying to survive and maintain fellowship in a harsh world over thousands of years in endlessly different circumstances. It also has had time to make a lot more mistakes.

But AA, in my opinion, has some traditions and understandings that keep it out of some of the traps the church keeps falling into. The church, for instance, thinks it has to have an opinion on everything (the right opinion, we might add). Ask the church a question, it will give you an answer—no matter how foolish or irrelevant the question. It's like a compulsion. AA has Twelve Traditions as well as Twelve Steps. The Tenth Tradition reads: "Alcoholics Anonymous has no opinion on outside issues; hence the AA name ought never to be drawn into public controversy." How chicken—and how effective. AA doesn't want to fight every battle. It has respect for the breadth of life, and it knows what its own purpose is, and means to stick to it. How refreshing. *I came for the lost sheep of the House of Israel,* said Jesus. (Matthew 15:24)

One of the things AA seems to know that the church has forgotten is that you can't recover for somebody else. Recovering alcoholics remember their drinking days. They remember what they themselves were like. They know that no power on earth could have helped them until they admitted their own powerlessness. So they have sayings like, "Carry the message, don't carry the alcoholic." Seasoned Twelve-Steppers operate in a way that would seem downright cruel to many church members. They do not offer a lot of help until they start seeing some response, some desire to work a program. Helping an alcoholic while he is still drinking is helping a person who intends to go on drinking. It is futile. It is called "enabling." It cooperates with the disease and encourages the disease to go on longer and get worse.

The church in our time majors in enabling. Any suggestion of a lifestyle change on the part of those we try to help is greeted with hoots and derision, charges of prejudice and inhumanity, accusations of being judgmental, lacking love, being unchristian. "Who are you to claim that your lifestyle is superior—blah blah blah." Do you know what would happen if somebody pulled that logic on an AA person trying to twelve-step somebody? "Who are you to claim that your sobriety is a better way than drinking? Just give the guy some money and keep your sermons to yourself." The AA person would say, "Then let him drink some more and see how it goes." And he would walk off without the slightest twinge of conscience— not because he has not been there, but precisely because he has. He knows it is futile to attack the outside of a problem. There are other people to help while this person is still managing his own life. Maybe later there will be another chance to help—a real one.

The church acts like it is afraid of its own message—like it hasn't bothered to look at the very message it carries. On the one hand, it scorns the love of money. Yet now it would save the world with money and the things money can buy—while soft-pedaling its message as if Jesus weren't really important anymore, or as if He were of no use to somebody with real problems. So the church tries to substitute its concerns for the condition of the world—its ideas about what everybody should be doing to improve things—in place of conversion and spiritual disciplines and a new Way of Life for anyone it comes in contact with, including those it tries to help. It is substituting fear for faith. We are afraid, so we try to save the world ourselves—try to substitute human wisdom and a humanistic program for the inner transformation of the soul and life in a New Kingdom.

I am not talking about worldwide programs or politics. I'm talking about you and the people you talk to and the people you try to help. Do you know nothing of Jesus—nothing of the New Covenant, the new Way of Life He brings? Does no Holy Spirit guide your daily path?

If you have a spiritual awakening, you have a message to carry. It has changed you. It will change others who hear the message. If they do not like or want the message, that is their choice. What has that got to do with your message?

But if you tell me that this individual, pietistic approach is foolish, old-fashioned and ineffective in the modern world we now live in, then I have a question for you: Can you name a movement in our time that has had more impact for good in our society than AA and the Twelve-Step movement? I can name only one—the Christian Church.

II Timothy 4:1-8; Colossians 1:3-12;
II Corinthians 5:17-6:10

IN ALL OUR AFFAIRS

Step Twelve B
*Having had a spiritual awakening as the result of these steps,
we tried to carry this message to alcoholics [sinners],
and to practice these principles in all our affairs.*

So we come to the end of this very brief and cursory look at
the Twelve Steps of Alcoholics Anonymous—Twelve Steps that
have now proliferated into a national and worldwide Spiritual
Growth Program, with applications so wide and varied that the
list often makes people chuckle in either derision or appreciation.
The last twenty years have seen AA and its many offspring sweep
into unprecedented popularity and acclaim. Those of you who
are students of history know this also signals a time of peril for
any movement. Great popularity frequently dilutes or even kills
the very heart and purpose of a spiritual movement. Many church
historians have mused that perhaps the conversion of the Emperor
Constantine was the greatest tragedy ever to befall the Christian
Church.

Likewise, it is proving well-nigh impossible to keep the
principles and traditions of AA intact under the onslaught of
widespread popularity and acceptance. For illustration, the
principle of "anonymity" is extremely uncomfortable under this
new limelight. Again we feel the strange links with Christian
heritage. Jesus said we should pray in the closet, in secret; that
we should do our good deeds in secret; that we should practice
our spiritual disciplines in a way that does not attract attention or
acclaim. Today we live in the midst of enormous religious
upfrontery. Religious advertising is commonplace and often
raucous. There is hardly any good deed the churches ever do

without publishing it far and wide—presumably to encourage others to come help and be helped. It sounds sensible. It just isn't how Jesus told us to live.

I am annoyed when people think our particular church does not do very much for others. The urge to tell them what and who, is sometimes nearly irresistible. Yet I constantly struggle to keep it quiet. Denominational leaders sometimes scold me for not being more willing to write articles about what we are doing and how we are doing it. They say it would be a help and an encouragement to our sister churches.

Well, I didn't get it from AA, but I find it in AA—in the Twelfth Tradition: "Anonymity is the spiritual foundation of all our traditions, ever reminding us to place principles before personalities." Or the Eleventh Tradition: "Our public relations policy is based on attraction rather than promotion; we need always maintain personal anonymity at the level of press, radio, and films." They didn't mention television because they didn't have television when this was written.

What happens if I go out and drink? What happens if people are drawn to *me,* instead of to the Program? What happens if people are drawn to me or to this church, instead of to Jesus and the Kingdom? You see, anonymity is not really about secretiveness or protection for the individual (though on the surface, that is sometimes helpful to an individual in the early phases). Anonymity in Christian language would be translated as "humility"—the first of the Christian virtues. And in our culture, the last thing anybody wants.

So we live in fascinating times. Will AA find a way to maintain its core principles—like anonymity—and still survive in our culture? Will some portion of the Christian Church find its way back to humility, and still survive in our culture? If not, then what remains of AA or the Church may be wildly successful and popular, but they will slowly lose the power that brought them to be—the power to save—the power that is not their own. Remember: "Institutions exist for the painless extinction of the ideas which gave them birth."

If you are a physicist, you are also fascinated by the widespread popularity of the Twelve-Step movement. "For every action, there is an equal and opposite reaction." It is not possible, then, for a movement based on powerlessness and humility to mushroom into such widespread acceptance—without the eventual "equal and opposite" reaction. It is predictable, then, that in the late 1990s and in the early years of the new millennium, there will be powerful leaders calling people into new movements that stress the need to claim personal power and build life on consciously chosen concepts of pride.

So the world does its thing, and we do ours. What we do here is claim the mercy and love of God as revealed in Jesus Christ, and that opens for us a new and different Way of Life. Jesus Christ saved and saves me first and continually, and His church has my primary loyalty in this world. But AA saved me from alcoholism, and so I have a lot of gratitude and loyalty toward AA as well. Since I find the two so complementary and helpful to one another—as should be the case between mother and daughter—I wanted to say something about it in case some of you would be as charmed as I am by the interplay between the two. So last October, on my tenth anniversary of joining AA, I decided to preach this series of sermons. I have always been amazed that you did not "throw me away" when I came out of the alcoholic treatment center at Cabrini Hospital. I was perfectly willing to leave here, back then; I hope I still am, in the Spirit's guidance. And I appreciate your patience over this long series, and hope it has been more of a blessing than a trial. Just because you have heard the sermons does not mean you are working the Twelve-Step Program. But you *have* heard about it, and know there are places to work it if and when you are ready.

Back to the Twelfth Step. We promised to talk about the second half of it today: *to practice these principles in all our affairs.* A friend of mine says, "You know, you just can't win. Ever since I started practicing these principles, I haven't had any affairs."

The real truth is, we all have lots of affairs: bills, plans, projects, organizations, relatives, vacations, appointments, responsibilities.

Keeping our affairs in order, or at least somehow managing to make it through our days, is everyone's challenge, and often it seems like it is an impossibility. That is the very setup for the greatest religious change/conversion/renewal/transformation of all. We wouldn't dare mention it anywhere near the First Step. We hardly dare mention it at the tail end of the Twelfth Step. We cannot keep up with all our affairs as it is. Now we are supposed to add this incredible, impossible, complex and confusing new maxim to every part of our lives? We must practice these principles in *all* our affairs? Barely able to shuffle and juggle and dance the whole array as it is, now we will do them all in the presence of God? For the sake of God? In a way we suppose will please God or be obedient to God's will for us? We couldn't even keep up with the way WE wanted to do it. Now we are supposed to keep up with the way *God* wants us to do it?

So what happens? For most people, most of the time, it's easy: In one ear and out the other. Even if they go to AA, or the church, or both—in one ear and out the other. They may agree with the sentiment, in a general sort of way—it sounds like a good idea, a decent, commendable concept, all right. So it gets thrown into the "yes" bin, along with motherhood and patriotism and honesty and love . . . and all the other things we vaguely approve of and believe in but pay no true attention to—things we have a vague and general allegiance toward and which, if we ever looked them straight in the eye, would change us forever to the very core of our beings. *Our Father who art in heaven, hallowed be thy name.* Really? All kidding aside? All the way and no-holds-barred? How long could we look even that one phrase full in the eye and not begin to feel all our old castles crumbling? Omnipotent, omniscient, almighty God . . . maker of heaven and earth . . . who personally loves you, forgives you, has a plan for your life . . . who sent Jesus Christ as surety on this pledge and as companion for the WAY—have we ever looked such a thing straight in the eye? Guess who would look away first?

In commenting on the Eleventh Step, I told you that AA is a religion, whether it admits it or not, because its adherents are instructed to listen for God's personal guidance and, when they find it, to obey it. Now we have the second proof. This is to be a way of life—in all we do and everywhere we go. This is not just a Sunday-morning affair. This is not just for when you are at an AA meeting. *Practice these principles in all our affairs.* It is definitely a religion when people enter a whole new way of life—just as it is definitely *not* a religion when people do not.

What *really* happens, when we contemplate practicing new principles in all our affairs, is that we are desperate to hedge the bet. We want to try it on a little at a time—try it out in this or that area first and see how it goes, see how it works, see what happens to us. And that is our biggest mistake. That is what makes it all terribly complicated and debilitating. It is far easier to handle all our affairs in the light of new principles than to test-drive them in just one or two categories. Trying to do everything in the light of God's guidance—in the light of trying to please God instead of ourselves—is easier than the practice of our own endlessly confusing and changing and contradictory moods and wills. For we are not, in and of ourselves, integrated. *My name is Legion.* (Mark 5:19) I am a walking civil war. I want one thing one moment, and a different thing the next. I want to be holy one moment, and talk myself out of it the next. It is far easier to practice these principles if I turn *all* my affairs over to the new WAY—it is much easier to live the Christian WAY than to live my own way. But it requires putting *all* the affairs into the new WAY. Otherwise, we get a terrible hodge-podge. The confusing conglomerate of twisted and competing loyalties and pressures and stress does not ease until we start practicing the new WAY in all our affairs. Only then do we begin to experience the peace, coordination, wisdom and power of the Holy Spirit at work in our lives.

What a terrible dilemma for us humans, who like to ease our way into things that scare us—into life-transforming changes, into the leap of faith. Are you still thinking you can ease your way into loving and serving God? As Jim Hightower says: "There are only two things you can find in the middle of the road—yellow lines and dead armadillos."

What aspect of our lives do we least often equate with the mission of the church? All of us seem to have lapses, times when we forget to let the Holy Spirit speak and direct us. All of us seem to have certain areas or categories of life where we have not yet let our spiritual practice penetrate. These areas are invariably holding us back from our true destiny and identity. But what aspect do most people most often fail to identify as part of God's mission? The church talks and talks about its mission, but it almost always means it as something extra—something after its people have already worked a full day and tried to take care of family and relatives and friends. Could the Holy Spirit really intend to save the world *after* its people are exhausted, and in the few minutes left over from already overly busy, stressful days? The power of the church is in the home and in the workplace. And the most neglected place of all is the workplace.

I am *not* talking about making a nuisance of yourself by trying to interject "Jesus remarks" at inappropriate times and into general conversations. But you don't *go* to church, you *are* the church. If every Christian went to work each day with a personal inner desire to do their job in a way and manner that would please their Lord—as if (to borrow from Paul) Jesus were their true boss, behind and more important than their human boss— that would transform the world!

I don't want to get you stuck there, but I will leave you there. Just trying to highlight a little of the meaning of this Twelfth Step: *to practice these principles in all our affairs.* It is not news to Christians that our Faith is a Way of Life, and a WAY we want to learn to walk at all times, and in every situation. Not news, but still Good News—for otherwise we must return to old ways: living for nothing . . . or living for ourselves . . . or living for other humans we have designated as more important than ourselves. Thanks be to God, who gives us *a new and living way.* (Hebrews 10:20)

I Peter 4:12-5:11

YOUR ADVERSARY

I.) YOUR ADVERSARY

I wonder how many people here this morning actually believe they have an adversary. Some of you have lived lives of such quiet competence, or have been born into circumstances of such harmony and blessing, that the thought of adversarial living—the contemplation of life as a struggle or a battle—is simply alien to your experience. And having found such favor yourselves, it does not throw you off very much to note that millions of other humans do not have any such harmony or blessing. If so, I'm afraid you will have to sit this sermon out.

The rest of us, I surmise, have experienced opposition in one form or another throughout most of our lives. We have found ourselves in competition with other people from time to time. We have had various sorts of struggles within ourselves, some of them rather severe. Some of you have been in wars where it became overtly obvious that some people were shooting at you, and others with you. Some of us have been in other kinds of wars— movements for racial justice, or efforts to feed hungry people, improve education, reverse the ecological crisis, and so forth. Some of us can even remember trying to defend ourselves or our friends or our siblings from some form of injustice as far back as the first or second grade.

The rest of us know that we struggle, at least from time to time, with adversaries. Some days it seems to us that life is hard enough, just taking it straight. And we wonder, perhaps, why we have to have adversaries. Why don't we all just cooperate and help each other? Why would anything or anyone wish to make things more difficult than they already are? Who has so much leisure time, and so few interests, that they can sit around with nothing better to do than make trouble for the rest of us?

Regardless of why, most of us know that with every endeavor we take into our lives, we find an adversary. Whether it is our attempts to grow and develop and fulfill our own lives, or our efforts to establish a career, build a family or accomplish some purpose of justice or compassion or improvement for our surroundings or the society we live in—something always interferes. We run into opposition, inside and out. Something blocks us, undoes part of our efforts, ridicules the approach, turns people against us, discourages us, or frightens us. What is it? Who or what is the adversary? We must name it—name our adversary—or we have no chance to win through or accomplish what we set out to do.

A dangerous thing, perhaps, to name our adversary. But far more dangerous not to. Sometimes we name the adversary and realize we have named a very small part of the trouble. We name a person. Or we name an inner fear. Or we name an attitude of the people around us. Nevertheless, it is a beginning, a starting place for knowing what we are up against and searching for what we can do about it.

In AA (which we have been using to compare and contrast some of the principles we know), the adversary is clear and specific. Actually, it is one of the under-adversaries of the true ADVERSARY. But since I am trying to get you to name your adversaries—the ones that trouble you in your life—AA is a clear illustration. In the passage from the Big Book of *ALCOHOLICS ANONYMOUS* that is read to open every AA meeting (Chapter 5, page 58), there is this intriguing sentence: "Remember that we deal with alcohol—cunning, baffling, powerful!" Some of us add "and patient." You see, now we know what we are up against. But our Scripture reading this morning goes further:

II.) YOUR ADVERSARY THE DEVIL

Our New Testament passage for today is not content to explain all the mayhem in terms of our own troubles and mistakes and inadequacies alone, not even if we add the troubles and mistakes of all the other people in the world. It puts it quite succinctly and unequivocally: *Your adversary the devil.* I wonder how many people here this morning actually believe they have an adversary greater than all the lesser enemies and struggles and issues—one who doubtless uses all of the lesser adversaries and issues, yet who is greater than all of them put together. Some of you do not, I know, because you are afraid it will turn into an excuse: "The Devil made me do it." And then you are afraid you will slough off your responsibilities and no longer try your hardest.

My mind has these things all twisted around backwards. I think people who do not take Satan seriously do not take the rigors of the spiritual life seriously either. They have a relaxed attitude toward evil. They can pay attention to prayer and maybe study the Bible and work the disciplines Jesus taught—when they feel like it, if they are in the mood. And if not, nothing very serious will happen. That is what they think. The fellowship of the church is nice, and it is a good thing for people to band together, to care about each other, to worship and play and pray together, and even to teach their children some of the basic Christian values—when it is convenient. And if not, nothing very serious will happen. I mean, it's not like it really and truly matters!

I have the impression that most liberal Christians take the Devil with a grain of salt, so to speak. An old New England saint used to chuckle and say, "If you do that, the Devil will return the favor." Meaning, he will gobble you up, tasty morsel that you have made of yourself.

Many of the people I know do not believe in the battle—do not identify with this bit about *your adversary the devil.* They imagine themselves living in the "middle" somewhere, so they are not living "at the ready." They are not alert. They do not expect a struggle or an attack at any moment, or under any circumstances—dark or light. So they have no particular religion. Or they gravitate toward one of the religions that does not believe in Satan. Or they go into standard churches but maintain for themselves a sleepy, comfortable approach—with minor spiritual disciplines and half-hearted measures—and they keep a camp with no sentries posted. After all, with no real enemy except ignorance and bad luck, a reasonable caution and a little common sense should do well enough. At work, at play, in relationships, in efforts to do good or be helpful, it ought to be sufficient just to give it an honest try—do a little bit when and where we can. But no "all night in prayer." No fasting. No full-hearted conversion or commitment. No daily disciplines of humility and study and forgiveness and thanksgiving. Don't you think ten percent is a little strenuous and inconvenient? After all, the Church of Jesus Christ is perfectly adequate as it is—against a symbolic or nonexistent foe—so two percent is more than generous.

In AA, the enemy is named. It is alcohol. In AA, alcohol is the Devil. Salvation means being saved from this Devil. All the steps and promises and hopes for a new and better life depend on finding release from bondage to this Satan. And it is a surprise somewhere along the line to discover that alcohol is the enemy. Many times, having named the enemy, it still takes considerable time to find some escape, some release. But it is fascinating and disconcerting to realize that for some extended period of time, we believed alcohol was our friend. We were convinced that it was doing wonderful things for us. Naturally, we were not marshaling any forces against it, since it was the welcome friend.

Satan *always* tries to operate under those exact same conditions. It is obvious, yet ever new, that the Devil never acts like the Devil. The Devil always smiles and talks and acts like a friend for as long as possible. Frequently, we have traveled a long way with the Devil before we even suspect that something is amiss. Sometimes nearly everyone around us can see the ugly reality, but we are still hypnotized by the smile.

Is alcohol really cunning? It sits there in a bottle, inert—just a chemical composition minding its own business. Is alcohol baffling? Is there really very much we don't know about it? In some ways, it's one of the more predictable substances on earth. It will treat you pretty much the same way every time, with only minor variations along the way. Powerful? In a reverse way. It surely has enormous impact on our society. But in AA we personify it, just as many of you feel Christianity personifies the forces of evil. And it works much better when we do. We have an adversary out there—those of us who are alcoholics. And it waits and watches—like a cunning, powerful, living being—for any careless moment, for just one split second of pride or self-control. It doesn't terrorize me in the least, not anymore. It's no problem at all—unless I forget! Forget that it is waiting for me—plotting, planning, waiting for me to neglect the steps, get careless with the principles that helped me, get forgetful of the Higher Power who saved me, get overconfident, get in the right mood: "I can handle it" or "What difference does it make?" You don't think alcohol is cunning, baffling, powerful and patient? You think it is just liquid in a bottle? This liquid in a bottle has destroyed the lives of millions of people? You must be pretty gullible if you think it isn't cunning, baffling, powerful and patient. Alcoholism has every mark and trace of Satan's ways and principles all over it. I name the outer manifestation of my enemy so that I know what I am up against, and I stop kidding around with the battle. That outer manifestation may seem foolish and small, but if I once identify it with the true enemy, then I know what I am up against, and I know that no half-measures will do. Shouldn't every Christian know that about Satan?

Let me ask you something: How do you explain God's compassion? Why do you suppose there is such deep and endless mercy and grace and forgiveness? Do you ever wonder why God would send his Son into such an ordeal? Jesus was sent out of love and concern for us? If there is no Satan—if it is merely our own stubborn, willful blindness and rebellion—why is God compassionate?

Some people do not have very much compassion or pity when they see others in trouble. Oh, there is a twinge of compassion here or there, but in many cases it is quite shallow and short-lived. I suspect it is because they do not believe in Satan. They explain the trouble or hunger or hurt in human terms alone, and think the people would be fine if they would just wake up and try a little harder. They have no real appreciation for what people are up against. Jesus did. Historically, the Christian Church has known. That is why it has seen itself as the product of, and known itself as a recipient of, the compassion of the God who has come to save us.

III.) YOUR ADVERSARY THE DEVIL PROWLS

We each call it as we see it. Anything else would be coercion, so indeed we are supposed to. But I know how this passage sees it. *Discipline yourselves, keep alert. Like a roaring lion, your adversary the devil prowls around, looking for someone to devour. Resist him, steadfast in your faith, for you know that your brothers and sisters all over the world are undergoing the same kinds of suffering.* (1 Peter 5:8) Satan is tracking all of them too. They get tempted to throw it away, or to go be self-centered and self-indulgent for a while, or to just relax and take it easy and try to live the good life for a while—just like you. And that is only the beginning, the seemingly harmless first whispers of the Evil One.

So when your children go into a new grade, or just plain off to school in the morning, do they expect the Devil to be prowling around, looking for somebody unwary? Naturally we don't want them frightened or troubled or overly concerned about things, do we? Well, maybe a little concern about drugs and sex and not doing their homework wouldn't hurt. But seeing themselves on a spiritual path, and being instant suckers for Satan if they step off of it? Is that what you teach your children? You don't worry about them being safe from Satan this summer, do you?

When you got married, did you consciously realize Satan would make that relationship difficult, turn it bad, ruin it entirely—if given half a chance? When you go to work in the morning, do you think your only adversaries are idiot drivers or the bad moods of fellow workers? When you try to help somebody—from a personal friend, to the homeless, to improving the community, to joining some group that's going to save the environment—do you think it will go easily, that everybody who understands will help, that you will have no serious adversary?

Satan prowls. Whether you personify him or not, he is cunning, baffling, powerful and patient. Any discipline you do not build into your Way, your temperament, your very lifestyle, he will eventually steal or ruin—from the weight you want to lose, to the good thoughts you want to think, to the purposes you want to live for.

Of course, we are not defenseless, if we do not wish to be. If we practice the disciplines, keep growing in faith and hope and gratitude and humility, Satan does not have an easy time knocking us off the Path. We also know who to call on for help and guidance, if Satan has not stolen our faith. Always, if we stop to notice, the Holy Spirit is there—trying to help and encourage and guide us. But always, your adversary the devil is prowling about, waiting for a careless moment or an opportune time. He did even with Jesus, if you remember the story. And you think *you* will escape his efforts?

Is there anything I can say—anything I can do—that will get you to name your adversaries, and then name Satan along with them and stop playing parlor games with the life Christ has invited us into? The ancient formula says, "Jesus came to save us from sin, death, and the Devil." Do you think that makes Jesus obsolete? *Discipline yourselves, keep alert. Like a roaring lion your adversary the devil prowls around looking for someone to devour.* I do not want it to be you.

Your adversary. Name it.

Your adversary the devil. Know it.

Your adversary the devil prowls . . . just waiting for any opportune moment . . . cunning, baffling, powerful and patient. Never forget it.

Matthew 7:13-14; John 10:7-9; Matthew 22:1-14

THE CAPACITY TO BE HONEST

We have done a lot of talking about the Pilgrimage, about the Christian WAY as a Path, and about how we must take steps if we want to be on this journey. Christianity was designed as a journey. Jesus used "journey" language and imagery from the beginning. *Come, follow me.* It is a "come as you are" party, but not a "stay as you are" party. It is incredible how often the church has developed a fortress mentality, and how often Christians have given the impression to others that faithful living is staid, boring—like believing in Jesus Christ means digging trenches in some safe place and staying put. For the most part, people who dislike Christianity, or who pay it only lip service or think of it as an unnecessary sideshow to life, have never seen it as a Pilgrim's Way. That is, they may have thought about it, but they have never tried it—have not practiced its spiritual disciplines, have not given any allegiance to Jesus Christ, have not taken any steps along the WAY, except perhaps in cursory or half-hearted ways. I know some people who once tried prayer for three or four days but, not getting the results they desired, gave it up.

One of the more debilitating experiences of Christianity is to come into an organization that calls itself a "church" and find no WAY—no Path being walked. It is possible to find churches in our time and culture where the members do not seem to have any clear or conscious notion of what they are doing, why they are there, or what the purpose is. They come to worship services and go to meetings from time to time, but most do not seem to know or care about each other very much; do not seem to carry any kind of message that means anything to them personally; do not seem to have any particular spiritual disciplines that govern or shape their lives. Doubtless in such a church there are members somewhere who mean business, who pray and read their Bibles and really seriously try to follow Jesus. But they keep quiet about it, and a new person could start coming to their church and take years to discover that there is any kind of Life or Pilgrimage going on. Some of us have experienced such churches, and hope not to have to ever again.

On the other hand, it is also possible to find some churches in our time and culture where the road is laid out in clear and no uncertain terms. If you want to participate, you will take certain steps—each described with precision. You will take this step today: wear these kinds of clothes, wear this kind of expression on your face, say these particular words, think these particular thoughts in the exact order and way you are told—and no others. By next week, here is where you will be on the path . . . and the week after that, here. When you study Scripture, here is what you will learn. When you pray, this is what the result will be. It's like a theme park—no matter who goes through the gate, the ride is always the same and always comes out in the same place. Some of us have experienced that kind of church too, and hope never to have to again.

It is not that we can claim any perfect balance at this church. People come here and, not finding the Path, leave. Or finding too much of the Path, leave. Even worse, some people don't find much of a Path and stay anyway. Yet the Spirit is among us, and working with us. So the Path is different for each one of us, even when we take the same steps. Yet from time to time, it seems like some people try to walk the Path and work the steps and still nothing much comes from it. Some days it may even seem true that we ourselves are going through all the motions, but nothing much is coming from it. How frustrating, or even disheartening, when a friend we encouraged to "come and see"—telling them in glowing terms how good it would be—how frustrating when they "try" the very thing we thought would be wonderful for them too, and nothing much happens.

Clearly it is not enough to work the Program, or walk the Path. Somehow it must be done in a special way, with an appropriate attitude. Hard to put such things into words, or to get it clear. *I am the door; anyone who comes into the fold through me will be safe. He will go in and out and find pasture.* (John 10:9) What in the world is Jesus talking about? A sheep is a sheep. A pasture is a pasture. The thing ought to either work or not work, if you go through the motions—right? Maybe it ought to be so, but it is not so. There is a nebulous or esoteric "extra" that seems to make all the difference. Have you ever seen a teenager do a right thing in a wrong or sullen way? Most of us could say we've not only seen one, we've been one. It is exquisite and obvious sabotage. Every motion may be done to match the precise instructions of parent or teacher, but the caricature produces anything but the desired result. It is possible to do all the right things and no good comes of it. Adults are perfectly capable of the same sabotage, but they do not always make it quite so obvious—at least not to themselves.

Enter by the narrow gate; for the gate is wide and the way is easy, that leads to destruction, and those who enter by it are many. For the gate is narrow and the way is hard, that leads to life, and those who find it are few. (Matthew 7:13-14) Have you ever wondered if maybe Jesus was talking here about an attitude? Is the narrow gate about good versus evil, or is it maybe more subtle? I suspect the gate is religion or faith itself. All people, at some point in their lives, want to be good and right and helpful and faithful. But many of us think this should be easy, that it should come naturally—that because we identify with "the good guys," walking the Path should be second nature to us. Everybody goes through the religious gate, but only a few go with humility—go with their whole heart, and willing to be changed—go with a total commitment to be with Jesus and to follow Him, come what may.

Maybe this passage isn't about being tossed into any extra fire. Some people walk the Path and take the steps and it opens out for them into a true and beautiful WAY. Others try the Path and seem to go through the motions of the steps, but nothing much happens. They find the pasture but don't come through the door, so there they are in the pasture but nothing much seems to be happening. They get to eat and play in the pasture, but undergo no transformation. They get to come into religion, but they miss the narrow door. So they get all the paraphernalia and ritual and worship services, and maybe even some of the fellowship. But the Living WAY and the power and presence of the Holy Spirit seem to elude them.

Here is this poor guy in the harshest parable Jesus ever told. He didn't ask to come to the wedding party. Nobody told him to get ready for the wedding party. It never crossed his mind that anybody would let him into the wedding party even if he had wanted desperately to be there. Then suddenly he is grabbed from behind, so to speak, right off the street—dragged to the wedding, thrown in with the rest of the guests. There he stands, too shocked and shy to adjust, when suddenly the groom's father spots him and yells, "Get that creep out of here, he's got no wedding garment!" And not just a simple bounce either—*Bind him hand and foot, and cast him into the outer darkness; there men will weep and gnash their teeth. For many are called, but few are chosen.* (Matthew 22:13-14)

This guy misses his chance. It's like he wins the lottery but doesn't turn in the ticket. He doesn't realize what he has missed until after it is too late. What is the wedding garment? People have wondered and discussed it for generations. It's the eerie twist that Jesus puts into all His teachings. What is the wedding garment? It can't be something outer. It has to be something about an attitude, an approach, a matter of the heart—a matter of the soul.

I'm simply saying that great as the spiritual disciplines are—and necessary as it is to take steps on any pilgrim's way—even these do not define or explain the WAY like we wish they would, like some mathematical formula would—where we can understand it all, and therefore be in charge. Some people work the steps and nothing happens. Others barely begin and miracles start happening all over the place. What is the elusive, extra ingredient—this door/narrow gate/wedding garment? Is it faith? Is it willingness? Is it humility? Even if these are the right words, do they define anything?

AA, as we have discovered, tends to echo the Christian Faith because that is what it came out of. But AA oversimplifies everything in its determination to be clear and practical. It shies away from too much God-talk because that has put so many people off, and because it does not want to erect unnecessary barriers or spend time in factionalism. So does AA have any awareness of this "extra" thing that is needed, this special attitude without which the Program would not work? If so, how will AA describe it? Will it still be in down-to-earth, simple terms?

I'll read to you a portion of AA's "Sermon on the Mount." That is, this passage of the Big Book which is read to open every AA meeting across the land: "Rarely have we seen a person fail who has thoroughly followed our path. [At least we got on the same subject, didn't we?] Those who do not recover are people who cannot or will not completely give themselves to this simple program, usually men and women who are constitutionally incapable of [are you ready for this?] *being honest with themselves.*" (Big Book of ALCOHOLICS ANONYMOUS, Chapter 5, page 58, opening paragraph)

Does that sound like a church making excuses for why its faith doesn't work with some people? Sure it does. And AA gets all the same cat-calls about it we do. And AA doesn't care any more than we should. It just calls it like it sees it, and experiences it.

To continue: "There are such unfortunates. They are not at fault; they seem to have been born that way. They are naturally incapable of grasping and developing a manner of living which demands rigorous honesty. Their chances are less than average. There are those, too, who suffer from grave emotional and mental disorders, but many of them do recover if they have the capacity to be honest." John Calvin lives on! Prove that you are among those destined to be saved by developing and demonstrating the capacity to be honest.

Every spiritual program requires more than the steps it says we must take. It also requires an attitude, a right approach. You cannot tithe out of just any old motive and still get spiritual benefit. Only gratitude produces the kind of allegiance that can sustain tithing as a way of life. All other motives backfire and, in the end, produce more harm than good.

Just so: the Program, the Path, the WAY, the Kingdom require more than their disciplines and rules and procedures. They take an attitude, a right approach, a stance of the heart and soul. Otherwise even the steps we take would get us nowhere.

In Christendom, we would claim a direct connection between faith and the capacity to be honest. That is, humans seem incapable of being honest until or unless they have some confidence, feel some assurance—we call it faith—that they will be loved, accepted, forgiven. **We cannot look at our dark side, or our true light, until *after* we trust the Love of God to sustain us.** We would also see great connections between humility and the capacity to be honest, since dishonesty is just a cover-up for our pride, or a buffer against our fear.

Staying with AA's summation of it, for the moment—what about the capacity to be honest? What do we mean when we say, "So-and-so is an honest man"? Shakespeare loved to play with the concept. In *MUCH ADO ABOUT NOTHING* (Act III, scene V), Verges says, "Yes, I thank God I am as honest as any man living that is an old man and no honester than I." Diogenes (of Sinope) is said to have carried a lantern through the streets of Athens, looking for an honest man. I don't think he was looking for an ethical man; it was something more than that. Paul says, "God must be true though all men be proved liars." (Romans 3:4) This thing about the capacity to be honest is bigger than we think.

It takes no great pondering to realize that our world is short on honesty; that we wish we could trust the people and the systems of our world to be more honest; that the future of the world would be remarkably improved and dramatically changed if a spirit of honesty were to sweep over the world. A slight increase in the amount of honesty would make vast improvements—even taking into account the damage and disruption of the adjustment period.

But contemplating such things is a parlor game, however intriguing. The only honesty we have any chance to improve is our own. For those of us who desire to work a better Program or to walk a straighter Pilgrimage—or if we get stuck or feel like we are making little progress for the energy we are putting forth—it may unstop the dam if we check our capacity to be honest.

There is outside honesty and there is inside honesty. An outer honesty is surely critical. The third of the Ten Commandments requires an outer honesty. Jesus makes it even more rigorous, if possible, in the Sermon on the Mount: *Let your "yes" be yes, and your "no" be no.* (Matthew 5:37) In other words, we do not even need to be under oath, but must speak the honest truth in all times and circumstances.

Great and important as outer honesty is—and blessing that it would be if the world ever moved toward it—an inside honesty is more fascinating, and even more difficult. An inner honesty is probably impossible if outer honesty is seriously neglected. Yet it is this inside honesty that is necessary to the spiritual path. What are the motives? What are the thoughts? What are the true purposes of the inner being—of the soul? Jesus frequently spoke of what came out of the heart. (Matthew 12:34; Luke 6:45) Much of His great Sermon is a directive to go behind the behavior to the inner honesty, to the motive or heart within. God, we are told, is not terribly interested in the outer behavior, in the results, in what we think we have accomplished externally (perhaps because God knows that control of the final results is not in our hands). Rather, *God looks on the heart.* The full quote is: *The Lord sees not as man sees; man looks on the outward appearance, but the Lord looks on the heart.* (I Samuel 16:7)

It is endlessly fascinating, and sometimes surprising to us as well, when we look to our inner honesty and really want to know our inner selves. It's surprising what we really care about, what we trust, what we believe, what we are trying to get and how. In any case, the steps don't work without the capacity to be honest.

Finally, I would mention that having the capacity to be honest does not mean we exercise it. It takes a lot of time and energy to be honest. It is not possible for us to know our motives or fears or hopes very well if we do not spend time on the inside—getting and keeping in touch with what is going on in our souls.

We live in a culture that gives no rewards for inner honesty, that has neither regard for nor interest in inside honesty. Furthermore, by accident or design, the American lifestyle does everything it can to prevent inside honesty. It provides no instruction, it acknowledges little value, it fills up every moment it can with noise or activity designed to prevent the necessary inner reflection. On top of that, it scorns or heaps guilt on anybody who is not "doing something"—something it can see. Yet we live in a Kingdom not of this world, and all of our highest values are things we cannot see. *The things that are unseen are eternal.* (2 Corinthians 4:18)

If you are a person with the capacity to be honest, and if you desire to be a person with inside honesty, you will have to fight for every minute you must spend to develop and exercise that capacity. After that, you will have to fight for the right to keep the time to maintain it. If you do not, the world will steal that inner time away, and you will have neither the inner honesty nor the time with the Spirit necessary to walk the Christian WAY. That is one of the things all of us learn on this Path. It is not just working the steps and keeping the spiritual disciplines—wondrous as they may be. It takes a certain attitude, a special approach. We call it humility. AA calls it the capacity to be honest.

ABOUT THE AUTHOR

Born and raised a Quaker, Bruce Van Blair had a "burning bush" spiritual awakening in the orange groves of Whittier, California at the age of twelve. Upon graduating from the University of Redlands, Bruce enrolled in Andover Newton Theological School from which he received a Master of Divinity degree in 1960. He was called to his first church, First Congregational Church of Paxton in Paxton, MA in 1959 and served as Minister in six succeeding churches: West Parish Church, Andover, MA (1963-66); Altadena Community Church, Altadena, CA (1967-73); First Congregational Church of Redlands, Redlands, CA (1973-1975); Redlands United Church of Christ, Redlands, CA (1975-80); Mercer Island United Church of Christ, Mercer Island, WA (1981-95); and Corona Del Mar Community Church, Congregational (UCC), Corona Del Mar, CA (1996-present). Bruce and his wife, Mariana, live part-time in Port Townsend, WA. His daughter and son-in-law, Willene and Russell Jaqua, his son and daughter-in-law, Brennan and Gretchen Van Blair, and his two grandsons, Lucas and Jared Van Blair, live nearby in Washington.